BIG WINGS

BIG WINGS

PHILIP KAPLAN

Pen & Sword
AVIATION

First published in Great Britain in 2005 by
Pen and Sword Aviation
An imprint of Pen and Sword Books Ltd
47 Church Street
Barnsley
South Yorkshire
S70 2AS

Copyright © Philip Kaplan 2005

ISBN 1 84415 178 6

The right of Philip Kaplan to be identified as the author
of this work has been asserted by him in accordance
with the Copyright, Designs and Patents Act 1988.

TO CLAIRE AND JOE

Grateful acknowledgment is made to the following for the use of
their previously published material:
Cumming, Michael, for extracts from his book *Pathfinder
Cranswick*, William Kimber, 1962.
Dabrowski, Hans-Peter, for extracts from his book *Messerschmitt
Me 321/323*, Schiffer Military History, 2002.
Falconer, Jonathan, for an extract from his book *Stirling Wings*,
Alan Sutton Publishing Limited, 1995.
Hersey, John, for extracts from his article *Hiroshima*, New Yorker
Magazine, August 1946.
Middlebrook, Martin and Everitt, Chris, for extracts from their
book *The Bomber Command War Diaries*, Penguin Books, 1985.
Peden, Murray, for an extract from his book *A Thousand Shall
Fall*, Canadas Wings, 1982.
Griswold, Wesley S., for an extract from his article *When Boats
Had Wings*, Popular Science Magazine, June 1963.
Sauer, Mark, and the San Diego Union-Tribune, for the use of the
article, 'Bail Out!', 25 August 2002 edition.

My thanks to the following people for their kind, generous help in
the development of this book: Joseph Anastasia, Hisham Atallah,
Dmitri Avdeev, Igor Babenko, David Batten, John Battersby, Don Bennett,
Bill Blanchard, Quentin Bland, Javier Bobadilla, Stephen Boreham,
Bristol Aero Collection, Alan Brown, Robert Cardenas, Tony Cassanova,
Amitava Chatterjee, James Covington, Michael Cumming, Hans-
Peter Dabrowski, Sven De Bevere, Ralf Drews, James Doolittle, Hans-
Joachim Ebert, Beryl Erickson, Chris Everitt, the Evergreen Aviation
Museum, Forest Industries Flying Tankers Limited, Sergio Gava,
Edwin Gehricke, Walter Gibb, Stephen Grey, Ed Gronenthal, Larry
Henderson, John Hersey, Eric Holloway, Katherine Huit, Tony
Iacono, S.J.S. James, Lynn Johnson, Kristof Jonckheere, Fred Kaplan,
Neal Kaplan, Cleon T. Knapp, Steve Knox, Florian Kondziela, Curtis
LeMay, T.G. 'Hamish' Mahaddie, Don Maxion, Martin Middlebrook,
Warren Mistler, John Mize, Marcus Neubauer, Michael Oakey, Michael
O'Leary, Murray Peden, Arthur Pegg, Peter Petrick, Jason Pineau,
John Powell, Dr. Raymond Puffer, Ted Quackenbush, Alan Renga,
Denis Richards, Mark Remmel, Philip Rowe, Hilary St George Saunders,
Michael Schmidt, Wouter Sikkema, Raimund Stehmann, Glen Stewart,
Paul Tibbets, Konstantin von Wedelstaedt, Luc Willems, Steve Williams,
Richard Wood, the Western Aeronautical Museum, Nancy Wyld.

A CIP record for this book is available from the British
Library

Efforts have been made to trace the copyright owners
of all material used in this book. The author apoligizes
to any copyright owners we were unable to contact
during this clearance process.

Typeset by Philip Kaplan
Printed and bound by
Kyodo Printing Co. (Singapore) Pte Ltd

Pen and Sword Books Ltd incorporates the imprints of
Pen and Sword Aviation, Pen and Sword Maritime,
Pen and Sword Military, Wharncliffe Local History, Pen
and Sword Select, Pen and Sword Military Classics
and Leo Cooper.

For a complete list of Pen and Sword titles please contact:
Pen and Sword Books Limited
47 Church Street, Barnsley, South Yorkshire,
S70 2AS, England

E-mail: enquiries@pen-and-sword.co.uk
Website: www.pen-and-sword.co.uk

Photography credits: Photographs by the author are credited PK.
Photographs from the author's aviation collections are credited
AC. Photographs from the San Diego Aerospace Museum are cred-
ited SDAM. Title page: PK, p6: both AC, p7: SDAM, pp8: Boeing, p9:
AC, p10-top: Boeing, p10-bottom-both: AC, p11- both: AC, p12-top:
AC, p12-13: Boeing, p14: AC, p15: AC, pp16-17: courtesy Jonathan
Falconer, pp18-19-all: AC, p20: AC, p21: courtesy Jonathan Falconer,
p22-top: AC, p22-bottom: courtesy Jonathan Falconer, p23-both:
AC, p24-both: AC, p25-all: AC, p26-top: PK, p26-bottom: AC, p27: AC,
p28-top: AC, p28-bottom: courtesy Jonathan Falconer, p29: AC, p30-
both: PK, p31: AC, pp32-33-all: AC, p34: AC, p35-both: AC, p36-
both: AC, p37: AC, p38: Harold Gronenthal courtesy Ed
Gronenthal, p39- both: AC, p40: AC, p41: AC, p42-both: AC, p43-
top: Fred Kaplan, p43-AC, p44-both: AC, p45: AC, p46-centre: PK,
p46-left: AC, p47-both: AC, p48-all: AC, p49: AC, p50-centre: courtesy Quentin Bland, p50-both: AC, p51-both: AC, p53-both: AC, p54-
both: AC, p55: Boeing, p56-both: AC, p57: AC, p58-top: AC, p58-bot-
tom: PK, p59: AC, p60: AC, p61: The Edwards AFB History Office,
pp62-63-all: AC, p64: SDAM, p65: AC, p66-both: AC, p67: courtesy
General Robert Cardenas, p68: AC, p69-all: Edwards AFB History
Office, p71: SDAM, pp72-73: SDAM, pp74-75-both: AC, p77: AC, p78:

CONTENTS

AC, p79: Steve Williams, p81: USAF, p82-both: AC, p85: AC,,p86: Steve Williams, p87: NASA Dryden,p88: AC, p89: AC, p90-top: PK, p90-bottom: NASA Dryden, p91: PK, p92: SDAM, p93-both: AC, p94-top: USAF, p94-bottom: AC, p95-top: Steve Williams, p95-bottom: courtesy Tony Cassanova, p96: Boeing, p97: AC, p98: NASA Dryden, p99: Steve Williams, p100: AC, p101: AC, p102-all: PK, p103-centre: Steve Williams, p103-right: AC, p105: NASA Dryden, p106: Edwards AFB History Office, p107: AC, p108-both: NASA Dryden, p110-111-all: NASA Dryden, p112-113-both: Edwards AFB History Office, pp114-123-all: Bristol Aero Collection, p124: AC, p125: AC, p126: Boeing, p127-all: AC, p129: AC, p130: NASA Dryden, p131: Boeing, p132: SDAM, p133: AC, pp134-135: Boeing, p137-both: Boeing, p138: Boeing, p141-both: AC, p142: Airbus, p143: AC, p144: AC, p146-147-all: Airbus, p149: AC, pp150-151-both: Airbus, p153-both: AC, pp154-157: Miami-Dade Public Library, pp158-159-all: AC, p161 and 163: courtesy Wouter Sikkema, p162: AC, pp164 and 166: Miami-Dade Public Library, p165: AC, p167-both: AC, p168: AC, p169: Tailhook, pp170-171-all: Stephen Boreham, p172-top left: AC, p172-top right: Edwin Gehricke, p172-bottom: Tailhook, p173: Edwin Gehricke, p174: AC, p175-top left: Edwin Gehricke, p175-bottom: Stephen Boreham, p176: Edwin Gehricke, p178: Stephen Boreham, p179: AC, p180: Edwin Gehricke, pp182, 186-187-all: Evergreen Aviation

Stephen Boreham, p176: Edwing Gehricke, p178: Stephen Boreham, p179: AC, p180: Edwin Gehricke, pp182, 186-187-both: Evergreen Aviation Museum, pp184-185: AC, p188-189-both: AC, p190: Ted Quackenbush, p191: AC, p193: AC, p194: courtesy Aeroplane Monthly, p195: AC, p196: AC, p196-203-all: Saunders-Roe, p205: AC, pp206-221-all: courtesy Hans-Peter Dabrowski, p208-top: courtesy Hans-Joachim Ebert and Daimler-Chrysler Aerospace, p212-bottom: courtesy Peter Petrick, p218: courtesy Peter Petrick, p207: AC, p208-left: AC, p209-right: AC, p211: AC, p216-left: AC, p217-right: AC, p219-right top and bottom: AC, p220: AC, p222: AC, p223, 224, 227, 228, 230: SDAM, p225: AC, p226-left-both: USAF, p229: AC, p231: Steve Williams, p233: courtesy Edwin Gehricke, p234: AC, p235: Florian Kondziela, p238-top left: Glenn Stewart, p238-top centre: Edwards AFB History Office, p238-bottom: PK, p239-top: Sergio Gava, p239-bottom: Michael Schmidt, p242: PK, p244-both: AC, p246: USAF, pp250-251: Marcus Neubauer, p254-both: Dmitri Avdeev, p255-top: Luc Willems, p255-bottom left: Sven De Bevere, p255-bottom right: Dmitri Avdeev, p258-right: Mark Remmel, p259-top: Sven De Bevere, p259-bottom: John Powell, p260: AC, p262-top: John James, p262-bottom: Alan Brown, p263: Hisham Atallah, p264: AC, p266-left: Ralf Drews, p266-bottom right: Steve Knox, p267-top: Bill Blanchard, p267-bottom: Amitava Chatterjee, p268: AC.

DOUGLAS

Donald W. Douglas Jr joined his father's company, Douglas Aircraft, in 1939, four years after the company had received a contract from the US Army Air Corps for preliminary and detailed design, mock-up construction and testing of components for what would be the largest land-based aircraft built in the USA during the Second World War, the B-19 bomber.

Douglas Jr was born in 1917, and was educated in mechanical engineering at Stanford University, Palo Alto, California. He continued his studies at the Curtiss-Wright Technical Institute in Glendale, California, where he read aeronautical engineering. It seems clear that his father, Donald Wills Douglas, intended to groom his son to become president of Douglas Aircraft and would brook no short-cut path to the top for the young man who began his association with the company as an engineer in the strength group. His father, determined that Don Jr would be well grounded in all aspects of the firm, saw that the young man was assigned a wide variety of positions in many different departments of the plant. Don Jr gradually rose through the ranks and in 1943, at the height of the war, was appointed to his first important supervisory job at Douglas, that of manager of flight test. In that role he oversaw the flight testing of nearly every aircraft type manufactured by the company. In the early post-war years he became director of the testing division and was responsible for type certification of the famous DC-6 and DC-7 airliners. He was made a company vice-president and board member in the early 1950s and in 1957 was named president of Douglas Aircraft, a role he served in until the company was merged with the St. Louis aircraft manufacturer, McDonnell Aviation, in 1967. He then served as senior corporate vice-president of the McDonnell Douglas Corporation until 1989. During his long career with the plane makers, Don Jr had an important role in the development of nearly all the significant Douglas aircraft models—except one. He had come along a little too late for the B-19.

In the mid-1930s the world was moving relentlessly towards war in both Europe and the Pacific and some American military planners believed it essential that the US Army Air Corps investigate the possibilities of building an experimental bomber with enormous range and hitting power. They wanted to find the limits of technology and capability in that time and get them all into one extraordinary aeroplane.

It was called Project D, classified top secret and visualized to be a "proof-of-concept" design and not necessarily a production aircraft. When the Army solicited involvement by the major aircraft manufacturers of the day, only the Douglas and Sikorsky companies expressed interest and preliminary discussions were held with both firms. Now known as the BLR, for Bomber, Long Range, the Douglas design proposal was designated XBLR-2.

Both Sikorsky and Douglas had been asked to construct wooden mock-ups of their proposed designs and these were evaluated by the Army Air Corps in March 1936. The Douglas design prevailed and the Sikorsky proposal was terminated. Douglas was given until 31 March 1938 to produce the prototype aeroplane.

The XBLR-2 was meant to be a kind of flying battleship, an advanced all-metal stressed-skin bomber capable of hauling up to 18,700 lb of bombs with a maximum range of 7,700 miles. Her cruising speed was to be 135 mph, with a top speed of 224 mph at an altitude of 15,500 feet. Her service ceiling was to be 23,000 feet and she would be powered by four Wright R-3350-5 18-cylinder air-cooled radial engines rated at 2,000 horsepower each, driving three-bladed constant-speed propellers. Her total internal fuel capacity of 10,350 US gallons would enable her to remain aloft for up to fifty-five hours. A low-winged monoplane, XBLR-2 was to be fitted with a retractable tricycle landing-gear arrangement, a system then considered relatively unconventional. Each giant main wheel was eight feet in diameter.

As the United States limped through the Depression years of the thirties, research and development funding for American military projects was necessarily quite limited, forcing a slow pace of progress on the new plane. Later in 1936, the BLR designation was superseded by the redesignation B-19 and the prototype under construction was

top: A publicity still, Betty Grable, from the movie *A Yank in the RAF*; above: Ad for the 1942 Oldsmobile . . . 'Power-Styled like the B-19'; right:Douglas employee Dorothy Rush with a B-19 main landing-gear wheel.

B-19

designated XB-19 in November 1937.

The Depression years dragged on and the XB-19 continued to slip further and further behind in its production schedule owing to the insufficient developmental funding by the Army Air Corps. The company had to use a lot of its own money to help in the funding of the project. And it had to divert a number of its key design personnel to the XB-19 from other aircraft development work with better prospects for eventual large-scale production than the big bomber offered.

Other problems dogged development of the XB-19, not least being the ever-increasing weight of the plane as its components and structures were refined. The added weight, of course, would result in diminished performance characteristics with the intended engines. This factor, coupled with various technological advances achieved in the aircraft industry during the three years since the start of the project, now rendered the XB-19 virtually obsolete even before she had been assembled. All of these considerations weighed heavily on the board of Douglas Aircraft, forcing a decision to recommend to the Army Air Corps in late August 1938 that the giant bomber project be cancelled.

The Army Air Corps, while cognizant of the Douglas company's position, and still unable to help with improved funding for the project, remained determined to see the XB-19 to fruition. The Army's Materiel Division instructed Douglas to continue the bomber project, albeit at a pace too slow to please anyone involved. But by 1940, with the war in Europe already a year old, it became clear to the Army Air Corps that the proposed performance of the B-19 would be insufficient to meet newly evolving needs, making the plane less important militarily, and eliminating the reason for the secret classification of the project. It was removed from that classification and soon became the subject of much media speculation about what was behind America's development of an extraordinary new ultra-long-range bomber by a nation not (yet) at war.

The work on construction and assembly of the big bomber went on inexorably in an enormous production hangar of the Douglas plant at Santa Monica's

left: The XB-19 under construction in the Douglas Aircraft plant at Clover Field, Santa Monica, California, in June 1941. More than three years behind schedule, the plane's maiden flight took place on 27 June 1941 piloted by US Army Air Corps Major Stanley Ulmstead. The bomber was flown that day to March Air Force Base, near Riverside, California, and turned over to the Army for thirty hours of evaluation.

'War doesn't determine who's right—only who's left.'
– Bertrand Russell

LB-47—New Black-Out Plant, Douglas Aircraft Corporation, Long Beach, California

Showing the Giant Bomber B-19 in Flight

PHOTO BY "DICK" WHITTINGTON

Clover Field and was finally completed in May 1941. To put her in a modern perspective, the physical dimensions of the XB-19 can be readily compared to today's Boeing 747-400 jumbo jetliner. The 212-foot wingspan of the Douglas bomber was slightly greater than that of the jumbo; her tail reached a height of just under 43 feet, while that of the 747 is 63 feet. The maximum gross weight of the B-19 was 162,000 lb, while that of the jumbo is something over 800,000 lb. The length of the bomber was 132 feet and that of the 747 is 231 feet.

The B-19 was meant to be capable of striking an enemy target thousands of miles from her base in the United States, and on such a mission she could accommodate either eight 2,000 lb bombs, sixteen 1,100 lb bombs or thirty 600 lb bombs in her internal bombbay. She could also carry up to 2,000 lb of bombs on ten underwing racks and her maximum bomb-load capacity was 37,100 lb.

To defend herself, the big plane was armed with one 0.37mm cannon and one 0.30 calibre machine-gun in the nose and forward dorsal turrets, one 0.50 calibre machine-gun in the tail position and one each in the ventral turret, the right and left fuselage positions and the rear dorsal turret. There were additional 0.30 calibre machine-guns on both sides of the bombardier's position and below the tail plane on both sides.

The bomber was to be operated by a crew of sixteen: an aircraft commander, a pilot, co-pilot, navigator, engineer, bombardier, radio operator, and nine gunners. Added capacity for an additional relief crew of eight including two flight mechanics, could be accommodated in a compartment over the bombbay, with six bunks and eight seats. The mechanics could access the engines in flight via passages in the wing. The plane was equipped with a galley for preparing in-flight meals, but the prototype aircraft did not have self-sealing fuel tanks or any armour to protect the crew.

Thousands of Douglas workers, Santa Monica residents and other southern Californians had gathered at Clover Field on 27 June 1941 to watch Army Air Force Major Stanley Ulmstead and a six-man crew take the XB-19 up for the first time. The maiden

flight was brief, uneventful and three years behind schedule. Major Ulmstead flew the huge bomber east to March Field in Riverside County, turning it over to the Army for Air Force evaluation and manufacturer flight testing. Donald W. Douglas received a telegram from US President Franklin D. Roosevelt congratulating Douglas on the achievement.

Following the period of testing, the XB-19 was conditionally accepted by the Army in October. When the Japanese attacked American naval ships and facilities at Pearl Harbor, Hawaii, on 7 December, it was decided to apply a camouflage paint scheme to the big plane while it underwent continued testing in southern California. Early war jitters also prompted Army officials to operate the bomber with her guns loaded through her last four test flights on the west coast. The plane was then transferred on 23 January 1942 from California to the Army Air Corps facility at Wright Field, Dayton, Ohio, out of any danger from Japanese aircraft. At Wright Field, the bomber was subjected to another broad range of tests which resulted in several relatively minor modifications and an improved braking system.

On formal acceptance of the plane by the Army in June 1942, Douglas Aircraft received payment of $1,400,000, but the company had by then spent nearly four million of its own dollars, incurring a dramatic loss on the project to that date.

As testing continued at the Wright Field base, the big bomber exhibited few significant faults other than a problem with engine cooling, reducing her maximum speed from 224 mph to 204 mph at an optimum altitude of 15,700 feet. In 1944, after completion of a lengthy period of operation as a flying laboratory at Wright Field, it was decided that the XB-19 would be converted to a cargo/transport aircraft. This modification included refitting her with Allison V-3420-11 turbo-supercharged 24-cylinder liquid-cooled engines. In this new version, she was redesignated XB-19A. With her modifications she achieved a new maximum speed of 275 mph and the engine

'War? My dear boy, it's awful— the noise, and the people!' – W.H. Auden

top left: The XB-19 at the March Field, California, base 27 June 1941; left: Donald Wills Douglas (right) in his Wilshire Boulevard, Santa Monica, factory in 1922; far left: The XB-19 over the Douglas Long Beach, California, plant in 1941.

cooling trouble was eliminated. During her time as a test aircraft, important data were accumulated that would later be used effectively in contributing to the further design development of the B-29 and B-36 heavy bombers.

The B-19 was not destined for actual production. She was underpowered for her weight and mission, but she had provided useful information that advanced the progress of the American war arsenal. The XB-19A was flown for the last time on 17 August 1946, from Wright Field to Davis-Monthan Air Force Base near Tucson, Arizona, where she was placed in

protective storage until June 1949 when she was scrapped. Or rather, most of her was scrapped. The forward fuselage had a brief additional career as a Tucson real estate office. It later turned up in a scrap yard in Los Angeles where it remained until at least the mid-1950s.

Specifications: Douglas XB-19
Engines: Four Wright R-3350-5 18-cylinder air-cooled radials rated at 2,000 hp each for take-off and 1,500 hp each at 15,700 ft
Maximum speed: 224 mph at 15,700 ft

Cruising speed: 135 mph
Initial rate of climb: 650 ft per min
Service ceiling: 23,000 ft
Normal range: 5,200 miles. Maximum range: 7,700 miles
Weight empty: 86,000 lb. Maximum weight loaded: 162,000 lb
Wingspan: 212 ft
Length: 132 ft
Height: 43 ft
Wing area: 4,285 sq ft
Internal bomb capacity: Maximum, 35,100 lb

Underwing bomb rack capacity: Maximum, 2,000 lb
Defensive armament: one 37mm cannon, six 0.30 calibre machine-guns, five 0.50 calibre machine-guns.

Specifications: Douglas XB-19A
Engines: Four Allison V-3420-11 24-cylinder liquid-cooled engines
Maximum speed: 275 mph at 20,000 ft
Cruising speed: 185 mph
Service ceiling: 39,000 ft
Normal range: 4,200 miles
Weight empty: 92,400 lb Weight loaded: 140,200 lb

below: The XB-19 landing at March Field during her brief Army Air Corps evaluation programme in summer, 1941.

SHORT

STIRLING

'The flashiest entry in my logbook was the day I flew what was perhaps the heaviest aircraft then in service, followed by the lightest. The heavy job was a Stirling bomber, full of parachutists newly arrived at Ringway and being given "air experience". This was the most boring of all the Ringway pilot's duties, as all he was required to do was fly the trainees anywhere for an hour, straight and level, and then fly them back. So the pilot was perfectly happy for me to fly the plane up and down the Welsh coast on his behalf while he put his feet up on the instrument panel and wrote to his wife.'   —from *A Kentish Lad* by Frank Muir

The brothers Eustace and Oswald Short knew their future would be in aviation when they experienced their first flight in a gas-filled balloon in 1897. They began making such balloons in 1902 and sold three of their creations to the Indian Army in 1905. Three years later their brother Horace joined them in the business and they incorporated to make and sell copies of the famous Wright Brothers *Flyer* under licence in a shop at Leysdown-on-Sea, Isle of Sheppey, in the Thames Estuary. By 1910 the Short brothers had relocated to larger facilities at nearby Eastchurch, where they designed and built the first tailless aircraft to fly, the Short-Dunne 5, and the following year they built the S-39, the first twin-engined aircraft. With the start of the First World War, their business expanded greatly, as they were providing the British military with the S.184, the first aircraft to sink a ship—a Turkish cargo vessel in the Dardanelles during the Battle of Gallipoli. The act caught the attention of the Royal Flying Corps, which purchased the plane and called it the Short bomber.

Until the late 1940s, there was no extensive worldwide infrastructure of airfields with substantial runways and facilities for commercial air travel. The only way such travel could be accomplished was by flying-boat and the Short brothers capitalized on that fact by designing and constructing the Singapore flying-boats, one of which attracted considerable interest when it carried Sir Alan Cobham on his 23,000-mile survey of the African continent. Next came the Short Calcutta, a larger and more powerful flying-boat that garnered the Shorts yet more fame when it was employed in commercial service by Imperial Airways in 1928 on routes around Greece and Italy, and in parts of the British Empire. The Calcutta was followed by the even larger Kent. With their growth and success, the Shorts opened a new and larger factory at Rochester, about ten miles from their Eastchurch location. Their progress allowed them to purchase the Pobjoy aero-engine company in 1934. They closed their Eastchurch factory, and two years later, joined forces with Harland and Wolff to open a Belfast facility known as Short & Harland Ltd, where they began producing the Handley Page Hereford bomber.

By the late 1930s, the experience the brothers had gained building large flying-boats enabled them to create the Sunderland, a flying-boat that was to distinguish itself as a premier anti-submarine patrol bomber in the Second World War. Along with the Consolidated PBY Catalina flying-boat, and that company's B-24 Liberator bomber, the Sunderland made life miserable for the crews of the German U-boats in the Battle of the Atlantic, contributing mightily to the Allied victory in that campaign. The Shorts' enhanced reputation through their work on the Sunderland led directly to their prestigious award of the contracts to develop the Stirling, the first heavy bomber for the RAF. The designers and engineers at Shorts struggled admirably to produce the bomber they visualized for Bomber Command, in spite of crippling specifications laid down by the Air Ministry for the plane. And to the extent that the Stirling failed to meet the performance demands put on it in wartime, blame should not be attributed to the Shorts design staff, who did their best, and indeed, created a very fine bomber.

In 1940 the German Air Force bombed the Short factory at Rochester, heavily damaging it and destroying a number of aircraft including several newly built Stirlings. The nearby Supermarine factory was also bombed and completely destroyed. Thereafter, primary emphasis was placed on the Short and Harland plant at Belfast for the production of Stirlings, as Belfast was beyond the range of the German bombers. By the end of the war, all Short aircraft production activity was concentrated in Belfast.

Maligned by many and denigrated during its military history and since, the Short Stirling was the first big, four-engined heavy bomber of the Royal Air Force in the Second World War, and the first of the RAF heavies to be designed from scratch as a four-engined bomber, capable of taking enormous bombloads to targets in the German industrial heartland. A total of 2,383 Stirlings was produced by Shorts at Rochester, Short & Harland at Belfast, Shorts at South Marston, and by Austin Motors at Longbridge. It was the Stirling to which Prime Minister Winston Churchill referred when he spoke of delivering 'the shattering strokes of retributive justice' to the Nazi enemy. He wrote to Lord Beaverbrook, his Minister of Aircraft Production, in July 1940 that, without an army capable of confronting German military power on the Continent, there was only one way that Britain could defeat Hitler: 'And that is an absolutely devastating, exterminating attack by very heavy bombers from this country upon the Nazi homeland. We must be able to overwhelm him by this means, without which I do not see a way through.' Churchill later summed up his view: 'The fighters are our salvation, but the bombers alone provide the means of victory.'

Royal Air Force Bomber Command had been specifically created for strategic bombing and the leaders of the RAF couldn't wait to get started. Since the beginning of the Second World War in September 1939, Bomber Command had been severely hampered in its role by the limitations of its equipment and the insistence of many in high places that 'one must not bomb private property,' a view also held by the American administration.

The operational bomber aircraft that could then be fielded by the RAF were the Bristol Blenheim, a small, relatively fast machine that carried a very light bomb-load and was clearly no match for German interceptors; the Bristol Beaufort, another twin-engined craft, designed to deliver torpedoes for RAF Coastal Command; the Handley Page Hampden, another twin with little carrying capacity; the Armstrong

'Nothing in life is so exhilerating as to be shot at without result.'
– Winston Churchill

left: The pilot of a Royal Air Force Stirling bomber in 1943. His eye level in the cockpit was nearly 23 feet above the tarmac.

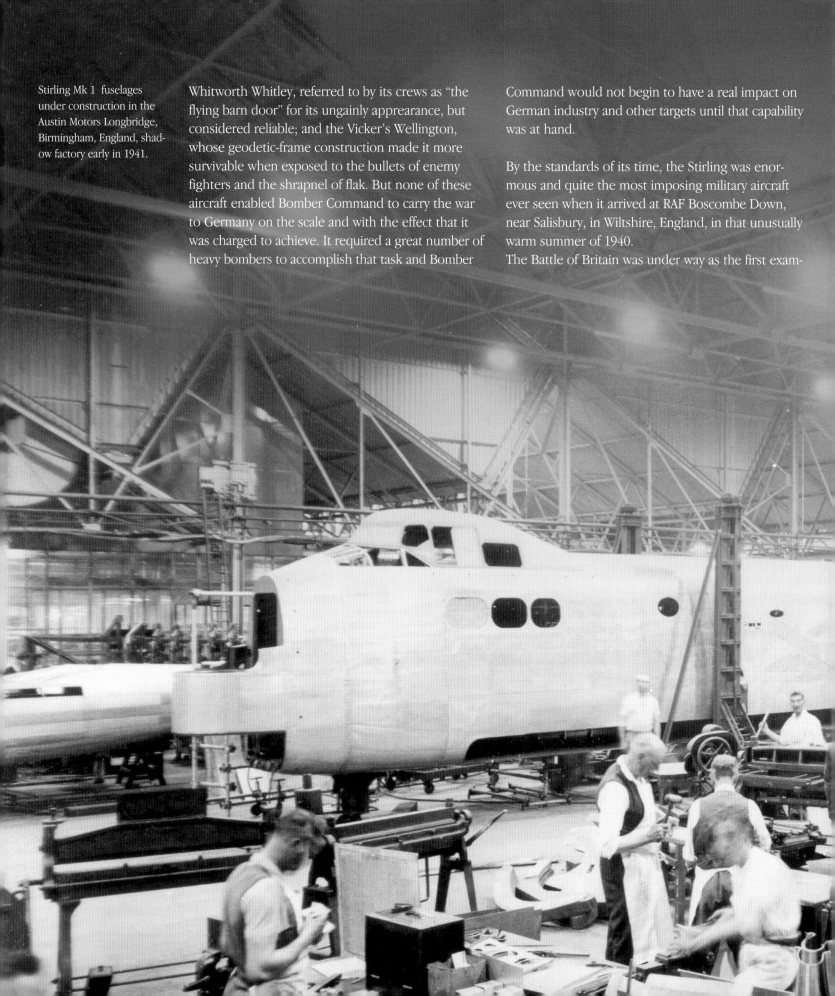

Stirling Mk 1 fuselages under construction in the Austin Motors Longbridge, Birmingham, England, shadow factory early in 1941.

Whitworth Whitley, referred to by its crews as "the flying barn door" for its ungainly apprearance, but considered reliable; and the Vicker's Wellington, whose geodetic-frame construction made it more survivable when exposed to the bullets of enemy fighters and the shrapnel of flak. But none of these aircraft enabled Bomber Command to carry the war to Germany on the scale and with the effect that it was charged to achieve. It required a great number of heavy bombers to accomplish that task and Bomber

Command would not begin to have a real impact on German industry and other targets until that capability was at hand.

By the standards of its time, the Stirling was enormous and quite the most imposing military aircraft ever seen when it arrived at RAF Boscombe Down, near Salisbury, in Wiltshire, England, in that unusually warm summer of 1940.

The Battle of Britain was under way as the first exam-

ples of the new bomber were completed in the Short Brothers aircraft production plant at Rochester, and delivered to Boscombe for evaluation by the Bomber Performance Testing Flight.

The big plane entered production at a point in the war when the morale of the British people was at a low ebb and, representing the nation's burgeoning offensive strength, it helped to boost that morale. Absurdly, though, the Air Ministry planners who developed the specifications for the new plane insist-

ed that it must fit into the standard RAF hangars of the time, thus limiting its wingspan to less than 100 feet. This silly requirement would seriously restrict the performance and severely limit the service ceiling of what might otherwise have been a superb bomber when one was sorely needed. Despite the legitimate protestations of the Short design staff, that the short-ened wingspan (from their original proposed design) would have a detrimental effect on the performance of the new plane, and on the service ceiling in particu-

Heavy "Stirling" bombers raid the Nazi Baltic port of Lübeck and leave the dock...

BACK THEM UP

BELT 'EM ONE!

lar, the Air Ministry remained adamant in its demand that the wingspan be less than 100 feet. Not only did it deny the plane a proper wing, it compounded the felony by requiring that it be able to maintain altitude with one of its engines shut down while carrying a heavy bomb-load, that it be capable of being launched from a catapult system, and that it double as a troop transport. The Stirling had the potential to match and even surpass the performance of the other British heavy bombers of that war, the Avro Lancaster and the Handley Page Halifax. Its Bristol Hercules engines delivered 6,000 hp. It was strong, well made, dependable, and highly manoeuvrable. It could take a lot of punishment, frequently completing its missions, though heavily battle damaged, and returning its crews safely to their bases. Even with its design limitations, it still proved to be the fastest of the three British heavies at low altitudes.

In the early developmental phase of the Stirling, Shorts actually built and test-flew a half-size prototype of the plane, the M-4, in 1938 at the Rochester factory field. This resulted in a number of design changes to the coming production aircraft, including lengthened undercarriage struts which, however, proved unreliable on several occasions during the operational lifetime of the big bomber. Still, the test flights of the M-4 confirmed most aspects of the design and the company was allowed to proceed with the construction of a full-size prototype that would fly for the first time on 14 May 1939, four months before the war with Germany began. Judging the handling characteristics of the new plane to be good, the test pilots of the Stirling prototype were surprised when the undercarriage collapsed on that first landing, for an inauspicious end to an otherwise trouble-free initial outing. The prototype suffered such severe damage in the incident that it had to be scrapped. In December, a second prototype test aeroplane was completed, flown and landed successfully, before being sent for evaluation to Boscombe Down in 1940. By May of that year, the first production Stirling, N3635, came from the factory and made her maiden flight.

No. 7 Squadron at RAF Leeming, in Yorkshire, was the first squadron in Bomber Command to be equipped with Stirlings and therefore, the first Royal Air Force squadron to have four-engined bombers. No one on the squadron, however, had any experience flying four-engined aircraft, so some pilots from RAF Coastal Command, who had been flying Short Sunderland flying-boats, were brought in to assist in the conversion training process at No. 7. But production and delivery of the new Stirlings was slow, and made even slower by German Air Force attacks on the Shorts assembly facilities. The company then set about establishing dispersed production of major components to spread the risk to its assembly effort, with new production facilities at Gloucester and Swindon. By the first week in September, though, 7 Squadron had received just four of the big bombers and one of these had already been lost in a training flight crash. These initial aircraft were fraught with mechanical problems including troubles with the Hercules Mk II engines, which had been fitted as an expedient until the specified engines were ready for use. As such, these early aircraft, called Stirling Mk 1s, were designated for training use only. At the end of the year, No. 7 Squadron had been reassigned to RAF Oakington, near Cambridge, and was at last receiving the Stirlings they would fly on actual operations, greatly improved machines powered by the Hercules Mk X. They would take their new bombers into combat for the first time in February 1941, when three of their Stirlings went to war on the night of 10/11 February as part of a forty-three-bomber force attacking an oil tank farm near Rotterdam.

The operational debut of the Stirling as a part of the Bomber Command Main Force took place on 24/25 February. Again, three of the aircraft of 7 Squadron, still the only squadron in Bomber Command to be operational with Stirlings, flew in a fifty-seven-aircraft main force to hit warships in the French port of Brest. In addition to the Stirlings, the force comprised thirty Wellingtons, eighteen Hampdens, and, making their operational debut, six Avro Manchesters, the twin-engined forerunner of the Lancaster. None of the aircraft were lost in the raid itself, but one of the Manchesters crashed on returning to England. The next raid in which a Stirling participated was on the night of 17/18 March, when one No.7 Squadron aircraft joined as part of another fifty-seven aircraft main force to strike a target at Bremen, the first time a Stirling bombed a target in Germany. The Stirling's first trip to Berlin, 'The Big City', occurred on 9/10 April when three No. 7 Squadron aircraft were part of an eighty-plane force of Wellingtons, Hampdens, and Whitleys dispatched to the German capital. In the attack, one Whitley was downed, as were three Wellingtons and one Stirling. The other two Stirlings had to abort. The raid marked the first loss of a Stirling to enemy action.

By the end of April 1941, a second Bomber Command squadron, No. 75, had become operational with Stirlings. It joined with No. 7 Squadron on the night of 2/3 May to provide three Stirlings for a ninety-five-bomber force hitting Hamburg. One of the No. 7 Squadron aircraft was shot down while in the landing circuit by a German intruder aircraft. Six of the Stirling crew members were killed and the seventh died the next day in hospital.

For several months the participation by Stirlings in Bomber Command raids was quite limited, as were deliveries of the new bomber to the squadrons. The delivery problem lay not with the aeroplane but with the method of manufacture. The new four-engined Lancaster bomber was being built using American-style assembly-line methods and was beginning to reach the squadrons faster and in far greater numbers than the Stirling, which was more of a made-by-hand production, utilizing the skills of many traditional craftsmen whose product was finely made but slower to complete.

On 12 February 1942, eleven Stirlings took part in a fascinating operation mounted when the German battle-cruisers *Scharnhorst* and *Gneisenau,* and the cruiser *Prinz Eugen*, sailed from Brest to Germany in what has become known as 'The Channel Dash'. The weather that day was poor over the English Channel, with low cloud providing good cover for the ships. In the late morning a patrolling Spitfire pilot sighted the enemy ships off Le Touquet and the call went out for all available RAF and Royal Navy units to attack the German warships before dark. With much of Bomber Command "stood down" for the day, it fell to 5 Group to answer the call for the Royal Air Force. From 1.30 p.m. until darkness, the squadrons sent 242 sorties

out to find and strike the warship targets in the largest Bomber Command daylight operation to date. In the difficult conditions, only a few of the bombers actually spotted the German ships and none did any real damage to them. However, the *Scharnhorst* and *Gneisenau* were both damaged and slowed, when they struck mines that had been laid by No. 5 Group bombers in the nights immediately preceding the escape of the warships. The ships reached the safety of German ports after having been trapped for months at Brest and bombed incessantly by the RAF during that time. In those attacks, both capital ships had been severely damaged. In that effort Bomber Command had lost 127 aircraft.

Two events early in 1942 signalled a sea change in the way that Bomber Command conducted its part of the war, and the results it achieved. On 8 January Air Marshal Sir Richard Peirse was replaced as Air Officer Commanding-in-Chief, RAF Bomber Command. His successor was Air Marshal Arthur T. Harris, the man who would come to be known by the crews who flew for him as 'Butch' (butcher) or 'Bomber' Harris. Peirse, who had been the chief of Bomber Command since October 1940, was replaced after several months of poor bombing results and a high rate of crew and aircraft losses. It was 'crunch-time' for the bomber force, as its very future was being debated by Churchill's War Cabinet and the Air Ministry, there being considerable feeling that it should be reduced from a substantial strategic force, to a much smaller tactical one. In the official history of the Royal Air Force the Chiefs of Staff took the view: 'We must first destroy the foundations upon which the German war machine runs—the economy which feeds it, the morale which sustains it, the supplies which nourish it and the hopes of victory which inspire it. Only then shall we be able to return to the continent and occupy and control portions of his territory and impose our will upon the enemy . . . It is in bombing, on a scale undreamt of in the last war, that we find the new weapon on which we must principally depend for the destruction of German economic life and morale.'

The second benchmark event for RAF Bomber Command came on 14 February 1942, when the Air

Two Victoria Crosses were awarded to Stirling pilots. In one of the incidents, an aeroplane of No. 218 Squadron on a mission to Turin, Italy, was piloted by Flight Sergeant Al Aaron DFM. It was August 1943 and Sgt. Aaron's Stirling was hit by a German nightfighter, killing his navigator. In the attack, a bullet shattered Aaron's jaw and he was also wounded in the chest and one arm. Three of the engines were damaged, one of them put out of action. Sgt Aaron put his bomb aimer in control of the plane and set course for North Africa. After five hours the Stirling reached a field there called Bone and the sergeant assisted the bomb aimer in making a wheels-up landing. All of the crew survived except Sgt. Aaron who died of his wounds nine hours later.

Ministry directed that a new policy, developed largely by Air Chief Marshal Sir Charles Portal after he had secured the approval of Churchill and the War Cabinet for the continuation of Bomber Command as a strategic striking force, should be implemented. It was a policy that was committed to the general bombing of Germany's forty-three leading industrial cities with their combined population of fifteen million people. The aim was to bomb them into sufficient chaos, disorganization and a breakdown of morale, as to end their ability to continue the war. The directive stated: 'It has been decided that the primary objective of your operations should now be focused on the morale of the enemy civil population and in particular of the industrial workers.' Thus was born the 'area bombing' concept, which has often been laid at the feet of Arthur Harris, but which, in fact, was the creation of Portal and the Air Ministry. It was Harris who would vigorously carry it out as C-in-C Bomber Command for the balance of the war and would receive both credit and blame for its results and consequences.

The implementation of area bombing coincided with the rapidly growing force of four-engined heavy bombers which, while mainly Lancasters, included large numbers of Halifaxes and Stirlings, and the retirement from most main-force action of the Manchester, Hampden, Blenheim and Whitley. When Harris came to the job, he had fewer than fifty heavy bombers at his disposal for an average raid and he demanded more, many more. Soon, far greater bomb tonnages could be brought to the targets. Improved bombsights and vastly improved navigation came about with the introduction of the "Gee" device, which allowed Bomber Command navigators to get a position fix from three stations in England and find their targets more easily. The weapons of choice now were the 4,000 lb blast bomb known as the "cookie", coupled with a great quantity of four lb incendiary bombs. And 8,000 lb "double cookies" came into use as well. The technique called for the first planes over the target city to drop high-explosive bombs intended to ruin and block as many roads as possible. This was done to deny access to the fire engines that would soon be needed to fight the massive fires started by the follow-

above: Stirling aircrew with
their bacon and egg meal
following a night operation
over Germany; right: Flt Sgt
George Mackie, pilot of this
Stirling Mk 1 at Waterbeach,
Cambridgeshire, in April 1942.

ing aircraft, dropping their blast bombs and incendiaries. Additionally, a new, seventh crew member was introduced to the big four-engined bombers, a bomb aimer, added to take that responsibility from the hard-pressed navigator. And as the new Lancaster heavy bomber came onto Bomber Command squadrons in substantial numbers, it brought a greater bomb-load capacity, a higher ceiling and better manoeuvrability than that of either the Halifax or Stirling. Perhaps the most significant improvement for the survivability of the crews, though, were the radio navigation aids like Gee, and later, Oboe, which dramatically reduced the number of air crews lost when their bombers crashed in England on the return flights from Germany. Many of these accidents occurred when navigational errors resulted from tired crewmen aboard aircraft running low on fuel. In a matter of months, however, the Germans developed a jamming technique that reduced the effective range of Gee, putting most targets within Germany out of Gee range.

But while Gee was still performing at its best, Harris was mounting major offensives against particular city targets, one being Essen, with its Krupp arms industry. A series of eight heavy raids were directed at Essen, in which a number of Stirlings took part. One typical attack took place on 8/9 March 1942, when a main force of 211 bombers, including twenty-seven Stirlings, struck through a heavy haze that caused inaccurate bombing and left the Krupps factories relatively untouched. Unfortunately for Bomber Command, none of the Essen raids produced the kind of results Harris was seeking.

The first months of Harris's command were marked by a relatively conservative approach to his task. He did, however, achieve especially good results with raids on Rostock and Lübeck, in which a large number of Stirlings took part. Buoyed by these successes, he conceived the idea of putting together 1,000 bombers for one massive raid on a German city target. Both Churchill and Portal enthusiastically supported the 'thousand plan' and Harris went to work on the details. While his actual available main force numbered only slightly more than 400 aircraft, he was able (just) to summon the balance of the 1,000 by leaning on the heavy conversion units, RAF Coastal Command

and Flying Training Command, to provide the additional planes and crews he needed. Many of these aircraft would be flown by pilots and crews who had already completed their combat tours, by instructors with crews still in training, and by any spare bods he could grab for the job.

The intent was not merely to launch one such major raid, but several. With the use of Gee navigation, and a new "bomber stream" concept, with all the aircraft taking a common route and speed to and from the target, with each plane allocated a height band and time slot in the stream, the risk of mid-air collisions and enemy interceptions was minimized, at least theoretically. Harris also planned for the entire bomber stream to pass over the target in an unprecedented ninety minutes, minimizing its exposure to enemy defences and, crucially, concentrating the amount of incendiaries dropped on the target city in such a way as to overwhelm the local fire services and cause great areas to be consumed in flames.

As planning and organization for the first "thousand" raid progressed, a snag developed when the Royal Navy suddenly balked at the participation of aircraft from Coastal Command. The Navy clearly feared that the success of such a major raid would hurt its chances of acquiring a large number of long-range aeroplanes for use in its war against the enemy's submarines. This naval intransigence forced Harris to re-scour his operational squadrons for even the most unlikely aircraft and crews to make up the shortfall, resulting in many largely untrained crews taking part in the first such raid.

As the end of May 1942 neared, the great force was ready and waiting to go. Harris wanted the target to be Hamburg because it was a major German port city, Germany's second largest city and the location of the construction facilities of more than 100 submarines a year. The weather, however, failed to cooperate and he elected to send the force to his second choice, Cologne. The attack was set for the night of 30/31 May and the force was comprised of 1,047 aircraft: 156 Wellingtons of No. 1 Group; 134 Wellingtons and 88 Stirlings of No. 3 Group; 131 Halifaxes, 9 Wellingtons and 7 Whitleys of No. 4 Group; 73 Lancasters, 46 Manchesters and 34 Hampdens of No. 5

'Procedure in the event of a bomb warning: in the built-up area, take cover inside the nearest building; inside rooms, open windows and close curtains; on the playing fields, continue games.'
– Eton College Diary

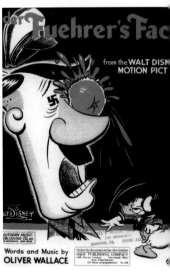

Group; 236 Wellingtons and 21 Whitleys of No. 91 Group (Operational Training Unit); 63 Wellingtons and 45 Hampdens of No. 92 Group (OTU) and 4 Wellingtons of Flying Training Command.

Of the aircraft force dispatched to Cologne that night, the records of Bomber Command indicate that 868 bombed the primary target and fifteen planes hit other targets. Two-thirds of the 1,455 tons of bombs dropped were incendiaries. In their superb reference work, *The Bomber Command War Diaries*, Martin Middlebrook and Chris Everitt describe the results: 'German records show that 2,500 separate fires were started, of which the local fire brigade classed 1,700 as 'large' but there was no 'sea of fire' as had been experienced at Lübeck and Rostock because Cologne was mainly a modern city with wide streets. The local records contained an impressive list of property damaged: 3,330 buildings destroyed, 2,090 seriously damaged and 7,420 lightly damaged. More than 90 per cent of this damage was caused by fire rather than high-explosive bombs. Among the above total of 12,840 buildings were 2,560 industrial and commercial buildings, though many of these were small ones. However, 36 large firms suffered complete loss of production, 70 suffered 50–80 per cent loss and 222 up to 50 per cent. Among the buildings classed as totally destroyed were: 7 official administration buildings, 14 public buildings, 7 banks, 9 hospitals, 17 churches, 16 schools, 4 university buildings, 10 postal and railway buildings, 10 buildings of historic interest, 2 newspaper offices, 4 hotels, 2 cinemas and 6 department stores. Damage was also caused to 17 water mains, 5 gas mains, 32 main-electricity cables and 12 main-telephone routes. The only military installation mentioned is a Flak barracks. In domestic housing, the following 'dwelling units' (mainly flats/apartments) are listed: 13,010 destroyed, 6,360 seriously damaged, 22,270 lightly damaged. These details of physical damage in Cologne are a good example of the results of area bombing. Similar results can be expected in those of Bomber Command's raids which were successful during following years.

'The estimates of casualties in Cologne are, unusually, quite precise. Figures quoted for deaths vary only between 469 and 486. The 469 figure comprises 411 civilians and 58 military casualties, mostly members of Flak units. This death toll was a new record for an RAF raid. 5,027 people were listed as injured and 45,132 as bombed out. It was estimated that from 135,000 to 150,000 of Cologne's population of nearly 700,000 people fled the city after the raid.

'The RAF casualties were also a record high figure. 41 aircraft were lost, including 1 Wellington which was known to have crashed into the sea. The 41 lost aircraft were: 29 Wellingtons, 4 Manchesters, 3 Halifaxes, 2 Stirlings, 1 Hampden, 1 Lancaster, 1 Whitley. The total loss of aircraft exceeded the previous highest loss of 37 aircraft on the night of 7/8 November 1941 when a large force was sent out in bad weather conditions, but the proportion of the force lost in the Cologne raid–3.9 per cent–though high, was deemed acceptable in view of the perfect weather conditions which not only led to the bombing success but also helped the German defences.

'Bomber Command later estimated that 22 aircraft were lost over or near Cologne–16 shot down by Flak, 4 by night fighters and 2 in a collision; most of the other losses were due to night fighter action in the radar boxes between the coast and Cologne. Bomber Command also calculated the losses suffered by each of the three waves of the attack–4.8, 4.1 and 1.9 per cent–and assumed that the German defences were progressively overwhelmed by bombing and affected by smoke as the raid went on. Further calculations showed that the losses suffered by the operational training unit crews–3.3 per cent–were lower than the 4.1 per cent casualties of the regular bomber groups and also that those training aircraft with pupil pilots suffered lower casualties than those with instructor pilots!'

A former Stirling pilot and author of *A Thousand Shall Fall*, Murray Peden, wrote: 'The Stirling was truly a wonderful aircraft which rendered great service as Britain's first four-engined bomber. But for its needless maiming at birth by the short-sighted planners who conjured up the Air Ministry specifications, the Stirling might well have out-performed even the great Lancaster. She assuredly was second to none as

top: Bombs on a trolley to be loaded aboard this Stirling as it is being refuelled for a night operation in 1942; above: A clever depiction of British Prime Minister Neville Chamberlain early in 1940.

a sturdy and dependable battler . . . The Short Stirling earned the highest honours, and never received them 'except from every pilot she ever bore aloft'.' In *Stirling Wings*, by Jonathan Falconer, Group Captain T.G. 'Hamish' Mahaddie wrote, 'I relish the opportunity to come to the defence of the Stirling, in spite of its operational shortcomings when compared to the Halifax and Lancaster. I find it most warming in the times since the end of the war to attend reunions of No 7 Squadron crews, where my keen interest and enthusiasm for the dear old Stirling is shared. True, we did suffer higher casualties than those above us, and from time to time we were party to damage by HE and incendiaries falling on us from above. In particular I remember a rear gunner in No 3 Group who, with his turret, was separated from his Stirling by a bomb from on high.

'It took the genius of Don Bennett, the Pathfinder Force leader, to add nearly 8,000 feet to the Stirling's meagre operating height of about 13,000 ft by the simple expedient of reducing the quantity of .303 ammunition (based on what was usually brought home), cutting the fuel reserve of 22 per cent by a half, and further removing all the armour plating including the vast door, which measured 7/8 inch thick, between the front cabin and the outer fuselage. I personally recall being at never less than 19,000 ft on any target during my PFF tour, except on the original PFF first sortie to Flensburg.

'One of the most remarkable features of the Stirling was its ability to absorb battle damage. I remember in the first months of the PFF one of its founder members, Flg Off Trench, suffered a direct hit from HE which dislodged the port inner engine and left a large hole and a mass of wires and ancillary gear waving about in the slipstream. Nevertheless, Trench made it back to Oakington, and was immediately awarded the DSO, an honour I believe he shared with Len Cheshire as the only junior officers to receive such an honour at such a rank.

'I would beg leave to present my personal experience, when my own Stirling, C-Charlie, got a squirt of 174 cannon shells from a nightfighter over the target of Cologne. It was clear that we must have been stalked by the Ju 88 prior to the actual strike, during which he used his upward-firing *Schräge Musik* twin

left: Air Chief Marshal Sir Arthur Harris, Commander-in-Chief, RAF Bomber Command; below left: Air Vice Marshal Donald Bennett, Commander, the Pathfinder Force.

above: A profile of Sir Winston Churchill.

'Like German opeara, war is too long and too loud.'
– Evelyn Waugh

top: The British Distinguished Flying Cross; right: A famous image by the renowned British aviation photographer Charles E. Brown, Stirling 1s of No. 1651 Heavy Conversion Unit over Cambridgeshire in late April 1942.

cannon. While the aim was very accurate, oddly enough the shells ended up in the region of the bombbay and happily not in the area of the fuel tanks. Nonetheless, the attack immobilized the entire aircraft and wounded four crew. With hydraulics shattered and the guns useless, instrument panel disintegrated and master compass U/S, the navigator still made it to base on the astro compass.

'In spite of the affection that crews had for the Stirling, it would be less than true not to stress how kindly they took to the conversion to the Lancaster. This was particularly so on No 7 Squadron, as I remember, when crews found that they were able to carry extra PFF stores further and higher than hitherto.

'The Stirling had a short but effective life during the Harris offensive. Then despite being relegated from the first division it came into its own once more on the ill-fated Operation 'Market Garden' when it towed gliders. Indeed, the Stirling became a warm favourite with the Glider Pilot Regiment. It is small wonder, therefore that Stirling crews testify to their undying faith in this fine old aircraft. Despite its limitations, it is remembered with pride and gratitude.'

The aeroplane has been remembered by former ground crew personnel for the risk involved in working on the engines from the upper surface of the wing. On the ground the nose of the Stirling reached nearly twenty-three feet high, and mechanics had to be constantly alert against the possibility of falling to the hardstand from its very high wing. It was not only the tallest, but also the longest of any aircraft in the RAF in the Second World War. Empty, the Stirling weighed more than twenty tons. When carrying a full load of bombs and fuel, the maximum height it could climb to was generally around 17,000 feet and frequently much less. The excessively short wing simply could not produce the lift required to take it higher in that condition.

The giant bomber was operated by a seven-man crew: a pilot, co-pilot, wireless operator/mid-upper gunner, navigator, bomb aimer/front gunner, flight engineer/mid-upper gunner, and rear gunner. It was armed with 0.303 calibre Browning machine-guns in three turrets: below the cockpit for the front gun-

ner, one in the top of the fuselage behind the wings and manned by the mid-upper gunner, and one in the tail for the rear gunner. The navigator sat at a table located just behind the cockpit and just in front of a heavy bulkhead where the wings joined the fuselage. The table for the wireless operator was situated just behind this bulkhead. The instrument panel for the flight engineer was located on the starboard side of the fuselage, to the right of the wireless operator's station.

The Stirling had commenced operations against the enemy in February 1941. With the ever-growing numbers of the better-perfoming Lancaster and Halifaxes on the squadrons of Bomber Command by the autumn of 1943, it was decided to reduce the employment of Stirlings as part of the bomber main force. The decision was based largely on an RAF study of the losses that Bomber Command experienced in its attacks on Berlin and Nuremberg between August and November 1943. It showed that the Stirlings involved in these raids suffered losses averaging between ten and fifteen per cent, a loss rate far higher than that of either the Halifaxes or Lancasters flying the same raids. By early 1944, the Stirling had been removed from bombing operations entirely, and for the remainder of the war it was re-assigned to special agent and supply drops over Nazi-occupied Europe, mine-laying, and electronic countermeasures activity for Bomber Command. It was also heavily used as a glider tug, a transport, and in the heavy conversion units for much of that period.

In August 1942, Acting Group Captain D.C.T. Bennett's Pathfinder Force was established from four Bomber Command squadrons, including the Stirlings and crews of No. 7 Squadron. But, as Denis Richards and Hilary St. George Saunders noted in *Royal Air Force, 1939–1945, Volume II, The Fight Avails*: 'The Pathfinders came into being only after protracted disagreement between Air Marshal Harris and the Air Staff. That the main force would have to be led by specially selected crews was not at issue, for this was already our practice. But the Air Staff's proposal to take these crews from their squadrons and concentrate them in a single corps d'élite seemed to

Harris—and to his Group Commanders—destructive of squadron morale. Throughout the spring and summer of 1942 the Bomber chief had accordingly fought the project with all his accustomed vigour; but his opposition, if spirited, soon developed into a rearguard action.' In *Pathfinder*, Don Bennett calls attention to a direct order given to Harris by Churchill, through the Chief of Air Staff, and since it 'was forced upon him, he insisted that I should command it, in spite of my relatively junior rank . . . He told me that whilst he was opposed to the Pathfinder Force and would waste no effort on it, he would support me personally in every way.' The Pathfinders were headquartered at RAF Wyton near Huntingdon, Cambridgeshire. Their bases included Oakington (with Stirlings), Gravely (with Halifaxes), Wyton (with Lancasters), and Warboys (with Wellingtons). Their initial remit was to precede the main bomber force to seek out the target and drop parachute flares for the bomb aimers of the main force to use as an aiming point.

Michael Cumming, in his fine book *Pathfinder Cranswick*, wrote: 'On a typical day, Pathfinder Force's leader learns during the morning the target selected for the night's operations. With his planning staff he works out the tactics his crews will use. These will depend on the size of the bombing force, the nature of the target and the anticipated weather conditions. The strength of the Pathfinders varies too. Sometimes the proportion of Pathfinders to Main Force planes is as low as one in fifteen; sometimes, when an attack is divided into several phases, Pathfinders' contribution may be as high as three in ten. When the general plan of attack has been decided, Bennett's squadrons receive their orders. At P.F.F. dromes all planes are checked on the ground and in the air so that they will be ready for the night's activities. The crews, eyeing the weather at frequent intervals, know that unless there is any deterioration in existing conditions they will be aviating tonight. In the squadron offices a list of stand-by captains goes up; the nominated captains move around the various sections notifying their crews—the navigators, the gunners, the wireless operators and the flight engineers—saying that they have been put down for flying tonight.

'For those who are taking part in the forthcoming raid there is the briefing session to be attended during the early evening when the crews gather to hear the targets chosen for them and learn about the arrangements for take-off, the route to be followed and the weather conditions forecast along the journey and over the target. They are told the method of attack and assessments of the enemy defences, too; meanwhile the aircraft are being loaded with the fuel, ammunition, markers and bombs. As darkness begins to fall the crews sit down to supper before collecting their flying kit, parachute, flasks of coffee, cans of fruit juice and chocolate and have a fitness check from the doctor before scrambling into the trucks that take them out to the waiting bombers.

'It is the turn of one of the Ruhr towns to receive a Pathfinder-led blasting tonight. There are a dozen Halifaxes forming the trailblazers, flying high above the Dutch coast, while the Main Force squadrons are still streaming over East Anglia and the North Sea. The Pathfinder planes are manned by operational veterans, expert in the triple arts of navigating, bomb-aiming and flying. Installed inside each aircraft are the scientists' latest contributions to the bombing campaign. The finest crews, the finest equipment; Bomber Command cannot afford mistakes in identifying and marking a target.

'Searchlights are weaving patterns in the night sky and the curtain of flak is drawn across the path of the Halifaxes. Each shell explodes with a sudden flash, heralding the thump that seems to come from just outside the aircraft. This is Happy Valley, Germany's most heavily defended area, but the Pathfinders have been here before many times and know what to expect in the way of a greeting from Jerry.

'A pilot needs fantastic guts to keep his bomber flying straight through a barrage as intense as Happy Valley. Jagged red-hot splinters from the bursting shells bombard the plane; blast sends it shuddering and skidding across the sky. But the pilot must ignore these distractions when he is trying to pinpoint a target with the precision of the Pathfinders. The Finders go in first, flying parallel a couple of miles apart, each releasing a stick of flares across the target area. These are special flares, hooded to stop their glare from blinding the next Pathfinder crews, who are known as the Illuminators; their task is to explore the ten miles of territory already lit up and then drop a close pattern of coloured flares round the point to be bombed.

'All the time the enemy guns are pumping up enormous quantities of shells, but the Pathfinders cannot waste time waiting for the barrage to ease because the flares will go out and the Main Force planes will arrive and not know where to drop their bombs. So in go the last of the Pathfinders. These are the Markers and their role is to put down a carpet of incendiaries so that when the flares indicating the actual target have burned themselves out there will be fires already raging on which the bombers can aim.

'Tonight the target is free of cloud but the Pathfinders are able to pave the way for the bombers even if the clouds completely mask the whole area. They locate the target with their instruments and drop a special type of parachute flare to mark a spot in the sky, above the clouds, which the bombers can use as a substitute aiming point. These sky-markers burn for four or five minutes—long enough for a stream of bombers to send down a sizeable weight of high-explosives on top of the unseen objective. Replenishing markers can be dropped by successive Pathfinders.'

With the appearance of the new Mk III Stirling on the squadrons, came the expectation of an improved performance for the aircraft, with greater speed, climb and maximum ceiling numbers, but despite the enhanced performance, loss rates among the Stirlings were growing. Eight Stirlings of eighty-three launched in an attack on Stuttgart in the night of 14/15 April 1943 were lost, or nearly ten per cent of the Stirling force dispatched. On 28/29 April, of thirty-two Stirlings sent on a mine-laying mission, seven were lost, for a loss rate of nearly twenty-three per cent. But as the year wore on, combat attrition among the Stirlings began to fall, particularly after the introduction of "Window", the fine strips of tin foil dropped in large quantities by the bombers to con-

TO OPEN THIS PACK TEAR DIAGONALLY FROM ANY CORNER AS INDICATED BY ARROWS.

FIRST AID OUTFIT FOR AIR CREWS

. . . CONTENTS . . .

AMPOULES SYRINGE (MORPHIA) . . . 2.   FOR SEVERE PAIN
ANTI-BURN MITTENS . . . . 2.   FOR HAND BURNS
ANTI-BURN JELLY IN 1oz. TUBES . . . 1.   FOR BURNS OTHER THAN
LARGE WOUND DRESSING . . . . 1.
SAFETY PINS . . . . 1.

NOTE:- SEE INSTRUCTIONS FOR USE ON EACH PACKET INSIDE.

ON BURNS OTHER THAN ON HANDS SPREAD ANTI-BURN JELLY OVER BURN AREA AND ALLOW TO DRY.

DO NOT USE ANTI-BURN JELLY WITH THE MITTENS

above: A standard issue Royal Air Force bomber air-crew first aid kit; right: A pair of RAF identification dogtags; far right: A Heavy Conversion Unit crew at a bomber station near Cambridge in the Second World War.

fuse the German radars. A total of 791 RAF bombers attacked Hamburg on the evening of 24/25 July 1943, including 125 Stirlings. Window was employed for the first time on this raid and just twelve bombers were lost from the entire force, with only three Stirlings among the losses. Thereafter, more than 100 Stirlings were regularly being dispatched in the big raids of Bomber Command. On 10/11 August 119 were sent to Nuremberg with the loss of just three. This was followed on 12/13 August by a raid on Turin in which 112 Stirlings participated with the loss of just two. Then came the memorable Bomber Command offensive against Berlin.

With the bloody Battle of Berlin, the losses of Bomber Command rose significantly and the losses of the squadrons operating Stirlings in the campaign were exceptionally high. It was simply a fact that the insufficient wing area of the plane meant that, in general, it could not climb to and maintain the bombing altitude of the other Bomber Command heavies, the Lancaster and Halifax. The Stirlings were forced to operate well below the altitudes of the main force bomber stream and as such were subjected to greater punishment from the enemy flak guns.

The first night of Bomber Command operations against the big city saw a large force of Lancasters attack the target while a force of 114 Stirlings and 281 other bombers struck Ludwigshafen and Mannheim in a diversionary raid. Ten Stirlings were lost in the effort. Four nights later, on 22/23 November 1943, fifty Stirlings joined 714 other RAF bombers as the main force in an attack on the German capital. Five Stirlings failed to return. Stirling losses were now averaging ten per cent a raid, clearly an unsustainable rate, and the decision was made to withdraw the big plane from bombing operations over Germany.

Stirlings continued to serve with the Royal Air Force in a variety of roles, including bombing. They were used effectively in attacks on the German V-1 flying bomb launch sites in France, including the raid of 16/17 December 1943, when twenty-six Stirlings bombed the V-1 site at Abbeville, a mission in which the force experienced no losses. In addition to such raids, the big planes participated in a number of mine-

laying operations. They were also utilized in the dropping of SOE (Special Operations Executive) agents into enemy-occupied territory. The Stirlings played a key role in the preparations for the Allied invasion at Normandy on 6 June 1944, when they performed a precision drop of Window to muddle the German radars in the area, causing the enemy to believe that the invasion force was coming into the Boulogne region, well down the coast from the Normandy beaches where the actual landings took place. On D-Day the Stirlings of No. 199 Squadron aided the main force bombers by effectively jamming German radar, and finally, No. 38 Group Stirlings supported the massive landing operations by towing a great number of gliders delivering troops to Normandy.

Following the D-Day landings, Stirlings continued in mine-laying operations and attacks on the V-1 sites in northern France. In the Arnhem operation of September 1944, Stirlings brought paratroops to their drop zones and towed gliders bringing supplies to help maintain the offensive. Meanwhile, Stirlings of Nos. 138 and 161 Squadrons, operating mainly from Tempsford in the Midlands, continued their SOE missions. In January 1945, No 38 Group Stirlings were again used as bombers, though not as a part of Bomber Command, in attacks on enemy troop concentrations in Belgium. By the end of the war in Europe the bombers had assumed a transport role,

left: The crew of a Stirling bomber is interrogated after a bombing raid; below: The results of an RAF Bomber Command attack on the German city Kaiserlautern.

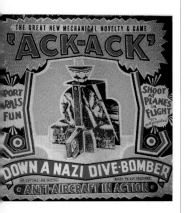

bringing in vitally needed supplies and carrying newly liberated Allied prisoners of war back to England.

Throughout the war, the Short Stirling served with distinction in a wide range of operational activities and was a much better aircraft than is generally believed. Had it been accorded appropriate and intelligent planning and consideration by the Air Ministry at its inception, the big bomber might well have been the best of the British heavyweights in that conflict.

Specifications: Short Stirling Mk 1
Engines: Four Bristol Hercules XI radials rated at 1,590 hp each
Maximum speed: 260 mph at 10,500 ft
Cruising speed: 200 mph at 15,000 ft
Service ceiling: 16,500 ft with maximum load
Normal range: 1,930 miles with medium load
Maximum take-off weight: 70,000 lb
Wingspan: 99 ft 1 in
Length: 87 ft 3 in
Height: 22 ft 9 in
Wing area: 1,460 sq ft
Bomb-load: 17,000 lb maximum.
Defensive armament: Two Browning 0.303 machine-guns each in nose and dorsal turrets; four Browning 0.303 machine-guns in tail turret.

Short Stirling Mk III
Engines: Four Bristol Hercules XVI radials rated at 1,650 hp each
Maximum speed: 260 mph at 14,500 ft
Cruising speed: 200 mph at 10,000 ft
Service ceiling: 17,000 ft
Normal range: 2,010 miles with 3,500 lb bomb load; 740 miles with 14,000 lb bomb load
Maximum take-off weight: 70,000 lb
Wingspan: 99 ft 1 in
Length: 87 ft 3 in
Height: 22 ft 9 in
Wing area: 1,460 sq ft
Bomb-load: 14,000 lb
Defensive armament: Eight 0.303 Browning machine-guns.

'An appeaser is one who feeds a crocodile, hoping that it will eat him last.'
— Winston Churchill

Right: A late winter afternoon on a Cambridgeshire hard-stand. A Stirling aircrew and the bombs they will drop on Germany that evening.

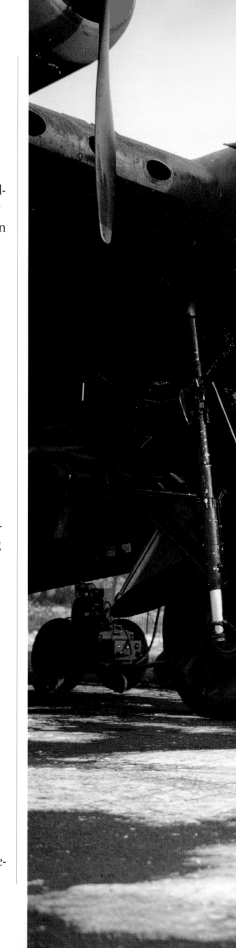

BOEING

right: B-29s of the 500th Bomb Group raining thousands of incendiary bombs on their target at Yokohama, Japan, on 29 May 1945. So prone to engine fires were the Boeing Superfortresses that air crews often referred to them as 'three turning, one burning.' Operating from bases in the Marianas Islands, the 500th was part of the 73rd Bomb Wing (VH), the first unit to fly the 1,200 miles from Saipan to attack Japanese target cities.

'The Reverend Mr Tanimoto got up at five o'clock that morning. He was alone in the parsonage, because for some time his wife had been commuting with their year-old baby to spend nights with a friend in Ushida, a suburb to the north. Of all the important cities of Japan, only two, Kyoto and Hiroshima, had not been visited in strength by *B-San*, or *Mr B*, as the Japanese, with a mixture of respect and unhappy familiarity, called the B-29; and Mr Tanimoto, like all his neighbours and friends, was almost sick with anxiety. He had heard uncomfortably detailed accounts of mass raids on Kure, Iwakuni, Tokuyama, and other nearby towns; he was sure Hiroshima's turn would come soon. He had slept badly the night before, because there had been several air-raid warnings. Hiroshima had been getting such warnings almost every night for weeks, for at that time the B-29s were using Lake Biwa, northeast of Hiroshima, as a rendezvous point, and no matter what city the Americans planned to hit, the Superfortresses streamed in over the coast near Hiroshima. The frequency of the warnings and the continued abstinence of Mr B with respect to Hiroshima had made its citizens jittery; a rumour was going around that the Americans were saving something special for the city.'
— from *Hiroshima*, by John Hersey

A strong case can be made that two aeroplanes, the P-51 Mustang fighter and the B-29 Superfortress bomber, contributed more to bringing the Second World War to a successful conclusion for the Allies than any other aircraft. In the European theatre of operations, the highly controversial daylight precision-bombing campaign of the American Eighth and Fifteenth Air Forces was in deep trouble at the end of 1943. Their heavily armed B-17 Flying Fortress and B-24 Liberator bombers had been billed as capable of protecting themselves from the fighters in the skies of Nazi-occupied Europe, but in fact they were incurring unsustainable losses in their frequent raids. Even the presence of their 'little friends', the P-47 Thunderbolt, P-38 Lightning and RAF Spitfire fighter escorts, was insufficient protection. None of the three types had enough range to stay with the bombers through the entirety of the missions,

which were then extending deep into Germany. The situation seemed all but hopeless and pressure was mounting in many quarters for the Americans to admit the failure of their daylight bombing policy and throw in with the British in their night-time area-bombing effort.

Then came the arrival of the first Mustangs in the ETO, P-51Bs and Cs, miraculous Merlin-engined melds of American and British thinking and technology, which for the first time in the war, made it possible for USAAF fighter groups to shepherd the American heavy bombers all the way to the farthest enemy targets and back. The P-51 Mustangs were soon providing a high level of protection from the German fighters. With the Mustang, the bomber boys knew they now had at least a reasonable chance of surviving their rugged tours of duty. With it the American daylight bombing campaign, coupled with that of the RAF at night, finally ended Germany's capability to wage war by crushing her industrial, transport and oil targets. Without the extraordinary range and capability of the Mustang, that goal would have been far more difficult, maybe even impossible to achieve.

In the Pacific theatre, the Japanese were proving even more difficult to overcome than the Germans had been. With fanatical determination they continued to pursue victory despite the utter hopelessness of their position at the end of 1944. Their military leaders vowed to make the Allies pay a staggering cost in lives and equipment by forcing a massive invasion of the Japanese home islands rather than submit to what they saw as the shame and indignity of surrender on Allied terms.

In Washington, a crisis of leadership loomed with the illness of President Franklin D. Roosevelt. US vice-president, Harry Truman, was an unknown quantity in the spring of 1945, having been in office only three months when Roosevelt died. Truman was left in charge of the American war effort at its most critical moment. One can only imagine the new president's emotions on being briefed, shortly after assuming power, about the existence of an entirely new and unimaginably powerful bomb believed capable of totally destroying a major city. Truman was

B-29

forced to ponder the pros and cons of invading the Japanese islands and suffering projected casualties of up to a million Allied military personnel, or employing the new untested weapon against one or more Japanese cities in the belief that that act would force the enemy to surrender unconditionally, ending the war.

Major-General Curtis E. LeMay arrived in the China-Burma-India theatre of operations in late August 1944 to take charge of the American Twentieth Bomber Command and its continuing series of attacks on Japanese targets. LeMay went along on some of the raids and quickly instituted a number of procedural changes. His primary emphasis was on daylight precision bombing, which he had helped to conduct so successfully in the European theatre. He brought in the technique of target marking by Pathfinder aircraft and his reforms were beginning to pay dividends, but the loss rate of his B-29s and crews was also growing rapidly and was soon unacceptably high. Finally, it was decided to concentrate all B-29 operations against Japan from the newly captured Marianas island group in the central Pacific, whose main islands of Saipan, Guam and Tinian would shortly provide ideal bases for the big bombers. From the Marianas LeMay would conduct a new series of fire raids with a ferocity even greater than that of the earlier attacks on German cities. Tokyo and sixty other cities of Japan had utilized a great amount of wood and paper in their highly combustible structures. The precision-bombing approach was not producing the desired results and a radical solution was under consideration. In the B-29 LeMay had a bomber with sufficient "legs" and bomb-load capacity to bring enormous quantities of incendiary bombs over great expanses of ocean, to hit Japan hard and often and make her burn.

The first B-29 bomber to arrive on Saipan was called *Joltin' Josie*. It was 12 October 1944, and *Josie* was the first of many hundreds of the planes coming to the Marianas for the final campaign against Japan. Her lineage went back to a project of the Seattle-based aeroplane maker Boeing. It was called Model 322.

left: A superb photograph of a B-29 at North Field, Guam in 1945, by Harold E. Gronenthal of the 70th Naval Construction Battalion; below: The book that told the story of the first US bombing raid on Japan in the Second World War, which was led by then-Colonel James H. Doolittle who would later command the US Eighth Air Force in England.

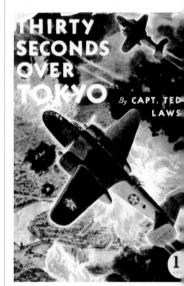

below: A B-29 bombardier at his Norden bombsight in the nose of the aircraft. The device was actually an analog computer which utilized air speed, drift, altitude and heading data to solve the bomb ballistics geometry for the bombardier during the bomb run to the target. Beginning in 1943, AFCE or Automatic Flight Control Equipment, was introduced in the European Theatre of Operations, linking the bombsight with the autopilot of the aircraft and virtually eliminating human error from the procedure, greatly improving results in so-called precision bombing. Another change in method during 1943 came when all the bombardiers in a heavy bomber formation released their bombs when the lead bombardier dropped his bombs, resulting in a much tighter bomb pattern on the targets and greater bombing efficiency.

The B-29 is considered by many historians and authorities to be the best heavy bomber of the Second World War. She was the last mass-produced big bomber of that conflict and the first such aircraft to utilize remotely controlled defensive armament, a central fire-control system, and fully pressurized crew compartments. The B-29 was the Boeing company's response to a 1938 US Army request for a new heavy bomber similar to the B-17, but pressurized. The company had already designed and built the first pressurized airliner to enter commercial service, the Model 307 Stratoliner, and was a logical choice to produce what the Army wanted. Boeing's design study called for a plane similar in appearance to the Stratoliner, but having a tricycle landing-gear instead of a tail wheel. Power was to come from four Pratt & Whitney R-2180 radial engines. The aeroplane was specified to have a maximum speed of 307 mph at 25,000 feet, and a maximum bomb-load of just under 10,000 lb. Though impressed with the aircraft Boeing was proposing, the Army was not then able to fund the project. Fortunately, the company chose to carry on developing the plane on its own.

The Model 322 evolved into the Model 333A, which examined the prospect of fully pressurizing the plane but discarded it because of the problems related to de-pressurizing the bombbays at high altitude for bombing. A decision was taken instead to link the

pressurized forward and aft crew compartments with a pressurized tunnel that passed over the bombbays, enabling crew members to transit between the compartments in flight.

Next came Models 333B, 334 and, in the summer of 1939, Model 334A, the aeroplane that would ultimately resemble the final B-29 design. It would be followed by Model 341, a turning point for the company in the evolution of the new plane.

In November, US Army Air Corps General Henry H. Arnold, concerned by information he had been receiving about rapidly developing new aircraft projects in Germany, requested and received authorization to engage major American aircraft companies in studies on the development of a new, very-long-range bomber. This was followed, in January 1940, with the issue of formal requirements for the VLR bomber to the Boeing, Douglas, Consolidated, and Lockheed aeroplane companies. Boeing was in the most advantageous position of the four, having begun work on its Model 341 project in August 1939. Model 341 featured a new high-aspect-ratio wing. The aeroplane was projected to have a top speed of 405 mph at 25,000 feet, with power coming from four Pratt & Whitney R-2800 radial engines rated at 2,000 hp each. 342 was to have a range of 7,000 miles with a one-ton bomb load, and a 10,000 lb bomb-load for shorter missions. Model 341 was reworked and refined into what then became Model 345, the design which would be submitted to the Army for final design approval. 345 called for an aeroplane powered by four Wright R-3350 Cyclone eighteen-cylinder radial engines, each with a pair of General Electric B-11 turbosuperchargers, for a rated take-off horsepower of 2,200. The maximum speed was to be 382 mph at 25,000 feet.

The new bomber featured a double-wheeled tricycle landing-gear arrangement that retracted into the engine nacelles, four retractable twin 0.50 calibre machine-gun turrets and a tail turret with two 0.50 calibre machine-guns and one 20 mm cannon. All of the retractable Sperry power-turrets were operated through remote control by gunners sighting through periscopes. Bombing capability was specified as 2,000 lb over a distance of 5,333 miles at a cruising

speed of 290 mph. The maximum bomb load was to be 16,100 lb. The Army received the Boeing design submission for the aeroplane on 11 May 1940. It then requested additional funded studies and in late June ordered preliminary engineering data for the new plane from all four plane makers, applying designations to their projected bombers in order of Army preference: Boeing–XB-29, Lockheed–XB-30, Douglas–XB-31 and Consolidated–XB-32. By 6 September, both Douglas and Lockheed had withdrawn from the competition for the new plane and two prototypes were ordered from Boeing. A further two prototypes were ordered from Consolidated, in case the Boeing design proved unsuccessful.

By late spring 1941, many in Washington foresaw US involvement in the war that had been going on in Europe and the far east for some time. Priority for the B-29 project began to rise. Fourteen test aeroplanes designated YB-29, were ordered, and the Army announced that an order for the first 250 production B-29s was forthcoming, to be confirmed in September. These planes were to be built at a new government-owned plant in Wichita, Kansas, which was being leased to Boeing specifically for B-29 production. With Japan's attack on US Navy ships and facilities at Pearl Harbor, Hawaii, on 7 December 1941, the Army increased its B-29 order to 500 aircraft. By February 1942, the Army had again increased its order for the new plane, to 1,500, and three additional aircraft manufacturers were asked to build B-29s–Bell Aircraft in Marietta, Georgia, the General Motors Fisher Body Division in Cleveland, Ohio, and North American Aviation at its new plant in Kansas City, Missouri. Before implementation of these plans, North American was asked to focus on the manufacture of its B-25 bomber at the Kansas City plant, and additional B-29 production was shifted to Boeing's Renton, Washington plant. The General Motors Cleveland plant was also asked later to concentrate production on fighter aircraft and the Glenn Martin Company was contracted to take GM's place in the manufacture of B-29s, at another new government plant in Omaha, Nebraska. A large subcontracting programme was also established to provide major B-29 sub-assemblies and components

from several companies including Goodyear, Cessna, and Chrysler.

In the course of testing and evaluating the new wing for the B-29, it was discovered that its very high wing loading would result in a nearly prohibitive landing speed. This led to the Fowler flap system which, when extended, added twenty per cent to the overall wing area and provided acceptable performance. To help maintain the critical balance of the aeroplane during actual bombing, when the gross weight would be suddenly reduced, the dropping of bombs was to be controlled through an intervalometer which alternated the release of the bombs between the two bombbays.

On most combat missions a crew of twelve would be carried, including two pilots, a bombardier, a flight engineer, a navigator, a radio operator, a radar operator and five gunners. The bombardier operated his bombsight and guns in the nose, ahead of the pilot and co-pilot, who rode behind armour panels and bullet-resistant glass. The navigator, radio operator and flight engineer rode in a compartment just behind the cockpit, and the radar operator and gunners were positioned in a pressurized section of the fuselage to the rear of the bombbays. The tail-gunner rode in his own tiny pressurized compartment under the towering vertical fin.

While the B-29 would ultimately prove an excellent bomber and a generally superb aircraft, through its development and the early part of its operational career, it had one terrible flaw–its engines. For much of the aeroplane's operational span it was referred to by wags, and many crew members, as "three turning, one burning", an epithet of some legitimacy. The Wright R-3350 was designed and initially tested in 1937. It demonstrated considerable promise, generating enthusiasm in the Army Air Corps. But by 1940 it had still not been put into production when American involvement in the war began to seem inevitable. Suddenly, Army pressure to get on with development of the engine led to a speed-up in production and some serious and persistent problems. The new, unproved powerplant, whose development was now being hurried by the exigencies of war, would cost the lives of many airmen and threaten

'Usually, when a lot of men get together, it's called war.' – Mel Brooks

above: Brigadier General Billy Mitchell was probably the best-known American proponent of air power and the bomber between the two world wars.

far right: A B-29 as depicted by illustrator Pvt. Fred Kaplan while serving with the 307th Bomb Group (H), a B-24 outfit on Guadalcanal during the war. There, he designed and painted many of the girls, ala Petty and Vargas, on the noses of the group's bombers.

the B-29 programme itself. Boeing was already under severe pressure from the Army to incorporate nearly 900 design changes in the plane between 1940 and 1942, including the elimination of the Sperry armament system in order to replace it with the new computer-controlled General Electric system. All of this and the on-going engine trouble were of extreme concern to the company.

When Boeing's Chief Test Pilot, Edmund 'Eddie' Allen began flying an XB-29 in September 1942, he must have been concerned about engineering projections that the engines were likely to become dangerously over-heated after little more than an hour of operation. He first flew the plane on 21 September for seventy-five minutes and was pleased with its performance. Both he and the assigned Army Air Force project officer, Colonel Donald Putt, were impressed with its handling characteristics and the lightness of the controls, remarkable for such a heavy aeroplane . . . and that it was 'easier to fly than a B-17'. Through the first eighteen hours of flight testing their impressions remained largely favourable, but on 28 December Allen was forced to prematurely abort a test flight of the prototype aeroplane when the number one engine caught fire. Another fire occurred two days later during the first flight of the Number Two XB-29. With that, further testing was suspended, to be restarted on 18 February 1943. In a disastrous resumption of the test programme, Allen experienced in-flight fires in two engines of the second XB-29. He declared the emergency but before he could return to the field, the fire burned through the wing. Allen, his entire eleven-man crew, nineteen workers in the Frye Packing Plant just north of Boeing Field, and five firemen died when the bomber fell on the packing plant after breaking up in the air.

The B-29 flight-test programme was halted. In Washington, General Arnold worried that the B-29 programme itself would soon be cancelled, with a profound and undoubtedly negative effect on the American war effort. He acted quickly to save the aeroplane, bringing in Brigadier-General Kenneth Wolfe to head a new 'B-29 Special Project'. Wolfe was given charge of the entire B-29 programme—aero-

plane production, flight testing and crew training. His remit was to have the B-29 ready for combat by the end of 1943.

Wolfe, Boeing, Wright, and literally thousands of people with specialized skills went to work, and slowly but steadily, progress began to result. The crew-training aspect proved one of the most demanding challenges issued by Arnold. With the substitution of the General Electric gun system in the aeroplane, the crew composition changed. It would be an eleven-man crew, with one less gunner required. The crew now comprised the aircraft commander, pilot, navigator, bombardier, flight engineer, radio operator, radar operator, central fire-control gunner, the left and right gunners and the tail gunner. The normal time scale to train specialist crew members then ran to between twelve and twenty-seven weeks, unacceptable within the constraints set by General Arnold. A partial solution came with a decision to enlist experienced volunteer B-24 bomber crewmen who were back in the States after completing their tours of duty in Europe and North Africa. All of these men, however, were new to the B-29, a far more complex and sophisticated aircraft than the one they were familiar with, and a long period of orientation and crew integration was required before they would be ready to go to war in the new bomber.

The training and crew integration was conducted at four air bases in Kansas under the direction of Colonel La Verne Saunders. Any shortcuts that could be justified were taken, but by December only a relative handful of crews were approaching readiness for deployment. Very few B-29s had arrived to be used in the training and much of it had to be flown in B-17s, good aeroplanes but far from capable of replicating the performance of the 29. The training programme, and the aeroplane production programme, were simply not proceeding at anywhere near the required pace. Boeing was under pressure to test, prove and produce in quantity, a totally new, incredibly complicated aeroplane in a time scale that did not allow for proper analysis, trial and error, bug locating and debugging. All new aeroplanes come with some built-in problems; complex planes tend to have more of them. The pressure on Boeing was exacerbated by the client's seemingly endless demands for modifications, which quite reasonably were based on experiences accrued in actual air-combat operations over Europe. At the Wright company an intensive effort was under way by the engineering staff on the engine overheating problem, and they were making progress, but throughout 1943 the engine fires persisted, with nineteen early-production B-29s being lost to that cause. Two new marks of the R-3350 were introduced, with modifications that did reduce both the tendency of the powerplant to overheat, and the related fire incidents. The originally specified three-bladed propellers of the XB-29s were replaced in the newer aircraft by four-bladed Hamilton Standard hydromatic propellers, 16 ft 7 in in diameter, with constant-speed governors and hydraulically-operated pitch and feathering control. However, a key effect of these and many other important modifications then being implemented was that General Arnold would not be getting the initial 150 B-29s that he was counting on for deployment to the China-Burma-India theatre of operations by April 1944. This new delay was more than he could tolerate, no matter how justifiable, and in February Arnold and Major-General B.E. Meyer left Washington to personally look into the troubled programme. They discovered at first hand that the modification programme was disorganized and almost totally inefficient. Arnold placed Meyer in charge of resolving the matter, insisting on a full report on the readiness status of every single B-29 by the next morning.

Hordes of additional personnel were quickly brought into the programme and the work pace at the various modification centres was increased to a no-nonsense round-the-clock routine. By the end of March the first combat-ready B-29s were available for delivery to the Army Air Force Twentieth Bomber Command, and by 15 April the required 150 aeroplanes were indeed ready for action. The modifications had been accomplished, deliveries were under way and Arnold's plans were back on track, but engine fires continued as did mounting aircraft and crew losses. In late April, all B-29s were grounded again pending the results of an immediate investigation.

The Wright company engineers went back to work

on the problem and this time designed new baffles to greatly enhance engine cooling. This appeared to help considerably, and by 8 May B-29 flights were resumed and nearly all of Arnold's 150 bombers had reached Indian airfields. Once operational in the CBI, however, new problems plagued the B-29 missions. Conditions on the Indian airfields were poor. They had been constructed for B-24 Liberator bombers and engineering difficulties had delayed their completion. The runways were being lengthened to 7,200 feet, which allowed the B-29s to operate, but not fully when loaded. At four principal airfield sites in China, the situation was worse. There the runways were literally being built by hand. Progress was painfully slow, even with 200,000 people working on the project. By May these new fields, though crude by any standard, were usable, but only just.

General Arnold had received the blessing of President Roosevelt to establish a special organization called the Twentieth Air Force which would operate in the Far East under Arnold's command. He committed the new outfit to 'the earliest possible progressive destruction and dislocation of the Japanese military, industrial and economic systems and to undermine the morale of the Japanese people to a point where

BIG WINGS

far right: A sweating USAAF armourer at work in one of the two bombbays of a B-29 Superfortress on a Pacific island base. Above him is the transit tube through which crew members traversed between the front and rear compartments of the fuselage in flight.

their capacity for war is decisively defeated.' To achieve these aims he was given total control of the B-29s in the CBI. Having this authority and making it pay off were entirely separate realities, as the CBI commanders and General Arnold were soon to learn. Supplying the B-29 bases there with high-octane aviation fuel, bombs, ammunition, spare parts, food, etc. was a monumental challenge. The first B-29 missions against Japan were to begin by 1 May, but supply delays compounded into further, greater delays. The first raid was not mounted until 5 June, an attack on the Makasan rail yards in Thailand. Of the 98 B-29s dispatched, fourteen aborted, mainly because of engine trouble. Weather problems resulted in radar bombing and chaos as very few bombs fell in the target area. On the return journey, forty-two of the B-29s ran short of fuel and had to land at bases other than their own, and five bombers crashed on landing. The few raids that could be launched from the CBI bases in the following weeks were even more disastrous for the Americans and as the problems of the CBI commanders grew, Arnold demanded more and more from them, including attacking the 'length and breadth of the Japanese Empire', an order that could not possibly be carried out in view of the shortage of critically needed supplies in the theatre.

The goal of developing a truly effective strategic bombing campaign against Japan itself would not begin to be achieved until the arrival in the CBI of Curtis LeMay in late August. General LeMay was a veteran air leader of the Eighth Air Force in England through the height of the American daylight precision-bombing campaign against Germany. He was legendary as a tough, innovative executive who seemingly thrived on the most difficult challenges. He demanded and got more from his men than did most of his contempories. Arnold brought LeMay in as a fixer, to prop up the Twentieth and produce the sort of results expected of the organization and the B-29. General LeMay participated in some missions and then set about reorganizing the Twentieth and instituting new procedures aimed at overcoming much of what had been hampering the B-29 operations from the CBI. By November his efforts were beginning to take effect, but continuing supply problems and air

craft accidents militated against the achievement of his goals. Added to that was increasingly effective resistance from Japanese fighters and interceptors, along with light bombers being used to drop phosphorous explosives onto the B-29 formations in order to disperse and turn them back. B-29 losses were now mounting appreciably owing to these factors and to air raids by Japanese bombers on the B-29 bases. By the end of the year 147 B-29s had been lost, a number equivalent to the entire force that had been sent over in May. None of this reflected on the nature or quality of LeMay's leadership, which was superb. But something had to be done to stem the losses and in Washington the Joint Chiefs of Staff decided to shut down the CBI bombing operation. In its place they would concentrate all future B-29 operations against Japan from the Marianas, which had only recently been taken from the Japanese after a month of fierce fighting. The raids flown by B-29s from the China bases had been largely ineffective, apart from providing experience for the crews and the planners. The B-29 had yet to live up to its billing.

In the Marianas the big bombers would soon have proper bases from which to strike the Japanese home islands, and crucially, the Marianas could be supplied by ship directly from the United States. Well before the principal islands of Saipan, Guam and Tinian had been secured and cleared of enemy troops, US Navy construction battalions were hard at work preparing new runways and lengthening existing ones to accommodate the heavy Boeing planes. It was heroic work, largely unsung, but mightily appreciated by the crews, who frequently needed every inch of the 9,000-foot runways being built there.

Major-General Haywood Hansell Jr was the man who had flown that first B-29 onto Saipan in October 1944 and it was he who would command the new Twenty-First Bomber Command in the Marianas. General Hansell was tasked with eliminating Japan's war-making capacity. By the end of November more than 100 new B-29s and crews had arrived on Saipan from their training bases in the USA. In naming the Japanese aircraft industry as the top-priority target for the B-29s, the Joint Chiefs expressed their support for Hansell's own operational preference—high-altitude

44

daylight precision attacks. But such attacks couldn't work, within the existing ground rules. Hansell's newly arrived bomber crews were inexperienced as far as the B-29 was concerned, and as the raids began from the Marianas it was immediately apparent that the new crews lacked the skills required for B-29 high-altitude precision attacks. A substantial number of engine failures and fires continued to plague them and the new airfield on Saipan was receiving a number of punishing low-level air attacks from Japanese bombers. With it all, bombing results for the B-29 raids were less, far less, than impressive. Now more was at stake than the future of the B-29, or even that of the air campaign against Japan. General Arnold was convinced that the reality of an independent, autonomous US Air Force was now wholly dependent on the success of the B-29 campaign against Japan. Never mind Hansell's problems; Arnold wanted results quickly. But Hansell was having to cope with crews who had been trained in Kansas, mainly in radar bombing at night and who were having trouble adapting to the high-altitude daylight techniques. Precision attacks were clearly beyond their capability. One example was the raid of 24 November when 111 B-29s were sent to attack the Nakajima Aircraft Company's Musashi aero-engine plant in the Tokyo suburbs. The plant produced approximately thirty percent of the engines for the Japanese Air Force. Things began to go badly wrong as seventeen of the bombers aborted the mission because of engine failure. Then, as the force approached the target area it encountered the phenomenon now known as the jet stream—high-altitude, high-speed winds from the west which were shoving the bombers across the Tokyo area at more than 450 mph, making accurate bombing impossible. In addition, patchy cloud was obscuring the Nakajima plant. In the end just twenty-four B-29 crews managed to drop their bombs in the vicinity of the target. All of the other planes released their loads over other parts of Tokyo. The target factory received very little damage that day. Fortunately for the attacking force, the Japanese put up little resistance, but one bomber was lost when it was deliberately rammed by an enemy fighter.

A number of subsequent raids proved far more

costly to the Americans, with forty bombers lost in eleven attacks. Hansell's efforts were not paying off and the B-29 losses were again mounting. In January General Arnold had had more than enough and recalled Hansell, replacing him with Curtis LeMay from the CBI. Before his departure, however, Hansell began a programme to reduce the weight of the B-29s. He, and then LeMay, considered the loss rate to date and reasoned that at least some of the persistent engine failures related to the excessive weight of the aeroplanes as they were then being employed. The rate

'You can't say civilization don't advance for in every war they kill you in a new way.'
– Will Rogers

below: Captain Colin Kelly, one of America's first heroes of the Second World War. B-17 bomber pilot Kelly attacked a cruiser of the Imperial Japanese Navy in December 1941. In the raid his plane was hit and on fire. He ordered his crew to bale out and remained at the controls while they did so. Before he could follow them, the plane exploded in mid-air. West Point graduate Kelly was posthumously awarded the Distinguished Service Cross; below right: A main landing-gear wheel from a B-29, this example is part of the collection of the Western Aeronautical Museum, Oakland, California.

Capt. Colin P. Kelly, Jr.

of engine-related aborts reached twenty-three per cent by mid-January, when the bombers were put on a severe weight-loss programme. By removing some of what he thought was an excessive amount of 0.50 calibre ammunition and other items, Hansell cut the overall weight of each bomber by 6,000 lb. This had the immediate effect of improving performance significantly, reducing scheduled maintenance and adding greatly to engine life. By July LeMay had the abort rate down to under seven per cent.

Hansell's and LeMay's improvements were enhanced with the completion in February 1945 of the largest bomber base ever built, North Field on Tinian. It had four parallel paved runways nearly 9,000 feet long and all the necessary base facilities to support the kind of operation that General Arnold was demanding. LeMay lost no time in taking full advantage of the resources at his disposal. On 19 February he directed that the priority thereafter in the raids on Japan would be to burn out the towns and cities that supported the aircraft and war-industry targets, rather than continuing with the precision-bombing effort. Initially these raids would be conducted from high altitude, but by the end of February LeMay had become convinced that the combination of the high operating altitude, the jet stream and the frequent cloud cover, was preventing the crews from achieving the objective. He shifted their operations to low-level, highly concentrated incendiary attacks, generally made from between 5,000 and 6,000 feet. He determined to try these attacks at night when, he believed, the enemy would offer the least resistance. On that basis he ordered the heavy General Electric gun systems to be stripped from the aircraft, retaining only the tail-turret armament for defence. This further weight reduction, together with the low bombing altitude, meant that the aeroplanes would be spared the strain of hauling their heavy loads to high altitude, which would save considerably on fuel and engine wear. He would also employ special pathfinder crews to fly ahead of the main bomber force and mark a central aiming point in the target area with high-intensity pyrotechnics. The first trial of this new approach took place on the night of 9/10 March when 279 Superfortresses

reached the target, Tokyo. When the attack began, surface winds were gusting at nearly 30 mph and the fires ignited by the thousands of incendiaries dropped from the bombers rapidly spread, becoming the same type of "fire-storm" that had engulfed much of Hamburg in July 1943. In the aftermath of the raid, 84,000 people had been killed and sixteen square miles of the city had been destroyed. It was and is the single most destructive air raid in history. Fourteen B-29s had been lost, but with this attack LeMay now felt that the bomber was beginning to prove its worth. In the following nights, similar large-scale raids were visited upon Nagoya, Osaka and Kobe, devastating large areas of each. Over the two-week period from 10 March, 120,000 Japanese civilians died in the raids. B-29 losses were relatively light for the scale of the attacks, and General Arnold was mightily pleased with the results of the Marianas forces.

The intensity of these early fire-bombing raids quickly depleted the supply of incendiaries at the B-29 bases, causing LeMay to mount a short series of tactical raids on the airfields of the Japanese home island of Kyushu, in preparation for the American invasion of Okinawa, then set for early April. The airfields were being used by Japanese 'kamikaze' suicide-planes in their attacks on US Navy warships about to take part in the invasion.

The B-29s were able to support the Navy in this way, but the Japanese managed to operate their suicide strikes from other, more remote airstrips and by mid-April the American bombers were back over Japan, bringing a new series of incendiary attacks, this time concentrating on the six major cities of Tokyo, Kobe, Nagoya, Osaka, Kawasaki and Yokohama.

At this point, General LeMay was able to call on the services of more than 500 B-29s and crews, and in fact, had more than 700 of the big planes on station in the Marianas. It had become clear that the fire-bombing by the B-29s was producing indisputably meaningful results which would lead shortly to the total destruction of Japan's cities. While Japanese air defences were also achieving greater success in bringing down the American bombers, with forty-three lost on the two Tokyo raids of 23 and 25 May, by the end of the month more than fifty percent of the city had been destroyed. In the hope that some diversionary daylight high-altitude attacks would confuse the enemy and reduce American bomber losses, a large raid involving 454 B-29s on Yokohama was staged on 29 May. This time the bombers were met and escorted by P-51 Mustangs operating from their forward field on Iwo Jima. The Mustangs engaged a large force of enemy fighters that had risen to defend the city. In the fight twenty-six Japanese planes were shot down for the loss of just three Mustangs and four B-29s.

It was the beginning of the end of Japan's Pacific war. Control of the airspace over her islands passed to the Americans in June as virtually all remaining Japanese aircraft were being saved for last-ditch suicide attacks to be unleashed during the expected Allied invasion of the home islands. At the end of June, all of the six Japanese prime-target cities had been largely destroyed and the B-29s were visiting many of the nation's other cities. LeMay now had the opportunity to utilize some of his best and most experienced bomber crews in a new series of high-level precision attacks on targets that had previously been beyond their ability to hit and hurt. The Musashi aero-engine plant was bombed again, this time with good results.

In another important role for the B-29s, LeMay involved them in a campaign of dropping acoustic and magnetic mines in the western approaches to the Shimonoseki Strait and the Inland Sea between March and August. More than 13,000 such weapons were laid and nearly all enemy merchant and military shipping in Japanese coastal waters was halted.

By July, despite the B-29 fire raids, mining operations, high-altitude precision attacks and a US Army Air Force prediction, Japan's leadership still showed no sign of capitulating to the Allies. Half a world away, in the desert of New Mexico, a group of scientists and engineers engaged in what was code-named the Manhattan Engineering District, or Manhattan Project, were nearing the end of their assignment—the development and testing of the first atom bomb. They exploded that initial device on a test stand in the desert at Trinity Site, Alamogordo, on 16 July 1945. The 100-foot steel tower on which the bomb was mounted was completely vaporized. The surface of the desert for hundreds of yards around the site was fused to glass.

At the time of the test, President Truman was in Germany attending a conference at Potsdam with Soviet Premier Josef Stalin and British Prime Minister Winston Churchill. The topic was the future of Europe. Having been thoroughly briefed about the potential casualties anticipated if the Allies had to invade Japan to bring the war to an end, Truman apparently had no qualms about authorizing the use of the atom bomb against a Japanese target city when he learned that the New Mexico test had been successful. The B-29 would soon perform the task for which it would always be remembered.

The Manhattan Project was, of course, cloaked in secrecy. Most people in the military whose participation was in some way required by the project, were told only that the work being done in New Mexico concerned a new weapon. Manhattan had been started after a group of scientists, alarmed at the apparent progress being made by Germany in nuclear fission, persuaded Albert Einstein to write to President Roosevelt warning him that a weapon of unprecedented power was now possible.

'Ready, fire, aim.'
– Spike Milligan

right: Enrico Fermi, the Italian-born American physicist and Nobel Prize winner, whose work in nuclear physics greatly advanced the American effort to build an atomic weapon in the Second World War; far right: US President Harry Truman who, on the death of President Franklin Delano Roosevelt, in 1945, had to make the decision on the use of the new bomb to end the war with Japan; below: General Curtis E. LeMay commanded the B-29 units in the Marianas and ordered the preparation of the 509th Bomb Group (H) for the delivery of the atomic bombs on the order of President Truman; below right: Then-Colonel Paul Tibbetts was commander of the 509th and was command pilot of the B-29 *Enola Gay* (named after his mother), which dropped the first atomic weapon, on Hiroshima in the morning of 6 August 1945. Two days later a second atom bomb was dropped on Nagasaki. The use of the two bombs resulted in the capitulation of Japan and the end of the war.

F.D. Roosevelt
August 2, 1939
President of the United States
White House
Washington, D.C.

Sir:

Some recent work by E.Fermi and L.Szilard, which has been communicated to me in manuscript, leads me to expect that the element uranium may be turned into a new and important source of energy in the immediate future. Certain aspects of the situation which has arisen seem to call for watchfullness and, if necessary, quick action on the part of the Administration. I believe therefore that it is my duty to bring to your attention the following facts and recommendations:

In the course of the last four months it has been made probable–through the work of Joliot in France as well as Fermi and Szilard in America–that it may become possible to set up a nuclear chain reaction in a large mass of uranium, by which vast amounts of power and large quantities of new radium-like elements would be generated. Now it appears almost certain that this could be achieved in the immediate future.

This new phenomenon would also lead to the construction of bombs, and it is conceivable–though much less certain–that extremely powerful bombs of a new type may thus be constructed. A single bomb of this type, carried by boat and exploded in a port, might very well destroy the whole port together with some of the surrounding territory. However, such bombs might very well prove to be too heavy for transportation by air.

The United States has only very poor ores of uranium in moderate quantities. There is some good ore in Canada and the former Czechoslovakia, while the most important source of uranium is Belgian Congo.

In view of the situation you may think it desirable to have more permanent contact maintained between the Administration and the group of physicists working on chain reactions in America. One possible way of achieving this might be for you to entrust with this task a person who has your confidence and who could perhaps serve in an unofficial capacity. His task might comprise the following:
a) to approach Government Departments, keep them informed of the further development, and put forward recommendations for Government action, giving particular attention to the problem of securing a supply of uranium ore for the United States;
b) to speed up the experimental work, which is at present being carried on within the limits of the budgets of University laboratories, by providing funds, if such funds be required, through his contacts with private persons who are willing to make contributions for this cause, and perhaps also by obtaining the co-operation of industrial laboratories which have the necessary equipment.

I understand that Germany has actually stopped the sale of uranium from the Czechoslovakian mines which she had taken over. That she should have taken such early action might perhaps be understood on the ground that the son of the German Under-Secretary of State, von Weizsäcker, is attached to the Kaiser- Wilhelm-Institut in Berlin where some of the American work on uranium is now being repeated.
Yours very truly,
Albert Einstein

Roosevelt set out to beat the Germans in the race to develop the atomic weapon and the Manhattan Project was launched. The responsibility for the project was given to the US Army Corps of Engineers and the work would ultimately involve more than 120,000 scientists and personnel. 'At no time, from 1941 to 1945 did I ever hear it suggested by the President or any other responsible member of the government, that atomic energy should not be used in the war.' – Henry Stimson, Secretary of War (1940–45). Brigadier-General Leslie Groves was named to head the Manhattan Project. He remarked to his key staff: 'If this weapon fizzles, each of you can look forward to a lifetime of testifying before congressional investigating committees.'

General Arnold was requested, in July 1943, to provide some specially modified B-29s for testing in the project. One such machine was under modification at

below: During the Second World War, gasoline sales in the United States were strictly controlled and priority was based upon individual need. A prority sticker was issued for every motor vehicle and had to be displayed in a corner of the windscreen.

'I don't know what weapon will be used in World War III, but I know that World War IV will be fought with wooden sticks.'
– Albert Einstein

'Only two things are infinite– the universe and human stupidity and I'm not sure about the former.'
– Albert Einstein

Wright Field in December of that year and in February 1944 the first drop tests of the weapon, whose final external shape had not yet been decided, were conducted at Muroc, California. As development of the weapon continued three more B-29s received modification in Nebraska to enable them to carry the final bomb types, of which there were two. The first, nicknamed 'Little Boy', was a uranium-based weapon weighing 9,700 lb. It was 120 inches long and 28 inches in diameter. The second bomb was called 'Fat Man' and weighed 10,000 lb. It was 128 inches long and 60 inches in diameter. Modification work at the Nebraska site was continued and by August forty-six B-29s had been converted into atomic bombers.

Training for the A-bomb air crews was assigned to Colonel Paul Tibbetts Jr, a veteran Eighth Air Force pilot who came into the programme after having flown a number of B-17 missions in Europe and North Africa and, crucially, participating in flight testing the B-29 for more than a year. Tibbetts had been briefed about the Manhattan Project in September 1944. In addition to the crew training, he was responsible for supervising the modifications necessary to make the B-29 capable of delivering the atomic weapon. His new command was designated the 509th Composite Group and was stationed at Wendover, Utah. There the group would function in total secrecy, supported by its own engineering, supply and military police elements. Tibbetts was told, 'You are on your own. No one knows what to tell you. Use normal channels to the extent possible. If you are denied something you need, restate that your need is for SILVERPLATE (a code name) and your request will be honoured without question.' The training, including a number of lengthy over-ocean flights, was completed by the spring of 1945. General LeMay had been briefed about the new weapon and the pending assignment of the 509th to North Field, Tinian. By July, the bombers, crews and support personnel of Tibbett's group were in place on North Field and beginning further drop tests and navigational training flights. Additional modifications were made to the group's B-29s, including a change to Curtiss electric propellers whose reversible pitch enhanced the braking capability of the bombers, as well as new cuffs for the pro-

peller blades, which improved the airflow and the cooling of the engines.

The participants and the aeroplanes were ready by 24 July when orders arrived from General Carl Spaatz, Commander, US Strategic Air Forces, Pacific, instructing the 509th to 'deliver the first special bomb as soon as weather will permit visual bombing after 3 August 1945 on one of the targets: Hiroshima, Kokura, Niigata and Nagasaki'. With arrival on 29 July of the components for Little Boy, assembly began and the weapon was ready for use on 2 August. General LeMay issued the field order for the mission, with Hiroshima the primary target, and Kokura and Nagasaki the alternates if poor weather should prevent a visual drop on the primary. The attack was scheduled for 6 August and Colonel Tibbetts selected himself to command the B-29 that would drop the weapon. That aeroplane was named *Enola Gay*, after Tibbetts's mother.

6 August. The mission take-off was set for 2.45 a.m. One hour earlier a flight of three reconnaissance B-29s (F-13As) left Tinian to scout weather conditions over the primary and secondary target cities. Concern about the possibility of a major accident on take-off had led to a decision to delay arming the atom bomb until *Enola Gay* neared the target. US Navy weapons specialist Captain William Parsons was on board the bomber to arm the weapon. *Enola Gay* would be accompanied by two additional B-29s acting as photographic aircraft.

Earlier in July, the Japanese government had received an ultimatum from the Allies demanding unconditional surrender and promising "prompt and utter destruction" if the ultimatum was not accepted. Japan rejected it. On 27 July B-29s were sent to drop leaflets on eleven Japanese cities, warning that they would be subjected to intense air bombardment. The next day six of these cities were bombed. On 31 July twelve additional cities received the leaflet warnings and on 1 August four of them were attacked. Then one final warning of impending attack was issued on 5 August.

In their mission briefing on the afternoon of 4 August, Tibbetts's crew was informed about the weapon they would be taking to Japan and the New

Mexico test success. They were forbidden to discuss or write about the coming mission. Tibbetts said that he was personally honoured, and was sure they were, to have been chosen to take part in this raid which would shorten the war by at least six months.

2.45 on 6 August, Paul Tibbetts released the brakes of the *Enola Gay,* and using nearly all of the long Tinian runway, the bomber was airborne in just over a minute. He climbed slowly, to preserve fuel and because two of his crewmen had to complete assembly of the bomb in the unheated, unpressurized bombbay. Shortly before 6.00 a.m., the *Enola Gay* passed Iwo Jima and began climbing to 9,300 feet, where it would rendezvous with the two B-29 photo-aircraft and continue on course to Japan.

At 7.30 a.m. Captain Parsons entered the bombbay and Colonel Tibbetts took the aeroplane on the long climb to the 31,500-foot bombing altitude. The latest report from Major Claude Eatherly, flying *Straight Flush,* one of the weather planes over Japan, indicated that the primary target city of Hiroshima was in the clear. Tibbetts then told the crew that they would make the bomb run on that city. The plane reached 31,500 feet and approached the aiming point over Hiroshima. There was no flak or enemy aircraft.

The target city was distinctively sited on a wide river delta and was divided by seven tributaries. The *Enola Gay* approached the city over the Inland Sea on a nearly due-West compass heading at a ground speed of 330 mph. Major Thomas Ferebee, the bombardier and a veteran of sixty-three combat missions in the European air war, was now flying the aeroplane through the Norden bombsight. His aiming point was the Aioi Bridge spanning the Ota River in the centre of the city. The headquarters of the Japanese Second Army was located near the bridge. With her bomb doors open, the Superfortress passed over Hiroshima on course, on time and at the prescribed air speed and altitude. As the plane crossed the aiming point at 8.15 a.m., Little Boy was released from the bombbay, dislodging the arming wires that would start its clocks.

Relieved of the weight of the bomb, Paul Tibbetts banked the plane into an extreme fighter-like turnaway from the coming blast. Forty-three seconds

after the drop, Little Boy exploded 550 feet southeast of the aiming point and 1,900 feet above the Shima Hospital. Tibbetts recalled, 'I threw off the automatic pilot and hauled *Enola Gay* into the turn. I pulled the anti-glare goggles over my eyes. I couldn't see through them; I was blind. I threw them to the floor. A bright light filled the plane. The first shock wave hit us. We were eleven and a half miles slant range from the atomic explosion, but the whole airplane cracked and crinkled from the blast. I yelled 'Flak!'

top: 'Little Boy', the first atomic bomb used against Japan; above: 'Fat man', the weapon dropped over the city of Nagasaki on 8 August 1945; far left: Another Pacific-based B-29 of the period in which the atomic bombers were operating.

below right: A B-29 crew inspects each other's parachute packs prior to boarding their aircraft.

'The best defence against the atom bomb is not to be there when it goes off.'
— Winston Churchill

thinking a heavy gun battery had found us. The tail-gunner had seen the first wave coming, a visible shimmer in the atmosphere, but he didn't know what it was until it hit. When the second wave came, he called out a warning. We turned back to look at Hiroshima. The city was hidden by that awful cloud. . . boiling up, mushrooming, terrible and incredibly tall. No one spoke for a moment; then everyone was talking.' 78,000 Japanese died instantly. Their city had been virtually erased.

'Early that day, 7 August, the Japanese radio broadcast for the first time a succinct announcement that very few, if any, of the people most concerned with its content, the survivors of Hiroshima, happened to hear: 'Hiroshima suffered considerable damage as the result of an attack by a few B-29s. It is believed that a new type of bomb was used. The details are being investigated.' Nor is it probable that any of the survivors happened to be tuned in on a short-wave re-broadcast of an extraordinary announcement by the President of the United States, which identified the new bomb as atomic: 'That bomb had more power than twenty thousand tons of TNT. It had more than two thousand times the blast power of the British Grand Slam, which is the largest bomb ever yet used in the history of warfare.' Those victims who were able to worry at all about what had happened thought of it and discussed it in more primitive, childish terms—gasoline sprinkled from an airplane, maybe, or some combustible gas, or a big cluster of incendiaries, or the work of parachutists; but, even if they had known the truth, most of them were too busy or too weary or too badly hurt to care that they were the objects of the first great experiment in the use of atomic power, which (as the voices on the short wave shouted) no country except the United States, with its industrial know-how, its willingness to throw two billion gold dollars into an important wartime gamble, could possibly have developed.'
— from *Hiroshima*, by John Hersey

By 8 August no official reaction to the atom bombing had come from Japan. No surrender. The second atomic weapon, the plutonium Fat Man, was prepared for use. This time it would be delivered by a B-29

named *Bock's Car*, after its commander, Captain Frederick Bock, but the plane would be flown on this occasion by Major Charles Sweeney. Kokura was selected as the primary target with Nagasaki the secondary. When *Bock's Car* approached Kokura in the early morning of 9 August, thick, patchy cloud obscured most of the city. Sweeney brought the bomber over the city on three separate bomb-run attempts, but the aiming point was still not visible. The target would be Nagasaki. Shortly before 11.00 a.m., the B-29 crossed the alternative target city and, although it too was mostly covered by cloud, the aiming point was sighted and Fat Man was released over it. Nagasaki suffered a similar fate to that of Hiroshima. A total of 35,000 people died. Many thousands more were injured at both Hiroshima and Nagasaki.

Now the Japanese leadership accepted the ugly reality of the new weapon. And on the same day that Nagasaki was attacked, the Soviet Union declared war on Japan and began a major invasion of Manchuria. Conventional B-29 raids on Japanese cities were continued through 14 August. After consultation with the Emperor, Japanese officials sent their acceptance of the Allied surrender terms. B-29 offensive operations against Japan ended and were quickly replaced with food and clothing drops to Allied prisoners of war being held in Japan, China, Korea and Manchuria. Nearly 4,500 tons of such supplies were provided to more than 63,000 prisoners. Eight B-29s and seventy-seven crew members were lost in these flights. During the bombing campaign against Japan from the Marianas, 23,500 individual B-29 sorties had been flown and 170,000 tons of conventional bombs had been dropped, as well as two atom bombs. A total of 371 B-29s had been lost to various causes, but the effort had eliminated the need to invade Japan with its undoubted catastrophic Allied and enemy casualties.

Sunday 25 June 1950. Squadrons of Russian-built T-34 tanks spearheaded an assault by units of the North Korean Army against Kaesong and Chunchon below the 38th Parallel in South Korea. Following the example of the Japanese against American forces at Pearl Harbor, Hawaii, less than a decade earlier, the North

Koreans attacked on a Sunday morning, when any resistance or response would be minimal. Initially, President Truman confined American participation in the United Nations' aid to South Korea to air action.

With the end of the Second World War, a great number of B-29s, many of them factory-fresh, had been put into long-term storage for possible re-use. An additional eighty-eight of the planes were transferred to the Royal Air Force in 1950. Many others were retained operationally in bomber squadrons of the new United States Air Force Strategic Air Command where they would serve until replaced by the very heavy B-36 intercontinental bomber. Still other B-29s were in service with the Far Eastern Air Forces of the USAF and a number of these aircraft were based at Anderson Field, Guam. They were within range of targets on the Korean peninsula. They were soon to be joined by B-29 wings transferred from SAC for a conventional bombing campaign that would last nearly three years during which the planes would again fill an important role. Apart from an early period when the B-29s were largely wasted in a fruitless series of tactical missions for which they had not

been designed and were completely unsuited, they performed impressively in a strategic bombing campaign against North Korean industry. They attacked armaments, aircraft and rail centres, sea ports, oil refineries, iron foundries, chemical plants, oil storage facilities and hydroelectric power plants.

It was 17 July 1953 and B-29 Superfortress command pilot Joseph Anastasia was flying from the 307th Bomb Wing airfield at Kadena, Okinawa, to attack a target in North Korea in what he regarded as 'the mission to end all missions'. 'The briefing was normal. We took off and flew at least fifteen minutes to cool the engines down and then began climbing to an initial altitude of 20,000 feet. As we climbed I had the gunners test-fire their guns to be sure they were working properly. They each had an extra twenty-five rounds for this purpose. Everything was going well. It was my sixth mission and I had no particular concerns about it. I had a flak vest under my seat and a steel helmet for my head. Now we were in the secondary climb and I was leading the last element of five airplanes up to 26,000 feet where we levelled off. This was to be

right: Assembly activity in a Boeing plant where the B-50 derivative of the B-29 was being produced. The B-50 differed in many significant ways from its predecessor, not least being the massive R-4360 aero-engines that powered it.

our bomb-run altitude.

'We were all set for the bomb run when suddenly the number four propeller went into an overspeed runaway condition. The only thing we could do was toggle it down electrically, and that didn't work. The engine would tear itself apart if we were unable to shut it down, so I ordered the engineer to feather it and he did so, I thought. We were on the bomb run and I had maximum power on (2,600 rpm and fifty inches of manifold pressure) to keep the lead, and I was doing pretty well, except things were a little hectic.

'We came to 'bombs away' and released our load, but nine bombs were hung up and didn't drop. I was running on three engines but I called the Group Lead and asked permission to make a second drop. He OK'd it so I race-tracked my pattern around and came in for a second try.

'Now the enemy radar guns were all turned into me. They knew my altitude and where I was going, so all they had to do was blast away and the chances were they would hit me, and hit me they did. They knocked out the number three engine and set fire to number two. With number four out of commssion I now had only one engine left. I ordered 'Salvo all bombs now' and they all dropped. At that point my airspeed was down to 150 mph and the bomber was about to stall. Then a burst of flak under the left wing lifted it up and over we went . . . into a spin to the right. I shut down the number one engine and alerted the crew for a bale out.

'Boeing had built a good airplane. She was strong and reliable, and could stand a lot of stress on her airframe. She had done about one full turn when I rang the bale-out bell. From back in the airplane came the voice of the radar operator: 'We cannot move. We are plastered against the sides of the fuselage. Help us. Don't leave us!' Centrifugal force had pinned them to the interior of the airplane. I took my flashlight from the edge of the seat and looked at the darkened instrument panel. The artificial horizon was tilted and all the other instruments were out of action except for the turn needle and ball. With all engines off and the props feathered, there were no generators on line and the over-loaded electrical circuits killed all the power on the airplane. The waist gates, which

below: The first atomic bomber, the *Enola Gay*, restored and preserved by the US National Air and Space Museum, Washington DC; bottom: Hot, difficult, demanding field maintenance work on a Pacific-based B-29 Superfortress.

close with power to keep the engines' turbochargers going, controlled the manifold pressure which gave power to the engines. Waist gates always failed in the open position, so I had four waist gates failed "open".

'This B-29 had Curtiss Electric four-bladed propellers which were set up to lose 35 rpm per 1,000 feet of altitude lost. We lost 16,000 feet, from 26,000 to a bit under 10,000 feet, losing 560 rpm per engine. The only information available to me was from my pressure instruments, the altimeter, airspeed indicator, vertical speed, and turn needle and ball. Using my flashlight I restored the bale-out bell. Our navigator was standing on the nose wheel door, waiting to bale out. I told him to sit down.

'All this was taking place in about four to six minutes. I studied the instruments and using the needle and ball determined that we were in a right turn, and so went with the controls in that direction. I jammed the rudder and counted fifteen seconds, then popped the nose forward with the control wheel. It stopped the spin. The bomber levelled off. We then glided back up to 11,000 feet. I had recovered from a three-and-a-half turn spin, a feat unheard of in the B-29. Fortunately, I was current in spins and spin recovery from flying P-51 Mustangs. I had a good number

one engine and, to my surprise, the number four engine was still running–the runaway prop had not feathered. So, I now had 1,975 rpm on two engines, was doing 147 mph and descending in a 'stalled' or burbelling condition . . . a juddering airplane.

'I got the plane onto a 150 degree heading for Kimpo Air Base in South Korea. I was letting down to land there when a B-26 on final, and on fire, crashed on the runway. Kimpo was then out of the question for us. We went on towards Suwon which is about forty miles south of Kimpo, and found it to be all fogged in, and as we still had about 7,000 feet of altitude, I decided to head for Taegu Airfield. When we arrived there, altitude 5,000 feet, it too was fogged in and of no use to us. I continued southeast toward the next possible landing site, Pusan. All this time another B-29 was flying 'S' turns near us. It carried a boat on the bottom of the fuselage that could be dropped to us in the ocean if we should require it.

'We were in a constant descent as I did not have enough power to fly level. We arrived at Pusan with 4,000 feet of altitude and solid fog and rain. At that point our alternative was to ditch in the Straights of Tsushima, islands between Korea and Japan. The airplane seemed to be shaking and vibrating severely and I commented on it to my co-pilot, who told me that it wasn't the airplane, it was my knees. I looked down and saw that my flight suit was quite bloody at my knees. I took my hands off the controls and held my knees to try to stop the shaking. We continued down toward the water to 1,000 feet. We could get only twenty-six inches of manifold pressure on the engines, barely enough power to keep the airplane above the stall by a few miles per hour. We were just about level at 400 feet over the water when I heard a radio call: 'Skipper Crystal Control calling Glad 35, can you hear me?' I answered on the emergency channel: 'I read you loud and clear.' He said that we were only ten miles from Itazuke, Japan, and asked if we thought we could make it there. I said I would try. I had only 200 feet of altitude when I saw the breakwater at Itazuke. There were also two towers in the harbor. I aimed at the one on the left, which aligned me with the runway. Seeing the green lights I called for gear down. We had no flaps and no electrical power, but the landing-gear was a free-fall type. The main wheels touched the runway. The nose gear wasn't locked down, but it had an over-centre lock on it and when it touched down it locked just fine. I pulled the air brakes after the roll-out and we finally came to a stop. We all climbed out and kissed the ground. We were so happy to be safely on the ground that we wept for joy. They towed the airplane off the runway and we were transported to the billeting area where we all flopped into bed completely exhausted.

'The next day we went back out to the airplane to look it over. What a mess. All four engines needed to be changed as well as the oil coolers and two of the propellers, which had holes in them. The sheet metal work on the wings and flaps was so badly holed that in some places you could stand on a ladder and poke your head through the wing.

'All of our gunners were flown back to Okinawa on a courier flight. The officers and our flight engineer remained at Itazuke with the airplane while maintenance people there worked on it. We had no clothes with us other than what we had on, and there were no clothes available to purchase, but we met a group of Red Cross girls who loaned us some jeans, boots and sweatshirts. We looked a mess but we were clean and alive. We stayed in Itazuke for a week while the B-29 was being repaired. The Japanese maintenance people there were very efficient and the airplane checked out OK when we flight-tested it. We then flew it back to Okinawa, landing at our home base, Kadena. We learned that we had missed three combat missions in the ten days' elapsed time that we had been away.'

The Korean War ended on 27 July 1953. In that conflict B-29s dropped 167,000 tons of bombs on enemy targets in 21,328 individual aircraft sorties. They accounted for the destruction of thirty enemy aircraft. Thirty-four B-29s were lost.

After the Korean War, most remaining serviceable B-29s were quickly retired from the USAF inventory. A number, however, were converted to specialized uses including aerial refuelling, search and rescue, weather reconnaissance, target towing, radar evaluation, and target drones. In October 1947, one B-29

was utilized as a 'mother ship' to carry the experimental Bell X-1 rocket-plane aloft. The X-1, piloted by then-Captain Chuck Yeager, was drop-launched from the bomber and became the first piloted aircraft to fly faster than the speed of sound.

The B-29 was recognized as having a really sturdy airframe, while also being somewhat underpowered for its weight. Those factors, coupled with the over-heating and other problems associated with the Wright R-3350 engines, led to the eventual development of the B-50, Boeing Model 345-2, an aeroplane with the basic B-29 airframe, but powered by the new Pratt & Whitney R-4360 Wasp Major air-cooled radial engines rated at 3,500 hp. Intended as an atomic bomber to be available should the new intercontinental B-36 programme not succeed, the B-50 looked a lot like the B-29 but was actually a very different aircraft. The wing was far stronger yet lighter than that of the B-29. The huge P & W engines provided 59 per cent more power than those of the B-29. The B-50 weighed more than the B-29 and required a higher vertical tail and larger flaps. The aeroplane also featured nose-wheel steering, faster activation of the landing-gear, hydraulic rudder-boost, electrical de-icing of the cockpit windows, wing and empennage de-icing, reversible-pitch propellers and other improvements. In all, just 25 per cent of the B-50 parts were interchangeable with B-29 parts.

The B-50 served along with the B-36 in SAC for several years until the introduction of Boeing's B-47 jet bomber. In February 1949 a B-50, *Lucky Lady II*, utilized aerial refuelling to make the first non-stop flight around the world, completing the 23,452-mile trip in 94 hours.

Another important evolution of the B-29 was the Model 367, the C-97/KC-97 Stratofreighter, whose maiden flight took place in November 1944. The 367 incorporated the wings, tail structure and undercarriage of the B-29. The new plane had a 'double-bubble' fuselage, the lower section having the same diameter as the B-29 fuselage. It was a cargo plane with its later examples having the R-4360 engines and the tall tail of the B-50. It took part in the great Berlin Airlift of 1949, carrying more than a million pounds of freight into the blockaded German city.

below: One of only a few remaining buildings in the city of Hiroshima after the atomic bombing of 6 August 1945.

'This war, like the next war, is a war to end all wars.'
– David Lloyd George

bottom: A gunner/observer's blister window on a B-29, this aircraft is in the collection of the American Air Museum, Duxford, England.

The Military Air Transport Service of the USAF operated C-97s during the Korean War and many of the planes supported the operations of the Strategic Air Command. More than 800 KC-97s served with SAC as aerial refuelling tankers and transports. With the coming of Boeing's KC-135 jet tanker aircraft, most of the KC-97s were transferred to Air National Guard units. By 1977, nearly all of them had been withdrawn from service, many ending their days in the 'aeroplane graveyard', the Military Aircraft Storage and Disposition Center (since renamed the Aerospace Maintenance and Regeneration Center), adjoining Davis-Monthan AFB, Tucson, Arizona. At MASDC, the big Boeings joined hundreds of other USAF, US Navy, US Marine and US Army aircraft considered surplus to requirements. Most of the C-97s and KC-97s were stripped of their engines and all valuable, resusable parts, before being chopped up by a giant guillotine blade and melted down into aluminium ingots.

A civilian commercial version of the C-97, Model 377, began service with Pan American Airways in February 1949. It was called the Stratocruiser and was spacious and well-liked by airline passengers of the day. They could enjoy a lower-level bar and cocktail cabin by descending a staircase from the main cabin. Airline seating arrangements varied, but the plane could readily accommodate 100 passengers and was operated by several airlines including British Overseas Airways

Corporation, United Airlines, Northwest Airlines, and American Overseas Airlines. The aeroplane had a top speed of 340 mph and a maximum range of 4,200 miles. Due to its relatively high purchase price, compared to that of the competing Douglas DC-6 and Lockheed Constellation, only fifty-five Stratocruisers were built.

An extreme derivative of the Stratocruiser was the Aero Space Lines Guppy, of which ten were built. The Guppy featured a lengthened fuselage and an enormous upper-bubble cargo section. It was powered by four Pratt & Whitney turboprop engines rated at 5,700 hp each. The nose could swing open to facilitate the loading of cargo which ranged from large-diameter rocket sections to fuselage sections of Airbus aircraft. The cargo flown by the Guppies was generally too large for road or rail transport.

The Boeing company had no part in another notable variation on the B-29. In late July 1944 a flak-damaged Superfortress was unable to make it back to its Chinese base following a raid on the Showa steel works at Anshan, Manuchuria. Captain Howard Jarrel elected to divert to a field at Vladivostok in the Soviet Union, where he landed a short time later. The crew was interned. Three weeks later another B-29 crashed in the foothills east of Khabarovsk. The crew had baled out and they too were interned. Another damaged B-29 had to land at Vladivostok in November and that crew was also interned. At that point the Soviets were then holding two intact B-29s, the remains of a third, and all the crews. In January all of the American airmen, by arrangement with the Soviets, 'escaped' to the west. The B-29s were not returned. In 1946 a journalist in Germany learned that the Soviets were then manufacturing an exact copy of the B-29 at factories in the Ural mountains. The report was discredited in the West, where it was believed that the Soviets were insufficiently competent to produce such a large, sophisticated aircraft. However, Soviet agents in the United States were discovered trying to purchase specific B-29 components including brake assemblies, wheels and tyres. When four 'B-29s' appeared in a low-altitude flypast on Aviation Day at Tushino Airport, Moscow, in August 1947, it was clear that the earlier report had been accurate.

The Soviet copy was designated Tu-4, a product of

the Tupolev Design Bureau, on orders from Joseph Stalin to produce a new strategic bomber for immediate manufacture. The bureau had the project well under way by early 1945 and began test flights in summer 1946. The aeroplane exhibited many faults with the remotely-controlled gun system, cabin pressurization, the landing-gear, propellers and, not unlike her American cousin, had serious engine defects. It was three more years before most of these problems were fixed and the Tu-4 was finally operational. With more than 300 of the bombers in service, the US then had to cope with an actual strategic bombing threat from the Soviet Union, forcing it to develop a new air-interception capability with ground radar stations, radar picket planes, Nike surface-to-air missiles, a Ground Observer Corps, and a force of jet fighter-interceptors. This costly effort was spurred in 1949 by the development of a Soviet atom bomb, putting the US under potential nuclear threat. It is believed that as many as 1,200 Tu-4s were built by the Soviets during the 1950s.

The last operational B-29 Superfortress was retired from the USAF inventory in June 1960. A number of B-29s lay in repose on the US Navy gunnery range at China Lake, California, for many years after the war. One of them was acquired by the 'Confederate Air Force' (now called the Commemorative Air Force), and is flown regularly in CAF air shows. Another of the China Lake planes was donated to the Imperial War Museum, Duxford, England, where it was restored and is displayed in the American Air Museum there. Others from the desert range have been acquired for display purposes by various private and Air Force base museums including the Castle Air Museum, California, the United States Aviation Museum, Inyokern, California, March AFB Museum, Travis AFB Museum, Warner Robins AFB Museum, Georgia, Hill AFB Museum, Utah, Kelly AFB Museum, Texas, Ellsworth AFB Museum, South Dakota, the 8th Air Force Museum, Barksdale AFB, Louisiana, the USAF Museum, Wright-Patterson AFB, Ohio, New England Air Museum, Connecticut, the Seattle Museum of Flight, Washington, the Pima County Museum, Arizona, Dobbins AFB, Georgia, the Strategic Air Command Museum, Nebraska, and the Smithsonian Air & Space Museum, Virginia.

Specifications: Boeing B-29

Engines: Four Wright R-3350 Cyclone 18-cylinder air-cooled radials, with two General Electric turbo-super-chargers, delivering 2,200 hp each for take-off.
Maximum speed: 357 mph at 30,000 ft
Cruising speed: 220 mph at 25,000 ft
Service ceiling: 33,600 ft
Normal range: 3,250 miles at 25,000 ft with a 5,000 lb bomb-load. Maximum ferry range: 5,600 miles.
Weight empty: 74,500 lb, Maximum gross weight: 120,000 lb
Wingspan: 141 ft 3 in
Length: 99 feet.
Height: 27 ft 9 in
Wing area: 1,736 sq ft
Normal bomb-load: 5,000 lb over a 1,600-mile radius at high altitude; 12,000 lb over a 1,600-mile radius at medium altitude
Defensive armament: Twelve 0.50 calibre machine-guns in four remotely controlled turrets (two above and two below the fuselage) and in the tail, each with 1,000 rounds of ammunition. Early production aeroplanes were equipped with one 20 mm cannon with 100 rounds of ammunition, in the tail position. Later production aeroplanes had four 0.50 calibre machine-guns in the forward top turret.

below: Another Marianas-based B-29 Superfortress bomber of the final air war fire raids against Japan in the summer of 1945.

NORTHROP

From the diary of Captain Glen Edwards, while he was serving as a United States Air Force test pilot:

4 May 1948 (at Wright Field, Ohio) 'Things are sure in a squeeze. We've got so many projects and so few pilots to perform same. If we don't get some relief pretty soon I may be forced to stay here while the B-45A service tests are going on. How horrible. Got to get to Muroc.'

18 May 1948 'Seems like I'm bound for Muroc tomorrow by fastest means possible. Plan to run sta-bility on the YB-49, performance on B-45A and Phase II on XB-35—What fun! Sounds like I'll be there for awhile. Packing like mad tonight.'

20 May 1948 'Got a short flight in on the YB-49 today—flew in the co-pilot seat with Bob Cardenas at the controls. Air speed indicator went out. So we ended up using an A-26 as pacer. Plan to fly again tomorrow.'

The aviation business has certainly nurtured its share of pioneers, innovators, geniuses and cranks. Among the most intriguing is John Knudson Northrop who was born in Newark, New Jersey in 1895. He was raised in Nebraska and later in Santa Barbara, California. Like so many others who made it to the forefront of aviation, he had always been fascinated with aeroplanes and the prospect of flying in them. Jack Northrop finished high school but his family lacked the means to provide him with further educa-tion. His early jobs, including a stint as an architec-tural draftsman, helped him develop the skills to become an exceptional designer, but it was his unbri-dled imagination that made him one of the great aeronautical innovators.

Northrop broke into the aeroplane business in Santa Barbara when the brothers Allan and Malcolm Loughead arrived there in 1916 to build a ten-seat flying-boat, the F-1, and a two-seat biplane, the S-1. In his design for the S-1, Northrop incorporated new construction techniques and an unconventional lateral control system, the first of many unorthodox direc-tions he would follow. But the Loughead brothers (later changed to Lockheed) did not prosper in their initial California venture and went out of business in 1921. Jack Northrop landed his next aviation opportu-

'The first rule of intelligent tinkering is to save all the parts.'– Paul Erlich

right: The Northrop YB-49 flying-wing bomber on the apron at the company's Hawthorne, California, plant.

XB-35
YB-49

above: Pioneering aviation designer John K. 'Jack' Northrop, who championed the development of the flying-wing aircraft. Northrop believed that an aircraft that lacked a conventional fuselage and tail assembly would be free of the associated drag and weight penalties and be lighter, faster and capable of carrying greater payloads than a conventional aircraft.

nity with Douglas Aircraft, also in southern California, in 1923. There he worked on the design of the World Cruiser biplane, four of which attempted to circumnavigate the globe in 1924. Two of them succeeded, completing the journey in 175 days. When the Lockheeds were re-established in aeroplane manufacturing during 1926, Northrop rejoined them as chief engineer. There his principal accomplishment was the sleek and swift Lockheed Vega executive transport, probably the best-known aircraft of the period between the world wars. Vegas were flown by several aviation celebrities to a number of long-distance speed records, most notably that of Wiley Post and Harold Gatty in the first circumnavigation of the world by a lone aircraft, their Vega *Winnie Mae,* in 1931. Post, and humorist Will Rogers, would die in an Alaskan air crash in 1935.

The Vega was a joint design effort of Northrop and his boss, Allan Lockheed. It was a high-wing monoplane without the external struts and wires associated with most earlier aircraft. Its moulded monocoque fuselage was carefully faired and crafted to minimize drag and establish a new standard for clean aeroplane design. It was ultimately powered by a 450 hp Pratt & Whitney Wasp engine that delivered a top speed of 180 mph.

Northrop was anxious to proceed with other innovative aeroplane design concepts, but Lockheed took a more conservative view and Jack left the company to start a new venture, Avion Corporation, where he began his early experimentation with flying-wing design, which he believed, was the best way to achieve higher performance and aerodynamic efficiency. The first flying-wing aircraft he built, however, gave an early indication of the inherent control problems that would come to be associated with the design.

With the financial crisis of October 1929, Northrop was unable to continue independent operation of Avion, but was able to arrange for United Aircraft, which included Boeing and Stearman Aircraft in its stable, to absorb Avion as a division that he operated as Northrop Corporation. As the great Depression engulfed America and much of the world in the early 1930s, Jack Northrop was forced to put away his exotic flying-wing concepts in favour of more conventional aircraft design. His next important project was the

Alpha, a single-engine all-metal passenger plane for Trans World Airline, which bought twenty of the aircraft. The Alpha incorporated many advanced features including de-icer boots on the wings and tail, but the sales were insufficient to put the Northrop division in profit. In September 1931, United Aircraft decided to consolidate Northrop Corporation with Stearman Aircraft and shift the newly combined division to Wichita, Kansas. Jack Northrop did not want to return to the mid-West and left UA to form another new company of his own.

In 1932 he began what would prove an inauspicious partnership with Donald Douglas. The new company was again called Northrop Corporation, but Douglas owned 51 percent of it. Years before this association, Northrop had designed a new, multi-cellular wing structure that would feature in the renowned Douglas DC-3 airliner of 1935, many of which are still flying in the twenty-first century. The continuing economic troubles of the 1930s affected Northrop and Douglas profoundly, and in 1937 Douglas bought out Jack Northrop's 49 per cent of the company and immediately dissolved Northrop Corporation. By January 1939, Northrop left Douglas, embittered by the partnership experience, but, because of the sale of his corporate interest, financially able to begin yet again, by forming Northrop Aircraft, Inc.

As war broke out in Europe and parts of the Far East, Northrop was just one of hundreds of American companies struggling to survive. Jack Northrop was eager to revive his flying-wing project, but at that time there was no Army or Navy interest in the scheme, so he took on all the sub-assembly work he could get for the aircraft of other planemakers, including part of the Consolidated PBY Catalina flying-boat programme and the Vultee Vengeance dive-bomber. The first important US Army contract that he received during the war was for 700 of his P-61 Black Widow nightfighters, which put the company on firm financial footing for the first time. In 1940 he also began work on what he called Model N-1M, the first true flying wing, with the consultation of California Institute of Technology aerodynamicist Dr Theodore von Karman and others. Wind-tunnel testing of various flying-wing models and experimentation with new concepts in high-lift devices, spoilers, flaps and low-drag airfoils seemed to indicate that an all-wing aircraft could indeed be operated successfully. Northrop was convinced that the saving in weight and drag achieved when the conventional fuselage and empennage of an aircraft were dispensed with in favour of containing all compartments, systems and components within the wing itself, would result in increased performance for the amount of power provided. The N-1M flew for the first time on 3 July 1940.

Jack Northrop believed that, unlike a conventional large bomber aircraft whose load of bombs, weaponry, ammunition and crew is carried within its fuselage, the flying wing, or span-loaded aeroplane, could have its load distributed across the wingspan. It would have no fuselage or empennage. But until the wartime technology of the 1940s, it was not possible to build a span-loaded airframe of sufficient size and weight to meet the requirements for such a bomber. In theory, the span-loader provides both low drag and high lift, enabling the aircraft to transport its payload farther, faster and more economically than a conventional aircraft and it should be less costly to build, being constructed as a single unit with no fuselage or tail structure. The weight distribution of the bomb load should be more efficient through the use of compartments along nearly the entire span of the wing. Defensively, the span-loader would present a far smaller target from the front or rear than a conventional aircraft. Northrop continued to develop the idea.

Early in 1941, the Army was developing requirements for a true intercontinental bomber, capable of attacking European targets from bases in the United States. It wanted an aeroplane with a 450 mph top speed and a cruising speed of 275 mph, a service ceiling of 45,000 feet, a maximum range of 12,000 miles while cruising at 25,000 feet, a normal bomb-load of 10,000 lb over a 5,000-mile combat radius and a maximum bomb load of 72,000 lb over a shorter radius. The Army invited Boeing, Douglas and Consolidated to do preliminary design studies to be followed by actual proposals. Douglas eventually dropped out of the competition when the Army Air Force showed no enthusiasm for the company's rather conservative proposal. In the end, Consolidated would win the com-

petition with its mammoth B-36, 383 of which were built by the end of production in 1954. The B-36, with four turbojets installed on its wings to supplement the power of its six R-4360 engines, served as the mainstay of the USAF Strategic Air Command during the early years of the Cold War until it was replaced by the Boeing B-47 and then the giant B-52 all-jet bomber.

On 27 May 1941 the Army asked Northrop to provide all relevant information about its flying-wing design, even though this theoretical aeroplane offered an estimated combat radius of only 3,000 miles with a 10,000 lb bomb load. While the Northrop aircraft would not come close to meeting the specified very-long-range requirement, the Army was sufficiently impressed with the concept to award the company contracts for two XB-35 prototypes in November 1941 and January 1942, and in September 1942 for thirteen YB-35 service test aircraft. In addition, funding was provided in October 1941 for the construction of four 1/3 scale flying-wing aircraft designated N-9M, for testing the design's performance and providing familiarization flying for programme test pilots. The first XB-35 was to be delivered in November 1943, with the second to follow in April 1944. Work began on the N-9Ms at the Northrop plant in Hawthorne, California, but a series of engineering related delays to work on the XB-35 prototypes hampered that programme schedule. When most of these problems were resolved, a production order for 200 B-35Bs was placed in June 1943, with the first of these planes to be delivered by June 1945. The Northrop Hawthorne plant was not large enough for full-scale manufacture of the production B-35s and expansion of the site was not practical at that time, so Northrop negotiated with the Glenn L. Martin Company to build the production airplanes at its Baltimore, Maryland, plant.

The 172-foot-span XB-35 was powered by two Pratt & Whitney R-4360-17 and two R-4360-21 Wasp Major turbo-supercharged radial engines, rated at 3,000 hp each, fitted into the trailing edge of the wing. Initially the engines drove dual contra-rotating three-blade pusher propellers, but serious and apparently unresolvable propeller gear box problems resulted in replacement of the dual-propeller arrangement by

'The guy who invented the first wheel was an idiot, but the guy who invented the other three, now he was a genius.'
– Sid Caesar

single Hamilton Standard four-blade reversible-pitch pusher propellers and a simplified gearing system.

The XB-35 was fitted with a set of double flaps on the trailing edges of the wing tips to do the work of conventional rudders. When, for example, the pilot depressed the left rudder pedal, the left split flaps opened in butterfly fashion, creating a braking effect that caused the aircraft to turn left. When both left and right rudder pedals were depressed, both sets of split flaps would open, reducing the airspeed and providing a glide capability. The split flaps system could also be employed to trim the aircraft. The wing had elevons on the trailing edge, inboard of the split flaps. As the pilot moved the control column forward or backward, the elevons caused the aircraft to descend or climb. When the pilot moved the control column to the left or right, the elevons on that side would cause the craft to bank in that direction. An additional set of flaps was located near the centre of the wing's trailing edge for use in take-off and landing.

The B-35 was to be operated by a crew of nine: pilot, co-pilot, navigator, bombardier, flight engineer, radio operator and three gunners, all positioned in a central crew cabin. Provision was also made for carrying six extra relief crew members on lengthy missions, with folding bunks located aft in the crew cabin.

The bomber was armed with dorsal and ventral remotely controlled barbettes, each housing four 0.50 calibre machine-guns. The tail cone carried four such weapons and four smaller barbettes were mounted, one each above and below the wing on both sides, outboard of the outer engines. The guns were controlled by gunners seated in a canopy near the rear of the crew cabin and by a gunner seated directly behind the pilot. The bomb load was distributed internally among eight bomb-bays outboard, and to the left and right of the crew cabin area. Fuel was distributed in self-sealing, leak-proof cells throughout the wing.

The four N9M flying-wing test aircraft were critically important to the overall programme in that they would provide the first opportunity for pilots to actually experience the handling of such craft and for the company to learn more about the feasibility of the concept. The N9M was originally powered by two 290 hp Menasco six-cylinder air-cooled engines, each driving a two-blade pusher propeller. The fourth test aircraft, the N9M-B, was fitted with two Franklin 400 hp air-cooled engines. These test aircraft had retractable tricycle landing gear and accommodated a pilot and one passenger. Intended as demonstration/ test vehicles, the N9Ms suffered a series mechanical failures, many of them related to the Menasco engines. The first of the craft flew on 27 December 1942 and was destroyed in a crash on 19 May 1943, killing the pilot. On 24 June the second N9M lost its canopy during the first flight but was landed safely. The N9M-B survived both the test programme and many years of neglect to be restored over a twelve-year period by Chino (California) Planes of Fame Museum volunteers. It was successfully flown again on 11 November 1994.

The N9M flight-test programme results were not encouraging. Projections showed that the full-size B-35 would be slower than specified and would have a range 1,600 miles shorter than required. The Martin Company was also reporting that a severe shortage of qualified aeronautical engineers (because so many of them had been drafted into military service), coupled with delays in the tooling process for the new bomber, were forcing the company to defer delivery of the first B-35 to 1947. Jack Northrop worried openly about the programme and now even he expressed concern that his design might be inherently unstable.

As the war entered its final year, it was apparent that the flying-wing bomber would not be operational in time for use in combat. More troubling for Northrop was the fact that other American aircraft manufacturers were already doing preliminary work on jet bomber prototypes that would make the propeller-driven XB-35 obsolete before it had even flown. At this point the Army Air Force cancelled the large B-35 production order and elected to continue the programme on a test basis only. It also directed that three of the YB-35s should be converted to jet-powered aircraft and redesignated YB-49 (bomber version) and YRB-49 (reconnaissance version). From that moment, XB-35 development slowed and the first flight of a prototype aeroplane didn't take place until 25 June 1946. It was a delivery flight from the Northrop Hawthorne factory

to the Muroc Dry Lake base in the California high desert. Northrop's test pilot Max Stanley was at the controls, assisted by flight engineer Dale Schroeder on the 45-minute flight. During the flight they experienced the first episode of the propeller gear box problem that was to plague the aeroplane throughout its test programme. The system of dual contra-rotating propellers and gear boxes quickly proved unsatisfactory, causing another substantial programme delay while single-rotation propellers and gearing were installed. The flight-test programme resumed in February 1948 and the revised propeller system was relatively trouble-free, but with it came a vibration problem and slightly reduced performance. In addition, on the resumption of flight testing, indications of metal fatigue were found in the cooling fans of the big R-4360 engines.

The maiden flight of the first YB-35 took place on 15 May 1948. It was mounted with single-rotation propellers and would be the only B-35 to be completed with the defensive armament package. The programme had definitely gone off the boil. Thirteen YB-35s had been ordered, but four of them were now designated as hangar queens, flightless birds whose only purpose would be to supply spare parts for the flight-test aircraft. For the Air Force and its suppliers the era of propeller-driven aircraft was essentially over. Only one of the YB-35s would ever fly. The Air Force view was that the plane was just too slow to be useful in the jet age and too unstable to be acceptable as either a bombing platform or a photographic reconnaissance aircraft. But the client had invested too much front-end capital in the plane to simply kill it outright, so it considered other possible uses for the big wing, including an air-refuelling role.

There would be no future for the propeller-driven B-35. In late 1948 the Air Force directed that nine YB-35s be converted to a turbojet design and reconfigured as photo-reconnaissance aircraft, designated RB-35B, later changed to YRB-49A.

Thousands of Northrop workers watched hopefully as Max Stanley taxied the first YB-49 eight-jet flying-wing bomber to the end of the company runway in Hawthorne that October day in 1947. Most were thrilled at the sight of the great wing trailing a thick

'If you build a better mouse-trap, you will catch better mice.'
– George Gobel

left: The Northrop XB-35 flying-wing bomber was powered by four Pratt & Whitney R-4360 engines, each driving a pair of contra-rotating pusher propellers. It was designed to carry a 52,000 lb bomb-load over a distance of 7,500 miles at an altitude of 40,000 feet.

right: General Robert L. Cardenas probably knows more about the flight characteristics of the YB-49 than anyone. He flew it from the Northrop factory to the Muroc Army Air Field test facility; he flew it in the test programme and he took it to Washington, DC on an impressive demonstration flight. After that flight he said, 'The YB-49 is no more difficult to fly than a B-29. On long flights at altitude, any plane is tiresome. The 49 is more sensitive than most planes and the pilot must be careful not to over-control'; below: A study of a bird wing by Leonardo da Vinci.

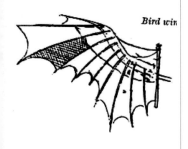

Bird win

WINGS OVER AMERICA

AIR CORPS U.S. ARMY

plume of black exhaust smoke as it began climbing on its brief maiden flight. Stanley was taking the aircraft to the Air Force flight-test facility at the Muroc base, just as he had done with its predecessor, the XB-35, in June of the previous year.

With the Air Force committing itself to a future of jet-powered aircraft procurement, the B-35 programme would end after a total of just thirty-six hours of flying, at a cost of roughly 1.8 million dollars per hour of flight, amortized.

US Air Force Major (now General) Robert Cardenas was in charge of the YB-49 flight-test programme and flew the second test aircraft from the Northrop plant to Muroc. The flight testing of the YB-49 was conducted in phases or test series. The first phase was flown by Northrop flight-test personnel to establish the airworthiness of the aircraft. The second phase, conducted by the Air Force, concerned the fundamental performance aspects of the aircraft including take-off speed, nose-wheel rotation, stall characteristics, speed in flight, rate of climb and others. The third phase dealt with issues of control and stability, the specialty of the test pilot, Captain Glen Edwards. Major Cardenas was conducting the performance test series and he recalled, 'The rate of acceleration of a jet aircraft, once it is in the air, is much faster than that of a prop job. You pick up so much airspeed so rapidly, you have two choices on take-off. If you took off [normally], you'd blow the gear doors off. [The YB-49] was a conversion from a prop airplane, the XB-35. When they converted it they changed the engines but they didn't change much else. So the landing gear took too long to retract. I had to pull up fairly steep, but not real steep. The only other thing I could do was pull back on the power, but no sane pilot wants to pull back the power on take-off. So, I left the power on and pulled it [the nose] up to keep the airspeed down till all the gear came up. Then, when you levelled off, you'd sit there rocking in your seat, back and forth, in unison with the slosh of the fuel (there were no fuel-cell baffles in the aircraft).'

When a conventional aeroplane is deliberately stalled, by reducing power and gradually pulling back on the control column, the wing loses lift and the aircraft begins to fall, virtually out of control. When you

release back pressure on the control column and resume power, the plane will normally regain airspeed and lift, and naturally resume level flight. The pilots who flew the N9M soon discovered that deliberately stalling a flying-wing aircraft in that time meant airflow separation, making the trailing-edge control surfaces ineffective, sometimes reversing the effect of the controls, sometimes causing the aircraft to enter a tail-slide, fall onto its back or slip into a left- or right-hand spin.

Major Cardenas: 'I did one stall which resulted in a gyration that was abnormal. The sucker flipped over. I wrote a report that, as far as I was concerned, the stall tests were finished and that the airplane should be placarded against any intentional stalls. I never stalled the airplane again.' Additionally, 'The cockpit layout was miserable. The crew could not escape. If anything happened in the airplane, you couldn't get out. I never wore a 'chute because I couldn't have gotten out anyway. You got in from underneath, a hatch underneath the airplane; walked about fifteen feet forward, put your rear end in the seat, pulled a handle and rotated the seat ninety degrees in the line of flight and, with the other hand you pumped yourself up four feet into the bubble, a bubble which could not be opened [and] could not be blown off. The only way you could get out was to rotate the seat, lower it four feet, get down on the walkway and walk back fifteen feet. In the event of an emergency, you couldn't get out.'

Cardenas later briefed a group of general officers about the YB-49, describing its landing-gear problems, engine problems, fuel-cell problems, etc. He said, 'All of these mechanical and design deficiencies in the airplane can be fixed. I have no doubt that Northrop can fix these deficiencies. The one thing that I can't even begin to tell you how to fix is that the airplane needs some form of stability augmentation. I cannot tell you how or with what. The airplane has basically exceeded the human sensory and response capabilities.'

Major Cardenas had completed about seventy per cent of the Phase-Two test series when he was offered an opportunity to return to the University of Southern California to complete work on his aeronautical engineering degree, provided he could replace himself on the YB-49 test programme. He had great confidence in Glen Edwards, and brought him out to Muroc from Wright Field to run the continuing flight testing. On 19 May 1948, Captain Edwards arrived at the Muroc base. The next day, Cardenas checked him out on the aeroplane. Edwards flew as co-pilot. On 21 May, Edwards took over as pilot, with Cardenas riding in the co-pilot seat. From Glen Edwards diary:

21 May 1948 'Got off another flight in the YB-49 today. This time I flew the airplane, and must confess it is something of an experience. Stability is poor all around—landing is peculiar. Has a great tendency to float.'

27 May 1948 'Got two flights off today with doubtful success. Darndest airplane I ever tried to do anything with. Quite uncontrollable at times. Hope to be more favourably impressed as time goes on.'

3 June 1948 'What a wonderful day this has been! Got off two flights on the YB-49, a lovely flight on the DC-6, one on the C-74—and I'm bushed. Col. Boyd flew the YB-49 for the first time today and wasn't too impressed. We all share the same views. A passable airplane in ideal circumstances.'

That was the final entry in Captain Edwards's diary. In the cool of the Mojave desert morning on Saturday, 5 June, Glen Edwards and a combined civilian and military crew prepared to take the YB-49 on another test flight from the Muroc Army Airfield.

The test pilots who flew the two YB-49 flying wings referred to them as 'One' and 'Two'. On Thursday 3 June, Captain Edwards had conducted in-flight tests on One for four hours. The tests included stalling the aeroplane with the landing gear down, with the landing gear up, and with flaps in all the possible settings. After that, Colonel Albert Boyd, chief of the Flight Test Division at Wright Field, took over and flew the plane for another hour. The point of these tests was to further explore the control, stability and stall characteristics of the YB-49, all of which were considered unusual and unacceptable by the Air Force pilots who had been flying it. At the end of the Thursday flight, One was turned over to Northrop, the manufacturer,

Even Jack Northrop had expressed concern that his flying-wing design might be inherently unstable. On 5 June 1948, a prototype YB-49, broke apart in mid-air, taking the lives of the test crew including that of Captain Glen Edwards, for whom the California high desert flight-test base is now named.

for additional testing of the stability, control and stalling characteristics.

Captain Edwards ran more tests in Two that Friday during a four-hour flight in which the aeroplane was put through high-power climb, high speed, and aileron responsiveness evaluations. The crew were evidently dissatisfied with the resulting data, and after consultation with both the Muroc and Wright Field Flight Test Divisions, it was decided to schedule an additional test flight for Saturday, 5 June. Major Daniel Forbes would fly Two as aircraft commander on Saturday with Captain Edwards as co-pilot. 1st Lt. Edward Swindell was along as flight engineer and two civilian engineers, Charles LaFountain and Clare Lesser completed the crew.

Saturday morning dawned clear, and at 6.44 a.m. Two lifted off from the dry lake-bed runway. Normal test procedure required the YB-49 to be accompanied by a chase plane, but as it was the weekend, and the flight had been scheduled at "the last minute", they had to fly without a chase plane.

On this flight, Lt. Swindell was responsible for balancing the aeroplane by controlling the fuel feed to the engines from the tanks forward and aft of the centre of gravity. The pilots were tasked with quite a large workload that morning, probably more than they could hope to accomplish in the time alloted for the flight. At 7.30 Major Forbes radioed the Muroc tower giving his position as over the north end of the Antelope Valley at an altitude of 15,000 feet, where they were to begin a series of stall tests. Forbes had flown as co-pilot to Major Cardenas on the YB-49 test flight in February when a stall test had resulted in the gyration mentioned earlier by Cardenas, who described the event further: 'After stalling the One, I found myself at the controls of an aircraft that was pointing almost straight up; refusing to respond to the controls. It was falling tail-first at 5,000 feet per minute. The aircraft then tumbled over backwards.'

It is thought by some that, when Major Forbes put the flying wing into a stall condition that June morning, he experienced another tail-slide which then led to the plane flipping over backwards or slipping sideways into an irrecoverable high-speed spin. Then, when he attempted to regain control, the outer por-

tions of the wings on both sides tore off as the aircraft exceeded its structural limit. In Air Force parlance, the aircraft, 'while undergoing a series of performance evaluations, departed controlled flight and experienced a catastrophic failure in the air.'

Shortly before 8 a.m., USAF Major Russell Schleeh was driving on California State Highway 466, and was startled to see several large pieces of metal plummeting to earth north of the Muroc base. The giant flying wing bomber had evidently displayed its instability one last time before disintegrating in flight and taking the lives of the entire crew. The centre section, containing the cockpit and crew stations, crashed within view of the base; the outer wing panels fluttered to the ground some distance away.

Major Cardenas returned to Muroc to take charge of the YB-49 test programme again. After the crash, Air Force confidence in the flying-wing bomber was at a low ebb. Northrop tried to save the day by having one of its test pilots demonstrate that the One could be safely stalled and the Air Force agreed to continue the test programme with bombing trials. It would be the last straw for the big wing. A level-bombing aircraft must provide a stable platform for the bombardier to aim and release his bombs accurately. The YB-49 did not meet that requirement. The Boeing B-47 jet bomber was superior in nearly all respects and in 1949, the B-49 programme was officially cancelled. The one remaining YB-49, a YRB-49, was placed in storage and was later scrapped. In August 1949, the two XB-35s and the first two YB-35s were scrapped. Between December 1949 and March 1950, all of the remaining YB-35 airframes were destroyed.

On 8 December 1949, Muroc Air Force Base was renamed Edwards Air Force Base in honour of Captain Glen Edwards. Jack Northrop's flying-wing bomber had come along forty years before the technologies that were needed to make such an aircraft operate successfully, as exemplified by the B-2 Spirit stealth bomber.

Specifications: Northrop XB-35
Engines: Four Pratt & Whitney R-4360 air-cooled radials of 3,000 hp each
Maximum speed: 391 mph at 35,000 ft
Cruising speed: 183 mph

right centre: USAF Captain Glen Edwards in 1948; far right: Two views of XB-35 test flights near the Muroc dry lake base.

Service ceiling: 39,700 ft

Range: 8,150 miles with a 16,000 lb bomb-load.

Weight empty: 89,560 lb. Maximum take-off weight: 209,000 lb

Wingspan: 172 ft

Length: 53 ft 1 in

Height: 20 ft

Wing area: 4,000 sq ft

Normal bomb load: 10,000 lb

Defensive armament: Twenty 0.50 calibre machine-guns in seven turrets

Specifications: Northrop YB-49

Engines: Eight Allison J35-A-5 turbojets rated at 32,000 lbs thrust each

Maximum speed: 495 mph

Cruising speed: 420 mph

Service ceiling: 40,700 ft

Range: 2,740 miles

Weight empty: 88,100 lb Maximum take-off weight: 213,500 lb

Wingspan: 172 ft

Length: 53 ft

Height: 15 ft 1 in

Wing area: 4,000 sq ft

Maximum bomb load: 16,000 lb

Defensive armament: Sixteen 0.50 calibre machine-guns in six turrets

CONVAIR

'. . . they shall mount up with wings as eagles'
– Old Testament, Isaiah

Beryl Erickson was chief test pilot for Convair, in charge of all flight testing for the B-36 programme. 8 August 1946: 'We were behind schedule. Our management considered the date to be a contractual imperative because the the programme was being threatened with imminent cancellation. The flight crew was ready at five in the morning, but we didn't receive flight release until just after noon. The ambient temperature was near 100 degrees. The plane's air conditioning system was not operable, and the temperature in the cabin was 140 degrees at take-off. The engines lacked the high-ratio cooling fans required for a hot day, so they were over-heated from the start. The engine oil pressure settled immediately below limits. That's bad. We advanced the six engines to full power and accelerated easily and smoothly to a take-off speed of 110 knots. The XB-36 controlled nicely in the take-off run and in the transition to steady climb. We flew conservatively with the gear down. The flight was uneventful and lasted thirty-eight minutes.'

Imagine a modern aircraft able to remain airborne for two entire days without refuelling. It seems impossible. And why should any aeroplane need to stay in the air for two days?

The earliest known consideration of aerial bombardment was a discussion by officers of the British Royal Engineers attending the 1893 Chicago Exposition. The first attempts at strategic bombing occurred in the First World War, when the British, French and Germans all conducted it with relatively little effect. The doctrine of strategic bombardment was the product of two military men, Italian General Guilio Douhet and American Colonel William Mitchell, both of whom had proposed the creation of independent air services for the most effective use of their nations' armed forces. Working within the system, Douhet published his theory that enemy cities, as well as military and industrial sites, were legitimate targets for mass bombing. He believed that such targetting would break the will of the enemy, whereas Mitchell believed in exclusively targetting industrial and military facilities with air power. Outspoken and considered rebellious, Mitchell was court-martialled for insubordination. By the mid-1920s, the philosophies of these two air-power pioneers had essentially merged. They agreed that the objective was to crush the will of the enemy to resist through the employment of strategic bombing and that the emphasis should be on precision attacks against specific military targets. This gradually evolved to include industrial facilities of military significance.

In the early 1930s, the US Army Air Corps had accepted Douhet's view that a proper defensive bomber formation could protect itself against attack by enemy pursuit formations without the help of escorting fighter aircraft. They also believed that 'a well-planned and well-conducted bombardment attack, once launched, cannot be stopped'. This perspective led to development and deployment of the generation of American heavy bombers that included the Boeing B-17 Flying Fortress and the Consolidated B-24 Liberator, both heavily armed. At the same time, development of long-range fighters was being de-

emphasized. It proved to be a costly mistake. The British Royal Air Force suffered heavy losses to German fighters and anti-aircraft fire when its Bomber Command tried to fly unescorted daylight precision-bombing raids in 1939 and 1940. The RAF then became convinced that such attacks were too costly and changed its operating policy to one of night area bombing. The American Eighth Air Force arrived in England to join the fray in summer 1942, refusing to accept the British perspective on bombing and proceeding to organize itself as a daylight precision force. It had no choice. The B-17 and

B-36

B-24, its only heavy bombers capable of attacking enemy targets in continental Europe, had been designed as day-bombers. They bristled with 0.50 calibre machine-guns and required ten-man crews for their operation and protection. As such, the bomb-loads they were able to carry were relatively small, at least when compared to those of the main force heavies of the RAF as the war continued. The Americans had to fly a daytime bombing campaign and they paid a heavy price for doing it. In four unescorted bombing raids deep into Germany in October 1943, the Eighth lost 148 heavy bombers—

most of them to enemy fighters—more than twelve per cent of the strike force. The Americans now understood that such daylight precision attacks could not be conducted without the aid of long-range fighter escort.

In 1940, when it seemed to many in the United States that England would be invaded and occupied by the Germans, the concept of a true intercontinental bomber began to develop. If England had fallen, the US would have had no air bases outside the Western Hemisphere. The Army Air Corps (it had not yet

above: All the Convair RB-36D strategic reconnaissance aircraft were delivered to the Strategic Air Command base near Rapid City, South Dakota during 1950 and 1951.

71

The design competition for the first intercontinental bomber–a high-altitude aeroplane with a heavy bomb load and unprecedented range–was initiated by the Army Air Force on 11 April 1941. This was eight months prior to the Japanese attack on Pearl Harbor, but at a time when Nazi aggression in Europe was achieving phenomenal success. America was faced with the overwhelming prospect of having to contest the Hitler war machine single-handedly. The defeat of Britain–which seemed probable–would leave the United States without European allies and with no bases outside the Western Hemisphere.

become the US Army Air Force) began drafting requirements for an aircraft capable of attacking targets in Europe from bases in North America. The new bomber was meant to have a 450-mph top speed, a 275-mph cruising speed, a service ceiling of 45,000 feet and a maximum range of 12,000 miles cruising at 25,000 feet. It was to carry a normal bomb-load of 10,000 lb over a radius of 5,000 miles, or a maximum load of 72,000 lb over a much shorter distance. Aerial refuelling was still experimental, and not considered practical in the planning of the new plane. Therefore it would have to be a very large and extremely heavy aircraft to accommodate the great fuel and bomb loads necessary for the plane to meet its performance specifications.

Boeing and Douglas were the only American companies with experience of building what were then considered very large aircraft. Their XB-15 and XB-19, respectively, were essentially flying laboratories and were much smaller and slower than the new bomber being planned by the Army. The largest bombers of the day, the B-17 and B-24, bore no relationship in size or performance to the new plane. The B-17E had a top speed of 317 mph, a cruising speed of 195 mph, a service ceiling of 36,600 feet, and a combat radius of 1,000 miles with a 4,000 lb bomb-load. The B-24D had a top speed of 303 mph and a cruising speed of 200 mph. Its service ceiling was 32,000 feet and its combat radius was 1,150 miles with 5,000 lb of bombs. Even the largest bomber of World War II,

the state-of-the-art Boeing B-29 Superfortress, which did not fly until 21 September 1942, could achieve a cruising speed of just 230 mph with a top speed of 361 mph, a service ceiling of just 32,000 feet and a combat radius of 1,900 miles while carrying a 16,000 lb bomb-load.

The Army asked both Boeing and Consolidated to undertake preliminary design studies for the big new bomber in April 1941 and Consolidated expanded work on a design it had begun in September 1940 for just such an aircraft. It was known as the Model 35 and was a high-wing design with a circular fuselage 128 feet long. It utilized twin vertical stabilizers like the company's B-24 and had a 164-foot wing. It had four engines arranged in two nacelles (one on each wing), each with one tractor and one pusher propeller. The aircraft would be slightly larger than Boeing's B-29, but it would not meet the Army requirements and would never be built.

Various manufacturers became involved to greater or lesser extents in the competition to design and build the new bomber. Baltimore's Glenn L. Martin Company was invited to participate, but declined owing to a shortage of engineering personnel. Douglas joined the project as did North American Aviation, but the latter did not submit any design proposals, and Northrop was asked for relevant information about the 'flying wing' design it was then developing. Finally, on 3 May 1941, preliminary design data for their proposals were submitted by Consolidated,

Boeing and Douglas.

All three planemakers were having trouble reaching the requirements laid down by the Air Corps for the very-long-range bomber. In its eagerness for an acceptable design, the Air Staff met in August to slightly relax their specification for the plane, reducing it to a 10,000-mile range with an effective combat radius of 4,000 miles with a 10,000 lb bomb-load. They respecified the service ceiling to be 40,000 feet and the cruising speed to be between 240 and 300 mph. The three contractors then revised their data and submitted new proposals in early September. After reviewing the new data and design proposals, and considering the recommendations of its experts, the Army Air Corps entered into contract negotiations with Consolidated which had, in fact, submitted two different proposals. The first was a revised version of its Model 35; the second, Model 36, was an entirely new design featuring six engines mounted in a thick wing, and driving pusher propellers. Douglas, it seems, elected not to pursue the 10,000-mile aircraft design, offering instead a plane with a 6,000-mile range, which the Air Corps rejected. The Air Staff officers were not impressed with Boeing's effort, judging it 'overly conservative'.

Consolidated was asked to submit detailed cost estimates for both of its designs in early October, and by the 6th, had requested $15 million plus a fixed fee of $800,000 for the development, mockup, tooling and production of two experimental aeroplanes. It also

stipulated that the customer must not 'entangle the project in red tape or continually changing requirements'. In fact, the new bomber was to become ensnared in more red tape than any other American defence project of that era.

A contract was issued to Consolidated on 15 November 1941 for two experimental XB-36 aircraft to be built at the company's San Diego plant. The first plane was to be delivered in May 1944 with the second due six months later. Two weeks after the contract was let, Army Air Corps engineers determined that the six-engined Model 36 design was the more promising of the two Consolidated proposals and the company began work on a full-scale mock-up of the bomber in San Diego. The mock-up would be used to check proposed equipment and armament installations. In their effort to design and construct an aircraft of the size and operating capabilities in the customer requirement, Consolidated engineers and officials knew they would be facing problems they had never before encountered.

No aeroplane had previously been built on a scale comparable to the Model 36. The wingspan was to be 230 feet, with an area of nearly 4,800 square feet. Power for the giant would be provided by six new 28-cylinder Pratt & Whitney air-cooled radial engines, each driving a 19-foot diameter, three-bladed propeller in a pusher configuration. They were to be accessible in flight through the 7.5-foot wing-root. The 21,116-gallon fuel load would be contained in six wing tanks. The 72,000 lb maximum-capacity bomb-

The Army Air Force was asking for a bomber that could (1) carry a 10,000 lb bomb-load to a target 5,000 miles away and return non-stop, (2) haul 72,000 lb of bombs at a reduced range, (3) travel at 300 to 400 miles an hour, and (4) take off and land on a 5,000-foot runway.

Several aeroplane makers had taken a look at the 10,000-mile range requirement, and had then resumed work on projects that they considered to be in the realm of possibility.

'Peace is when nobody's shooting. A 'just peace' is when your side gets what it wants.'
– Bill Mauldin

'. . . the Americans may be throwing away a lot more good money after bad in a determined effort to save face by putting the big piston-engined bomber on the global map. One gets the impression, in fact, that the Air Force top planners, having spent so much already on their favourite weapon, and with the 10,000-mile goal clearly in sight, are loath to cut their losses and start on a fresh trail. Judged, of course, by present jet fuel consumption figures, one can fully appreciate their dilemma– although it is a tolerable certainty that by the time the Convair B-36 is in full operation, the pure jet bomber will have reduced the range gap to a negligible quantity.

'Range, undoubtedly, is the red warning light that now overshadows American global strategy and, clearly, from the military planners' viewpoint it cannot be lightly brushed off. From the design standpoint, too, it is like a recurring decimal–difficult to shake off and forget; the

load would be carried in four seperate bombbays in the 163-foot fuselage, which would have pressurized forward and aft crew compartments connected by an 80-foot-long pressurized tube containing a wheeled trolley on which crew members could slide back and forth. In addition to crew positions, the aft section contained a galley, a toilet and four rest bunks. The bomber's defensive armament consisted of five 0.37 mm cannon and ten 0.50 calibre machine-guns distributed in four retractable turrets, two on top of the fuselage and two on the bottom. There would also be a radar-directed tail gun turret. At this stage of development, it was anticipated that the gross weight of the plane would be 265,000 lb and the top speed would be 369 mph at the service ceiling of 40,000 feet.

One of the greatest challenges faced by Consolidated engineers was how to achieve the 10,000-mile range requirement. Basic drag on the aircraft had to be kept to an absolute minimum. Smoothness of the skin and joints of the craft was essential. Every effort had to be exerted to minimize the weight of the plane. The elimination of thousands of drag-inducing pop-rivets from the assembly process was made possible by the development of an experimental new metal adhesive, Metlbond, the creation of Dr Glenn Havens, a research scientist hired by the company. Ultimately, about one-third of the exterior skin of the new bomber would be assembled using the Metlbond technique. The criticality of drag and weight reduction to the achievement of the range requirement was underscored frequently by company officials who constantly reminded the engineering staff that every pound of extra weight required two pounds of fuel to complete the 10,000-mile mission.

Several new systems had to be developed for the B-36, including a 3,000 psi hydraulic system (1,500 psi was the standard of the time), with new pumps, valves and actuators to move the enormous landing-gear and flaps. A special methyl bromide fire-extinguishing system was designed to replace the conventional carbon dioxide system then available. Methyl bromide offered a lower boiling point and was safer, lighter and easier

to store than carbon dioxide. This system was not developed in time for the prototype XB-36, but was installed in all subsequent B-36s.

In the first six months of development, the company concentrated on refining the design of the gargantuan bomber, controlling its weight, reducing drag and tackling the many challenges common to the early stages of such mammoth projects. A full-size wooden mock-up of the plane was constructed in a large building next to Consolidated's engineering department in San Diego. It included the fuselage, one entire wing and the twin vertical stabilizers, with the defensive armament and landing-gear installations receiving particular emphasis. By late July 1942 the mock-up had clearly demonstrated that initial weight estimates for the aircraft had been optimistic. The 10,000-mile range requirement was in jeopardy and members of the company's Mock-up Committee were split on the issue of how to trim weight from the plane. Some of them favoured reducing the amount of defensive armament and the size of the crew, while others felt that such changes would emasculate the B-36, making it tactically useless. Eventually, they reached a compromise, agreeing to eliminate only certain items they considered less than essential, such as certain crew comfort and survival installations and equipment. The accompanying weight reduction proved less than sufficient and the range requirement remained a nagging problem for Consolidated. Even so, the client approved the mock-up in September and, buoyed by the progress, the company elected to move the XB-36 programme from the home plant in San Diego to its newest facility, Government Aircraft Plant No. 4, at Fort Worth, Texas. This would free up considerable manufacturing and assembly space in San Diego for the company's other pressing committments, Catalina flying-boats and Liberator bombers. It was also thought a prudent move in light of the perceived threat of attack by the Japanese on the major coastal cities of California. The XB-36 mock-up was dismantled and shipped by rail to the Fort Worth facility. The move itself, and the project set-up reorganization in Texas was accomplished in just thirty days, but once established there, progress on the programme ground nearly to a halt as the B-36 was forced to take a back seat to demands of Consolidated's B-24 and B-32 lines.

In wartime, priorities rule and expediency is all. Before construction was to start on the two XB-36 prototype aircraft, officials of Consolidated were lobbying the government to place a firm production order for the B-36. They claimed that, by beginning preliminary work on production aeroplanes in parallel with work on the experimental planes, at least two years could be saved along the way to an operational bomber. But at that point the Pacific war was going badly for the Allies, and the government believed that it could not accede to the Consolidated request. There was only so much money and manufacturing capacity available and priority then had to go to the B-24, B-29 and B-32 programmes.

In March 1943, the Consolidated Aircraft Corporation merged with Vultee Aircraft, Inc., to become Consolidated Vultee Aircraft Corporation, a name that was soon shortened to Convair. Now world events began to change the prospects for the B-36. In spring 1943, China was on the verge of being conquered by the Japanese. The Boeing B-29, the only bomber theoretically capable of operating over the great distances of the Pacific, was in its early production but was wracked with growing pains, not the least being a rash of engine fires. Bases for the B-29s within operating range of the Japanese home islands were not yet available; the battles for the Marianas Islands were yet to be fought. The only hope for the American effort in the Pacific appeared to rest on accelerating development of the very-long-range B-36, a weapon that could attack Japan from bases in the United States. US President Franklin Roosevelt met with British Prime Minister Winston Churchill in May and they discussed the critical Pacific situation. US Secretary of War Henry Stimson then circumvented normal procurement procedures and authorized the Army Air Force to order the B-36 into production without any further delay caused by the completion of the two prototype aircraft. Convair received a letter of intent in July for the purchase of 100 B-36s at a then phenomenal cost of

$1,750,000 per aircraft. Priority for the B-36 was officially raised, though still not to the level of the B-29.

As Convair hurried to advance the development of its bomber behemoth, significant changes were showing in the fundamental design. The twin vertical stabilizers, reminiscent of those on the B-24, were a concern for the company engineers who now believed that a hard landing or severe flight conditions might cause the stabilizers to shear off. The twin tail soon gave way to a single, 47-foot-high vertical fin which, while providing increased directional stability, decreased the structural weight of the aeroplane by 3,850 pounds and reduced drag as well. This design change would add 120 days to the scheduled delivery date of the first XB-36 and an actual contract was issued for the production aircraft on 23 August 1943.

Despite a greater emphasis on production of the superbomber, progress was slow. Vital wind-tunnel testing was delayed for several months as all appropriate facilities were tied up with higher-priority work, and development of the new Pratt & Whitney engine for the B-36 was slow and behind schedule. The Pacific war began to turn in favour of the Allies, and by mid-1944, with the Marianas campaign concluding, it would soon be possible to launch B-29 strikes on Japan from new airfields on Tinian. The teething problems of the B-29 had been resolved to the satisfaction of the Army Air Force, which now no longer saw the operational deployment of the very-long-range B-36 as an urgent matter. The contract for production of the initial 100 B-36s and related spare parts, was finally signed on 19 August 1944. It carried no priority rating, making the procurement of parts and materials for the new plane virtually impossible for the duration of the war. Strangely, however, the delivery schedule was unchanged. Convair was still expected to deliver the first production B-36 in August 1945 and the last aeroplane of the order was to be completed by October 1946.

When the European war ended in May 1945, total aircraft production in the United States was cut back by thirty per cent; 17,000 aircraft were taken off the

more you keep pushing up the tankage, the poorer becomes the relative military load, and the bigger and clumsier the air frame. One penetration sidelight on this is that a 10,000-mile piston-engined bomber is forced to carry an oil tankage of greater weight than its own bomb-load. The XB-36 for example, was originally designed to accommodate 1,200 US gallons of oil weighing some 9,000 lb, while the B-36B is millstoned with at least 11,000 lb.'
- from *Flight and Aircraft Engineer*, official organ of the Royal Aero Club, 1 July 1949; far left: Women at Consolidated in San Diego assembling B-24 Liberator bombers in World War II.

'How do you get that non-stick stuff to stick to the frying pans?'
– Steven Wright

'Lately a few critics of air power have stated their fears that strategic bombers will become 'a new maginot Line.' This is one of the strangest of all comparisons. I do not think it is fair to say we Americans think that way. We have profited by the lessons of recent history. We know that no line of any kind, natural or man-made, can be depended upon to keep us safe.

'The Air Force has been careful to reiterate that no defense is a complete defense today. This is unfortunately true even of air defense by high-performance fighters. In a heavy, determined attack, some planes will probably get through. This is a fact which must be faced. We do not refer to our radar net as a radar 'fence.' There are no fences against airplanes. Our air defenders are not trying to build a 'Maginot Line' out of radar beams, airplanes, or anything else.

'The best defense is an active defense in depth and a powerful offense in depth. I think everyone will agree that this is true of our entire land, sea and air team. Each member of the team can perform that position of the task for which it is best fitted. References to strategic bombers as evidence of 'Maginot Line psychology' are difficult to understand. Such references are usually accompanied by another statement that is equally confused. Someone in the armed services, so these statements read, is now advocating complete dependence upon strategic bombers to guarantee the security of the nation. I am not sure just who this is supposed to be. All military

manufacturers' order books in the next year and a half. In yet another U-turn, however, the B-36 programme was left untouched. Now the government saw a renewed need for a very-long-range bomber in view of the great losses suffered in the fierce campaigns to seize the islands from which the B-29s were operating against Japan. With the coming of the atomic bomb, which informed government officials knew would not long be an American exclusive, the B-36 was further justified as their only likely means of retaliating against a nuclear aggressor. Finally, when compared to the B-29, America's only other heavy bomber, the B-36, significantly outperformed the Boeing plane and was cheaper by half to operate in terms of cost-per-ton mile.

The engineers at Convair pressed ahead on the bomber project with renewed vigour, but were still faced with the fact that their big baby was considerably overweight. This more than any other consideration, prevented their progressing at the necessary pace for the schedule. They were especially concerned about the weight of the huge P&W R-4360-25 Wasp Major engines, and the nose guns, a recent equipment addition stemming from the experience of the B-29s in the Pacific. These items, together with new and heavier radar and radio equipment, were adding substantially to both the weight and the drag problems of the plane.

The next major challenge confronting the Convair people was the landing gear. In the retracted position, the main wheels and gear had to fold up into the wing. For proper fit, the engineers decided to use a single 110-inch-diameter main-wheel tyre. Another factor in the choice was that the industry was not yet able to provide adequate brakes for a multi-wheel gear system, as has since become standard on very large aircraft such as the Boeing 747. But such huge tyres (one under each wing) would concentrate most of the aeroplane's weight onto just two rather small contact patches. At that time, only three runways in the entire world were capable of withstanding the stress that would accompany B-36 operations: Carswell Air Force Base at Fort Worth, Eglin Field, Florida, and Fairfield-Suisun AFB in California. It was a ridiculous limitation that was exacerbated by the

planners recognize that there are certain purposes bombers can accomplish and certain purposes they cannot accomplish. Strategic air power is a powerful weapon. In the hands of the United States, strategic air power is primarily a deterrent to war. It is a means of quick retaliation against any aggressor. Air power alone and unassisted is scarcely capable of winning a complete victory. A strategic air force is designed to destroy the means of making and supporting an attack against ourselves. This accomplishment would

significant risk to the aircraft and crew should one of the two main tyres fail on a landing. The tyres, weighing 1,475 lb each, were the largest tyres ever made for an aircraft. Each main landing-gear with wheel, tyre, dual multiple-disk brakes, struts and ancillary equipment weighed in at a staggering 8,550 lb.

After a strong recommendation from the Air Force Chief of Air Staff for Materiel that a new landing-gear be developed to better distribute the weight of the B-36, thus eliminating the need for specially built runways, a new four-wheel bogie-type undercarriage was designed which utilized 56-inch-diameter tyres and enabled the new bomber to operate from any runway that a B-29 could use. The new undercarriage meant that a slight bump would have to be designed into the top surface of the wing on each side, but the new gear also produced a 2,600 lb weight saving.

By 1945 the big bird was still too heavy, but making some progress towards getting into trim. At 278,000 lb, her performance projections had to be revised once again. The top speed was now to be 323 mph, down from 369 and uncomfortably close to that of the latest model B-29. The service ceiling had also dropped, from 40,000 feet to 38,200, but the B-36 was still impressively superior to the Boeing plane in range and payload. Her cost would be three times that of the B-29, but she would be able to haul a 72,000 lb bomb-load an estimated 5,800 miles. The B-29 could carry just 20,000 pounds of bombs 2,900 miles. In terms of airframe weight, the B-36 weighed less than twice as much as the B-29, but it could carry more than ten times the bomb-load to a distance of 5,500 miles. The programme in 1945 was continually plagued by late or substandard materials from suppliers and there were concerns that the prototype aeroplanes might have resultant structural limitations.

On 8 September 1945, nearly six years after the signing of the original contract for the big plane, the first example, XB-36 (42-13570) rolled out into the Fort Worth sunshine. It began to be called "Jesus Christ", after the most common reaction of people the first time they saw it. There followed a lengthy series of delays and postponements, until 8 August 1946, when Convair chief test pilot Beryl Erickson lifted the

largest and heaviest aircraft ever flown, from the Carswell runway, accompanied by a seven-man company crew, on a generally uneventful 37-minute first flight over the plains of west Texas. What followed, however, was quite worrying for the company and the customer. Subsequent test flights revealed the aeroplane's actual top speed to be just 230 mph. This, along with a severe propeller vibration and ineffective engine cooling, meant the burning of considerably more midnight oil for Convair engineers. The cooling problem was soon solved with the use of a two-speed cooling fan, but there was little to be done about the vibration apart from strengthening the affected structures, which added still more weight.

A lot of time, effort and money went into finding and fixing the early problems of the first production B-36s. After resolving chronic fuel-tank leaks, troublesome alternating-current electrical systems and recurrent engine-cooling problems, however, the postwar years became a time of high achievement for the plane and her crews. In May 1948 a B-36A, again piloted by Beryl Erickson, made a 36-hour flight hauling a 10,000 lb dummy bomb-load and 5,796 lb of simulated 20 mm ammunition 8,062 miles at an average speed of 223 mph. The gross weight of the aircraft was just under 300,000 lb. The flight proved the B-36 a genuine intercontinental bomber.

On 8 July 1948 the first greatly improved version of the plane, the B-36B, made her maiden flight. Using uprated 3,500 hp Wasp Major engines, the new mark had a top speed of 381 mph with a service ceiling increased to over 42,500 feet. It could maintain an average cruising speed of 300 mph at 40,000 feet, and its bomb-load was increased to 86,000 lb, enabling it to carry two 43,000 lb Grand Slam bombs. Like the earlier B-36s, the new model was operated by a crew of fifteen: a pilot, co-pilot, radar bombardier, navigator, flight engineer, two radiomen, three forward gunners and five rear gunners.

The giant plane came with its own set of particular maintenance challenges. It required special work stands, jacks and dollies. It was too big to be sheltered in most existing hangars and construction of new, tailor-made hangars was financially prohibitive. New, high-capacity fuelling pumps had to be designed, and in 1949, a radical new 'maintenance dock' had to be created that covered most of the wing and three engines. Each aeroplane required a pair of these docks when major service was done on it and such work could thereafter be conducted in virtually all weather conditions.

After years of secrecy, the Air Force finally invited the press to spend a day with the big bomber in October 1948. Some of what appeared in American newspapers the next day follows. 'Uncle Sam's newest, biggest bomber–the B-36–is a long, slim Texas gal with a wiggle to her rear. She's a little on the skinny side, but she's beautiful. Pilots of the bombers which carried newspapermen were unanimous in their admiration for the plane.'
– *New York Daily News*

'War is hell . . . but if a war has to be, the Eighth Air Force's B-36 groups are going to the scene in comfort, with plush leather seats, built-in ash trays, food lockers, gadgets for heating food, wash basins, beds, and above all, leg room. One well-planned attack by B-36s carrying atomic bombs could virtually bring down the curtain on any nation's hope for victory.'
–United Press

'The B-36 can put the world in its bomb sights. From the crew's aft compartment, a look out the observation blisters turns your mouth dry. The nose of the plane is a couple of Pullman car lengths in front of you. Twenty feet behind you is the 47-foot tail, high as a four-story building. And the horizontal control surface is as long as the entire wing of the old Convair B-24.'
–Associated Press.

Most military aeroplanes have had nicknames– Spitfire, Mustang, Lancaster, Liberator, Catalina, etc. The B-36 never had an official nickname. In late 1948, however, Convair mounted a contest in which all its employees could enter their suggested names for the bomber. The contest rules stipulated that 'The name should be appropriate to the size and purpose of the plane, and in keeping with the fine, historic traditions of Convair's fighting aircraft. It

not solve all problems. The restoration of peace and security to the world must necessarily be our ultimate goal in any future war. The accomplishment of this aim would most certainly require land and sea forces under any circumstances we can now foresee.

'Without a powerful and successful strategic air attack, our position in a possible future conflict would be a most difficult one, as you are well aware. If conflict were forced upon us, our strategic force would pass from the role of deterrent to that of heavy retaliation. Our insurance against defeat and our hope of future victory would depend in large measure upon the effectiveness of this attack.'
– General Hoyt S. Vandenberg, Chief of Staff, U.S. Air Force, 9 February 1949

should be one word and should not be a "made-up" combination. Duplication or possible confusion with other Army or Navy aircraft names should be avoided. Preference will be given to names which relate to the size, weight, power, range, purpose, and mission of the B-36.' The deadline for submitting names was 28 February 1949. The panel of judges included Major-General Roger M. Ramey, commander of the Eighth Air Force; Amon Carter, publisher of the Fort Worth *Star-Telegram*; and LaMotte T. Cohu, president and general manager of Convair. A $50 prize would be awarded to the winner along with a special certificate. Fort Worth employees submitting the top five entries would be eligible for a ride in a B-36. The rules also stated that the name selected would not become official until approved by the Air Force Munitions Board Aircraft Committee. Of the 797 names submitted, sixty were 'Peacemaker', the name which, on 13 April the judges declared the winner. Five employees were chosen in a draw from the sixty who had submitted Peacemaker, and the company then respectfully recommended the name to the Air Force for adoption. In the end, some religious groups objected to the name and the Air Force deferred an official decision. The B-36 went through its entire lifespan without an official name, but was generally referred to as Peacemaker.

The bombers of America's Strategic Air Command have always been protected by a shroud of secrecy. It was an exceptional circumstance in March 1949, when Arthur "Bill" Pegg, chief test pilot of Britain's Bristol Aeroplane Company, was allowed to fly the B-36 to evaluate the handling characteristics of a very large aircraft prior to embarking on the testing of Bristol's huge new airliner, the Brabazon. 'Before flying the Brabazon, I wanted to find out from your people who fly B-36s if there is anything particularly difficult, anything peculiar to flying such a large aircraft. I found out. So far as the B-36 is concerned, there isn't. The B-36 flies beautifully, and I was very impressed both with its performance and its handling. Everything about it seems to be completely normal, which is why I say that it is surprisingly unsurprising.' Pegg was the first foreign pilot to fly the B-36. Later

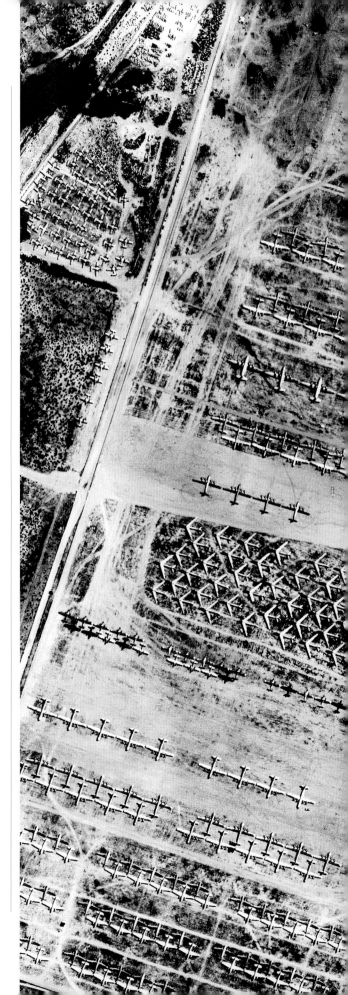

that year, he hosted Beryl Erickson on an inspection tour of the Brabazon in England.

Probably the best of the B-36 line was the D model. The D incorporated the advanced K-3A bombing and navigation system. All of the flying control surfaces were now covered with magnesium skin instead of doped fabric. Snap-action bomb doors had been fitted and their two-second operating time minimized the drag normally associated with the bomb-run. The aeroplane was delivered with the capability of carrying the Mk III/4 atomic bomb, a weapon which, at that time, still had to be armed in flight. The conventional bomb capacity was the same as that of the B model. Additional fuel cells were installed in the wing inboard sections, enhancing the already amazing range of the plane.

The most important modification of the aeroplane began in 1951. In a major effort to improve its take-off and "dash" speed and compensate for the ultimate weight of the aircraft through its operational career, a programme was initiated at Fort Worth to add two General Electric J47 turbojet engines in an aerodynamic pod under the outer portion of each wing. The power of the four jets, when added to that produced by the six R-4360 reciprocating engines, gave the bomber a top speed of more than 400 mph which could be sustained for vital short periods. General Curtis LeMay, head of the Strategic Air Command in the 1950s, recognized that in the ultra-long-range, high-altitude B-36, he had something really special and he championed the aeroplane through its many ups and downs. The B-36D, and all subsequent marks, benefitted from greatly improved performance mainly because of the addition of the four GE jet engines. Now the aeroplane could attain a top speed of 406 mph at 36,200 feet, and a service ceiling of 43,800 feet. Using the jets reduced the take-off run by 2,000 feet and doubled the rate of climb. The jets were normally used only on runs into the target and on take-offs and climb-outs. As the B-36 flew quite well on only three of its six piston engines, it was common practice to shut down some of the engines during cruise. With the advent of the B-36D, the plane was no longer as vulnerable to attack by enemy fighters. The best operating altitude for most fighters

of the day was between 20,000 and 25,000 feet, while the B-36 could easily operate at 40,000 feet. On 16 January 1951, six B-36Ds staged through Limestone AFB, Maine on a flight from Carswell AFB, Texas to RAF Lakenheath, England, in the first B-36 deployment outside the United States.

The lengthy B-36 missions during its operational decade pointed up the exceptionally high fatigue factor carried by the crewmen. In 1951, Convair human factors personnel were engaged in a programme to improve the interior environment of the aeroplane. Involved in the effort was the installation of many wool and fiberglass sound-deadening panels in each pressurized compartment, ninety-seven forward and fifty-nine aft. Additionally, vinyl carpeting was installed in both crew compartments. It helped to keep the interiors warm, increasing crew comfort. Other improvements included better bunks and mattresses, blankets and pillows, an improved galley facility with two electric burners, skillets, pots, pans, silverware and utensils. There were two plug-in hot cups for heating soups, coffee and other hot liquids, and an electric oven as well as a refrigerator. Folding tables near the bunks allowed crewmen to eat in relative comfort. More personal storage capacity was added, and the aft cabin lavatory was improved with a sink, mirror, toilet and privacy curtains.

There was considerable dissatisfaction with the quantity and quality of target intelligence available to the American strategic bombing force going all the way back to the B-29 raids on Japanese cities in the final months of the Second World War. General Curtis LeMay had commanded those B-29 missions, and when he was put in charge of SAC after the war, the provision of highly competent strategic reconnaissance aircraft was among his highest priorities. LeMay's enthusiasm and respect for the B-36 and its superb altitude and range capabilities led him to insist that approximately one-third of the entire B-36 force be dedicated to the reconnaissance role and the advent of the RB-36 line. The mission of the reconnaissance version was 'to carry cameras and electronic equipment which, in the event of war, would gather

information about the enemy'. Through much of the first decade of the Cold War, RB-36s roamed over much of the globe, keeping an eye on the activities of various nations in a manner similar to that of their successors, the Boeing RB-47 and the Lockheed U-2 and SR-71. For most of that decade, a period before the deployment of intercontinental ballistic missiles on land or at sea by members of the "nuclear club", the ultra-long-ranging B-36 force patrolled the skies and were the modern version of Teddy Roosevelt's "big stick." Certainly, much of the credit for the lack of another world conflict, possibly nuclear, is due the B-36 and the credible retaliatory threat it provided in that tense time.

'The sky was clear and the August day warm as the big bomber descended towards a routine landing at San Diego's Lindbergh Field. The flaps of the B-36 were down and the airport in sight when the eight-man civilian crew, returning from an eight-hour test flight, felt a massive shudder. The intercom came to life: 'Dave, we have a problem,' said Walt Hoffman, a flight engineer who somehow managed to keep his voice calm. 'The number five engine has fallen off the wing and we have a fire.' Pilot Dave Franks, who had spent thousands of hours flying B-24 Liberators, Catalina flying boats, Navy transports and Convair 240 airliners, suddenly had a life-and-death decision to make.

'Few people took note this past August 5, 2002 of the 50th anniversary of the day a US Air Force Convair B-36 simply fell apart on final approach and crashed into the ocean a few miles off Mission Beach. Don Maxion remembers though. The 76-year-old retired flight engineer feels a kind of duty to tell what happened on that day so long ago. He is the only one left who lived through the tragedy. 'I loved my job. We all did. We felt so fortunate to be doing something we loved with guys we respected and liked so well, and to get paid for doing it. We really were like a family up there. But this event changed everything. I still have my parachute. The kids, when they were little, used to use it as a tent in the back yard.'

'The B-36—the largest bomber ever built by the United States—never dropped a bomb in anger. Yet many still regard the enormous plane as a main reason the Cold War never turned hot, hence the nickname, 'Peacemaker.' Early in 1941, when Europe was dominated by Germany and Britain's very survival was in doubt, the US Army Air Corps decided it needed a long-range bomber the likes of which the world had never seen. This aeroplane would need to take off from U.S. bases, fly 5,000 miles at 300 mph at a ceiling of 35,000 feet, drop its 72,000-pound bomb-load on targets in Europe and return home without refuelling.

'Consolidated Vultee, forerunner of Convair, with plants in Fort Worth, Texas and San Diego, won the contract with its design for a bomber with a 230-foot wingspan, a length of 162 feet and a height of 47 feet, bigger overall than the intercontinental B-52 which replaced the B-36 and is still in use today.

'With World War II raging, production of the B-36 was put on hold because the need for conventional bombers was too great. The first B-36 was not delivered until 1948.

'The big plane spent a decade as the backbone of the US Strategic Air Command, constantly airborne with nuclear payload, ready for a bombing run on a moment's notice. When production ceased in August 1954, more than 380 B-36s had been built at a cost of $3.6 million a piece.

'By the time it was declared obsolete and taken out of operation in 1959, the B-36 had gone through several modifications and upgrades at Convair's San Diego plant, with each new design requiring extensive flight tests. It was such a flight that Don Maxion and his seven buddies from Convair were completing that August day in 1952, when an engine of their bomber inexplicably caught fire and fell off.

'The aircraft they flew that day, B-36D-25-CF 49-2661, was the 121st B-36 built at the Consolidated Vultee plant in Fort Worth. Originally a B-model, it had been sent to San Diego for conversion to a D. Essentially, four jet engines were added (in pods of two, one under each wing) to the six existing 3,500-hp reciprocating piston engines.

'Maxion, then 26, was one of four engineers aboard (in addition to two pilots, a radioman and radar tech-

With the imminent collapse of China in the summer of 1943, the need for a bomber able to hit the Japanese home islands became obvious to US Army Air Force planners. America still had no bases from which to reach Japan. That July, Convair, then the Consolidated Vultee Aircraft Corporation, was given an order for 100 production model B-36s. But with subsequent gains by US forces in the Pacific, the priority for the B-36 fell as limited resources were needed for production of bombers that were already operational.

With the potential of atomic war after August 1945, a new emphasis emerged for B-36 production, the need for immediate retaliation if the United States was attacked.

'Everybody's a pacifist between wars. It's like being a vegetarian between meals.'
– Colman McCarthy

8 August 1946. 7,000 employees of the Convair Fort Worth, Texas, plant watched from a fence beside the runway as the prototype XB-36 roared into the air on its maiden flight with Beryl Erickson at the controls. The first production B-36 was flown for the first time on 28 August 1947. It differed in many ways from the XB-36, most notably with its new bubble-type cockpit canopy that provided far better visibility for the flight crew, and its four-wheel main landing-gear which greatly improved weight distribution and enabled the plane to operate from nearly any runway that could accommodate the weight of a medium bomber.

The B-36 demonstrated its load-carrying capability on 30 June 1948, when it dropped 72 1,000 lb bombs. It later dropped an 84,000 lb bomb-load from high altitude, and on 28-30 July 1949, a B-36 flew more than 10,000 miles carrying a 10,000 lb bomb-load half that distance.

Seven years after the first B-36 had been delivered to the Air Force, Convair rolled the final production B-36 from the Fort Worth assembly plant. It was the 383rd B-36 built and delivered.

The last operational flight of a B-36 was on 12 February 1959, when an aircraft from Biggs AFB, El Paso, Texas, flew to Fort Worth, where it was retired from service. It was later installed at Amon Carter Field as a memorial to all who built, maintained and flew the giant bomber.

nician). He was the youngest member of the San Diego-based crew.

'Tests that day included a simulated bombing run over Plaster City, California, a desert outpost near El Centro in the Imperial Valley. 'That was exciting', Maxion said, 'because of an automatic-pilot manoeuvre in which the giant plane dropped its bomb and turned and twisted at a seemingly impossible angle, roaring heavenward to escape the faux mushroom cloud and blast effect.' They also did a high-speed run 500 feet above the ocean's surface and an emergency landing-gear drop, in which a member of the crew had to climb out into the great wing, without a parachute and in the open air, to ratchet out a pin holding up the gear. 'First time for me was scary', said Maxion. 'Second time was even scarier because I knew what to expect. But I'd done the parallel bars and rings in high school, so I knew I could handle it.'

'When Walt Hoffman reported the missing engine and fire, pilot Dave Franks stood and looked over the right wing. Then he yelled "bale out" over the intercom.

'Next came Hoffman's voice again: 'The right wing is on fire and the number four engine is falling off the wing.'

'When the incident began, the giant bomber was heading southeast along the coast; it was just over La Jolla at an altitude of 2,500 feet. Franks banked the aeroplane 90 degrees, a hard right turn that carried it away from the heavily populated beach communities and out over the ocean. In the next day's San Diego *Evening Tribune*, Captain J.D. Baker, pilot of an Air Force training plane that was slightly above and a mile behind the stricken B-36 described what he saw: 'Flames shot out of one engine. Soon the burning engine fell out of the plane and there was an explosion. The whole right wing was wrapped in flames."

'Franks now reiterated his order to bale out and the crew wasted no time.

'Maxion's job in such a situation was to open the left forward emergency hatch by the main landing gear. The crew had been warned not to bale out of the plane there if the landing gear was down and the number three engine was running; there wasn't enough clearance. 'But we had no choice,' Maxion

said. 'There was no time to get to our bale-out position, the emergency hatch by the nose gear.' Roy Sommers, the radioman, jumped out first, followed by Maxion.

'The crew typically did not wear their parachutes or bulbous Mae West flotation devices during long test flights over land because they were hot and uncomfortable. But crew members slipped into their parachutes quickly. Some also strapped on their Mae Wests, but Maxion didn't bother. He leaped out of the hatch—the only time he has ever jumped from a plane—and concentrated on counting. 'We had been trained to count to ten and then pull the rip-cord,' he said. 'I got to about 2 and yanked on it. Roy Adkins, the co-pilot, later told me that I missed the landing gear by a couple of feet, with a better margin for the engine propeller.'

'Aeroplane parts rained from the sky as Maxion slowly descended. Metal panels large enough to decapitate a man went whizzing and whistling by. In an attempt to steer clear of the debris, Maxion yanked on one side of his parachute risers, but gave that idea up when the chute momentarily collapsed.

'He watched in shocked disbelief as the B-36, now a disfigured hulk of fire and smoke, spiralled into the sea. Hundreds of people watched from the shore as the plane hit the water in a tremendous explosion, sending a mushroom cloud of smoke and water skyward. 'Flames went up 20 or 30 feet when the plane struck the water,' said Clifford Dodson, who was watching from the porch of his West Point Loma home.

'Drifting down toward the sea, Maxion realized he had no flotation device and would wind up miles off shore. He got rid of his heavy oxygen bottle and high boots. He hit hard and went deep underwater. By the time he reached the surface, his parachute was sinking fast. He disentangled himself from the chute, slipped out of his flight suit, tied the legs together and used it as a crude buoy. The water was cool, but not terribly cold, and the swell was gentle.

'A Coast Guard helicopter came by before long and plucked Maxion and Roy Adkins, the co-pilot, out of the water in a sling, winched them aboard and flew them to the Naval Hospital in Balboa Park. June Maxion, who was at the couple's Robinson Street apartment with their three children, said she got a call from a supervisor at Convair. 'I was desperate to know if Don was all right. People in the neighbourhood started coming by, the phone kept ringing and it was all over the radio. I called the Naval Hospital and said I needed to talk to my husband right away. I just had to hear his voice.'

'Word came quickly that one by one the other fliers had also been rescued. 'I thought everybody made it. A few guys had some scratches, but nobody was really injured,' said Maxion. 'But then we learned that three guys were still missing.' One of the missing, radioman Sommers, got picked up by a passing fishing boat, was dropped off at a nearby pier and hitch-hiked home, carrying his sopping parachute. But Hoffman and Dave Franks didn't make it. Their bodies were never found. Maxion and his mates speculated that Hoffman may have gone to the back of the air-craft to retrieve his Mae West and couldn't get back to the emergency hatch in time. But everyone agreed Franks stayed with the plane till the last pos-sible moment to make sure all crew members got out and the plane was well clear of land. 'Dave just waited too long,' Maxion said. 'I truly believe he gave his life to save us.'

'The spot where the bomber went down is more than three miles off Mission Beach in about 250 feet of water. Local fishermen, most of whom are too young to remember the B-36 crash, call it 'the Airplane Hole,' and know it as a great place to catch rock cod.

'Determined to learn what caused the huge plane's engines to fail, the government sent Navy divers down day after day in the weeks following the crash. In pres-surized suits weighing hundreds of pounds and breathing a mixture of oxygen and helium, the divers searched the silty bottom and retrieved sections of engine, fuselage and wing in an attempt to piece together what had happened.

'The B-36 had been plagued by minor engine fires, which crews generally had been able to extinguish in the air. Discarding several other theories, Maxion said, officials traced the fire to the engine alterna-tors. 'The alternator housings were made of mag-nesium. The failure of the alternator could have started an uncontrollable magnesium fire. But they

were never certain.'

'Maxion and the other surviving flight test crew members were given the option of transferring to jobs on the ground. They opted to keep flying, though Maxion added some equipment to his kit, including flares and shark repellent. He remained close to his fellow B-36 fliers for many years, even when work took them to opposite compass points on the globe. 'Roy Sommers was the last one. We were buddies forever; he died eight years ago. Our wives still have lunch together regularly. When you fly that often with guys, risk your lives together and come through something like that, well, you'll never have friends like that again. I still miss those guys very much.' —article by Mark Sauer in the *San Diego Union-Tribune*

Specifications: Consolidated B-36J

Engines: Six Pratt & Whitney R-4360-53 Wasp Major 28-cylinder air-cooled radials rated at 3,000 hp each and four General Electric J-47-GE-19 turbojet engines rated at 5,200 lb thrust each
Maximum speed: 406 mph at 36,200 feet
Cruising speed: 391 mph
Service ceiling: 43,800 ft
Normal range: 6,800 miles with a 10,000 lb bomb-load
Weight empty: 171,000 lb Maximum take-off weight: 410,000 lb
Wingspan: 230 ft
Length: 162 ft
Height: 46 ft 8 in
Wing area: 4,772 sq ft
Normal bomb load: 72,000 lb Maximum bomb-load: 86,000 lb
Defensive armament: Six retractable, remotely con-trolled fuselage turrets, each with twin 20 mm can-non; similar weapons in nose and tail

In 1949, aviation legend Charles Lindbergh was sent to Convair in Fort Worth by the Pentagon. His remit was to review the entire B-36 pro-gramme. Chief test pilot Beryl Erickson hosted Lindy for two days. 'We treated him like any-body else. He flew as my co-pilot, and he was impressed with many things. He operat-ed the overhead controls for the jet engines on the B-36D. When we told him there was no mechanical connection between the controls and the engines, he understood that that was an innovation. Those controls were the forerunner of fly-by- wire controls.'

Beryl Erickson retired from General Dynamics, the parent company of Convair, in 1962. He had accumulated the astounding total of more than 25,000 flying hours in his long career, which included 7,000 hours in B-36s.

BOEING

The B-52 is the largest bomber ever built, with some of the later models having a gross weight of 488,000 lb. Across a series of seven models this extraordinarily capable, adaptable and durable aeroplane has proved itself in so many ways a brilliant design and a wise choice as both a nuclear and conventional weapons-delivery system.

The Boeing Airplane Company of Seattle, Washington, may be best known today for its array of highly successful jet airliners, ranging from the first 179-passenger 707 that entered service with Pan Am in October 1958, to the 568-passenger 747-400 jumbo. But from the mid-1930s to the early 1960s, the company's primary activity was the design and production of superb bomber aircraft.

Like most American companies in the 1930s, Boeing suffered the effects of the great depression era as it struggled to survive the worst economic decline in history. The key to its survival and ultimate rise to pre-eminence in its field was its unbending commit-ment to the 'big bomber' concept and its determina-tion to build the finest examples of the type in the world. The effort began in 1935 when the company was awarded an Army Air Corps contract to design and construct what would be the largest and heaviest aircraft yet built in the United States. The 150-foot span, 38,000 lb XB-15 served Boeing as a flying labora-tory, providing a useful research and development function and pioneering many features that would become part of the company's famous B-17 Flying Fortress bomber of Second World War. Boeing's big bomber lineage continued with the various wartime versions of the B-17, followed by the ultimate bomber of that conflict, the B-29 Superfortress, best known for its delivery of the two atomic bombs which brought the war to an end in August 1945.

One of the aviation world's best-kept secrets was the Boeing Model 450 until it was rolled out of Seattle Plant Two in September 1947. It was Boeing's first jet aircraft, the six-engine B-47 Stratojet bomber, a radical-looking plane that would bridge the Cold War gap for the US Air Force Strategic Air Command (SAC) between the service of the huge ten-engine B-36

right: NASA's venerable B-52 air launch carrier or "mother-ship." This B-52 has been used for more than forty years to launch NASA experi-mental aircraft and for other flight research projects. It is both the oldest B-52 still fly-ing and the B-52 with the lowest amount of flight time. Among the many projects to which it has been assigned, it served as the launch plane for 106 flights by the X-15.

B-52

'The object of war is not to die for your country, but to make some other bastard die for his.'
– General George S. Patton

Peacemaker intercontinental bomber and that of the eight-jet B-52 Stratofortress. Preliminary design studies for the B-47 were begun in 1943 at the height of the war. The design was revolutionary, with ultra-thin wings that were swept back 35 degrees, six turbojet engines slung in pods under the wings and an unusual tandem bicycle landing-gear arrangement with additional balancing outrigger wheels that were housed in the inboard engine pods. The high-speed bomber was lightly armed with just two tail-mounted remotely operated guns, in the belief that it would not be subject to enemy fighter interception at the altitudes where it would operate. The B-47 had a crew of just three—a pilot, a co-pilot and a navigator/bombardier. Like its B-36 predecessor, the B-47 was a nuclear bomber, but much faster. By the end of its production run in 1957, 2,032 B-47s had been built, and of these about 1,800 served with SAC up to and into the transition to the mammoth B-52.

From 1946, when the Strategic Air Command of the US Air Force was formed, it served as America's Cold War nuclear deterrent, in combination with submarine-launched and land-based ballistic missiles, for forty-four years. In a time when the doctrine of both the American and Soviet superpowers was "mutually assured destruction" (MAD), each side counted on

the premise that it would survive a first-strike nuclear attack by the other, and would then launch an overwhelming retaliatory strike. One part of the SAC bomber force was on constant airborne-alert status while one-third of the force was on permanent ground alert, armed with nuclear weapons, with the crews on stand-by for immediate take-off. SAC bombers and their aerial-refuelling tanker planes were strategically based in the United States, Britain, Spain, Morocco and in the Pacific. With the collapse of the Soviet Union came the end of the Cold War, and in 1992, the Strategic Air Command was deactivated. In 1997 a new organization, the Air Combat Command, was formed, incorporating the aircraft of the former SAC.

For nine crucial years of the Cold War, from 1948 through to 1957, General Curtis E. LeMay served as commander of SAC. LeMay had been a key figure in the main Allied bombing campaigns of the Second World War in both the European and Pacific theatres of operations. A high-achieving, no-nonsense, tough taskmaster, LeMay was known as a 'big-bomber man' and as such, disliked the relatively small B-47 for its inability to carry a 10,000 lb bomb-load over a 3,500 mile radius of action, which he considered an essential SAC requirement. LeMay favoured a much larger, more threatening all-jet bomber and was influential in

the October 1948 Air Force decision to reject a Boeing design for a new straight-winged bomber powered by six turboprop engines. This was the Model 462. It looked like a larger B-29, having a 221-foot wingspan and a length of 161 feet. It was specified for six Wright XT35 Typhoon turboprop engines rated at 5,500 hp each and driving six-blade propellers. To meet the Air Force range requirement, Boeing elected to go with turboprops instead of the extremely fuel-hungry turbojets then available. The gross weight of the Model 462 was to be a hefty 360,000 lb. As the story goes, the Boeing people who had come to Wright Field, Ohio, to try to sell the design, repaired to their hotel and within a few days returned to the base with a new bomber design concept, the Model 464-49, and a balsa-wood model of it, based on power provided by eight jet engines. It was projected to have a maximum speed of 565 mph at 46,500 feet and a combat radius of 3,550 miles carrying a 10,000 lb bomb load. The gross weight was estimated at 330,000 lb. This 'instant revamp' was immediately accepted by the Air Force, marking the moment when it committed itself to jet-powered aircraft for the future. It soon contracted with Boeing for two jet-powered prototype aircraft, the XB-52 and the YB-52.

Actually, it was not that easy. A lot of important Air Force toes had been stepped on along the way to the jet B-52 decision, including the important armament, powerplant and propeller divisions at Wright Field, and extreme budgetary constraints were in place on Defense Department spending in the Truman administration, threatening the entire B-52 programme. With completion of the XB-52 mock-up in late April 1949, heated wrangling broke out within the Air Force hierarchy over the apparent range of the new plane, which was actually a combat radius of only 2,700 miles, instead of the promised 3,550. One faction favoured reviewing the whole programme and even organizing yet another manufacturer competition, but General LeMay, who was by now commanding SAC, staunchly advocated the B-52, making the case that the continuing development of the J57 engine would, in reasonable time, provide the required range. By November 1949, Boeing had helped its own cause by proposing a change (and a new model designation,

464-67) in which the fuselage length of the new plane was increased to 152 ft 8 in, providing additional space for fuel and increasing the combat radius to 3,500 miles, with a new gross weight of 390,000 lb. The Air Force internal argument over the advantages and disadvantages of the B-52 continued into 1950, the year in which the Korean War began. LeMay took full advantage of this new threat to world peace and persuaded USAF Chief of Staff General Hoyt Vandenberg to authorize approval of the B-52 to replace the B-36 as the mainstay of the American strategic bombing force. The initial production batch contract for thirteen B-52As was signed in February 1951, agreeing delivery of the first production aeroplane by April 1953.

The XB-52 emerged from Plant Two in November 1951 and brought with it a range of problems so extensive as to delay its first flight until after that of the number two prototype, whose maiden flight took place in April 1952. With major American aeroplane manufacturers vying for dominance in the Air Force heavy-bomber procurement plans, the Convair entry, an eight-jet swept-wing version of the B-36, called the YB-60, also flew for the first time in April of that year. Unfortunately for Convair, its big jet proved to be more than 100 mph slower than the B-52 and was eliminated from contention. That first B-52 was designed with a tandem cockpit layout similar to that of the B-47, another characteristic that LeMay hated. The cockpit layout of the production aeroplanes would change to a conventional side-by-side arrangement at his insistence. The forward fuselage was also lengthened to accommodate additional equipment and one new crew member, the electronic warfare officer, who was responsible for electronic defence of the aircraft including radar jamming. The crew now consisted of a pilot, a co-pilot, a navigator, a radar navigator, an electronic warfare officer and a tail gunner.

The first B-52s were powered by eight Pratt & Whitney J57 turbojet engines rated at 8,700 lb thrust each. They were mounted as pairs in four pods hung beneath the 35-degree swept wing of the big plane. Defensively, it had only a tail turret containing four 0.50 calibre machine-guns that could be fired manually or automatically with tail-warning radar-directed fire.

Of the thirteen B-52A aeroplanes, three would be

below left: Boeing's six-jet B-47 was the forerunner of the B-52, leading the US Air Force into the age of the big jet bomber. below: The American popular singer Doris Day was probably the biggest name in her profession in the 1950s when the giant B-52 entered the Air Force inventory and became the mainstay of the USAF Strategic Air Command.

retained as developmental aircraft. The last of these three would later be modified to carry the North American Mach 7 X-15 air-launched, rocket-powered research plane. The other ten were completed as RB-52B reconnaissance/bomber aircraft. They were fitted with uprated engines and other improvements over the A model, and were the vanguard of an expanded 53-aircraft initial order. The 93rd Bomb Wing (H) of the Strategic Air Command took delivery of the first B model planes at Castle Air Force Base, California, in June 1955. While an operational unit, the main role of the 93rd BW was to provide transition training for new B-52 crews. In January 1957, three B-52s of the Castle AFB Wing made history by flying non-stop around the world in 45 hours 19 minutes, being refuelled in flight just three times.

Subsequent marks of the Boeing bomber were produced through the next decade, aircraft of increased power and greater weight through the B-52F with Pratt & Whitney J57-P-43W engines that, with water injection, were rated at 13,750 lb thrust each, or a total thrust of 110,000 lb for an airplane with a combat weight of 293,100 lb.

Until the introduction of the B-52G model late in 1960, all B-52s had been jointly built in both Seattle and Wichita, Kansas. With the G, all B-52 production took place at Wichita. The G looked different from all earlier B-52s. Its vertical tail fin was reduced in height

by nearly eight feet and its chord was increased. The fuel capacity of the aeroplane was increased significantly with the elimination of the self-sealing bladder-type fuel cells, in favour of sealing the entire wing to hold fuel as a "wet" wing. The maximum combat radius without in-flight refuelling was extended to 3,600 miles and the maximum speed became 634 mph.

The last model of the B-52 series was the H, 102 of which were built by Boeing-Wichita and delivered to SAC in 1961 and 1962. The principal feature of the H model was the switch to the Pratt & Whitney TF33 turbofan engines, which were rated at 17,000 pounds thrust each. These new powerplants provided greater fuel efficiency, were quieter and much more powerful than the J57s they replaced, and they gave an unrefuelled range of 8,800 miles. The defensive armament was also changed; from the four tail-mounted 0.50 calibre machine-guns to a multi-barrel, quick-firing Gatling gun. B-52 production ended in October 1962 with 744 aircraft delivered. The B-52H continues to serve the USAF in the twenty-first century, and with various upgrades and service-life extension programmes it is expected to remain operational until 2040, giving the plane an incredible service career of at least 85 years.

It had been designed as a high-altitude nuclear bomber, but the first major combat assignment for the B-52 came in the Vietnam War in June 1965, with the dispatch of two wings of B-52Fs to the American base on the Pacific island of Guam. They were there to take part in a series of thirteen-hour missions to drop high-explosive conventional bombs on targets in Vietnam. At the same time the entire fleet of B-52Ds underwent modification to enable them to carry an increased load of conventional 'iron bombs' in both the bomb-bay and under the wings for a maximum bomb-load of 60,000 lb. These D model aircraft replaced the B-52Fs in the bombing campaign over Vietnam in 1966. Operating from Guam and Thailand, B-52s began strategic attacks on North Vietnamese targets that year and came under threat from Soviet-built SA-2 surface-to-air missiles (SAMs) which had a 28-mile range and an 82,000-foot ceiling. At least seventeen B-52s are known to have been brought down by the SAMs, with many others damaged by them. The B-52s

operated over Vietnam for eight years, flying a total of 126,615 sorties.

No B-52s were lost in South Vietnam to enemy fire. In a bizarre incident at U-Tapao air base in Thailand, there had been a discrepancy between the airspeed instruments of the two pilots in a B-52 that was nearing take-off speed. As the bomber reached the midpoint of the runway, the pilot aborted the take-off and the aeroplane hydroplaned off the strip and into the grass. It had a full bomb load on board. When it came to a stop the crew was able to safely evacuate the plane, but the pilot of a nearby rescue helicopter mistakenly believed that the tail-gunner was still trapped in the bomber. As the helicopter moved over the burning B-52 to drop fire retardant on it, the bomber exploded, taking the lives of both helicopter pilots.

Conditions and facilities were crowded at Anderson Air Force Base on "The Rock", as Guam was referred to by the B-52 crews stationed there. The Buff (Big Ugly Fat Fellow, to use the polite form) bombers were required to share parking slots, fuel and other facilities with many other resident aircraft, including SR-71, RC-135, and U-2 spy planes. At one point in the operations, Anderson was having to house 12,000 more men than it could accommodate in billets, making the establishment of tent cities necessary.

A force of 206 B-52 Stratofortress bombers was based in the western Pacific by June 1972 and was operating in an expanded war zone of four countries: Laos, Cambodia, and North and South Vietnam. Serving the aerial-refuelling needs of the big bombers were 172 Boeing KC-135 tanker planes. With the bombers having to fly much farther from their base on Guam to the war zone, mid-air refuelling was essential, where it had not been needed for the B-52s flying from U-Tapao, Thailand. At this point, SAC KC-135 tankers were having to provide up to 130 air-to-air refuellings a day. The KC-135 Stratotanker was operated by a five-man crew—two pilots, a navigator, a flight engineer and a boom operator—on their vital missions filling the giant B-52s with JP-4 jet fuel. In the course of the Vietnam War, the KC-135s performed an amazing 813,878 refuellings.

B-52 bombing attacks in the Hanoi-Haiphong area of North Vietnam had been halted in October 1972. But

top left: The remains of a B-52 being scrapped in the AMARC facility near Tucson, Arizona. bottom left: The instrument panel of the NASA B-52. That aeroplane was used in some of the most significant research projects in aviation history. below: A detail of the massive landing-gear of the big Boeing Stratofortress.

below: A B-52 bomber under construction at a Boeing facility in the 1950s.

'As I hurtled through space, one thought kept crossing my mind–every part of this rocket was supplied by the lowest bidder.'
– John Glenn

by December, President Richard Nixon was ready to resume the attacks with a renewed vengeance. Linebacker II was Nixon's eleven day, round-the-clock, maximum-effort bombing campaign against the two cities. He believed that such a demonstration of force could end the war, and the Strategic Air Command was required to utilize half of its entire worldwide B-52 force in that final campaign.

The bombing missions of Linebacker II began on 18 December 1972 and continued through 29 December, with a stand-down on Christmas Day. By mid-December, there were so many extra B-52 crews on Guam that, in addition to the tent-city billets that had been in place as the personnel build-up had progressed, the gymnasium had to be used as a makeshift dormitory.

In the bombing campaign, B-52Ds were bringing massive loads of 108 bombs each to their targets, the heaviest bomb-load ever carried to a target by a war plane. North Vietnamese defences were particularly effective and fifteen B-52s were shot down by their surface-to-air missiles in the Hanoi area. On the American side, Staff Sergeant Sam Turner, tail-gunner of a B-52D out of U-Tapao on 18 December, became

the first B-52 gunner to shoot down a MiG-21 fighter.

Defensively, many of the B-52 crews and tacticians participating in this Linebacker campaign may have, to some extent, contributed to exposing their aircraft to the thousands of deadly SAMs in the Hanoi-Haiphong region. The practice of turning on and testing their electronic countermeasures equipment several minutes before the bomb release, together with repeatedly using the same approach to the targets there, undoubtedly increased the possibility of their being shot down by the missiles. The old debate about the effectiveness of taking evasive action in the target area resurfaced with the practice of B-52s approaching their targets in a straight line or trail formation of three-ship cells, and taking no evasive action, which must have made the work of the North Vietnamese SAM teams a bit easier. The Air Force came in for considerable criticism over the quality of its internal communications, inflexibility, unrealistic prioritizing, failure to use surprise tactics, and piece-meal attacks. The exhausted U-Tapao crews probably suffered the most, as they were much closer to their targets than the B-52 boys out in Guam, and sometimes had to fly one or more missions a day, while

their Guam counterparts were flying just once every second or third day.

In one of the more dramatic incidents of the Linebacker II operation, a U-Tapao-based B-52D under the command of Captain John Mize approached Hanoi, the North Vietnamese capital, in the evening of 27 December. It was the ninth day of the bombing campaign and much of the enemy SAM capability had been degraded after numerous attacks on it. The North Vietnamese SAM crews had resorted to firing salvoes of their weapons; a new and frightening prospect for the B-52 crews.

Seconds after bomb release, Mize witnessed fifteen SAMs rising towards his aircraft. Shortly after that, the bomber lurched in concussion as a SAM exploded, driving bits of shrapnel through the thin skin of the plane and into the legs of the pilot and the navigator. The tail-gunner was also wounded. In the cockpit, fire warning lights came on and three of the plane's eight engines failed. The B-52 slid into a steep descent, falling several thousand feet before Mize was able to bring the bomber back into level flight. He checked on the condition of the rest of the crew and pondered the odds of making it to the nearest Thai airbase. He had lost three engines on the port side and now the last engine on that side was misbehaving. The crippled plane soon lacked all power on one side, was on fire and was shaking violently as he struggled to keep it flying.

There was some thought among the crew of ejecting, but they were still about thirty miles from the relative safety of flatter terrain. An hour after releasing its bombs, the B-52 was back over Thailand and the pilot was now certain that it could not be landed safely. In addition to his other problems, the electrics of the big plane went wild. Some systems quit. The bombbay doors fell open and one landing-gear began cycling up and down, again and again. If the intercom failed, Mize would be unable to order the crew to eject, so he ordered them to do so. Three of the crew ejected, but the ejection seats of the co-pilot and the navigator would not function. Mize ordered them to climb out and waited for them to leave the aeroplane. By now the bomber was falling and the pilot could do nothing to stop it. Then the electrical system failed completely and he ejected.

Unknown to Captain Mize and his crew, the largest rescue effort of the war was being mounted for them while he had been struggling to bring the B-52 back into Thailand. Within fifteen minutes of his bale-out, Mize and all of his crew were picked up by USAF helicopters from the Thai jungle, thanks in large part to the URC-64 beeper radios that all B-52 crewmen carried.

Larry Henderson was an Electronic Warfare Officer in B-52s and flew two tours during the Vietnam War, in 1969 and 1971. 'My experiences with flak and triple A were very limited, as we flew our combat missions at altitudes of 36,000 to 38,000 feet. We could see flak going off well below our aircraft, but it was never considered a threat. The surface-to-air missiles, however, were quite different; they had no trouble reaching us. Normally, the B-52 was not flown into a SAM threat area, but this was not the case on the first three missions of my second tour in the Vietnam arena. Our first mission was to lead a flight of three bombers, together with Ironhand (Wild Weasel/defence suppression F-105s) to southern Laos in support of US Marine forces.

'As we began the bomb run, I detected SAM radars tracking our aircraft from our 11 o'clock position. Just as we released our weapons I picked up a signal that indicated missiles were airborne and being guided at us. I called over the radio for all aircraft to break left due to the threat, and within ten seconds two SAMs exploded high and to the right of our aircraft. No injuries were suffered. The Ironhand aircraft had been out of position and had not seen the missiles.

'During the debrief [it was clear that] no one outside of our three aircraft had seen the missiles and 7th Air Force Intelligence could not confirm the presence of the missiles on the ground. The actions were listed as 'unknown'. With typical military [logic] we were scheduled to lead the same mission the next day, at the same time, same altitude and same attack heading. Again, we were fired upon; this time by at least six missiles; again, with no damage. On the third day of flying the exact same mission and again being fired on by the SAMs, the 7th Air Force finally confirmed the presence of the [missile] threat and cancelled further missions in the area until the threat

below: The brothers Wilbur and Orville Wright first flew their powered aeroplane at Kill Devil Hill, Kittyhawk, North Carolina, in December 1903, less than fifty years before the initial flight of the Boeing B-52.

below: Boeing's B-17 bomber of World War Two fame; bottom: A popular American soft drink of the B-52's early years.

had been suppressed.

'We were known to the rest of the crews as the 'Blytheville Missile Magnets' (as we had been part of the 97th Bomb Wing from Blytheville AFB, Arkansas. Actually, the B-52s were rarely under threat of attack until they were released to operate in North Vietnam, where they came under very heavy attack from all types of SAMs and enemy fighters.

'During my first Vietnam B-52 tour in Guam, we were scheduled to be a runway spare one day, rather than fly the primary mission. We would only launch if one of the primary aircraft aborted within fifteen minutes after take-off. One of the primary aircraft had an 'unsafe gear' indication and was going to abort if recycling the landing-gear did not cure the problem. While he was performing this action, we taxied to the end of the runway and were within one minute of launch when the primary called to tell us that his problem was fixed. We were released and taxied back to the parking area. The aircraft we had been about to fly was scheduled as a primary for the evening mission, and we were at an outdoor movie when that mission launched. As the number two bomber lifted off, the left wing fell off and the plane exploded in a fireball that was visible over most of the island. I was stunned to learn that the aircraft we had almost launched in earlier in the day was the one that had been lost. None of the crew was ever recovered as the plane went down in the Marianas Trench.'

Less than two hours after the opening shots of the Operation Desert Storm air war on 17 January 1991, seven B-52Gs of the 2nd Bomb Wing at Barksdale AFB, Louisiana, arrived over the Persian Gulf to launch a total of thirty-one Conventional Air-Launched-Cruise-Missiles at Iraqi communications and power station targets. They were taking part in the longest combat bombing mission in history, a thirty-five-hour, 14,000-mile round trip requiring four in-flight refuellings. Such ultra-long-range raids would not be repeated, but in that first Gulf War, seventy-three B-52s participated, bringing 72,000 bombs to Iraq from bases in England, Spain, Saudi Arabia and the island of Diego Garcia in the Indian Ocean.

B-52s have been used in other conflicts since Desert

Storm, including the May 1999 Nato air campaign against Serbian targets in Kosovo. Again, Barksdale B-52s operating out of RAF Fairford in England, in company with five North American B-1B bombers, flew nightly raids carrying cruise missiles and 3,000 lb Hav Nap long-range precision-strike missiles, along with 500 lb general-purpose bombs, cluster bombs, and even leaflets intended to persuade the Serbs to quit their fight with the Kosovo Albanians. The B-52 went to war again in 2003, to help bring down the Iraqi regime of Saddam Hussein.

Phil Rowe was an electronic warfare officer in B-52s during the Cold War years. 'Early in the B-52 programme, with memories of the lumbering B-36 still fresh in our minds, we followed the long-time practice of a lengthy pre-flight of our airplanes. I mean really lengthy. For a typical training flight we began the procedure of checking out aircraft equipment and systems over four and a half hours before each scheduled take-off. Strategic Air Command policy for crews in the heavy bombers required extensive pre-flight checks. Just before 0400 hours, well ahead of our planned 0830 take-off, we would arrive at the squadron area to pick up our gear, which included more stuff than Aunt Bessie needed for a wedding. That was but a part of the preparation for routine training missions. We had already spent the whole day earlier on mission planning and briefings to senior squadron staff to describe every aspect of the scheduled mission.

'There were six of us on the crew, not including any extras that frequently came along. Extra people might include an instructor pilot or evaluator, if this was a check ride, and there might be an instructor/evaluator/navigator, or a similar extra for the electronic warfare and gunner's positions. Seldom did we carry more than nine folks. Regular and extra crew members carried a briefcase, a parachute (plus three spare parachutes; two for the forward compartment and one for the aft tail-gunner), heavy clothing, one or more flight lunch boxes each, and two large thermos jugs and one small one were brought as well. There would be one or two sextant cases, each half the size of a footlocker and, of course, there were sometimes whole footlockers full of spare parts for the old MA-6 radar

system, depending on how important the mission was. We literally filled the whole back of the crew bus with the stuff we brought along. In the early days, before 1958, we also carried duffel bags with extra clothing, shaving kits and such, in case we landed some place other than our home base.

'When we arrived at the airplane, which was parked way out, a mile or so from the squadron buildings, we immediately unloaded all the equipment and lined it up under the wing of our bomber. Each man would place his own stuff in front of where he would stand for inspection by the aircraft commander. Then came another briefing, by the AC, and his inspection to make sure that everything needed was present and in good condition. The process was more easily endured if the weather was good. Then the crew would separate and the loading process began. Most of the stuff went into the forward crew compartment, where five of the six would fly, as would any extras. The tail gunner flew all alone in the aft compartment some 100 feet away in his own pressurized world and facing rearward. Some of the stuff not needed in flight was stored in the section aft of the rear landing gear and forward of the gunner's position. No wonder the B-52 grossed out at 450,000 pounds or more.

'Then it was time to start the exterior inspection, an important stem-to-stern external examination of the aircraft. The two pilots divided the walk-around checks, one taking the starboard side, the other the port. The electronic warfare officer and the tail-gunner checked their exterior portions of the plane too, like radomes, radio antennae, guns, ammo compartment doors, chaff dispenser ports. The ground power carts had not been started yet, so there was no electrical power or cooling air supplied to the interior equipment. Only in severe winter conditions would there be special carts running to pump warm air into the cockpit or essential equipment areas.

'It was time to climb aboard. Each man headed for his assigned crew station. The two pilots went to the upper flight deck, followed by the EWO and any extra folks. The gunner went aft to the tail. The fuselage between the forward and aft compartments was not pressurized in flight, nor was it heated or cooled. Each man now followed his own printed checklist,

carefully positioning switches sequentially, attaching helmet and oxygen mask to the communications and life support systems. An hour or more might pass from when the crew arrived at the airplane to when the first systems were powered-up by the ground equipment. There was much more to do. The B-52 is a huge, complex piece of hardware and systems.

'When the Power Off checklists were completed, the pneumatic carts were readied or started. The crew would complete the system checks without the engines being started or the use of aircraft generators (alternators). Each crewman would report over the interphone to the AC that he was ready to proceed. Next were the engine starts and system checkouts on aircraft power. All systems were exercised and checked except those which could only be checked in flight. For safety reasons, some systems could not be tested. These included the high-powered electronic transmitters, armaments and, of course, things like gear door and retraction mechanisms.

'Then everything was shut down. The engines were stopped and electrical power turned off. The Power On and systems checks were completed. Noted discrepancies were entered in the aircraft systems and equipment logbook and things that had to be fixed before the flight would be attended by maintenance personnel. Very few discrepancies were allowed to

top: A B-52H on final approach into RAF Fairford, Gloucestershire, England, in 1999; above: Another H model, delivering its bombs.

remain as open items. Safety-of-flight and mission-critical items had to be fixed or the flight might be cancelled. Sending a B-52 crew on an eight-hour training mission was expensive, so all had to be in order to preclude a wasted effort.

'After the plane was powered down, there were a few moments for a coffee break, another crew briefing and a report by the pilot to the Wing Headquarters Command Post about the status of the airplane, whether it was ready to go or not, how long it would take to make any necessary repairs.

'About 45 minutes before the scheduled take-off time, the crew would return to the airplane, climb aboard and start the checklists all over again, only this time they would continue through all pre-take-off phases and then move the airplane out to the end of the runway.

'A lot of work had been done by a lot of people to get that big bomber to the ready line at the end of the runway, including ground crew, maintenance teams and the flight crew. At 0830 the Stratofortress accelerated down the runway. Non-flyers may think it was merely a matter of kicking the tyres and roaring off into the wild blue yonder on another glamorous flight.

'Unlike our normal practice of reporting for training missions four and a half hours before take-off, we were required to show up for airborne alert flights just one hour before take-off, because fellow crews performed the lengthy B-52 pre-flight checks for us. It sure helped. An ordinary eight-hour training flight meant a fourteen-hour day or longer, with pre-flight, the mission itself, and the post-flight debriefing. For a twenty-four hour airborne alert flight, normal practice would have meant a thirty-hour day. Much too much.

'A dozen B-52s, fully loaded with weapons, armament and fuel, headed down the taxiway for a noon lift- off. We couldn't be airborne any too soon for our sister ships that were still aloft. If we delayed, they could not land, or the alert force would be degraded by a number of missing airplanes.

'At two minute intervals we turned onto the active runway, roared off into the Washington skies and were soon lined up in a loose trail formation, one mile apart and stacked up 500 feet. The lead ship flew slightly below the optimum cruising altitide for our gross weight and the last one slightly above it. We

left: A striking image of a Wichita-built B-52D during a SAC mission in the 1960s; below: A still from the movie *Strategic Air Command*, in which Jimmy Stewart, playing a major league baseball player and Air Force Reserve pilot, watches as a B-36, the predecessor of the B-52, passes low over the ball park.

turned west and headed out over the Pacific, loaded with nuclear destructive power we hoped would never be needed.

'Our crew flew twenty-eight of the noon-to-noon missions over a seven-month period. The first half dozen missions were really tiring for we hadn't yet mastered our pacing. None of us got much sleep until we had adjusted to the routine after several more flights.

'Down on the lower deck we stored a lot of stuff. Three wooden footlockers were stowed in the galley area. One of them, double-locked with two combination padlocks, held the war-mission folders. We would not open that box unless we got an authentic GO-CODE radio message. Another footlocker held spare parts for the K-System radar bombing equipment. In those days of vacuum tube electronics and analogue electro-mechanical computers for navigation and bombing calculations, spare parts were essential. Many times we had to remove and replace circuit boards or vacuum tubes to keep the system running. The third footlocker was the most important, to us at least. It was full of inflight meals especially created for SAC's finest aircrews. There were meals for all five of us in the forward cabin, sort of like tv dinners, but much more deluxe. The steak meal was my favourite. In the aft compartment was another food and beverage supply for the tail-gunner.

'On the upper deck of the forward crew cabin, just to the right of my seat and about eight feet aft of the pilot, was the only bunk on the plane. On the early alert missions I was able to get to the bunk before any of the others. But after about the tenth mission I had to be really quick to beat the co-pilot to it or I slept on the cold floor atop an air mattress. We were required to have two people awake at all times in the forward cabin, meaning one of the two pilots plus one of the remaining three, the navigator, radar bombardier, or myself. Back in the tail, our gunner could sleep whenever he wanted, though he was frequently interrupted by intercom checks to make sure he was alive and kicking. During take-off, landing, and the two aerial refuellings, we all had to be awake and in our seats. Out of the twenty-four hours aloft, each of us got a full eight hours sleep, once we got the routine down.

left: Another view of the NASA B-52 mothership, this from a KC-135 tanker over mountainous terrain in California. This B model is powered by eight Pratt & Whitney J57-19 turbojet engines, each developing 12,000 lb thrust. below: the nose of a B-52D.

'Someone in headquarters had the bright idea to give EWOs like me enough training in the pilot's flight simulator to be able to monitor the fuel, electrical and hydraulic systems in the cockpit. The plan was to have one non-pilot sit up front to keep the pilot awake and help monitor things, while the other pilot got some rest. But, since they never asked the nav or radar bombardier to participate, I usually did that job. On one of the twenty-eight missions, my limited pilot training came in handy. Our auto-pilot failed just after take-off and the bird had to be hand-flown for the full twenty-four hours. I got about five hours at the controls on that flight. For a guy who had only flown light planes, that B-52 seemed like a Mack truck, and about as responsive.

'Most of the missions were routine, even boring at times. But occasionally we had a little excitement. We once had an engine fire shortly after climb-out. Things got pretty tense for a while, but after burning off fuel for four hours to get light enough to land, we got home okay. A strange and interesting thing occurred on two successive missions along the same part of the Canadian west coast, just off the Queen Charlotte Islands. We were flying south, parallel to the coast and over water. Our B-52s were in trail formation. It was routine for the radar operator to monitor the one-mile spacing of the planes ahead of us on his scope. B-52s looked like bright dots on the radar screen, clearly visible against the blackness of the ocean below. Suddenly, and unexpectedly, another radar return appeared off to our two o'clock position. It was about fifty miles away when first spotted and headed straight for our formation. The radar operator alerted the pilot to look out for another plane, but none could be seen. The target flew diagonally across our string of bombers, passing just ahead of our plane and then disappearing to the rear. Nobody ever had a visual sighting of it, just the radar image. Even our tail-gunner turned on his radar, but saw nothing. The same phenomenon visited us again on our next flight, down the same part of the coast. This time the radar operator turned on his scope camera to capture the images. He wasn't seeing things. We radioed our sister ships to verify the target. They too, only saw it on radar. We never learned what it was.

'It was late spring and we were flying alert missions north of Alaska. The ice near the shore, not far from the mouth of the Mackenzie River, began to break up. Supply ships that were headed for the coastal radar site at Tuktoyaktuk, Tuk Tuk for short, stood off, awaiting the gradual ice melt. We flew past that ice-bound hamlet every third day that spring of 1959. The slow ice melting process was of great concern to the small group of radar operators and support personnel at Tuk Tuk, a station that was part of the vast network of North American Air Defense Command's Cold War skywatch effort. They were always glad when we checked in with them as we turned onto our southbound leg of the flight path. We swapped sports news, weather reports and, most importantly to them, ice pack status reports. From our lofty altitude, we could see the full expanse of the ice pack in the area and the re-supply boats headed for Tuk Tuk, impeded by the ice. Each day we reported the progress of those much anticipated supply vessels. We readily appreciated how important our conversations and those status reports were to the men stuck down there in the frozen north. We would be back home in a matter of hours, but they were confined there for months at a time. For a brief moment we brightened their lives, and they ours.

'After each alert mission we still had to attend maintenance debriefings, to report on the condition of the plane and its systems. That took about forty-five minutes, unless extensive equipment write-ups had to be explained.

'After debriefing, crews were offered the opportunity to have a relaxing steam bath and a rubdown at the gymnasium, all free of course, but most headed for home and their families. In forty-eight hours they would have to take off again. After a string of four missions, crews were given a week of free time. Because our schedules were stable, most of us were able to plan ahead for family or personal activities. My co-pilot and I took a couple of fishing trips to northern Washington.

'SAC eventually discontinued the airborne alert missions. They were horrendously expensive, wore out the planes and equipment, and really protected only a quarter of the bomber force. It was limited nuclear deterrence at best.'

Lieutenant-Colonel Joseph Anastasia is the bomber pilot's bomber pilot. In his long career in the United States Air Force, Col. Anastasia flew as command pilot in B-29, B-36, B-45 and B-52 aircraft, encountering and surviving some incredible adventures. 'I was flying a B-52 night training mission out of Bergstrom Air Force Base, Austin, Texas. After the usual lengthy pre-flight, the crew boarded the airplane. We stowed our equipment and strapped ourselves in our ejection seats. We ran the checklists and, with all eight engines running, completed the taxi checklist and received clearance into the number one position for take-off. I aligned the bomber with the runway heading and set the brakes. I set the power, released the brakes and we started to roll.

'The co-pilot adjusted the engine pressure ratios evenly, and all engine instruments checked OK. A hundred things were going through my mind . . . acceleration, engine output, exhaust gas temperatures, what to do in case of an emergency, and many more. I was watching the runway marker boards as they flashed by, 1–2–3–4–5–6–7, 12,000 feet of runway with a 2,000-foot overrun marker at 180 knots of airspeed as the airplane got light and began to fly. I climbed to 1,000 feet and started my flaps-up profile, trying not to lose too much altitude. I climbed out to 37,000 feet on an easterly heading and then started a long navigation leg toward Albany, New York. We completed the take-off and climb checklist and settled down for the long, twelve-hour flight.

'At about the four-hour mark, I had to go downstairs to relieve myself. There was a fireplug urinal that you could stand at, and while doing so I decided to flip on the bombbay lights and look in there. I was shocked to see a three-inch stream of jet fuel running on top of the alternator bay to the deck underneath, which had a four-inch lip. The fuel was pouring over the edge onto the tyres in the wheel well, and down into the bomb bay. I let junior go and snapped up as I studied the situation. I went over to where the navigator was sitting and told him what was happening. His eyes got as big as saucers and he said something about baling out. I said, 'No, but plot me a course that will take me back to Bergstrom, avoiding any populated areas.' I went back up the ladder to my seat and told Tom, my

co-pilot, about the situation in the bombbay and asked him about the fuel state. He said that about 10,000 gallons or 60,000 pounds were missing. I didn't know then that the Marmon clamp, which held the three-inch fuel lines together at the top of the fuselage, had come apart and no amount of valve closing or cross-feeding would stop the flow of fuel.

'Tom brought up the question of our ejecting, and I said, 'No, not yet.' I banked the airplane five degrees and headed back to Texas. I then called the SAC Command Post and told them about our problem. I said that I was not transferring fuel across the airplane and that I had more than 10,000 gallons of JP5 running out into the alternator bay. They asked about my intentions and I said I would continue the flight back to Bergstrom. They asked if we intended to eject, and they left that to my discretion.

'We arrived back in the Bergstrom area where it was still dark. We had returned there at 44,000 feet to conserve fuel, and we were still losing fuel at the same rate and had now lost some 20,000 gallons. We had a major leak.

'As the sky became lighter, I called our base. They knew what was going on as they had been monitoring the SAC Command frequency. I set us up in a holding pattern in the Bergstrom area and asked the radar operator to go take a look in the bombbay. He said I would have to give him a direct order to do so, and I decided to go myself. I went back downstairs and saw to my dismay that the fuel was still pouring out of the three-inch pipe at the same rate. I then returned to my seat, strapped in with oxygen mask on and the bale-out bottle knob in a handy position, and advised everyone to get ready for a quick ejection. Some of the crew said they wanted to eject, but I told them that there was nothing electrical that wasn't vapour-protected, and that it was safe. They reluctantly agreed. I then ordered the radar operator to open the bombbay doors. At Bergstrom they had a telephoto camera aimed at us and we were in good range as we had now descended to 6,000 feet, the minimum bale-out altitude. The bomb doors opened and all 20,000 gallons of fuel seemed to evaporate in an instant, but some of it covered the airplane. The engine exhaust then

'Normal people believe that if it ain't broke, don't fix it. Engineers believe that if it ain't broke, it doesn't have enough features yet.'
– Scott Adams

Some of the many B-52s that flew the Rolling Thunder and Linebacker missions of the Vietnam War, as well as those of Operation Desert Storm, lie beneath the Arizona sun while awaiting their fate. They will be cut up in compliance with the US-Soviet Strategic Arms Reduction Talks agreement.

ignited it and there was a big flash, but we flew out of the flash in one piece.

'All of the fuel that had accumulated in the bomb bay was now gone, but there was a fuel stream coming out through the bombbay doors, which could certainly be lethal. We were now very low on fuel, having flown some seven hours, and we needed to land soon. I had Tom lower the flaps and they worked fine as the flap motors were sealed. Next came the landing gear. We had steel-impregnated tyres, which meant that we could land on ice, snow, or a wet runway and have a good co-efficient of friction for stopping the plane. But all of the four forward tires were saturated with jet fuel and I expected them to lay a trough of fire when we touched down. I lowered the gear and again nothing happened, except for more streaming fuel. I flew the downwind leg to land to the north, turned base and final and approached the end of the runway at 145 knots indicated. We touched down at the 1,000 foot marker. It was a smooth landing, but as soon as we touched, a streak of flame erupted from the tyres and they began to burn the fuel that had soaked into them.

'I braked hard and had Tom pull the drag 'chute; we stopped in 7,000 feet. I immediately cut the eight engines and rang the bell to evacuate the airplane. I was out of my harness and behind Tom as we jumped down the ladder and out of the bottom of the plane, where the fire was burning real well. We ran ahead of the airplane and off the left wing to our crew assembly point in case of a crash-landing.

'The crash crew arrived with their foam and hoses. They had to go into the bombbay to squirt foam up into the alternator deck. It took them thirty minutes to get the fire under control and put out all of the smouldering tyres. A crew bus picked us up and took us to the maintenance debriefing room. All the "wheels" were there wanting to know what had happened. After cleaning up the foam, the maintenance inspectors looked at the Marmon clamps and saw what had happened. They wired SAC headquarters and Boeing in Seattle. All B-52s were promptly grounded until they had been inspected. A permanent fix was made and all of the clamps were changed. For us it had been a rather hair-raising experience.'

Specifications: Boeing B-52B

Engines: Eight Pratt & Whitney J57-P-1W turbojets rated at 11,000 lb thrust each, with water injection
Maximum speed: 630 mph at 20,000 ft
Cruising speed: 525 mph
Service ceiling: 47,000 ft at combat weight of 272,000 lb
Normal range: 3,600 miles combat radius at combat weight of 272,000 lb
Maximum take-off weight: 420,000 lb
Wingspan: 185 ft
Length: 156 ft 7 in
Height: 48 ft 4 in
Wing area: 4,000 sq ft
Bomb load: 43,000 lb
Defensive armament: Four 0.50 calibre M-3 machine-guns in tail turret

Specifications: Boeing B-52H

Engines: Eight Pratt & Whitney TF-33-P-3 turbofans rated at 17,000 lb thrust each
Maximum speed: 650 mph at 23,800 ft at combat weight of 306,350 lb
Cruising speed: 530 mph
Service ceiling: 47,700 ft at combat weight of 306,350 lb
Normal range: 4,300 mile combat radius
Maximum take-off weight: 488,000 lb
Wingspan: 185 ft
Length: 159 ft 4 in
Height: 40 ft 8 in
Wing area: 4,000 sq ft
Bomb load: 70,000 lb
Defensive armament: One General Electric M61 Vulcan 20 mm cannon

'If it's good, they'll stop making it.'
– Herbert Block

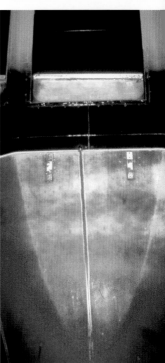

NORTH AMERICAN

The B-52 bomber had not even begun service with the US Air Force in 1954 when General Curtis LeMay went shopping for an entirely new and more capable strategic bomber to replace it. By 1955, LeMay's Strategic Air Command was involved in preliminary work on three major nuclear delivery system programmes. The first was the development of an intercontinental ballistic missile (ICBM), the second a chemically-propelled intercontinental supersonic bomber, and the last was a nuclear-powered bomber able to fly to any target in the world and back without having to be refuelled. The history of the ICBM through the Cold War years is well known. That of the nuclear-powered bomber is not.

With the first atomic bombs, American industry became interested in the possible application of nuclear propulsion for ships, submarines, trains, cars and even aeroplanes. In 1951 the US Joint Chiefs of Staff came out in favour of a high-priority programme to develop an atomic-powered aircraft or ANP (Aircraft Nuclear Propulsion.) In a joint effort of the US Atomic Energy Commission and the Air Force, a plan to develop a flight-test programme utilizing a Convair B-36 bomber and a small nuclear reactor was initiated and Convair received a contract for the project in November. A B-36 would be used as it could be readily modified to carry the reactor. It was intended as a flying laboratory to monitor the reactor in flight and the radiation levels produced; the aircraft would not receive any power from the reactor. The particular B-36 chosen to become the Nuclear Test Aircraft (NTA) had suffered damage in a tornado that struck Carswell AFB, Texas, on 1 September 1952. The nature of the damage made it an ideal choice for reconstruction to the special airframe requirements of the NTA.

The completed aeroplane was designated NB-36H. It carried a 35,000 lb, 1,000 kW air-cooled reactor in a container installed in one of the bombbays. Extensive shielding was provided around the reactor and the crew compartment. The maiden flight of the NB-36H took place on 17 September 1955 and the aeroplane flew a total of forty-seven test flights. The data gathered indicated that the aeroplane would pose no special threat even when flying at low altitude, but that an accident could cause the release of fission products and radioactivity from the reactor.

Following the launch of the Soviet *Sputnik 1* satellite in October 1957 came the beginning of the US–Soviet technological space race. It was then that General LeMay declared SAC's desire for an advanced jet heavy bomber, to be operational by 1963, and replacing the B-52 and B-58 bombers by 1965. LeMay wanted a high-altitude, very-long-range Mach 3 aeroplane that could deliver both nuclear and conventional weapons. The competition would be between a conventionally-powered aircraft and a theoretically possible nuclear-powered one. The programmes proceeded slowly, with little real progress on the nuclear side and in March 1961 President John Kennedy ended the nuclear-powered aircraft programme with a statement which included the comment: 'Nearly fifteen years and about $1 billion have been devoted to the attempted development of a nuclear-powered aircraft; but the possibility of achieving a militarily useful aircraft in the foreseeable future is still very remote.'

North American Aviation of El Sugundo, California,

would design and build the plane that LeMay wanted, but he would never have it. The B-70 *Valkyrie* had evolved from a concept of the North American design staff in which a bomber was composed of three parts: a long central pod containing the crew, the engines, some fuel and the bombs, along with two large left and right side units comprising most of the wing and tail structure, and housing the bulk of the fuel. It was visualized as a canard design of enormous size, larger than a Boeing 747-400 jumbo and weighing a million pounds at take-off. The idea was that the giant combo-plane would approach enemy airspace subsonically. At that point the large outer-portion structures would have been depleted of their fuel and would be discarded. This would leave a much smaller inner-pod aircraft with stubby wings and tail and such a great power-to-weight ratio that it could accelerate to Mach 3 and dash to its target and then out of the enemy airspace. General LeMay's reaction to the design: 'Hell, this isn't an airplane. It's a three-ship formation.'

In 1957, North American presented the Air Force with a new design that pleased LeMay and that December work began on two prototypes of the XB-70. They would cost approximately $1.5 billion and would be the most expensive two aeroplanes built to date. Like the earlier rejected design, the XB-70 would feature a canard, or horizontal stabilizer, mounted just aft of the crew compartment. It would have a long, narrow, elegant fuselage and a large delta wing fitted with twin vertical stabilizers. The power would be supplied by six General Electric J93 turbojet engines with afterburning, rated at 30,000 lb thrust each. The six huge powerplants were to be contained in an engine box beneath the wing to generate maximum compression lift. The company believed that the trick to making such a big aircraft fly at three times the speed of sound without using three times as much fuel as in subsonic flight, was what they called 'wave drag'. In simple terms, they found that it takes much more fuel to fly at high subsonic speed than at much higher speeds and, with sufficient power to fly through that wave drag, their plane could then go much faster without excessive fuel demand.

The designers thought that the plane should be built of stainless steel to better resist the extreme

below: The XB-70A on the ramp at the NASA-Dryden Research Center, Edwards AFB, California. The aeroplane was capable of flying at three times the speed of sound. Two XB-70A aircraft were built, one being lost in a mid-air collision with a NASA F-104 chase plane on 8 June 1966.

XB-70

heat of high-speed flight. Their design would have tilting wing-tips to help trap more compression under the big delta wing, for added lift. Their timing coincided nicely with new developments in high-performance aviation fuels (specifically an ethyl-boron type), leading to the conclusion that the new fuel, in combination with the compression lift produced by their design, would indeed make it possible to achieve sustained flight at Mach 3. They projected that the new bomber would be capable of flight to an altitude of 100,000 feet, a cruising speed of Mach 2 with Mach 3 "dash performance" and a 6,000-mile range without refuelling.

The harsh realities of high-supersonic flight meant that an entirely new approach to aircraft construction would be required for the B-70. Nearly three-quarters of the plane would be made of light, ultra-thin, extremely strong brazed-steel honeycomb sandwich, with titanium utilized in the most heat-critical nine per cent of the aeroplane. The company had to pioneer many of the new construction techniques and encountered a number of difficult problems with them. Other troubles were brewing for the project in Washington where, in 1959, some highly vocal members of the pro-missile lobby were extending their influence and bringing into question the expenditure on the B-70. Many believed that the day of the manned bomber had passed, and with sentiment growing to end the project, the Air Force and North American were dealt another blow when the very expensive boron fuel programme was cancelled.

In December, the axe fell on the B-70. Only the completion of a single prototype was retained in the project, with the first flight now set for the end of 1962. Later, however, B-70 funding was partially restored, with provision for the building of twelve operational bombers in addition to the prototype aeroplane. But Kennedy administration's Secretary of Defense Robert McNamara soon reasserted the view that continued B-70 development could not be justified in light of the emphasis being placed on ICBM systems. McNamara changed the B-70 to a Mach 3 research project, lowering its priority status. Only two aeroplanes would be built.

North American's problems with construction of the prototypes escalated in late 1962 when a form of

'The future is not what it used to be.'
– Yogi Berra

left: One of the two XB-70As after its rollout at Air Force Plant 42 in Palmdale, California, on 11 May 1964.

electrolytic corrosion was discovered in the structure of the first aircraft. This major setback required substantial rebuilding of the plane. It would be a further two years before the first prototype was ready to fly. The roll-out finally occurred on 11 May 1964 at the company's Palmdale, California, facility.

The pilot and co-pilot sat in cocoon-like capsules whose clamshell doors would close to become sealed individual escape pods if depressurization should occur. They were equipped with emergency supplies, oxygen bottles and limited throttle and trim controls for use in an emergency descent to a safe altitude where, if necessary, the escape pods could be rocket-ejected through jettisonable overhead panels.

The initial flight of the first prototype aeroplane was on 21 September 1964. The pilots were USAF Colonel Joe Cotton and North American chief test pilot Al White. It was a memorable maiden flight. The two men started their pre-flight checklist at 6.10 a.m. and began the engine starting procedure at 6.45. A warning light in the cockpit came on as the second engine was started, causing both running engines to be shut down. The trouble had been a faulty circuit breaker and all six engines were then started beginning at 7.14. Taxiing the XB-70 out to the runway was quite an experience for the pilots. As they sat in the nose compartment, nearly 110 feet in front of the main landing-gear wheels, they bobbed up and down each time the nose wheels rode over the concrete joints in the taxi-way. Taxiing at low speed also brought on a brake chattering effect which made ground manoeuvring a tiresome chore. Al White turned the great plane into the wind on the runway at 8.24 and rolled the six throttles all the way into afterburning for maximum power. Rotation came as the XB-70 reached 193 mph, and the 387,000 lb *Valkyrie* lifted off to become airborne for the first time.

The flight was to be a short hop from the Palmdale factory over to the Flight Test Center at Edwards AFB in the Mojave desert. The airspeed was kept to about 300 mph. When the plane was over the Edwards base, and had been joined by chase planes whose pilots would observe and assist White and Cotton, it was time to try retracting the landing-gear. One of the chase pilots notified Cotton that the right-side main gear had only cycled half-way through the retraction, and that fluid was leaking onto the fuselage behind the landing-gear doors. Cotton cycled the landing-gear to the fully extended down position and the pilots continued the test schedule with low-speed handling and stability tests in which the aeroplane performed very well. In the following half-hour the number three engine began to overspeed and had to be shut down. The two men now set up the XB-70 for its first landing, grateful for the three-mile-long dry lakebed runway at Edwards. Being so far ahead of the landing- gear, judging their height over the runway as they approached it was a real concern. They required the assistance of a chase plane pilot who called out their altitude in feet as the great white plane descended.

When the landing gear touched down, the two rear main wheels on the left side locked up owing to a pressure surge in the braking system. Fire erupted immediately from the left landing gear and White and Cotton were informed of it by a chase plane pilot. White allowed the big plane to roll out for more than two-thirds of the runway, where fire crews extinguished the blazing tyres.

In the test flight of 12 October AV/1 (Air Vehicle 1), as the number one prototype was now called, attained Mach 1, the speed of sound, for the first time.

All went reasonably well in the flight-test programme until 7 May 1965, the twelfth flight. AV/1 was cruising at Mach 2.58 when a section of skin known as the horizontal splitter broke away, severely damaging four of the six engines and forcing the pilots to shut them down. However, they were able to restart the number five engine to provide some lift and stability to the right side of the aeroplane, and bring it in for a safe landing. All six engines had to be replaced. The portion of the aeroplane that failed and separated in flight was a part of the honeycomb construction, causing grave concern about the integrity of that material and construction technique, and by extension, the ability of the prototypes to reach and sustain Mach 3.

By mid-July 1965, both aeroplanes were participating in the flight test programme. On 14 October her crew took AV/1 through Mach 3 briefly. 'On this flight the XB-70 proved its capability of attaining Mach 3 at

left: An XB-70A rolling out after landing. The objectives of the XB-70 flight research programme were to study the aeroplane's stability and handling characteristics, to evaluate its response to atmospheric turbulence, and to determine the aerodynamic and propulsion performance. The secondary objectives were to measure the noise and friction associated with the airflow over the aeroplane, and to determine the levels and extent of the engine noise during take-off, landing and ground operations; bottom left: To the left and right sides of the XB-70 cockpit are the pilot and co-pilot's control yokes. Between them is the centre console with the six throttles for the General Electric jet engines. Above this is the centre instrument panel. The bottom panel contains the wing-tip fold, landing-gear and flap controls, as well as the hydraulic pressure gauges. In the centre are the three rows of engine gauges. The top row are tachometers, below that are exhaust temperature gauges, and the bottom row are exhaust nozzle position indicators. Above these are the engine-fire and engine-brake switches.

far left: An XB-70A climbing out on take-off from Edwards on the morning of 17 August 1965; left: In flight with the wing-tips lowered in the 65-degree configuration for high-speed stability and increased lift; below: Parked on the Edwards ramp in 1967. The aeroplane never went into production but was used for flight research involving the Air Force and NASA's Flight Research Center, a predecessor of today's NASA-Dryden Flight Research Center at Edwards.

below: A great pall of smoke marks the crash site of the AV/2 near Barstow, California; right: The XB-70A Valkyrie during take-off rotation. The high angle of attack results from the combined effects of the aircraft's weight and the performance of the propulsion system.

70,000 feet!', from Al White's pilot report. However, minor damage to an outer wing panel occurred in the test and AV/1 would never be flown above Mach 2.5 again. As testing continued with both aircraft at speeds in excess of Mach 2, concerns arose about the severe heat buildup on the aircraft. Efforts were made to condition or "heat-soak" the AV/2 for dashes at Mach 3 by running it for prolonged periods at Mach 2.8 and 2.9. The temperature of the nose and leading-edge surfaces of the plane rose to 625 degrees with the rest of the aircraft skin reaching 450 degrees. One way of taking advantage of this phenomenon was the employment of "heat sinks" in the fuel tanks. As the fuel absorbed heat from the fuselage, it was drawn into the engines and burned away, leaving the cooler fuel behind. With this procedure, the pre-heated fuel was used more efficiently. To prevent an explosion, however, the growing void in the tanks had to be filled with nitrogen.

Important lessons had been learned during the fabrication of AV/1, which were applied to AV/2 and as the testing continued, AV/2 proved able to tolerate the effects of Mach 3. But both of the giant aircraft, like most new and complex machines, were subject to a variety of glitches and system failures. Both hydraulic systems failed on the 37th flight of AV/1, preventing the landing gear from deploying properly. A safe landing was made at the Edwards Flight Test Center, but it required nearly the entire three miles of runway for the landing roll-out. A similar problem happened aboard AV/2 on the test flight of 30 April 1966. In the preparation for landing, the nose gear failed to go down. The crew tried two rather hard touch-and-go landings on the main wheels in an effort to pop the nose gear down, but without success. To land the aeroplane without the nose gear down was out of the question. The only apparent option for the crew was to bale out, saving themselves but losing the extremely valuable aeroplane. With ample fuel on board, the crew were instructed to circle in the Edwards area while staff on the ground worked on the problem. After a lengthy discussion an engineer suggested a way of bypassing a circuit breaker in one of the plane's backup electrical systems. Joe Cotton was flying as co-pilot that day and he managed to improvise a "jumper" with a paper clip. Down came

the recalcitrant nose gear. Newspapers the next day referred to the incident as '39 cent paperclip saves $750 million aircraft!'

Earlier in the spring, the AV/2 *Valkyrie* made its only non-test flight when the Air Force presented the aeroplane to the public at a Carswell AFB, Texas, airshow. Pilots Fitz Fulton and Joe Cotton took the plane from Edwards to Carswell in just fifty-nine minutes at speeds up to Mach 2.6. They displayed the amazing aircraft for the Texas crowd before landing. The return flight to Edwards was flown subsonically, taking three hours.

As the testing continued, results improved and in May AV/2 was flown at Mach 3 for a sustained thirty-three minutes, ending any remaining concerns about honeycomb skin separation. Phase 1 of the flight test programme was nearly finished. Phase 2 would see the participation of the National Aeronautics and Space Administration (NASA) and its chief test pilot, Brigadier-General Joe Walker, in the B-70 programme. Walker had flown the X-15 research aircraft to beyond Mach 6, (4,100 mph) in level flight.

In the test flight of 8 June, AV/2 had completed the tasks assigned to it for the day. It was then to join a small group of other jets—all of which were powered by General Electric engines—in a publicity photo shoot for GE. Al White was the pilot of the XB-70. USAF Major Carl Cross, new to the B-70 programme, was his co-pilot. The other aircraft in the formation were a Northrop F-5, a Northrop T-38, a US Navy McDonnell F-4 and an F-104 flown by Joe Walker. The photo session was completed at 9.30 a.m. when, inexplicably, the F-104 began moving in close to the right wing tip of the bomber. The wing-tips of the XB-70 were in a 30-degree down position, and a heavy vortex effect generated by the *Valkyrie* wing threw the F-104 over on its back and over the top of the bomber's wing, shearing off most the big plane's twin tail fins and part of its wing. The F-104 then exploded in a fireball killing Walker instantly.

Joe Cotton, flying the T-38, called to White and Cross in the B-70, '207 . . . you've been hit! You've been hit!' And then, 'Okay, you're doing fine. He got the verticals, but you're still doing fine.' The giant plane continued on for several seconds, almost as normal. Then it entered the first of two slow rolls before

yawing violently and slipping into a spin whereupon a large portion of the left wing broke away. Al White managed to eject in his escape pod. The drogue parachutes of his pod deployed properly, but the airbag beneath it, intended to cushion the impact of the landing, failed to inflate. White survived the incredible 33 G impact but was badly battered and required lengthy hospitalization. He would never fly the XB-70 again. Major Cross, a veteran pilot of more than 8,500 flying hours, failed to eject and, trapped in his seat, rode the slowly rotating bomber down to the ground. He died when the B-70 crashed four miles north of Barstow, California. The entire event had lasted seventy-six seconds.

Following the tragedy, modifications were made to AV/1, including the ejection system. But as this aeroplane was no longer approved to fly at speeds above Mach 2.5, it was not acceptable to the Air Force for continued high-speed testing, and it dropped out of the B-70 programme. But the testing continued, with NASA conducting an additional thirty-three research flights investigating sonic booms, clear-air turbulence, flight controls, aerodynamics and propulsion-system performance, and operation in relation to super-sonic transport aircraft, until February 1969. That month AV/1 was flown for the last time, to the USAF Museum at Wright–Patterson AFB, Ohio, where it remains on display.

Specifications: North American XB-70
Engines: Six General Electric YJ-93 turbojets rated at 30,000 lb thrust each with afterburner
Maximum speed: 2,056 mph at 73,000 ft
Cruising speed: 2,000 mph at 72,000 ft
Service ceiling: 77,350 ft
Normal range: 4,288 miles
Weight empty: 300,000 lb Maximum take-off weight: 534,700 lb
Wingspan: 105 ft
Length: 185 ft 10 in
Height: 30 ft 9 in
Wing area: 6,298 sq ft

BRABAZON

Six months before he was scheduled to take the giant Bristol Brabazon airliner on her maiden flight, company chief test pilot A.J. "Bill" Pegg was given the opportunity to fly another mammoth aeroplane, the Convair B-36 intercontinental bomber, to get a sense of how really big aircraft could be expected to handle and behave. Pegg went to Fort Worth, Texas, to take the controls of the US Air Force Strategic Air Command's plane and was surprised by the relative ease with which the B-36 could be flown. His verdict: 'It flies beautifully.' The Convair bomber happened to have the same wingspan, 230 feet, as that of the Brabazon, but they had little else in common. The bomber was fifteen feet shorter than the airliner and weighed 40,000 lb more. It had six 3,000 hp Pratt & Whitney R-4360 air-cooled radial engines mounted as pushers on the trailing edge of the wing, while the Brabazon was pulled by eight 2,500 hp Bristol Centaurus radials coupled in pairs behind four nacelles, with each pair driving two contra-rotating propellers. Pegg was comfortable with the challenge awaiting him when he returned to England after his B-36 experience. When asked about the coming first flight of the Brabazon, he said, 'I will fly the cockpit and I imagine the rest of the aeroplane will follow.'

Some called her 'the beautiful dream'. She was the largest land-plane in the world at the time of her first flight in 1949. The Bristol Brabazon project started during the Second World War when a committee in Britain under the chairmanship of Lord Brabazon was formed to plan the future of British aircraft production after the war. In the pre-war years Brabazon had crossed the Atlantic on the liner *Queen Mary,* and visualized a post-war world in which those who could afford it would be treated to the same level of comfort and luxury on that journey in an elegant airliner. In 1942, the committee recommended the development and production of such a plane, capable of crossing the Atlantic non-stop in all weathers, and they authorized the Bristol Aeroplane Company to begin preliminary work on it, the Type 167, provided the effort did not interfere in any way with the company's current war production activity.

The Type 167 was to be modelled on two of the

left: Construction began on the Bristol Brabazon Type 167 airliner fuselage and wing in October 1945 in an eight-acre assembly building that adjoined the newly-strengthened 8,000-foot runway at Bristol's Filton, England, facility. The structural components of the plane, including the skin, were designed to meet load requirements while having minimal weight. The weight savings through innovation and sophistication could be measured in tons.

The Bristol Aeroplane Company had done a design study in 1937 for a long-range strategic bomber. When invitations were extended in 1942 for studies relating to a new heavy bomber, Bristol had the advantage of its earlier work, which led to a design for an aircraft with a 5,000-mile range, a 225-foot wingspan and eight engines buried in that wing, driving four pusher-propellers. The Bristol bomber was not produced, but much of the work was later applied to the Brabazon project.

company's heavy bomber designs that had been rejected by the Royal Air Force in favour of the Avro Lancaster and the Handley Page Halifax bombers. One of these designs was the Type 159, proposed in 1939 as a 300 mph four-engined bomber with a 114-foot wingspan. The second proposed aircraft was not allocated a company type number but did bear a passing resemblance to the final design of the Brabazon.

Bristol planners had considered the realities of transatlantic flight in the early 1940s. To achieve a non-stop capability from London to New York with the technology of the time required a very large aeroplane with a range of 5,500 miles. It was thought then that the new plane would weigh about 330,000 lb. The economics of such a venture dictated that it would need to accommodate a minimum of 100 passengers to produce a profit for an airline operating it.

Edward P. Warner, vice-chairman of the Civil Aeronautics Board of the United States, and one of the leading aviation authorities of the time, offered this estimate of post-war commercial aviation in his 1943 Wilbur Wright Memorial Lecture to the Royal

Aeronautical Society: 'A substantial proportion of the tourists undoubtedly welcome the sea voyage for its own sake, and will prefer to keep it as a part of their holiday. The necessary length of the non-stop flight from eastern-most North America to the British Isles imposes an economic burden which is likely to reflect itself in rates of fare considerably higher than those charged for covering the same distance in Continental air transport. Nevertheless I believe that it would not be too sanguine to anticipate that half of the maximum pre-war ocean travel in the first and cabin classes (139,000 transatlantic passengers in 1936) will be shifted into the air. Certainly the factor of newly created travel will be an important one in this case; for just as statesmen and soldiers have learned in the past two years to run back and forth across the Atlantic when there is need for discussion, so in future business men having negotiations afoot in New York or Detroit will board a plane where once they would have sent a cablegram. It does not seem over-optimistic to anticipate that newly created travel over the Atlantic will equal twice the amount diverted from the previously existing channels.

'There is another way of arriving at a figure for the volume of trans-Atlantic air travel. In September, 1940, the average travel between the cities of the Pacific coast of the United States and those of the eastern third of the country averaged 250 passengers per day. I have little doubt that after the war the figure will be increased to 1,200. That represents the prospective interchange of persons between two regions, one of about 10,000,000 population and the other of about 90,000,000, with their centres of population located about 2,400 miles apart. In considering transatlantic traffic, on the other hand, we are reckoning with the interchange between populations of about 90,000,000 and 250,000,000 respectively—considering only the eastern third of North America and the western half of Europe as being major contributors to transatlantic movement—with their centres of population separated by about 3,700 miles.

'Upon all these bases I believe it reasonable to anticipate a post-war average of 600 passengers by air per day in each direction between the United States and Canada and the British Isles and the Continent of Europe. The daily average will, of course, be subject to substantial seasonal fluctuations from the annual mean, unless we make even better progress than I expect in eliminating irregularities of service due to the weather . . . Upon the assumption that the apparent time from London to New York will be 14 hours, which I believe is compatible with the conclusion I shall later develop on the relations between speed, non-stop distance, and economy, a departure from London at six in the afternoon will permit arrival in New York at eight in the morning . . .

'Upon that basis I can look forward to departures from London at 5, 6, 8 and 10 p.m. and midnight as offering as much frequency as anyone could reasonably desire. Allowing for flights that may start from points on the Continent, an all-inclusive year-round average of eight schedules each way each day between North America and Europe seems a reasonable goal.' So much for best estimates!

Bristol native Roy Fedden was the acknowledged genius behind most of Bristol's aero-engine success. He joined the company in 1920 and guided it through the development of a series of excellent air-cooled radial aero-engines. By the late 1930s Fedden was beginning work on his most important design, the 2,000 hp Bristol Centaurus, a superb engine that powered the Hawker Tempest II fighter-bomber in the Second World War. It was the engine that would power Brabazon Mark I, though it was not intended for the ultimate passenger transport, Brabazon Mark II. That aircraft was to have had four coupled pairs of Bristol Proteus 710 turboprop engines, but as the Proteus was unlikely to be available before the early 1950s, it was decided to equip the Brabazon Mk I with Bristol's next most powerful engine, the Centaurus. It looked like a four-engined aircraft if one simply counted the nacelles, but the Brabazon Mk I was powered by eight Centaurus radials, buried in the wing in pairs set at 45-degree angles to the propeller shafts. Each of the four shaft systems drove a pair of contra-rotating three-blade propellers and each propeller was linked to an individual engine. If, as an air show tee-shirt of the 1990s proclaimed, HAPPINESS IS A PAIR OF BIG BRISTOLS, the eight-engined Brabazon must surely have portended ecstasy in the offing.

The Proteus-equipped Brabazon Mk II was to have operated at a top speed of 360 mph. The Centaurus-powered Mk I had a maximum speed of 300 mph with a cruising speed of 250 mph at 25,000 feet. While the Proteus was not ready in time for Brabazon, it did power another giant aircraft of that era, the Saunders Roe Princess flying-boat. Years later a redesigned and refined version of the Proteus would provide power for the "whispering giant", the Bristol Britannia airliner.

The exigencies of war had forced Bristol to spread its design and other activity to several locations in England. Design work for the Blenheim, Beaufort and Beaufighter, for example, was being done in the Walton Park Hotel at Clevedon. Ivor House, a large private home in the Clifton area of Bristol, had been requisitioned to house the design team for the Brabazon in 1943. During the first two years of the project, progress was delayed by problems associated with where to build an aircraft of the size being contemplated; how to power such an enormous creation and what size and strength runway was needed for it.

below: After the Brabazon, the Bristol Aeroplane Company developed and produced the Britannia four-engined turboprop airliner which first flew in August 1952.

'I always sit in the tail end of a plane, always, 'cos you never hear of a plane backing into a mountain.'
— Tommy Cooper

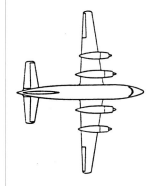

In addition to the construction of the aircraft itself, and an enormous new assembly hall for quantity production, another aspect of the project was the enlargement and lengthening of the company runway at Filton.

Clearly, the Bristol company had no facilities large enough to cope with the assembly of such a big plane, let alone a quantity of them. One possibility was to build the Brabazon at the company's Banwell plant at Weston-super-Mare near the Severn estuary. While the factory sheds there were large enough, it was believed that the runway would have to be strengthened to support the weight of the new airliner. Finally, a decision was taken to expand the main Filton site to accommodate the Brabazon.

With its wartime manufacturing committments, including the Blenheim bomber, the Beaufort and the Beaufighter, Bristol's progress on the airliner of the future was frustratingly slow. The full-size wooden mock-up of the airframe, which allowed technicians, engineers and designers to precisely fit the various components and furnishings of the plane in exacting detail, had to be constructed in Filton's old Number Two Flight Shed. No other existing company facility was large enough to house it. An essential aspect of the overall Brabazon programme was the design and construction of a gigantic new assembly hall, specifically tailored for production of the new plane. Under construction in 1946, this building would become the largest hangar in the world at 1,054 feet in width. It would occupy seven and a half acres of what had formerly been a golf course. Fitted into its roof was a crane system capable of moving a twelve-ton load around the interior. A 50-foot-high wall of glass ran the entire length of one side of the structure, providing an extraordinary amount of daylight for the workers.

The completed design and a working model of the great assembly hall were ready in June 1946. The building was divided into three bays of equal width, with the centre bay considerably deeper than the two end bays. The roof was 117 feet over the floor and the total working area was 290,000 square feet, nearly seven acres. The aim was to provide ample space for the assembly of as many as eight Brabazon airframes and the building would front a six-and-a-half-acre con-

'Seeking after that sweet golden clime, / Where the traveller's journey is done.' – from *Ah, Sun-flower* by William Blake

crete apron utilized as an aircraft-handling facility. Each of the three giant bays provided aircraft access through a pair of folding doors which were driven by six 5 hp electric motors.

The third aspect of the Brabazon project was the lengthening and widening of the Filton runway to allow for taxi trials, ground-handling and manoeuvring tests and an appropriate safety margin for take-offs and landings. Calculations had determined that the runway would have to be extended to 8,250 feet and widened to 300 feet, twice the width of the runways at most major airports today. It was estimated that Brabazon would require 3,000 feet to take off when fully loaded and the remaining mile of runway would be available for braking in an aborted take-off and additional safety overrun. In addition, a turning circle 600 feet in diameter was built at each end of the runway. The construction contract for the runway went to John Laing and Company, which began work in September 1946 and completed it on schedule in April 1948. In the course of this construction, it was necessary to demolish the small village of Charlton, which partially lay in the path of the runway extension. The demolition had been highly controversial, but the decision was ameliorated somewhat by the many requisitioning precedents established during the war. The displaced Charltonians were rehoused in a new fifty-home estate at nearby Patchway.

Before and during the period of construction on the new assembly hall, and the extension/expansion of the Filton runway, work proceeded on the Brabazon Mk I fuselage in the Number Two Flight Shed, with the tail structure and the inner wing sections built as an integral part of the fuselage and the outer-wing sections built alongside it. The construction of the major portion of the aircraft was a new and greatly simplified procedure, incorporating a number of manufacturing efficiencies. The use of rivets sealed in dope resulted in far fewer rivets being required for the airframe assembly. The company also employed revolutionary machining methods to drill, mill, fold and roll the many components of the streamlined airframe.

Weather played a dramatic part in the concurrent multiple construction projects, severely hampering completion of the assembly hall, the runway and taxi

ways. The winter of 1946/7 was among the worst on record and the various work schedules relating to the Brabazon were hopelessly delayed. To partially offset the impact of the delays, the company arranged to lease the completed west bay of the new assembly hall to British Overseas Airways Corporation for the sheltering of aircraft from their fleet of Lockheed Constellations and Boeing Stratocruisers.

The Brabazon Mk I was an advanced aircraft in many ways. It featured a fully automatic hydraulic control system which had previously been tested on an Avro Lancaster bomber by Bill Pegg. The system enabled the pilot to actuate all of the control surfaces with power-assisted ease, like the power-steering system in a car. It was duplicated to provide a fully operational back-up should the primary system fail. With a 55-foot undercarriage track, the aeroplane was suitable for ground handling on most principal airports. The plane was also equipped with powered nose-wheel steering and automatically synchronized propellers.

Among the more innovative ideas implemented in the Mk I was the gust-alleviating system in which a gust-sensing vane was mounted on the exterior skin just outside the cockpit. The vane was electrically linked to the ailerons which were raised by an impulse when the device sensed an upgust, and were lowered in a downgust. The device had also been flight tested on the Lancaster and was one of the few appendages hung on the otherwise clean Brabazon airframe. It was considered an appropriate gust-limitation method relative to the 250 mph cruising speed of the Mk I at 25,000 feet. A more sophisticated, advanced gust warning and fully automated trimming system was intended for the Proteus turboprop-powered Brabazon II aircraft with its specified cruising speed of 330 mph at 35,000 feet, the altitude commonly flown by current jetliners. But this automated system proved too challenging to develop and ultimately figured in the 1953 decision to terminate the Brabazon project.

Bill Pegg became chief test pilot of Bristol's in December 1945 and the Brabazon project became

above: Lord Brabazon of Tara, Chairman of the Brabazon Committee, pointing out features of the aircraft that bears his name, to the Minister of Supply, the Right Honourable F.R. Strauss, Viscount Addison, and Lord Pakenham, Minister of Civil Aviation; above left: The cockpit and instrument panel of the Brabazon.

right: The Brabazon fuselage resting on its own undercarriage, outside the unfinished Filton assembly hall on 4 October 1947; below: The Brabazon 1 flying low over Heathrow airport, London, during a demonstration flight 15 June 1950; far right: The famous Bristol Aeroplane Company logo.

his baby.

With so much riding on the success of Brabazon for the company, the British aircraft industry and for national pride, Pegg was aware of the scrutiny he was under and the pressure to perform, and make the aeroplane perform, to a very high standard. The attitude of BOAC towards the Brabazon was less than enthusiastic and Pegg knew it would take a powerfully impressive performance to change that. He approached the coming flight-test programme with calm and cool professionalism. He needed to find out what the handling of a giant aeroplane felt like before he would take Brabazon up. In the entire world there were only a few aircraft comparable in size to the big Bristol plane. In southern California there was the Hughes HK-1 flying-boat, known as the Spruce Goose for its largely wooden construction, an effort to conserve strategic materials for the US war effort. It was actually made mostly of birch. The HK-1 had been the brainchild of the American industrialist Henry J. Kaiser, who had pioneered the Liberty ship design and construction programme of the Second World War. Designed and built by Hughes Aircraft, the flying-boat was the largest aircraft in the world when completed in 1947. It had been intended for the transport of 750 fully equipped troops to distant battle zones, but became highly controversial when the war ended with the aeroplane still unfinished. The US Congress was eager to grab a peace dividend by killing the funding for the flying-boat. Howard Hughes flew the HK-1 once, in November 1947, for slightly less than one mile at an altitude of 70 feet and an airspeed of 80 mph. He proved it could fly, but Congress killed it anyway and it never flew again.

Another airplane of comparable size to Brabazon was the Saunders-Roe Princess flying-boat, a ten-engined 105-passenger sea plane built at Cowes on the Isle of Wight, not that far from Bristol. But the maiden flight of the Princess would not come until 22 August 1952 and she would not be providing Bill Pegg the big aeroplane hands-on experience he wanted. The only real possibility was the American B-36 bomber, with six engines and 22,800 hp. Pegg was invited by Convair to go to Fort Worth, Texas, and fly the Peacemaker, as the B-36 was called. After

flying it several times, including one eight-hour hop, he returned to Bristol with new confidence in what he was soon to do with the Brabazon.

As the summer of 1949 wore on, ground testing of Brabazon Mk I continued. The first flight of the plane was tied to the early-September flying display at Farnborough. It was essential that Pegg fly Brabazon before Farnborough and that he display it there. On Saturday 3 September, Pegg, co-pilot Walter Gibb, and a Bristol flight-test crew of eight engineers and observers, took the instrumentation-laden Mk I on a series of taxi trial runs to a maximum speed of 75 mph. At that speed the nose began to lift and Pegg had to reduce power to keep the big plane from becoming airborne before he was ready. All went well, except for the nosewheel steering, which was not working properly. At the end of that day, it was decided to steer the plane on the ground by means of differential braking, and the nosewheel steering system was disconnected.

Approximately 10,000 people from Bristol and beyond appeared around Filton on Sunday, the 4th, anxious to witness the history-making maiden flight of the Brabazon. They would not be disappointed. A large tow tractor dragged the heavyweight airliner to the eastern end of the Filton runway in the late morning. After a thorough pre-flight check the eight massive Centaurus engines were started and Pegg slowly taxied the Mk I the length of the runway and carefully took her through a wide turn to the east-bound centreline. He rolled the plane into a seven-knot crosswind on take-off power. It looked as if this might be another taxi trial. As the speed approached 80 knots, the nose began to rise and it became obvious that Brabazon was going to fly. Pegg: 'We decided that if all the conditions were suitable, we would have a go today and she was off the ground in some 500 to 600 yards.' He took the plane on a leisurely 140 mph circuit over the Severn estuary and back into Filton in an elapsed time of twenty-seven minutes. The Brabazon floated in to a gentle 88-knot landing and rolled out in just 600 yards to a stop.

The company's Reginald Verdon Smith exclaimed, 'A splendid run. Well done.' And to Lord Brabazon he declared, 'This will make a lot of chaps gay today.'

'Experts say you're more likely to get hurt crossing the street than you are flying, but that doesn't make me feel any less frightened of flying. If anything, it makes me more afraid of crossing the street.'
– Ellen DeGeneres

top right: Half of the Brabazon wing, showing the propellers that were driven by the huge 2,500 hp Bristol Centaurus 18-cylinder radial piston engines. The narrow nacelles indicate that they served merely as housings for the contra-rotating propeller drive shafts, each pair of props being linked to a pair of Centaurus engines buried in the wings; bottom right: A.J. 'Bill' Pegg, chief test pilot of the Bristol Aeroplane Company, in the foreground, and Walter Gibb, captain of the Brabazon reserve crew and Pegg's co-pilot on this demonstration flight from the Filton factory to London.

The maiden flight, statistically was: aircraft weight 210,000 lb, fuel carried 4,000 gallons, take-off distance 500 yards, take-off speed 85 mph, highest speed attained 158 mph, highest altitude reached 4,000 feet.

Four days after the maiden flight, Bill Pegg flew the Mk I to Farnborough as planned. He did a spectacular display, filling most who saw it there with a sense of patriotism and pride.

It became company policy to conduct much of the Brabazon flight-test programme over British cities. Like the B-36 that Pegg had flown in Texas, the Centaurus-powered Mk I made a distinctive drone as she approached, and as the flight plan normally called for an operating airspeed of only 150 mph, the residents of a town or city being overflown by the Brabazon would hear her long before she passed overhead.

Walter Gibb flew the Brabazon as pilot in command on some of the test flights. He recalled, 'It was very comfortable. It flew very well. It was big. You didn't whip it round a corner like a Tiger Moth or a Spitfire, but as long as you treated it like a double-decker bus or a large aeroplane, you had no trouble at all. You could do some beautiful landings on it, because it was quite close to the ground, and when it had the full flaps down you were on a big air cushion. In fact, there was one peculiarity we had to add to the cockpit. That was a light to show when the main wheels were on the ground. There were times when you did a really nice landing and you couldn't tell when the main wheels were on the ground. You wanted to know because you had to push the control column forward to get the nose wheel on the ground and get reverse pitch to stop. So, if you didn't know, you kept holding off and holding off, when you were on the ground all the time.' Gibb took the airplane through a series of stall tests at an altitude of 20,000 feet and was pleased with its behaviour, commenting later that the Brabazon recovered from a stall on her own, losing at most 2,500 feet in the stall.

As flight testing continued into 1950, some ominous signs appeared. It became clear that delivery of the new Proteus turboprop engines to power the Brabazon II would be greatly delayed through developmental problems. The key selling features of the Proteus were its ability to provide substantial power at altitudes well above the levels where gusting had been a problem, and the relatively vibration-free operation of the turboprop powerplant. After earlier generations of piston-engine airliner travel, the smooth-running turboprop would offer welcome relief from the fatigue of lengthy air journeys. But Proteus, by the summer of 1950, was overweight and underpowered. It was then that another aeronautical genius played a part in rescuing Proteus, and Bristol, from imminent disaster.

Stanley Hooker had been a colleague of Sir Frank Whittle during the early years of turbine engine development and was in charge of gas turbine development at Rolls-Royce in 1948, when he resigned following a disagreement with Rolls chairman Lord Hives. With Proteus in deep trouble, Reginald Verdon Smith brought Hooker into the Bristol fold with a remit to fix the promising engine. He set about redesigning the powerplant and eventually saved it, but in the interim, the Bristol company nearly went under.

Another problem, fatigue of the Mk I engine support mountings, coupled with other fatigue problems in the inner-wing box structure, troubled company officials, and of an equally serious nature, the operating costs of the plane were proving considerably higher than anticipated. These factors exacerbated BOAC concerns about the aircraft's viability as a transatlantic airliner. And across that ocean the Americans had fully committed to the coming jet age with the continuing development of their Boeing 707 and Douglas DC-8 jet airliners, which in another eight years, would completely change the nature of air travel for the next fifty years and beyond.

Walter Gibb: 'The spec wasn't correct for immediate post-war flying. The people who wrote up the specs were the high-ups in aviation and business and when they had crossed the Atlantic pre-war, they'd gone on the *Queen Mary*. They conceived of an aeroplane with all this comfort, bunks and a great dining room to eat in. And, of course, come the day, that wasn't what the airlines wanted. They wanted to ram as many passengers as possible into the tube and give 'em lunch on their laps.'

Despite Bristol's programme to show off Brabazon around Britain and build enthusiasm for the big plane, BOAC remained unconvinced and eventually declined to purchase it. There were no other orders for it on the books and in 1952, engineering analyses had established that the projected life of the airframe would be only 5,000 flying hours, a figure far too low to enable airworthiness certification for the plane.

Bill Pegg was now working on the test programme of Bristol's promising new airliner, the Britannia, which he flew for the first time on 16 August 1952. The company was very enthusiastic about Britannia and was now focusing almost exclusively on it. On 20 September, after 164 flights and more than 382 hours in the air, Brabazon Mk I took off for the last time, three years after her maiden flight. Both the Mk I and Mk II were placed in storage in the assembly hall. On 17 July 1953, the House of Commons formally ended the Brabazon project. In October, workers from the firm of Coley of Hounslow, specialists in salvaging scrap metal from unwanted aircraft, came to Filton to begin demolition of the two airframes. In the hangar where they were built, both planes were cut up for scrap. In two weeks the work was completed and the Brabazon was no more.

Specifications: Bristol Brabazon Mk I
Engines: Eight Bristol Centaurus piston radials of 2,500 hp each
Maximum speed: 300 mph
Cruising speed: 250 mph
Service ceiling: 25,000 ft
Range: 5,500 miles
Weight empty: 145,100 lb Maximum take-off weight: 290,000 lb
Wingspan: 230 ft
Length: 177 ft
Height: 50 ft
Wing area: 5,317 sq ft
Passenger capacity (Mk II): 100

BOEING

By February 2004 the Boeing company had delivered 1,341 of its 747 jumbo jet aircraft to customers worldwide. The 747 is the favourite airliner of most passengers, having carried them in comfort and safety to destinations around the globe for more than thirty-five years. Since beginning airline service in 1970, the 747 has travelled the equivalent of 74,000 round trips to the moon. It has created a world market for air travel. The number of passengers who have been transported by the plane is equal to more than half of the entire world population. It gave meaning to the term "jumbo jet", which was first coined about the Boeing giant. So important is the 747 to world air travel it has been honoured by the United States of America with a postage stamp as one of the most significant technical advances of the twentieth century, along with the first flight of the Wright Brothers and Charles Lindbergh's solo flight across the Atlantic.

When the 747 was designed, a lot of people (including

many at Boeing) thought that the company would be financially ruined by the project. The origin of the aeroplane was a hotly contested US Air Force competition for the design and construction of a new strategic heavy-lift transport with the ability to carry fully equipped troops and heavy weaponry to Europe and other potential zones of conflict. Boeing was beaten in that 1965 competition by Lockheed with its C-5 Galaxy design. The Boeing 747 is a derivative of its Air Force competition design, and on reflection, the company may well have come out ahead of Lockheed in the long run as just 131 examples of the C-5 were built, against more than 1,300 747s delivered by 2004, with more on Boeing's order books.

In 1965 the head of Pan American World Airways, Juan T. Trippe, was talking with Boeing about the possibility of the plane maker developing a stretched version of the 707 airliner to accommodate 250 passengers. Trippe had been the first to order earlier Boeing aeroplanes including the 307, 314, 377 and 707. The company responded that Trippe's request was not technically feasible and he then asked for an entirely new airliner capable of hauling 400 passengers over a distance of 5,000 kilometres; he also wanted a cargo version of the new plane. Boeing's President William Allen, later phoned Trippe to ask if he was serious about the request. Trippe said he was and in December 1965 they began negotiations on the project. In April 1966 they signed a sales contract for twenty-five of the new planes at a total cost of $550 million, then the largest ever single purchase by an airline. They agreed a target date for the first flight of the new 747 of 17 December 1968, the 65th anniversary of the Wright brothers' first flight.

Unlike virtually all of his competition in the airline industry, Juan Trippe believed that the new Boeing plane would be economically viable. It would provide him with the ability to serve the fifteen percent annual rise in passenger growth that he was predicting, and would be able to seat three times as many passengers as the existing 707s flown by most of his competitors. Then came the world economic downturn of 1970 and the oil crisis that followed it. But despite these circumstances, some of Pan Am's international competitors were eager to purchase the new 747 so as

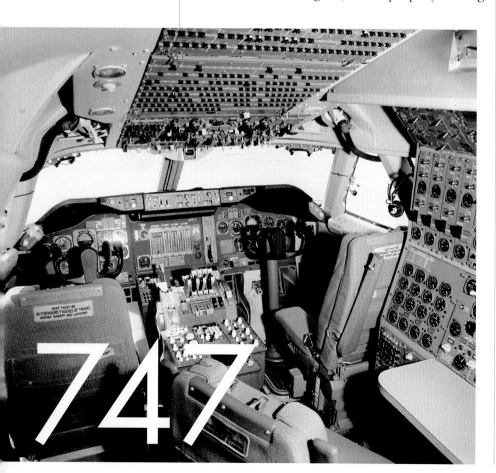

not to be left behind by the American carrier in the race to dominate the international air routes.

It was Boeing's intention that the new plane should have a double-deck fuselage, but when Trippe was shown a mock-up of the design, he rejected it for Pan Am in favour of a single-deck layout with the famous 'hump' in the forward portion. Actually, the Pan Am president wanted to use the hump space behind the cockpit as a special area for passengers, possibly as a bar, reminiscent of that feature on the earlier Boeing Stratocruiser, but above rather than below the main cabin. Other possibilities for the space included a cinema, a restaurant or even a casino.

Boeing put 50,000 employees on what would be the largest aircraft project in history. It recognized in 1964 that its Renton, Washington facility, then producing 707-, 727- and 737-type aircraft, could not be expanded to facilitate 747 production and began a search for an appropriate site on which to build a new assembly plant. A location forty miles north of Seattle, at Everett, Washington, was selected, despite its lack of a rail link. Boeing spent $5 million to build such a link, to what would become the largest industrial building on the planet at 5.5 million square feet. The construction project proved to be extraordinarily difficult, with 2,800 workers struggling in seemingly endless rain, snowstorms and deep mud, in a superhuman effort to turn 700 acres of pine forest into the huge complex within the established schedule. Boeing workers started construction on the 747 line even before the completion of the new $200 million plant.

In charge of the huge company staff on the 747 was Mel Stamper, a Bill Allen appointee who was tough, tireless and utterly disciplined. Stamper ran the operation for four years around the clock, frequently sleeping in the office when unable to return home. He was a high achiever and set such an outstanding example that his work force emulated his dogged determination to build the great plane as perfectly as possible and right on schedule. They impressed him to the extent that he began referring to them as the 'Incredibles'.

That first 747 was essentially made by hand, as were the 75,000 construction drawings. On 30 September 1968 the first of the new jumbos, *City of Everett*, was rolled out of the plant as Boeing 707, 727 and 737

airliners celebrated the occasion in a flypast. It was less than three years after the signing of the contract for the initial 747 order.

Jack Waddell, head of flight testing for Boeing, had been concerned about flying the aircraft from a cockpit that was more than thirty feet above the ground, and to get used to the position, he had the company build a special movable-platform mock-up of the cockpit to the exact height of the actual aircraft cockpit.

The prototype 747 was two months behind schedule on 9 February 1969, when Waddell took it up for the first time. He returned full of praise for the aeroplane. But as flight testing began, it was clear that there were serious problems with the early Pratt & Whitney JT-9D engines. Fifty-five engine changes were required during the 1,013-flight test programme.

In a less than perfect debut performance, Pan Am began the commercial airline service of its first 747-100 with a 21 January 1970 flight from New York to London. As often happened in the early days of jet airline operations, there were teething troubles. A malfunctioning cargo door delayed the departure of *Clipper Young America* with 336 passengers on board. Then, when the problem was fixed and the aircraft was taxiing out to the runway, an engine overheated, requiring a replacement aircraft and an additional delay of nearly seven hours. Malfunctions caused delays on many jumbo flights in that period, with a lot of the problems being engine related. It began to appear that too much emphasis on producing the new plane in just thirty-four months may have led to shortcomings, at least in the engines. The growing recession of the late 1960s, coupled with the cancellation of Boeing's supersonic transport programme by the US government in March 1971, and declining commercial orders, led to the company shouldering a debt burden of $1 billion and a staff cutback from a total of 101,000 to 38,000 in 1971.

A turnaround came as sales of the company's highly efficient three-engined 727 airliner took off in the early 1970s. That, together with Pratt & Whitney resolving the problems with its JT-9D engine, which substantially improved the reliability of the 747, allowed the company to introduce the 747-200, which offered a greater payload capability and

lower left: The 747 flight deck. The Boeing giant was nearly stillborn. In 1965, when Boeing agreed to develop the big plane at the urging of Pan Am's Juan Trippe, the administration of US President Lyndon B. Johnson had just initiated a major austerity programme for America. Trippe had to personally intervene to persuade Johnson that the 747 was in the country's best interests and the plane's economy of scale would enable more people to fly for less money; below: The lineage of the 747 includes early pursuit craft like these 1930s Boeing P-12s built for the US Army Air Corps.

'The first piece of luggage on the airport carousel never belongs to anyone.'
– George Roberts

range. Beginning in 1970, Boeing offered the 747-200 with a choice of engines provided by Pratt & Whitney, General Electric or Rolls Royce. Nearly 400 examples of the 747-200 were produced for Boeing's expanding list of customers. Meanwhile, the reputation of the 747-100 was enhanced as it proved able to be operated for an average of fourteen hours a day with reliability.

In the mid-1970s, the company introduced the 747SP (Special Performance), an adaptation of the -100, which was 48 feet shorter in fuselage length and capable of carrying 300 passengers over a range of 7,600 miles. It was offered with a choice of General Electric or Rolls Royce engines and was utilized on such routes as New York–Tokyo non-stop.

Boeing began studies in 1956 on how to meet a demand the airlines had identified for an airliner that could combine jet speed, quiet and comfort with the ability to operate from the shorter runways of smaller airports. However, the company was not then in a financial position to fund the development of such a plane and its directors were determined that they would only proceed with the project when they had a minimum of 100 firm orders for the new aircraft.

That new aeroplane was the 727. It would utilize a fuselage similar to the earlier 707 and share a common flight deck with it. It differed principally in the number and position of its engines: there were three, and all were tail mounted. Positioning engines on an airliner in this way was not new. The French Sud Aviation group had mounted two engines at the tail of its Caravelle jetliner in 1955, and the British Hawker Siddeley Trident airliner also had three tail-mounted engines. The positioning of the engines at the tail of the 727 brought several advantages to the aircraft, including substantially reduced noise levels in the passenger cabin, especially on take-off, improved aircraft handling and safety when operating with one engine shut down, greatly reduced risk of ingesting debris from the runway, and greatly increased efficiency of the wing without the restrictions imposed by engines and their mountings there.

The second most important distinction between the 727 and its 707 predecessor was the wing itself, which was designed to incorporate a new and highly com-

left: The 747-400 model can carry up to 568 passengers and has a range of up to 7,670 nautical miles on routes such as San Francisco to Sydney and London to Singapore.

'Gunter's Second Law of Air Travel: the strength of the turbulence is directly proportional to the temperature of the coffee.'
– Nicholas Gunter

A Boeing 747-400 is made up from six million separate parts, half of them being fasteners. The aeroplane has 171 miles of wiring and five miles of tubing. 147,000 lb of aluminium is used in its construction. 75,000 engineering drawings were used to produce the first 747. The original 747 flight-test programme, which led to the aeroplane's certification for commercial service in December 1969, used five aeroplanes, lasted ten months and required more than 1,500 hours of flying. The engine thrust has grown from 43,500 lb per engine on the early 747s, to as much as 63,300 lb on the current model. Engine noise from the current 747-400 is half of what it was on the original 747s that were delivered in 1970.

plex system of flaps and high-lift devices that enabled the aeroplane to operate safely and efficiently from runways as short as 5,000 feet. Prior to the introduction of the 727, only propeller-driven aircraft had been able to operate from runways of that length.

The unique design of the 727 presented certain potential disadvantages too, not least being a tendency for the aeroplane, with its "T" tail, to be subject to a "deep stall" condition in which it entered a high nose-up attitude and the turbulence off its wing prevented the tail plane (horizontal stabilizer) from functioning. Boeing design engineers minimized this characteristic with the design of their tail unit and they fitted the aircraft with a system to warn against an impending stall condition. Another problem that came with the design of the new plane was a tail-heavy condition with so much weight concentrated there, which led to critical balance considerations in the loading of passengers, fuel, baggage and cargo. On the plus side, the 727 came with the first installed airliner auxiliary power unit (APU) and an integrated access stairway at the rear of the plane between the body-mounted engines. These two features made the aircraft practically independent of airport ground facilities.

By 1960, Boeing had recorded more than the initial 100 orders for its 727, and in 1962 the first such aircraft was rolled out at the company's Renton plant where it was being produced on an assembly line parallel to that of the 707. That first 727 began service with United Airlines in February 1964. It is now part of the collection of the Museum of Flight in Seattle, having been retired from airline service by United in 1991 after 64,500 flight hours and 48,000 landings. Such first-generation 727s could seat a maximum of 131 passengers and were powered by three Pratt & Whitney JT8D engines rated at 14,000 lb thrust each. With the outstanding success of the aeroplane, Boeing introduced the stretched 727-200 in the summer of 1967. With up-rated engines of 16,000 lb thrust each, this bigger sister had a passenger capacity of 189 and a 600 mph cruising speed over a 2,800-mile range.

Most pilots who flew the 727 praised its excellent handling qualities, while passengers were amazed by the quiet in the cabin, both on take-off and in flight. So popular was this aeroplane that the company con-

tinued to produce it for twenty-two years, delivering the last of 1,831 aircraft, (an air freighter version), in September 1984 for Federal Express. As of 2003, more than 900 of the aircraft were still flying, most of them as cargo carriers.

Following on the success pattern of the 727 was Boeing's "baby" airliner, the model 737, not the loveliest creation of the Washington state plane maker, but by far its biggest selling airliner. In a time of feverish design activity at the company, with its personnel resources stretched to capacity on the 727 and 747 programmes, as well as that of the supersonic transport, there was little room for a major new project. But again, a promising new market had emerged, this time for a small, 100-passenger, twin-jet airliner. This market had already been addressed by Douglas, with its DC-9, and by the British Aircraft Corporation with its BAC 111, when Boeing announced the new 737 in 1965, two years behind its competition. Again, the company relied on the basic fuselage width of the 707, which afforded a substantial saving in manufacturing over that of an entirely new fuselage and allowed its airline customers to configure their aeroplanes with six-abreast seating as opposed to the five-abreast layout of both the DC-9 and the BAC One-Eleven.

The 737 airliner, in its various marks, ranging from the smallest 737-500, which seats 110 passengers, to the 189-passenger 737-900, has resulted in more than 4,000 aircraft sales at prices ranging from $38.5 million to $85 million as of 2003. In a joint venture of General Electric and SNECMA of France, CFM56 turbofan engines power the 737-500. The company also offers the Boeing Business Jet derivative of the 737-700 for the executive jet market. Priced at $34.25 million, plus the cost of the custom interior, Boeing had orders for forty-six of the planes within a few months of the model's first flight in September 1998. The 737 is the best-selling commercial jetliner of all time, and like its giant 747 sister ship, has carried the equivalent of more than half the world population. Boeing 737s are serving more than 250 airlines in ninety-five countries.

It is perhaps inevitable that in the course of more than three decades of flight operations, any aeroplane, and especially a very large and complex one, would experience its share of accidents and incidents. Twenty-seven times between 1974 and 2002, 'events' occurred involving 747s that resulted in the deaths of passengers, crew and, in some cases, people on the ground. In most cases the fault lay not with the aircraft, but with human error, terrorism, or other non-mechanical causes.

A Lufthansa 747-100 had not been properly configured for take-off from Nairobi, Kenya on 20 November 1974. Just after it became airborne, the aircraft stalled and crashed less than 4,000 feet beyond the end of the runway, killing fifty-five of the 140 passengers, and four of the seventeen crew.

On 27 March 1977, a bomb attack by Canary Island separatists on the Las Palmas airport caused the diversion of two 747 flights, both non-scheduled. One was a KLM 747-200 from Amsterdam to Las Palmas; the other a Pan Am 747-100 from New York to Las Palmas. Both of these aircraft, and many more, were diverted to nearby Tenerife that day. The runway was shrouded in dense fog as both aircraft awaited clearance to depart Tenerife. The KLM flight was heading back to Amsterdam and had instructions to depart before the Pan Am jumbo. The KLM 747 then taxied to the end of the main runway and awaited take-off clearance. The visibility on the airfield was extremely limited and there were communications difficulties between Tenerife air traffic control and the KLM flight.

Meanwhile, the Pan Am aircraft was instucted to taxi down the same runway as far as Exit 3, where it was to move onto a parallel taxiway and continue to the take-off point. In the heavy fog, the Pan Am pilot missed the turnoff and elected to go on to Exit 4 and move onto the taxiway at that point. Tenerife air traffic control then gave the KLM flight clearance for the route it was to take after take-off, but the KLM crew mistakenly believed they had also received permission to take off and began their roll. The KLM pilots could not see the Pan Am jet ahead of them in the fog, nor could anyone in the Tenerife control tower see either aircraft on the runway, and the tower was not equipped with runway radar. When the Pan Am pilots finally spotted the approaching KLM jet, they attempted to manoeuvre sharply off the runway, but there was insufficient time to complete the turn. The KLM

jumbo was partially rotated and nearly airborne when it slammed into the fuselage of the taxiing Pan Am 747, ripping it apart. In the ensuing fireball, 321 of the 380 passengers, and nine of the sixteen crew of the Pan Am plane died. All 234 passengers and fourteen crew of the KLM jumbo were killed. The Pan Am captain was among the few survivors. This incident took the greatest number of lives of any air disaster until the terrorist attacks of 11 September 2001.

A Korean Air Lines 747-200 was shot down by a Soviet air-to-air missile near Sakhalin Island, Soviet Union, on 1 September 1983 after the aircraft had strayed into Soviet airspace. All of the 240 passengers and twenty-nine crew were killed.

In August 1985, a Japan Air Lines 747 experienced a sudden decompression, which caused major damage to the flight controls. The aircraft had suffered an earlier hard landing, which had caused substantial damage to the fuselage section beneath the tail. The rear pressure bulkhead was not repaired properly and failed during the 12 August flight from Tokyo to Osaka. The fractured bulkhead allowed pressurized cabin air to blast through, severely damaging the vertical tail fin and the multiple hydraulic systems it contained. After disengaging the autopilot, the flight crew struggled to regain a measure of control over the big plane through the use of engine power adjustment and the wing control surfaces. The captain had managed to slowly turn the aircraft to a heading that he hoped would allow him to make a crash-landing at Haneda, but the increasing loss of hydraulic fluid soon rendered his remaining controls useless. Unable to maintain sufficient altitude to clear the 5,000 foot Mt. Ogura, or to manoeuvre around it, the plane shortly hit the mountainside. All nineteen crew and 505 of the 509 passengers died when the plane crashed. It was the highest number ever killed in one aircraft.

In an event witnessed by this author at Bangkok, Thailand, airport on 5 April 1988, a Kuwait Airlines 747-200 was hijacked. The aircraft took off for Kuwait and landed in Cyprus. Two of the hostages were killed before the hijackers surrendered to the authorities.

The most infamous event involving a 747 was that of the Pan Am aircraft that exploded and crashed at Lockerbie, Scotland, only thirty minutes after taking

'The head cannot take in more than the seat can endure.'
– Winston Churchill

below: The US space shuttle *Endeavour* mounted atop one of NASA's specially modified Boeing 747 Shuttle Carrier aircraft, at the Dryden Flight Research Center, Edwards Air Force Base, California; right: A night view of a 747 through open hangar doors at the immense Everett, Washington, facility. By the early 1990s, the 747 fleet had flown 3.6 billion people–the equivalent of more than half of the world's population.

'As the Spanish proverb says, 'He, who would bring home the wealth of the Indies, must carry the wealth of the Indies with him.' So it is in travelling; a man must carry knowledge with him if he would bring home knowledge.'
– Samuel Johnson

off from London Heathrow airport bound for New York on 21 December 1988. A bomb was detonated in the forward cargo compartment, causing the plane to break up in flight with the loss of 243 passengers, sixteen crew and eleven people on the ground.

Just after taking off from Amsterdam's Schiphol Airport on 4 October 1992, an El Al 747-200 freighter suffered the separation of its number three engine and pylon from the wing. In parting, the engine caused the separation of the number four engine and pylon and further damage to the right wing and some of the aircraft systems. Struggling to return to the airfield, the crew lost control of the plane which then crashed into a large apartment building. Four aboard the 747 and forty-three people on the ground were killed.

At 8:22 on the evening of 17 July 1996, TWA Flight 800, a 747-100, took off from JFK Airport, New York, for Paris. The aircraft had arrived in New York from Athens at 4.31 that afternoon and was serviced and refuelled prior to its scheduled departure for France at 7 p.m. Concern about a piece of 'suspect' luggage delayed the departure for more than an hour. The jumbo took off at 8.19 p.m. At 8.29 the captain of the flight said to the co-pilot, 'Look at that crazy fuel flow indicator there on number four . . . see that?' Two minutes later the crew of an Eastwind Airlines 737, flying in the same area as the TWA flight, saw an explosion. The crew of an Alitalia flight behind the TWA plane, confirmed the Eastwind report, as did the pilot of a Virgin flight. Eight miles off the coast of East Moriches, Long Island, New York, the TWA jet had suffered a catastrophic explosion and broken up in the air. All 230 people aboard the plane died.

Like the gigantic Antonov An-225 heavy lifter, a version of the 747 was developed as a platform for transporting the space shuttle orbiters. The intention was to ferry the American shuttle orbiters from Edwards Air Force Base in California, where they were sometimes required to land when returning to earth from their space missions, to their home base at the Kennedy Space Centre in Florida. It was in February 1977 that a flight-test programme began at the National Aeronautics and Space Administration's Dryden Flight

Research Facility, Edwards, AFB, on the shuttle/747 "piggyback" combination, with the shuttle being unmanned in the initial testing. This was followed by a test in which two crew members were aboard the shuttle, and that by a final test phase in August when the manned shuttle orbiter was actually released from the 747 mother ship to glide to a landing on the Edwards dry lake bed. Initially, the last phase of the testing was viewed with considerable apprehension by some of the pilots involved, but the work ultimately went according to plan with the shuttle making a proper separation from the mother 747. Much of the credit for the success of the separation testing is due to the Second World War ace and first test pilot to fly

faster than the speed of sound, Chuck Yeager, who suggested that a positive angle of attack be employed when mounting the shuttle orbiter onto the back of the big Boeing. The attitude eased separation of the two craft.

Two 747 aircraft were acquired by NASA to be transformed into ferry platforms for the shuttles. They had formerly served with American Airlines and Japan Air Lines. With the shuttle mounted in place on the back of the 747, airflow to the vertical tail of the airliner was seriously disrupted and to counter the negative effect this had on the lateral stability of the big jet, large end-plate fins were fitted to the horizontal tail tips. According to one of the NASA 747 pilots, there was considerable buffeting in flight with the shuttle mounted. And with the shuttle on top, the 747 was performance limited to a maximum altitude of 26,000 feet and an indicated maximum air speed of 250 knots.

In 1990, Boeing modified and delivered two 747-200B aircraft to the US Air Force to replace the elderly 707s which had served seven US presidents since 1962 as 'Air Force One'. The new presidential jumbos have an air-refuelling capability, giving them nearly unlimited range. They are equipped to seat up to seventy passengers and are operated by a crew of twenty-three. The Air Force also operates four E-4Bs (747s) as National Airborne Operations Centers for the coordi-

'I like terra firma. The more firma, the less terra.'
– George S. Kaufman

below: An American Airlines
747 descends to San Diego's
Lindbergh Field, an
approach that to pilots
resembles that of an aircraft
carrier landing. A 747-400
takes off at 180 mph, cruises
at 565 mph and lands at 160
mph. The 747 fleet has
logged more statute miles
than the equivalent of 75,000
trips to the moon and back.

nation of a response to any national emergency, including terrorism and nuclear war. One such aircraft is maintained on permanent alert status with a crew of up to 114 personnel.

An entirely new and greatly improved 747 took to the air for the first time on 29 April 1988, the 747-400. It looks much the same as earlier 747s, except for the six-foot-high drag-reducing winglets affixed vertically to the wing-tips. This advanced jumbo can carry 416 passengers over a maximum range of 8,300 miles and is powered by still more efficient engines made by Rolls Royce, General Electric and Pratt & Whitney. Clearly different from that of its predecessors is the 'glass cockpit' with television-like screens displaying the information that had previously been shown on conventional instruments. It is operated by a cockpit crew of two.

Boeing builds different versions of the -400: a Domestic version with a 568-passenger capacity over a 2,075-mile range; a Combi with options for carrying either 266 passengers and seven cargo pallets or 410 passengers; and the Freighter, capable of hauling a 285,000 lb load over a 5,000-mile range.

Can planemakers build aircraft even larger than the 747, the Airbus A380, and the An-225? Aircraft engineering and design experts argue both sides of the question. Imaginative concepts abound including air-cushioned vehicles, twin or multi-body vehicles, span-loaders with immensely capable wings for lifting enormous cargoes, and surface-effect vehicles at projected gross weights of up to 900 tons, able to skim the surface of oceans with great efficiency. In 1929 one of the design world's most innovative and original thinkers, Norman Bel Geddes, put his dream of a gigantic 'flying-wing, flying-boat airliner' down on paper, to the amazement, amusement and admiration of many. Geddes had become known for his extraordinarily imaginative set designs for New York stage productions, but by 1929 he was heading a major American industrial design firm. There he visualized the mammoth flying-boat that would carry hundreds of well-healed travellers back and forth 'between New York and Paris'. Just where such a craft would land in the Paris area was unclear, but his vision certainly was. With a wingspan of nearly 600 feet and weighing 1.4 million pounds, the plane was meant to be pow-

ered by twenty large engines mounted on an airfoil attached by pylons above the main plane. It would carry 451 passengers in great luxury, served by a crew of 155 and would offer facilities such as a gymnasium and a 200-seat formal dining room. With nine decks, there would be amenities like promenades, a games area, a bar, a solarium, a lounge and a cafe, rivalling the grandest luxury liners afloat at the time.

The notion that the most important reason for crossing an ocean by aeroplane is to get to the destination as quickly as possible, didn't seem to matter much to Geddes, whose 'Air Liner Number 4', as he referred to it, was intended to cross the Atlantic at a mere 90 mph, taking more than a full day to make a flight from New York to London, for example. This would have been ten miles an hour slower than the average achieved by Charles Lindbergh on his 1927 Atlantic crossing. Geddes may have been influenced in his planning of the Number 4 by the German passenger airship *Graf Zeppelin* and by Claudius Dornier's luxurious DO-X flying-boat, both of the same period as his design.

Of the Number 4, Geddes wrote, 'For a number of years I have been working on plans for a big plane. It is not "big" for the sake of being big but for other factors which will be apparent as I describe it. It is my firm belief that this is in no sense a mad or foolish idea but sound in every particular. It represents my idea of what the intercontinental air liner of 1940 will be like.

'As a premise one must accept the fact that the air liner I am going to describe will fly, and fly just as readily as any other plane. In fact, I have every reason to believe that it will fly much more smoothly than any plane that has yet been built, if for no other reason than because of its enormous size . . .

'In the design of this plane, two major elements have had foremost consideration: first, safety; second, comfort of passengers. Both of these factors have been solved mainly by her immense size. As regards the safety factor, it has been possible to make elaborate provision. While twenty 1,900 hp motors are required to raise her from the water, twelve are sufficient to fly her at cruising speed. Thus, counting the six reserve motors, she is equipped with more than twice as many motors as will be necessary after once rising from the water—a safety factor of over 100 percent . . .

'No airplane or airship has yet offered to passengers comfort equal to that provided by steamship or even railway travel. Tomorrow's air liner will offer facilities and comforts that are in every respect identical with those offered by the most advanced ocean liner. Passengers aboard this air liner are able to move about as freely as on an ocean liner, enjoying recreations and diversions similar to those to which seagoing passengers are now accustomed . . .

'The main promenade deck is four hundred and fifty feet long and seventeen feet wide. Running nearly the full length of the main wing on the forward side, with large windows of shatterproof glass along its entire length, passengers are provided with the same view and conditions as on the finest ocean liner. Besides providing ample space for passengers to stroll, it accommodates at the same time one hundred and fifty deck chairs. On this deck there is a veranda cafe with tables for ninety persons . . .

'This plane has been designed on the basis of the latest developments in aviation known today. Every detail and every principle involved has been tested in one form or another. It is merely the combination that is new.

'As to whether, exactly, this type of air liner is the next step in solving the problem of intercontinental aviation is beyond calculation. What can be reasonably anticipated is that a liner its equal in size, facilities, and comfort will be a common means of intercontinental transit in the not very remote future. Whether the development of such liners will follow the identical trend I have indicated is problematical. I am inclined to believe that the principles I have followed will be utilized for a few years and that engineers will then have at their command new principles which will make possible further advances and simplifications.'

It is and has always been the payload requirement and range that define the size of an aircraft. The nature of the cargo, its weight, the radius of required range, the engine and fuel requirements, all combine to influence the design. The 747-400, for example, was designed with the requirement that it should be able to fly an extremely long route such as from San Francisco to Sydney. A part of what enables such range is its ability to carry up to 3,300 gallons of fuel

in the horizontal (tail plane) stabilizer, in addition to that in all its other fuel cells. Its engines, depending on which are chosen by the customer, give it up to thirteen per cent greater fuel efficiency than that of the 747-300. Since the 1970s, the Boeing company has been through a seemingly neverending series of planning exercises relating to how the 747 might be enlarged to meet new requirements of the world's airlines, requirements which have also changed many times in that period. In the 1990s the company saw its share of the world market for passenger aircraft eroded by the growing sales of the four-partner European aerospace consortium, Airbus. Boeing has struggled to regain the position of market leader.

In the 1970s, Boeing launched a number of studies into the feasibility of enlarging their 747. One such plan called for an extended-length wing fitted to a double-decker fuselage, resulting in an aircraft with a 300,000 lb payload, improved range and a hefty gross weight of more than one million pounds. It was way ahead of the engine technology it would require. The company then focused on several options, all of which enlarged the aeroplane through the insertion of fuselage-extending "plugs" of various lengths, offering different combinations of range and passenger capacity, the largest of which provided seating for 732 passengers on long-range routes and up to 1,000 on shorter routes. But the harsh effects of the 1970s oil crisis, together with lagging engine technological development, resulted in these schemes being shelved. While Boeing did make a major impact on the air travel market when it introduced the popular, efficient and highly advanced 757 and 767 twin-engined airliners, their very success caused many in the airlines community to question Boeing about why the 747 had slipped behind the technological curve in areas like 'glass-cockpit avionics', carbon-composite construction and other advances. In the view of many, Airbus was taking the lead.

By the late 1980s, the explosive tiger economies of Asia had prompted Boeing to re-examine the evolving requirements of the airlines serving the Pacific Rim nations. The effort identified a need for a new airliner with a capacity for between 600 and 800 passengers, with a range of 7,500 nautical miles or more. The

'If God had intended us to fly, he would have made it easier to get to the airport.'
– Jonathan Winters

right: The space shuttle Columbia is carried atop a specially modified 747 on a flight from Palmdale, California, to the Kennedy Space Center, Florida, in March 2001; bottom: Another view of a 747/ shuttle pair departing the Palmdale facility; far right: The 747-400ER prototype taking off on a test flight.

'Try flying on any plane with a baby if you want a sense of what it must have been like to be a leper in the fourteenth century.' – Nora Ephron

Since it entered airline service in 1970, the 747 has been produced in more than twenty versions, including freighters, combis, convertibles, and many special-use models such as the US presidential aircraft, Air Force One; top right: An early 747-100 on the Everett ramp; bottom right: A manufacturing view of the 747's ancestor, the highly successful 707 jetliner.

company organized meetings in 1992 where representatives of the airlines serving the large trans-Pacific market discussed more than one hundred design proposals for stretching and reconfiguring the 747 in various ways and in sizes all the way up to a giant with a 290-foot wingspan and a take-off weight of 1.7 million pounds, with seating for 750 passengers. The delegates considered many issues, including the characteristics of the major world airports relative to ground manoeuvring, docking, loading, fueling and, crucially, turnaround times. The airline people were insistent that the turnaround for any new superjumbo must not exceed that of the 747-400 aircraft. That meant that such a 600-plus passenger plane must be serviced, loaded with 3,000 cubic feet of luggage, at least 1,800 meals and 75,000 gallons of fuel, and fully prepared for a transoceanic flight within one hour of arriving at the gate.

At about the same time that the Boeing-customer meetings were going on, Airbus was talking with airlines that were currently flying 747s to glean what information they could about what these airlines wanted in a future high-capacity airliner, one that might seat upwards of 800 passengers. It would lead to the development of the A380. Airbus had previously concerned itself strictly with smaller-capacity airliners, but was now clearly on the path toward direct competition with the Boeing jumbo.

In the 1990s some of Boeing's biggest customers for the 747 were apparently more interested in the possible development of an entirely new large airliner, than an enlarged, evolved 747. Once again the company went back to the drawing board, but this time under the spectre of direct competition from Airbus.

In the aftermath of the terrorist attacks of 11 September 2001, the business of most major airlines suffered a dramatic decline as many travellers simply stayed at home. The deserts of Arizona and southern California bloomed almost overnight with hundreds of airliners that were surplus to requirements. The air travel business gradually recovered, and for Boeing it finally seemed clear that a new direction was necessary. The aviation industry had been through a three-year downturn and the airlines evidenced little interest in either an extra-long 747 or a faster-than-the-competition Sonic Cruiser, as the company referred to yet another of its

stream of airliner proposals. Enter the Dreamliner.

Prospects for the commercial division of Boeing finally improved in April 2004 when the company announced that it had entered into a $6 billion agreement with Japan's All Nippon Airways for the purchase of fifty new 787 airliners, which Boeing calls the Dreamliner. It was an important achievement for the Seattle planemaker in its effort to re-establish itself as the world's premier airliner manufacturer and a major sale in the rich East Asia market. Under the agreement, one-third of the 787s would be built in Japan. In the still difficult economic climate of the aviation world, Boeing managed to post a $623 million net income for the first quarter of 2004, compared with a $478 million loss in the same quarter of the previous year. While it has done quite well in defence contract work in the early years of the twenty-first century, it has been surpassed by Airbus in the commercial jet field and was buoyed by the warm reception accorded the 787 by ANA.

By contemporary standards the 787 is a mid-size plane intended to carry 200-300 passengers over an amazing 8,000-plus-nautical-mile distance, non-stop, a much greater range than that of any other aircraft its size. It is an ideal vehicle for serving a rapidly growing market of important secondary cities throughout Asia that are prospering as both high- and low-tech industry arrives. Business travel should flourish in these markets and Boeing anticipates selling roughly thirty per cent of its 787s to airlines in that part of the world.

The Dreamliner is to make its maiden flight in 2007, and begin customer delivery the following year. Of the new plane, Boeing states that it will be roomier and quieter than currently serving airliners. It will be slightly wider, with more 'wiggle room' for passengers in a sexy new interior. It will be wired to provide so-called 'e-enabled' passengers additional entertainment choices in the air and the aircraft will be capable of self-diagnosing problems in flight and calling ahead to order spare parts for installation at the next airport.

For the airlines, the 787 will be far more fuel efficient and so cheaper to operate. A part of this efficiency will result from the aircraft being made largely of light, composite material rather than traditional aluminum. Part plastic resin, part carbon fibre, it is the same strong, black material used to make the shafts of golf clubs and fishing rods, and can be formed to any shape. Long used in the manufacture of military aircraft, these composites are lighter, stronger and more durable than aluminium. Construction of the 787 with composites will eliminate the need for the millions of rivets used in conventional aluminium aircraft construction, as the airliner industry evolves once again, having started with aircraft made from wood and fabric before shifting to rivet-fastened aluminium. As most of the 787 primary structure will be made of composites, further manufacturing efficiencies will acrue. Unlike most metals, the new materials do not require heavy machining. Boeing is not new to building aeroplanes with composite structure, having used it in the massive tail section of the 777 jetliner. In addition to their being lighter, thereby making the 787 more fuel efficient, aerostructures made of composites do not corrode like metal, thus affording the airline customers considerable savings in maintenance. One of the more dramatic aspects of employing the composites in the manufacture of the new plane is the expectation of performing the final assembly of the relatively large structural units in just days rather than the weeks that are normally needed for traditional aircraft assembly.

Boeing is going truly global in sourcing the parts for its 787. While final assembly will take place in Seattle, parts for the Dreamliner will come from suppliers in Britain, France, Italy, Japan, North Carolina, Oklahoma, Arizona and Connecticut. Nearly two-thirds of the plane will be provided by contractors. The company has a history of co-manufacturing with Japanese industry; throughout the 1990s, Mitsubishi Heavy Industries, Fuji Heavy Industries and Kawasaki Heavy Industries manufactured parts for the big Boeing 777 twin jet. Boeing anticipates a production period running for as much as forty years and a world market for the Dreamliner of up to 3,500 aircraft.

Until the immense Airbus A380, enters service, the Boeing 747 will continue to be the largest civil airliner in operation. It has been in continuous production for more than thirty-five years and is flown by more than eighty operators worldwide. Its design and size make it the most readily recognized airliner flying

today. Nearly 70,000 Americans are involved in the production of the 747 and another 10,000 people working for Boeing suppliers around the world contribute to it. While nearly bankrupting Boeing in the early days of the project, the 747 has long been hugely profitable for the company, allowing it to enter into many new and potentially profitable ventures such as the Dreamliner. And, in July 2004, Boeing once again raised the prospect of a new, advanced version 747 in another effort to reclaim some of the market share for jumbos sought by the A380 makers. This new big Boeing is the 747A (Advanced). A little larger and technically superior to the 747-400ER, the 747A would seat 450 passengers and would combine some of the Dreamliner technology with the size of a 747. It would be quieter and have greater range than the current 747. The company claims that the 747A would be considerably cheaper to operate than the A380 super-jumbo and would offer (revenue-creating) Sky Suite dormitory rooms in the top of the aircraft, similar to those in a Pullman-style railway carriage. Other options for the large 'attic' space behind the cockpit, stretching nearly the entire length of the fuselage, include business suites, state rooms or additional stowage. In the wake of the airline industry interest in the A380 superjumbo, Boeing believes it has identified a market gap for an airliner of the 747A type with potential sales of 350–450 aircraft over the next twenty years and will likely decide whether to build it by some time in 2006.

Specifications: Boeing 747-400

Engines: Four Pratt & Whitney PW4062 rated at 63,300 lb thrust each, or Four Rolls Royce RB211-524H2-T rated at 59,500 lb thrust each, or Four General Electric CF6-80C2B5F rated at 62,100 lb thrust each
Cruising speed: 567 mph
Service ceiling: 45,000 ft
Range: 7,260 nautical miles
Maximum take-off weight: 875,000 lb
Wingspan: 211 ft 5 in
Length: 231 ft 10 in
Height: 63 ft 8 in
Wing area: 5,500 sq ft
Passenger capacity: 416–524

left: In April 2004, the Boeing board approved the launch of the 787 Dreamliner passenger jet based on firm orders for fifty of the new planes from ANA (All Nippon Airways). Intended as a super-efficient 200 to 250-seat airliner, the Boeing 787 is somewhat smaller than the current 747 and 777 jetliners. It employs new engine and materials technologies that allow it to burn significantly less fuel per passenger, and fly farther without refuelling. The company expects the airline users of the 787 to fly it on new nonstop links between mid-size cities. Its 9,000-plus mile range would, for example, take it from Singapore to Denver without a layover.

Development of the new 787 is a part of Boeing's response to the coming Airbus A380 superjumbo jet-liner. The company is hoping to build the 787 to be so efficient as to provide ample incentive for airlines to retire their 767's, A300s and A310s, and replace them with 787s.

The Dreamliner production is scheduled to begin in 2006 with the first flight of the new twin-engine plane in 2007.

AIRBUS

One of the world's great industrial rivalries is that of Airbus and Boeing. Since the 1990s, the two aviation giants have been trying to outdo each other in the race to design, build and sell the next really important airliner. For a long period the Boeing people pursued the idea of offering the airlines of the world a new, stretched version of their veteran 747 jumbo, the 747X, but the concept met with little interest from their potential customers. In designing and launching the A380, Airbus is trying to end Boeing's long monopoly of the large airliner market. One model of the Boeing 747 can accommodate 416 passengers in a three-class configuration, whereas the new Airbus A380 will easily accommodate 555 in a relatively standard seating arrangement. In January 1997, Boeing put aside the notion of a 747 superjumbo and instead focused on what it believed to be a better alternative, a twin-jet mid-size aircraft that it calls the 787 Dreamliner, designed to carry between 200 and 300 passengers more than 8,000 nautical miles (see the Boeing 747 chapter). Boeing now sees a much more limited potential market for giant passenger planes, while Airbus clearly disagrees. But industry sources indicate that most, if not all, of the more than 150 A380s that Airbus has on its order books have been sold at deep discount prices in order to get the necessary number of aircraft orders and important customers on board, to go ahead with the new plane. Industry insiders wonder if, when the discount honeymoon ends, Airbus will be able to sell the A380 at the full price. Many believe that US airlines in particular, will not be ordering A380s in the present economic environment, until the economy and travel demand improves dramatically. Some feel that the big plane will not sell in the USA other than to cargo carriers, and that for passengers, *non-stop* is the real answer, not *bigger*. Current customers for the A380 aeroplane include: Emirates, Air France, Lufthansa, Qantas, Qatar Airways, Singapore Airlines, Virgin Atlantic, Federal Express, Etihad, and International Lease Finance.

The A380 is the biggest passenger jet in the world and may well retain that crown for many years to come. With so much cabin space, it is only to be expected that Airbus would talk up the big plane, at least theoretically, in terms of thick carpeting, on-board

lounges, bars, gyms, casinos, boutiques, sleeping rooms, business centres, showers and other lavish amenities, but for most airline customers the harsh realities of airline industry economics seem to point to a far more traditional, maximum-number-of-bums-on-seats approach to operating the new plane.

The consortium Airbus was formed in 1970 when French, German, Spanish and British aviation organizations joined forces in a direct challenge to the principal airliner makers of the United States—Boeing, McDonnell Douglas, and Lockheed. The first product of the consortium was the 250-seat A300B1, whose maiden flight took place in October 1972. Classified as an intermediate-to-long-range passenger transport, the A300B1 evolved in time into the A300-600, an airliner manned by a crew of two, with six cabin crew and seating for up to 361 passengers. With a top speed of 554 mph and an operational ceiling of 40,000 feet, the A300-600 has a range of 4,260 miles. Airbus has built and sold more than 500 of its A300 type, the forerunner of an extensive family of short, intermediate and long-range jetliners.

In 1987, long before its development of the A380, Airbus launched the A340 project, the largest commercial aircraft to enter production to that date. The A340 has been offered in several versions. Initially, the reduced-capacity -200 led the parade, followed immediately by the -300, which was first operated by Singapore Airlines in 1996 (A340-300E). The standard long-range -300 seats up to 440 passengers and is flown by a crew of two. Lufthansa became the first customer for the A340, which began replacing the airlines McDonnell Douglas DC-10s in 1993.

An enormous new purpose-built facility near Toulouse in southern France, the Jean-Luc Lagardère industrial site has been created as the final assembly plant for the world's largest airliner, the A380. Lagardère, who died in 2003, was a visionary French industrialist and a leading figure in Anglo-French industrial co-operation. His efforts led in large part to the creation of the Airbus company, initially through the merger of Matra and Aérospatiale, and later by merging that new company with Germany's DASA and the European

A380

Aeronautic Defence and Space Company. Lagardère also figured prominently in the Airbus decision to go ahead with the A380 programme, one of the biggest aeronautical ventures of all time.

Airbus builds and sells half of the world's commercial airliners, and employs 48,500 people at sites around the world. Since entering the airliner market in 1974, it has sold more than 4,800 aircraft to more than 180 customers. Along with its commercial aircraft activity, the company is managing the development of the A400M military transport programme, an aircraft that is being assembled in Seville, Spain. Its first flight is scheduled for 2008.

Construction on the Lagardère site at Toulouse began in 2001, a year after the formal launch of the A380 programme. By the spring of 2004, most of the major site buildings were completed and the remaining structures and facilities of the 360 million euro complex were due for completion in 2005. The focal point of the huge facility is the ten-hectare U-shaped final assembly hall for the A380. One of the largest buildings in the world, the assembly hall was begun in March 2002 and was finished in just under two years, in time for the arrival of the first large sections of the new plane. The site also includes the A380 static test building and apron areas where assembled aircraft will be ground-tested (fuelling, cabin pressurization and weather-radar) and prepared for their first flights, and the A380 general-purpose hangar for short-term work on newly assembled aircraft. A new 200,000-square-foot building has been constructed at the nearby Toulouse Saint Martin location to house the A380 cockpit simulator and a test rig for systems-integration simulation and verification. An A380 major component assembly hall was completed at the major Airbus Hamburg site in 2003 for the structural assembly of the forward and aft fuselage sections and the fitting of their flight systems. In addition, the Hamburg site provides facilities for interior finishing, paint shops, an engine run-up facility, a pre-flight hangar and a delivery centre. A mammoth 900,000-square-foot West Factory facility at Broughton, England, was completed and opened in 2003 for the manufacture and assembly of the A380 wing, and another new building to house the world's largest

landing-gear test rig was completed at the Filton, Bristol facility in England in 2002. The horizontal tailplane and belly fairing are assembled in new halls at Getafe and Puerto Real in Spain, while large all-carbon-fibre fuselage sections emanate from a facility in Illescas, Spain. The centre wingbox is produced and assembled in a large workshop at Nantes, France, while the forward and centre sections of the aeroplane are created at Saint Nazaire. Further fuselage work is done at the Méaulte, France facility. The production of completely equipped A380 sections occurs at sixteen Airbus facilities across Europe. These sections are then transported to Toulouse for final assembly. While most sections of the new plane are brought to the Lagardère facility by sea and river, some of the smaller components, like the nose section, from Méaulte, and the vertical tail fin, from Stade in Germany, are delivered by the Airbus Beluga super-transporter aircraft. The other, larger A380 sections, however, arrive at Toulouse from the sub-assembly manufacturers in Spain, France, Germany and the United Kingdom on specially built barges, ships and road vehicles over the rivers, seas, canals and roads of Europe. The wings, for example, are

'Always choose the oldest customs official. No chance of promotion.'
– Somerset Maugham

below: The interior of a French Goliath bomber, converted for use as an airliner after World War I. Though relatively comfortable for its day, it was a far cry from the pioneering French-British-Spanish-German giant of today, the Airbus A380.

moved by truck and trailer from the Broughton plant to the river Dee. There they are loaded on a barge for the 24-kilometre trip to the river's estuary, from where they travel by large ship to the port of Pauillac, near Bordeaux. From there the wings are moved by barge up the Garonne river to the harbour at Langon where they are transferred to special truck-and-trailer vehicles for the remainder of their journey to Toulouse. On the road trip from Langon to the Toulouse factory, the giant A380 sections travel over a special 'outsize convoy itinerary' route, most of it roads frequented by normal traffic, but traffic disruption is minimal as the aircraft sections move only at night on the route. The A380 section convoys are made up of three truck-and-trailer units that carry the front, centre and rear fuselage sections, with two further units carrying the wings and one carrying the horizontal tailplane. The 240-kilometre journey from Langon to Toulouse takes several nights, with the convoy stopped in specially built parking areas during the daytime.

In the 1990s, such major aircraft manufacturers as Airbus, Lockheed Martin, and McDonnell Douglas were involved in studies about the viability of a flying-wing airliner. The Airbus concept bore some resemblance to the Northrop Grumman B-2 stealth bomber. The wingspan was to be 340 feet and the passenger capacity, on two decks, was up to 900. It was called the FW-900 and had an estimated take-off weight of 1.3 million pounds. Power was to come from three engines of 120,000 lb thrust each, mounted above the rear fuselage. The McDonnell Douglas design, a beautiful thing called BWB-1 (Blended-Wing Body) was to have a 289-foot wingspan and looked a lot like a giant ray. Intended to carry up to 800 passengers over a distance of 7,000 nautical miles, the BWB-1 was also to be powered by three jet engines, but of just 50,000 lb thrust each, as the company believed that the superior aerodynamics of their wing design would translate into a jetliner with much better fuel economy than that of the competition. When Boeing took over McDonnell Douglas later in the decade, it refocused its approach to the BWB-1 concept, emphasizing potential military and commercial

freight applications as opposed to passenger utilization. In that period, a two-pronged effort got under way to revive the concept of a giant supersonic jetliner, one that would be both economically viable and environmentally friendly, following the retirement of the Anglo-French Concorde. Coordinated through NASA, the US National Aeronautics and Space Administation, the project was divided into two programmes: HSR-1 (High-Speed Research) which concentrated its efforts on the noise and pollution issues, and HSR-2, which looked into the technologies that would be needed to produce such a high-speed civil transport aircraft. An industry team headed by Boeing and McDonnell Douglas took on the airframe technologies study, while a similar team formed by General Electric and Pratt & Whitney studied the potential engine technologies. The goal was a plane with a passenger capacity of 300, three times that of Concorde, and with twice the range. The cruising speed was to be Mach 2.4, reducing the average flying time from San Francisco to Tokyo from more than ten hours to just over four hours. The world awaits this supersonic wonderjet.

Airbus has chosen a different path to the future. In its view, air traffic control systems and airports the world over were [and continue to be] struggling with an ever-increasing number of commercial aircraft. It reasoned that this congestion could be reduced through the operation of a new, very large long-range jetliner, able to carry more passengers than the largest airliners currently in operation. The A380, it believes, will carry more passengers farther, allowing for growing passenger numbers and helping to ease an increasingly congested environment. It claims it will achieve this without increasing the number of air traffic movements and without having a negative impact on the environment, thanks to significantly reduced noise and emissions levels. It says that, with its new-generation engines and advanced wing and undercarriage design and technology, the A380 will not only comply with current noise limits but will be quieter than today's largest airliner. It will meet strict local regulations such as QC2 for departure at London airports. The new aeroplane will generate half the noise at take-

left: The beautifully clean, efficiently designed flight deck of the A380. With this cockpit layout, its procedures and handling characteristics, pilots will be able to make the transition to the A380 from other Airbus fly-by-wire aircraft with minimal additional training. Utilizing new-generation engines and advanced wing and undercarriage design and technology, the aeroplane is expected to be quieter than today's largest airliners.

The new superjumbo has been planned in collaboration with some sixty major airports to ensure a smooth entry into airline service.

Airbus is offering a baseline passenger A380 with a 555-seat capacity in three classes and a range of up to 8,000 nautical miles. There is also a freighter version, the A380F, that will carry a 150-ton payload. Power for the new Airbus can be provided by either Rolls-Royce Trent 900 engines or GP7200 engines from The Engine Alliance, a General Electric and Pratt & Whitney joint venture.

The top speed of the A380 is to be 595 mph with a 560 mph cruise speed at a flight altitude of 40,000 feet.

'France was discovered by Charlemagne in the Dark Ages. Other important historical figures are Louis XIV, the Huguenots, Joan of Arc, Jacques Cousteau and Charles de Gaulle, who was President for many years, and is now an airport.'
– Terry Jones

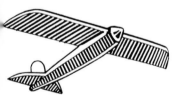

'I suppose we shall soon travel by air-vessels; make air instead of sea voyages; and at length find our way to the moon, in spite of the want of atmosphere.'
– Lord Byron, 1882

off and carry thirty-five per cent more passengers than its competitor over routes such as London–Singapore.

While interest in the new megacarrier Airbus is high, there are those in aviation circles who agree with Boeing that the industry and the world are not ready for such a giant people-mover. Airbus takes the view, however, that in making the commitment to the A380, it has positioned itself very well to take full advantage of what it predicts will be a burgeoning market for such planes in the next few decades. It has worked closely with its current and prospective airline customers, with sixty major airports and the airworthiness authorities, in the preliminary planning of the A380, which flew initially in April 2005.

How is such a product planned? To be successful it must incorporate state-of-the-art technologies in materials, systems and industrial processes. It must be compatible with existing airports. It must be roomier, have more passenger seating, floor space, comfort and amenities than today's jetliners and, crucially, it must bring its airline customers a much lower seat-mile cost and greater range than the most efficient jetliners flying today, so that those airlines can afford to offer their passengers a higher standard of comfort, luxury, safety and efficiency than has previously been available–at affordable prices.

In today's world of air travel, a new, expensive passenger plane like the A380 has to be a friend of the environment. Never mind how big and powerful and capable it is. It simply must be quieter, have greater fuel economy and a lower impact of exhaust gases on the atmosphere. On a fuel-consumed-per-passenger-mile basis, the A380 is expected to have a 'fuel burn' comparable to that of today's most efficient small turbo-diesel cars. On the ground, the aeroplane can taxi using only two of its four engines and is equipped with a low-noise auxiliary power unit. With this new giant, Airbus clearly feels it is on course to deliver the plane of the near future that many, if not most, major airlines will want for the coming years. Thus far, in spring 2005, the company has announced firm orders on its books from eleven customers for a total of 154 A380s, several of which will be an air freighter version. The FedEx Express subsidiary of FedEx (Federal Express) Corporation has ordered ten

Airbus A380-800F air freighters, with options for ten more. Delivery of their aircraft is to begin in 2008. FedEx operates a wide range of aircraft in its current fleet of more than 600, from major hub locations at Memphis, Paris, Anchorage, and Subic Bay in the Philippines. The A380 is the first major commercial jetliner to have an air freighter version co-developed with it as a part of its launch. The freighter version will have a 150-ton cargo capacity over a range of 5,620 nautical miles and will use standard interline containers and pallets. The plane will be able to offer one-day trans-Pacific service, cutting as much as a full day off door-to-door time.

The A380 is very big indeed, but it is still essentially a conventional airliner design. It has a wide-body cylindrical fuselage just slightly longer than the big Boeing 747. Like that rival plane, it is powered by four engines, either Rolls-Royce Trent turbofans or Engine Alliance (a co-venture of General Electric and Pratt & Whitney), with total thrust ranging from just under 268,000 lb to just over 299,000 lb, depending on the model ordered. It is expected to cruise at 560 mph at 35,000 feet and have a top speed of 595 mph, faster than many of today's jetliners. The service ceiling will be 43,000 feet and the range of the -800 model with seating for 555 passengers is to be 7,800 nautical miles.

Excess weight being the enemy of all aircraft, the designers of the A380 have been careful weight watchers in their effort to create an airliner with amazing spaciousness as well as excellent performance, reduced emissions into the atmosphere and relatively low operating costs. Airbus estimates that forty per cent of the aeroplane's structure and components are to be made from carbon composites and advanced metallic materials, all of which bring the advantages of lightness, reliability and ease of repair. An example of the design ingenuity in the A380 is the use of a carbon-fibre-reinforced plastic central wingbox, for a weight saving of one and a half tons over a comparable aluminum alloy structure. Carbon fibre is also used for the finbox, the rudder, the horizontal stabilizer, the elevators, the upper-deck floor beams and the rear pressure bulkhead. Thermoplastics are employed in the construction of the fixed-wing leading edge and the secondary bracketry of the fuselage.

A new, light material called Glare is being used for the first time in a civil airliner, a laminate with alternating layers of aluminium and glass-fibre-reinforced adhesive, which is utilized in the upper fuselage shell of the A380. The new material is more fire-, damage-, and corrosion-resistant than standard aircraft aluminium and weighs ten per cent less than the traditional aircraft metal. While being manufactured with a hot bonding process, Glare is repaired using the same methods as standard aircraft aluminium.

Another important innovation in the manufacturing of the A380 is laser beam welding. The process is being applied to the attachment of the longitudinal reinforcement stringers of the lower fuselage shell, rather than traditional riveting. This highly efficient fastening method is far faster than riveting and results in another weight saving. A safety benefit of laser beam welding accrues through the elimination of fasteners which are a major source of corrosion and fatigue cracking.

It is hoped that, with the A380, Airbus and its customer airlines will show more consideration for the economy-class passenger and provide more comfort for this poor, beleaguered soul, than has been the airline and aviation industry norm to date. The company states that the new plane will have twin-aisle cabins on the upper and lower decks, with forty-nine per cent more floor space for thirty-five per cent higher seating capacity. The three-class layout will provide seating for 555 passengers with a typical upper-deck layout providing 96 business-class and 103 economy-class seats. The main deck will provide seating for twenty-two in first class and 334 economy-class seats. There will be two stairwells between the passenger decks, as well as a lift system between them to provide access for passengers with limited mobility. The great size of the plane makes possible a number of seating-configuration/passenger-facility combinations.

There are eight full-size cabin doors on both sides of the A380, with two doors on the main deck and one door on the upper-deck forward of the wing, which can be used simultaneously for embarking or disembarking passengers. Two in-hold loading belts, one at the forward end and one at the rear under the fuselage, can be utilized simultaneously to speed baggage transfer.

The designers of the A380 appear to have taken on the issue of long-haul passenger comfort and convenience with enthusiasm, their overall aim being to provide these travellers with the quietest, most comfortable and enjoyable journeys possible. They are striving to enable Airbus customer airlines to offer unrivalled standards of space, comfort and amenity in each cabin class. That all-important feeling of spaciousness is conscientiously addressed in the economy-class sections. Spacious overhead stowage is designed for ease of access without limiting headroom or passenger movements in the cabin. The stowage bins can accommodate more roll-aboard bags than any other widebody aircraft. The lighting and air conditioning are extremely important to the maintenance of passenger comfort throughout long-haul flights and Airbus provides localized control of these elements within each of the separate zones in the aeroplane.

On short-, medium- and long-distance flights, the cabin air must be clean, pressurized, draft free and maintained at a comfortable temperature. On average, all the air in the cabins is completely changed every two minutes. At a cruising altitude of 40,000 feet, with air pressure one-quarter of the normal pressure on the ground, the outside air temperature is -56°C and the humidity is around two per cent. The cabin air has to be a mixture of outside air with filtered and recirculated air from the cabin. In normal operations, more than half the air is taken from outside. Airbus states that none of the air that is supplied to the aircraft toilets, galleys and cargo holds is re-circulated, but is instead dumped directly overboard. The system allows Airbus cabin air to be maintained at comfortable levels of temperature, humidity and pressure, while high-efficiency particulate arrestor filters remove nearly all bacteria, dust and airborne microbes, providing passengers with one of the cleanest environments possible. The re-circulating air also optimizes the humidity within the cabin environment.

The company has come up with an innovative

Airbus is stressing passenger comfort in the design of the new A380 superjumbo. Cabin air, for example, is an important element for both long and short-distance travellers. Airbus plans to keep its cabin air clean, pressurized, draft-free and at a comfortable temperature with a highly efficient air conditioning system which will change the cabin air completely every two minutes.

'No man needs a vacation so much as the the person who had just had one.'
– Elbert Hubbard

'Heaven is an English policeman, a French cook, a German engineer, an Italian lover and everything organized by the Swiss. Hell is an English cook, a French engineer, a German policeman, a Swiss lover and everything organized by the Italians.'
– John Elliot

ACCÈS INTERDIT -
AVION SOUS
TENSION

'The scientific theory I like best is that the rings of Saturn are composed entirely of lost airline luggage.'
– Mark Russell

Lavatory Urinal Freshening-Up Area concept for the A380. It is a three-room design that lets its airline customers provide passengers with more room and cleanliness in such important facilities, something especially welcome over really lengthy trips. An up-market lavatory is provided for the needs of first-class passengers, offering what Airbus refers to as fine materials, new surface appearance, and special focus on illumination and noise reduction.

In the run-up to the A380's interior design process, Airbus brought large cabin mock-ups to eight major cities on three continents and solicited the opinions of 1,200 frequent travellers, male and female, of different cultures and nationalities, on their likes and dislikes in the presentations. This exercise proved to the company's satisfaction that it was on the right track to bring unmatched levels of comfort to passengers on the new plane—without adding unnecessary weight or drag to increase the running cost. It added to the Airbus designers' understanding of passenger reaction to the various elements in the cabin and how each of them varies according to the local culture. With forty-nine per cent more floor space and thirty-five per cent more seats than the Boeing 747-400, the A380 main deck is the widest in the air, making it possible for Airbus customer airlines to offer wider seats and provide each seat with its own armrest; a frequent passenger demand. Another significant space feature of the new plane is the lower deck which can accommodate sleeper cabins, lavatories, crew rest areas, business centres, more space for more passenger amenities, or more seats.

Airbus has long been committed to equipping its big A330 and A340 jetliners with the latest in-flight entertainment systems offering on-demand video and audio, ready access to many high-quality movies and audio programmes, all stored digitally on the system servers. The passengers are able to access live television broadcasts, films and games on their individual liquid crystal displays, all controlled through a handset. The Airbus Flight Information System allows customer airlines that equip their aircraft with laptop power outlets and PC data connections to let their passengers transmit and receive messages from their usual e-mail addresses. They are also able to connect to a standard internet browser to navigate websites and the passenger information stored in the on-board server.

The passengers aren't the only element in the A380 equation intended to benefit from the forethought and planning that has gone into the design of the new superjumbo. In 1994, Airbus put together an A380 Airport Compatibility team, twelve years before the giant aircraft was scheduled to enter airline service. The team has established a well-developed dialogue with representatives of many of the world's major airports, which are now using the A380 as the reference aircraft for their master planning. Facing the prospects of heavy passenger growth, ever-increasing congestion and limited expansion potential, most of these airports are having to plan for the operation of very large aircraft like the A380. And, with a relatively small increase in the budgeting of their existing infrastructure, they foresee increased revenue with the introduction of the giant airliners. Thus far, the dialogue developed by Airbus with the sixty major airports seems to be helping considerably in shaping both the new plane and the master planning of the airports.

These major world airports are, in many cases, already compatible with the requirements of the new Airbus plane, and of those that are not yet compatible, many have already begun the necessary work to achieve the upgrade. Additionally, other significant airports have been involved with Airbus based on the interest of airlines in establishing future A380 routes.

The extensive consultations with airports and regulatory agencies has substantially influenced the final characteristics of the new plane; such as its certification for unrestricted operation on 45-metre-wide runways and the width of its landing-gear whose twenty-wheel arrangement lets the A380 manoeuvre on a 23-metre-wide taxiway while carrying a pavement-loading factor no greater than existing large airliners. At the terminal gate, the interior cabin layout and the door locations of the plane will enable a comparable turnaround time to that of the current Boeing 747-400, but with thirty-five per cent more passengers being boarded. Existing ground servicing equipment can be utilized with the A380, whose ground servicing points are located in positions similar to those on existing wide-body airliners. The aeroplane can be operated from any airport that currently serves the 747 jumbo, but there are certain aspects of airport ground facilities that, in some cases, will require atttention and possible modification. Some terminal facilities, including the gate departure lounges, the parking stands themselves, as well as bridges, overpasses and certain taxiways with load-bearing concerns may need work to bring them up to a new standard.

From the cost standpoint, many major airports see the modification and reworking of some of their terminal facilities to make way for the new, bigger jets as far more efficient, less expensive and easier than the alternative—a massive replication of runways, parking stands and gates. In some cases, it is a choice of spending many billions or mere millions of dollars to achieve compatibility with the coming growth that the arrival of the superjumbos will mean. Compared to the costs, and the time involved in developing new airports, such 'compatibility adjustments' must seem like bargains to the airport authorities. According to the company, Airbus people have been working, and continue to work, with customer airlines, airports, ground handling companies, and ground servicing equipment manufacturers, to help coordinate and facilitate all aspects of airport ground operations for compatibility with the A380 by its entry into airline service. Airbus has created a full-scale partial mock-up at the Toulouse facility for the operational testing and evaluating of the catering vehicles to be used in servicing the aircraft's 26-feet-high upper deck.

Thanks to the mid-deck positioning of the cockpit, A380 pilots should like the visibility from it and the ease of ground manoeuvring compared to that of the 747. This mid-deck cockpit position also eases the transition for pilots from other Airbus aircraft to the new A380. In ground manoeuvring, the clearance of the A380 between the main wheels and the edge of the taxiway is greater than that of other wide-body airliners thanks to its shorter wheelbase, allowing it to be manoeuvred on taxiways without restriction. To simulate different full-scale landing-gear layouts and weights, Airbus built a landing-gear-configuration test vehicle, using A340 Airbus wheels and tyres and various tyre pressures to simulate different types of aircraft. In the testing, up to 32 tons of load per wheel was

simulated through the addition of ballast to the vehicle. The results of this testing were validated using both Airbus and other aircraft. It was then possible for the company to simulate any landing-gear configuration, including the associated aircraft weight and load factors transferred through each wheel. Conforming to the needs of airlines and airport authorities, the A380 has been designed to fit within a 'horizontal box' 262 feet square, to make the most efficient use of existing taxiways, runways and gate parking stands. The plane will use the same runway length as the Boeing 747.

Airbus has addressed the issue of aircraft noise on the environment with a determination to make the A380 significantly quieter than current large aircraft, and give it substantial margins in relation to current and future noise limit regulations. In addition to international aircraft noise regulation, the new plane has a significant advantage over existing large aircraft based on very stringent local noise regulation such as the Quota Count (QC) system of the London airports at Heathrow, Gatwick and Stansted. In the design of the A380, the lower noise levels have been achieved through the optimization of the engines, the nacelles, and the airframe itself. Besides these physical design characteristics, the A380 is being fitted with a unique feature in which the Flight Management System is programmed with 'optimal noise trajectories', enabling the plane to continuously and reliably adhere to the Noise Abatement Departure Procedure while accounting for the aircraft parameters and ambient conditions.

A380 pilots making the transition from the current new-generation family of Airbus aircraft, should easily and readily familiarize themselves with it. Airbus provides airline customers with a wide range of training courses utilizing advanced technology and training media. It operates training centres in Toulouse, Miami, Florida and Beijing, China. For convenience, the ground-school phase can be taken at the airline's base of operations. Other courses for flight and cabin crew and maintenance staff are also available. The typical transition training time from the A330 or A340 aircraft is anticipated to be much less than the twenty-five days normally needed for a transition from aircraft

'Never go abroad. It's a dreadful place.'
– Earl of Cardigan

without this commonality. The instrumentation of the A380 cockpit is similar to that of its predecessor Airbus aircraft, but more advanced. In the A380 there is a direct dialogue between the pilot and the systems. Ergonomic research undertaken by Airbus, together with the opinions of pilots from many major airlines, has contributed to the final cockpit design. The handling of the aeroplane is similar, and with the flight deck located halfway between the two passenger decks, the eye-level view of the pilot is virtually the same as in current aircraft, making taxiing relatively easy. And the placement of the flight deck at this mid-deck position reduces the cockpit noise levels through improving the aerodynamics at the nose of the aircraft.

Airbus sees the commonality of its new generation of jetliners, developed thanks to the introduction of fly-by-wire technology, as one of the keys to its success and ability to offer airlines increased cost-efficiency and flexibility. The company developed full design and operational commonality with the introduction of digital fly-by-wire technology on civil airliners in the 1980s, and as a result, ten of its aircraft, from the 100-seat A318 to the 555-seat A380, feature quite similar flight decks and handling characteristics. Airline operators of these Airbus jetliners benefit considerably from this commonality through the shorter training and transition time for pilots and flight engineers moving from one type of plane to another. Other operator benefits include significant cost savings through streamlined maintenance procedures and reduced spare parts holdings. Such commonality appears to be bringing important commercial and economic advantages to Airbus aircraft operators. Within the operator organizations, added flexibility can be achieved as aircraft types of various sizes and seating capacities may be serviced and maintained by the same teams of personnel as a single-aircraft-type fleet. It also provides pilots the possibility of flying a range of routes, including both short and long-haul trips.

Two concepts developed by Airbus and seen by many airlines as beneficial to their operation, are Mixed-Fleet Flying and Cross-Crew Qualification. Cross-crew qualification makes it possible for pilots to transition from one Airbus fly-by-wire aircraft type to another with less training time than that required in

left: Take-off on the maiden flight of the first Airbus A380, 10.29 a.m., 27 April 2005 at the Blagnac Airport, Toulouse, France. The flight lasted nearly four hours.

The A380 entered production in January 2002. Final assembly began in May 2004 and the first flight of the new superjumbo took place in April 2005 with entry into airline service to begin in early 2006.

Airbus Industries is building the huge plane at its Toulouse, France, plant and is a consortium formed by the European Aeronautic Defence and Space Company and BAE Systems of Britain.

Pre-assembled sections of the A380 are transported from manufacturing sites in Broughton, England, Hamburg, Germany, Puerto Real, Spain, and St Nazaire, France, to the final assembly line in Toulouse on a huge, specially built roll-on roll-off vessel made in China.

Airbus have announced firm orders for 124 A380 aircraft from customers that include Singapore Airlines, Lufthansa, Emirates, Air France, Qantas, Malasia Airlines, Etihad, Virgin Atlantic, Korean Air, Qatar Airways and International Lease Finance.

'Why is it called tourist season if we can't shoot them?' – George Carlin

full transition training. Approved by the Federal Aviation Administration in 1991, cross-crew qualification enables pilots to transition from the A320 aircraft to the larger A330 or A340 in just eight working days, rather than the twenty-five days required for the full type-rating course. The transition time from the A330 to the A340 is only three days and from the A340 to the A330, just one day. The reduced training times can result in substantially lower training costs and higher crew productivity. It can mean increased mobility as well as improved employment prospects for the pilots.

Airlines are able to take advantage of the Airbus operational commonality through the implementation of mixed-fleet flying, in which their pilots are able to remain current on more than one fly-by-wire aircraft type simultaneously. This allows them to switch readily from the short and medium-haul operations of the Airbus A320 aircraft to the long-haul trips of the A340. In moving back and forth from, say, long-haul trips to short, a pilot gets more take-offs and landings than he would otherwise have, eliminating the requirement for currency training. Also, his sleep-cycle disruption is lessened. Short-haul crews changing to long-haul operations benefit by having less fatigue from high-cycle operations. The airlines benefit through increased revenue hours flown by their pilots for the same number of on-duty hours, owing to less standby and 'dead time', resulting in increased productivity. An added benefit from mixed-fleet flying is the ability of an airline to interchange aircraft of different sizes and passenger capacities at very short notice, with no crew-scheduling problems. Major cost savings can result for airlines utilizing cross-crew qualification and mixed-fleet flying.

Airbus first introduced 'fly-by-wire' electronically managed flight control systems on a commercial jetliner, the A320, in 1988. The system utilizes computer technology to improve aircraft handling and safety. The fly-by-wire system operates the aircraft's moving flight-control surfaces by means of converting the pilot's commands to electronic impulses through electrical wiring, rather than mechanical linkages to the cockpit. The technology was employed initially on jet fighter aircraft and its later adaptation for commercial jetliners has brought lower operating costs to airline operators through reduced aircraft weight

which has meant less fuel consumed. The environment has benefited too, with a smaller volume of exhaust gases being generated. The safety factor for fly-by-wire is a monitoring system that Airbus calls 'hard protection.' It effectively oversees the pilot's commands to the plane's control surfaces, providing a 'flight protection envelope' which maintains a safety margin for the aircraft. Thus, the pilot is able to maximize the performance of the aircraft in emergency situations without over-stressing the aircraft. One of the greatest benefits achieved by Airbus with its applications of fly-by-wire technology has been the ability to create a family of aircraft types ranging from the 107-seat A318 to the new 555-seat A380, all having very similar cockpit layouts and handling characteristics. It is thereby able to pass along the advantages of shorter, more cost-effective training and conversion of crew to its airline customers.

Another fascinating member of the Airbus family is the Satic A300-600ST 'Beluga' super-transporter. Since the early 1970s, Airbus has been transporting major assembly portions of its planes between its various manufacturing and assembly locations. In those early years, the company operated a small fleet of specially-converted Boeing Stratocruisers, called 'Super Guppies'. But by late 1997 these planes were in need of replacement and no suitable aircraft existed offering such an enormous open-fuselage cross-section for the hauling of outsize cargo shipments. Airbus designers set to work on the development of the company's own outsize transporter aircraft, the Satic Beluga. Satic stands for Special Aircraft Transport International Company and was established jointly in 1991 by Aérospatiale and Deutsche Aerospace Airbus, specifically to build the new super-transporter.

Starting with a basic A300 airframe, the Beluga design team identified and shaped five primary conversion areas which, collectively, resulted in one of history's most unusual and utilitarian vehicles. Among the interesting alterations made to the original airliner airframe is the extreme lowering of the flight-deck/cockpit area to a position below and forward of the cargo compartment floor level. Loading and unloading of the oversized cargoes takes place through the main forward freight door, above the cockpit. The cargo hold can accommodate a 45-ton shipment, and just two men are needed to load or unload the giant cargo in a forty-five minute turnaround, an effort that had previously taken two hours with the Super Guppy. The Beluga crew consists of a pilot, co-pilot and two cargo handlers. The plane is powered by two General Electric 59,000 lb thrust turbofan engines. It cruises at 484 mph and has a range of 1,035 miles. Airbus operates a fleet of five Belugas, which also serve the needs of other clients, such as the European Space Agency, through charter services offered by a company established in 1996, Airbus Transport International.

Long-range aircraft operations, and the attendant safety considerations, have motivated Airbus to re-evaluate the regulations governing such operations over remote and inhospitable areas. This led to the company proposing new safety-related concepts to the various regulatory agencies, suggesting the development of new regulations for operating in such extreme regions. The company refers to these rules as LROPS, Long-Range Operations. The proposals have been accepted by the US Federal Aviation Administration, the European Joint Aviation Authorities and the International Civil Aviation Organization, which began work on new LROPS rules with a goal of 2003 for implementation.

Rules in effect prior to the adaptation of LROPS, were called ETOPS, for Extended Twin Operations, and related to twin-engine aircraft operating over areas with few airports. These FAA and JAA rules require such aircraft, in an emergency, to land at 'the nearest available diversion airport'. If that airport is closed, the pilot is required to fly on to the next closest diversion airport and such diversions are not to exceed 180 minutes in flying duration. The reality of such remote airfields, however, is that they are often ill equipped to cope with an aircraft in an emergency situation, having poor-quality, unimproved runways and few or inadequate facilities for accommodating and feeding passengers and providing them with medical care and supplies—all critical requirements, especially in poor weather conditions. In some areas, there simply are no airports. Under the new LROPS concepts, the flight crew in an emergency situation, is charged with selecting the safest and most appropriate diversionary airport to land at, and not nec-

essarily the nearest one. This liberalized approach is intended to improve the safety of passengers and crews wherever they fly. LROPS regulations are meant to apply to all flights having diversion times of three hours or more, regardless of the aircraft type or its number of engines and to all flights over designated 'extreme regions.'

Airbus has been developing an On-Board Oxygen Generation System for use under LROPS, especially for operations on routes crossing the Himalayas. With such a system, a depressurized aircraft may be flown at an altitude higher than 10,000 feet, requiring lower fuel reserves. Also under development is a long-range communication system known as Aircraft Dependent Surveillance (ADS), using global positioning satellites and radio links to give pilots more reliable communications with air traffic controllers in remote and inhospitable areas. A340 and A380 aircraft will have LROPS certification with options of up to eight hours of diversion time. Special LROPS design packages are available to airline customers who want to fly such routes with A340s or A380s. These aircraft will then be able to operate over new polar routes through Russia, from Asia to and from Europe and the USA.

Airbus describes the A380 as the 'flagship of the 21st century' and 'the most advanced, spacious and efficient airliner ever conceived.' One of its main goals with the new giant plane is to make it the most pleasurable flying experience possible, regardless of a traveller's size or class of ticket. The A380 is scheduled to enter airline service in 2006.

Specifications: Airbus A380-800

Engines: Four Rolls-Royce Trent RB-967 turbofans or four Engine Alliance GP-7267 turbofans, both rated at 70,000 lb thrust each
Maximum speed: 595 mph at 35,000 ft
Cruise speed: 560 mph at 35,000 ft
Service ceiling: 43,000 ft
Normal range: 7,800 nautical miles with 555 passengers
Weight: empty, 606,000 lb, maximum take-off 1,190,495 lb
Wingspan: 261 ft 10 in
Length: 239 ft 6 in
Height: 79 ft 1 ins
Wing area: 8,920 sq ft

below: The inventor, Sir Hiram Maxim and his huge flying machine, tested in 1894. It weighed 3.5 tons and developed 360 hp.

31

'To travel hopefully is a better thing than to arrive, and the true success is to labour.'
— from *El Dorado* by Robert Louis Stevenson

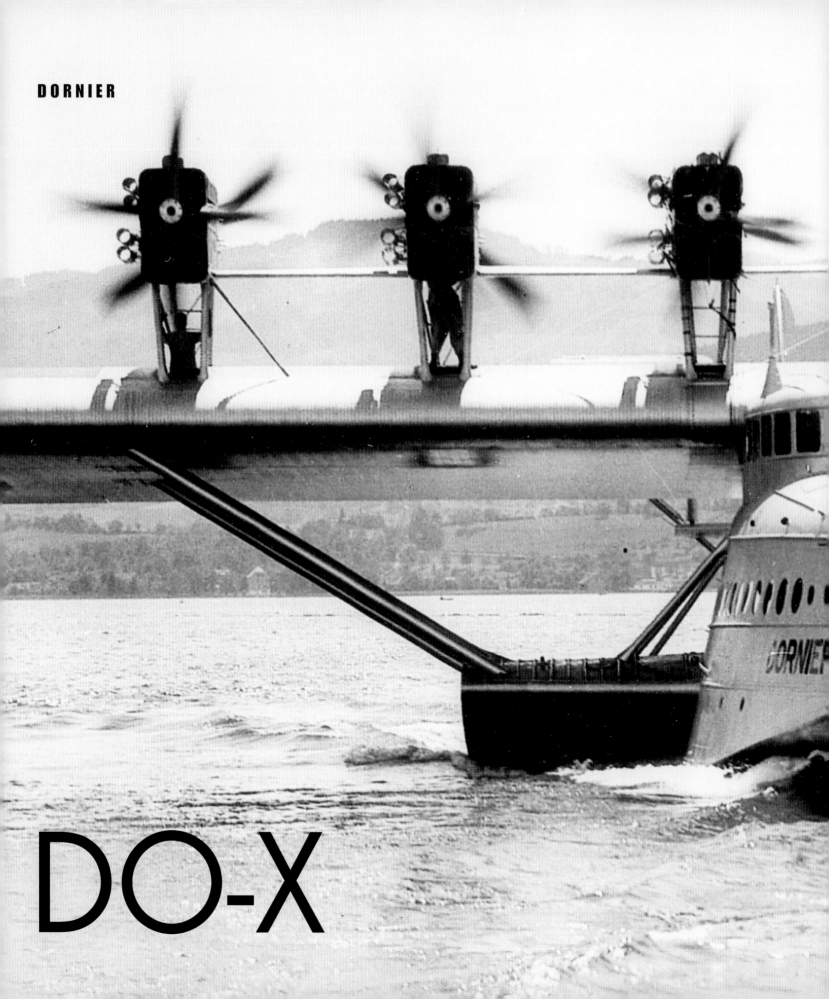

DORNIER

DO-X

overleaf: The Dornier DO-X flying-boat taxiing on Lake Constance in 1929; top right: On the factory ramp at Lake Constance; bottom right: The first flight, 12 July 1929.

DORNIER

'I have recently been all round the world and have formed a very poor opinion of it.'
—Thomas Beecham

Even before the end of the First World War, the German aircraft designer Dr Claudius Dornier was thinking seriously about building a large, all-metal flying-boat. In 1922 his first effort, the twin-engined monoplane flying-boat called the *Wal* (whale) flew for the first time. The engines of this pioneering aircraft were mounted in a single nacelle on top of the wing in a tractor-pusher format. The design led to improved variants which continued in production until 1936.

Claudius Dornier was born in Kempten, Germany, on 14 May 1884. His early fascination with engineering and metal construction led to his education at the Munich Institute of Technology, where he was well prepared for the career he would enjoy in the design and construction of advanced aircraft. Following a short apprenticeship with the Graf Zeppelin Company, where he failed to persuade officials to expand their business to include aeroplane manufacture, Dornier left Zeppelin and, with his brother, formed Dornier Metallbauten GmbH, to design and build all-metal flying-boats. In 1919 they began their research on his dream project.

From the article *When Boats Had Wings*, by Wesley S. Griswold, first published in the June 1963 issue of *Popular Science* magazine: 'Fifty thousand people crammed New York's Battery Park. They peered down the busy harbor through a haze of August heat. Suddenly, a few minutes past noon, they spotted what they had been eagerly expecting. Out of the seaward murk emerged the biggest, noisiest airplane that anybody there had ever seen or heard. The perspiring crowd burst into wild shouts and cheers. Bands struck up *Die Wacht am Rhein* and *Deutschland über Alles*. Tugboat and ferry captains tied down their whistles.

'This raucous welcome, on August 27th, 1931, was for the German Republic's monstrous, 12-engined Do-X. It was the world's largest flying-boat. It was also, up to that time, the biggest heavier-than-air aircraft ever built. Escorting planes looked like gnats beside it, an observer wrote. Its great wing, with six pairs of engines perched back to back in a row along the top, stretched nearly 158 feet. Its three-decker hull, made of duralumin braced with steel girders, was 131 feet long. Loaded to capacity, it weighed 52 tons.

'The throbbing, silvery Do-X slowly settled to a sedate landing off the Battery. Seventy-two passengers and crewmen—an astonishing number for the time—climbed out. Their stories were conflicting. Passengers (some had just been dancing to accordion music over the ocean) said they'd had great fun. But they had shared only the easiest part of a long, troubled journey. The crew, which had nursed the flying-boat all the way from its home berth on Lake Constance, were far less enthusiastic. They had plenty of reasons to be sour. The Do-X, said to be capable of crossing the Atlantic in 40 hours, had taken nearly 10 months for its first trip.'

It was one of the most impressive aircraft ever built. Its construction began in 1927 and it first flew in 1929. It was Dornier's spectacular attempt to design and build a large, trans-oceanic passenger aeroplane. With twelve Siemens-Jupiter engines of 525 hp each, a 157-foot wingspan, a length of 131 feet, a height of 33 feet and weighing up to 61 tons fully loaded, the Dornier Do-X was by far the largest aeroplane in the world and caused a sensation wherever she went.

Like other aerial giants considered in this book, the Do-X was ahead of her time. She was designed with a series of well-furnished luxury compartments to transport forty passengers in great comfort at 110 mph. Full-course meals were cooked on board in an all-electric galley. Drinks were served from a fully stocked bar and both washrooms were equipped with showerbaths. The ship-like cockpit, a control room really, was called the pilot house, and except for dead astern, the view from it was almost unobstructed. The controls and instrumentation were minimal, with just two throttles, each controlling an entire bank of six engines and a panel of lights to indicate which engines were running and which were not. The chief engineer and his assistants monitored their instruments and were responsible for other controls in the motor control room behind the pilot house. From there, mechanics could clamber out into the thick, fabric-covered wing during flight and crawl along a passageway to the engine pylons. An accessory unit at the rear of each engine could be worked on in flight, but the

In 1929 she was the largest aeroplane in the world and she generated excitement wherever she went. On 20 October of that year, the DO-X took to the air with 169 passengers, crew and stowaways on board for a one-hour flight over the Bodensee.

The 1920s was an era of post-war devil-may-care living and free spending for many. The '20s and '30s were the zenith of the flying-boat era and many examples plied the popular passenger routes.

engines themselves were not accessible in flight.

The fuselage was composed of three decks with the upper deck housing the pilot house, the navigation room, the flight engineer's compartment, a radio office and the captain's cabin. The spacious wood-panelled passenger compartments were located on the second deck, with seating and sleeping accommodation, a bar, smoking room and a writing room. Much of the fuel, cargo and other stores were carried on the lower deck.

Under construction for nineteen months, the Do-X made her first public appearance at the Dornier facility in Altenrhein, Switzerland, on 12 July 1929. She slipped into the waters of Lake Constance with the bright morning sun reflecting gloriously from her aluminium fuselage. Technicians tended her for the next hour as taxi-testing on the lake continued. Then at 9 a.m. came what Claudius Dornier later referred to as 'one of the biggest moments of my life.' His chief pilot, Richard Wagner, applied the full power of the twelve engines, took the flying-boat across the water at near take-off speed, found 'the step' and lifted it from the surface of the lake. The journalists, photographers, officials and guests were ecstatic. One local paper reported, 'Do-X, the hotel ship. A miracle of German technology. A tremendous novelty in aviation history. This is no longer a plane, but a ship, a real ship, which is able to lift out of the water and will fly through the air. If you look at it, this giant, incomparably bold work, visions of reality, which were fiction only three years ago.'

On a foggy morning in October, before the lavish interior of the Do-X had been installed, 149 employees of Dornier and members of the press, along with ten crew members and several stowaways, boarded the aircraft, sat in light wicker chairs and awaited the take-off, which took less than a minute. In a brief 53-minute flight over Lindau and Friedrichshafen, the plane broke the unofficial record for carrying passengers, a record that then stood until 1949.

As the testing phase progressed, Wagner reported that the big flying-boat performed well and was an easy plane to fly, even though it was not equipped with any servo motors or mechanical control assists. With a light load, she could get off the lake surface in 30 seconds or less, but when fully loaded, she was

once run along at full power for twelve minutes without becoming airborne. Despite her great array of engines and the 6,300 hp they supplied, some of that power was wasted in an effort to overcome the substantial drag created by the engines and their mountings on the top of the wing, which also reduced the lift efficiency of the wing. A further power-loss problem occurred as the rear row of fixed-pitch wooden propellers could not achieve full thrust in the turbulence created by the propellers of the front row. Testing of the aircraft revealed a number of relatively minor problems, which were readily corrected by Dornier engineers. After seventy-one test flights, the Do-X was declared fully tested by the German Aviation Test Centre and was turned over to the commissioning authority, the German Reich, in February 1930.

During the testing phase, it was found that the Siemens-Jupiter engines delivered declining performance when run continuously for long periods. In the tests, the problem was dealt with by compensating for the power loss with higher revs, but this led to overheating which could not be corrected. As the German government insisted on using only German-built engines, no solution was available until the German Navy, which had funded trials of the flying-boat for possible long-range reconnaissance and torpedo-bomber functions, announced that it was no longer interested in the plane. Thereafter, the company was able to borrow the Do-X from the Reichs Ministry of Transport, which was paying the development costs of the project, and Dornier decided to replace the problematic powerplants with American Curtiss-Conqueror engines of 660 hp each, on loan from the Curtiss company. These new engines would provide the added power and safety factors the aircraft needed, although their added weight meant that most performance characteristics remained unchanged. The top speed, though, was now 150 mph.

Following further alterations, and the fitting out of her luxurious interior, the flying-boat now designated Do-XIa, flew with her newly increased power on 4 August 1930. In an attempt to garner maximum publicity for 'the magnificent achievement of the Reich', the plane was flown from Lake Constance, under the command of former Navy pilot Friedrich Christiansen, to

IMPERIAL AIRWAYS EMPIRE FLYING-BOAT "CALEDONIA"

DEUTSCHE LUFT HANSA: DORNIER DO. 18 FLYING-BOAT

1930 NATIONAL AIR RACES 10TH ANNIVERSARY

THRILL FOR THE NATION!

CURTISS-REYNOLDS AIRPORT --- CHICAGO

PAN AMERICAN AIRWAYS: MAIN AISLE, "CLIPPER" CLASS FLYING-BOAT

PAN AMERICAN AIRWAYS: GLENN MARTIN 130 FLYING-BOAT "CHINA CLIPPER"

AIR FRANCE: LIORE-ET-OLIVIER H. 24-2

IMPERIAL AIRWAYS FLYING-BOAT "SATYRUS"

S.A. NAVIGAZIONE AE... GENOVA

The AIR TRAVELER in CUBA

HAVANA
PINAR del RIO
VARADERO
ISLE of PINES
CIENFUEGOS
SANTA CLARA
CAMAGUEY
MANZANILLO
SANTIAGO

right: A wonderful photo of the DO-X, made on the Ijselmeer, The Netherlands, in the mid-1930s by the grandfather of photographer Wouter Sikkema.

'It is not worthwhile to go round the world to count the cats in Zanzibar.'
– Henry David Thoreau

Amsterdam and then on to Calshot, England, Bordeaux, France, Santander and La Coruna, Spain and Lisbon, Portugal. Hundreds of people came out to see the Do-X, whose fame was rapidly growing as members of the press, invited by Dornier, spread the word about the fabulous flying-boat. However, the show ground to a halt in Lisbon, when an accidental fire broke out causing damage to the left wing. Repairs kept the plane in the Portuguese port until the end of January 1931. The Do-X left Lisbon for South America, via Africa, on 31 January.

Trouble struck again on 3 February, when the plane hit a heavy swell during her take-off run from Las Palmas, suffering severe wing damage that laid her up there for three months. Bad weather then stranded the plane at Bolama, West Africa, until 30 May, when the Atlantic leg of her journey could be undertaken. On 5 June she arrived to considerable fanfare at Natal, Brazil, and in the next two months called on Trinidad, Puerto Rico and Cuba, before arriving in Miami on 22 August. Dornier's goal, and the final destination for the flying-boat in the epic flight, was New York harbour where she landed on 27 August after brief stops at Charleston and Norfolk. US President Herbert Hoover greeted the Dornier crew at New York in a jubilant welcome. But even in this triumphant accomplishment, trouble loomed for the Dornier as the world economic collapse, spurred by the 'Wall Street Crash' shortly after the Do-X came to town, threatened the company with financial ruin. Dornier could not afford the heavy costs involved in continuing the journey of the Do-X. No financial angels appeared to save the day for the plane and her maker, and plans were made to lay her up in storage in the United States when the Reichs Ministry of Finance intervened to provide an additional loan to Dornier to cover the continuing operating costs of the plane. Following an eight-month stay in a New York dry dock, the big flying boat left the city on 19 May 1932 and, after a 22-month odyssey, arrived in Berlin, landing on the Müggelsee on 24 May to the delight of 200,000 cheering Germans who had come out to see her.

The marvellous Dornier flying boat had gained wide recognition and fame in her lengthy tour, but no sales. Two additional examples of the Do-X had been built, the X-2 and X-3, and were sold to the Italian government, whose military used them briefly for

right: Another fine Sikkema image of the DO-X on the Ijselmeer. The large flying boat was equipped to carry passengers in the utmost comfort and luxury. The hull contained three decks, with sleeping quarters, bathrooms, writing rooms, a bar, a kitchen and a dining salon sixty feet long; below: Even more famous in the late 1920s than the big Dornier was the pioneering American aviator Charles Lindbergh, whose record solo flight from New York to Paris in 1927 fascinated the entire world.

prestige flights, scrapping them in 1934.

Impressive achievement as the aeroplane was, its great weight, limited payload capacity and poor fuel economy (its engines used 400 gallons of aviation spirit an hour) destined it never to have the successful transatlantic operation that many had hoped for it. Indeed, Claudius Dornier always maintained that he had meant the plane to only be experimental and not for regular commercial service.

In an attempt to recoup some of the vast investment in the Do-X, the plane was sent on a five-month tour of Germany in June, during which fares were charged for pleasure flights. Thereafter she remained at Altenrhein until 19 April 1933, when she embarked on another tour, this time around Europe, but major damage to the tail control surfaces resulted from a bad landing on the Danube, curtailing the tour. The flying-boat then came into the possession of the Reichs Aviation Ministry in October 1934 and the following May it became part of the German Aviation Collection in Berlin, and was the focal point of the museum in its entrance hall. During the Allied bombing campaign against Germany in the Second World War, a direct hit on the Museum by an RAF aerial mine destroyed the Do-X, one of the most extraordinary aircraft in history. Claudius Dornier designed and built two important twin-engined bombers for the Luftwaffe in the war, the Do-17 and the Do-217, but with the war came the end of his company, and in 1947, he moved to Switzerland, where he worked as an aeronautical engineering consultant until his death in 1969.

From an article in *Aircraft Engineering*, December 1929, here are comments by Claudius Dornier about the design of his Do-X flying-boat: 'The leading thought in the design of the Do-X was that, to lead to the desired goal, only that which had been technically proved could be used. Every kind of "experimenting" was ruled out from the beginning. There is no doubt that through this precaution creative work was, to a certain extent, handicapped. The fact, however, that from the commencement of the tests of the flying-boat, up to their completion, only about one hundred working hours were occupied in alterations, proves, in conjunction with the results achieved, that the

below: DO-X crewmen row
out to their aircraft on Lake
Constance.

plan adopted was correct.

'The preliminary work towards the building of the new flying-boat goes back to the year 1924.

'That the aeroplane must be a boat was obvious from the beginning. Not so simple was the question, monoplane or biplane, but here, also, comparatively quickly came the decision for the monoplane. The first plan drawing bears the date September 27, 1924. A so-called self-stabilizing boat was first thought of, which on account of its great breadth would need no further lateral support. It would take too long here to discuss the manifold variations which were worked through before we arrived at the final plan, dated June 21, 1926. I should like to remark that in these design plans considerable use was made of models. Both the originally planned 6-metre-wide boats, as well as the hull which afterwards came into use, were first mocked up in full size, with complete steering gear, etc., in wood.

'On December 22, 1926, work was begun in the constructional departments. In the course of the work, with the exception of an alteration of the outline of the wing stump—about which I shall speak later—there were very few deviations from the plan.

'The project as well as the working out of the plans, was kept secret for a long time. The very first design of the year 1924 had seven engines of 4,200 total hp but we finally arrived at twelve engines with, originally, a total of about 5,800 hp. Owing to later improvements in these engines we now have about 6,300 hp available.

'The final decision to have twelve engines is due in the main to the fact that units of 800/1,000 hp, which would have been necessary, cannot be reckoned as safe a proposition as engines of about 500 hp. One of the most difficult decisions we had to make was the choice and arrangement of the engines. The questions, water-cooled or air-cooled, super-imposed, or built into the wings or into the hull itself, occupied us for two years. That the decision finally arrived at was for the arrangement in use is due to the fact that this solution seemed to me then, and still does today under the given conditions, the best possible compromise.

'The deciding factor for the choice of air-cooled engines for the first flying-boat was the fact that with these, compared with water-cooled engines, a weight saving of over 3,000 kg (6,600 lb.) was possible.

'The tandem arrangement of the engines was practically forced on to us owing to their large number. This arrangement has been familiar to us with all its pros and cons for more than ten years now. As soon as one is compelled to use a large number of engines, this is the simplest, lightest, and safest method of mounting them, and is, therefore, coming more and more into use. One can almost say that the tandem arrangement reduces the number of units by half, in that they work practically as a 'double engine.' A tandem unit of two, each with nine cylinders, is very little more complicated than a single engine of eighteen cylinders and it is considerably more reliable.

'One sees that small angles of attack in the auxiliary wing connecting the engines cause a slight lessening of resistance. To this small lessening of resistance is added, at larger angles of attack, a not unnoticeable increase of lift. The ideal can, naturally, never be achieved practically. The engines, whether in wing or in hull, must be cool. This, if one disregards pure superficial cooling—which can only be used in the case of racing machines—costs power, and therefore loss of speed. If one arranges the propellers free, one must have in the case of engines lying in the interior

of the plane, heavy driving gear, easily liable to break down, and, in addition, because of their bearings, causing added resistance.

'As a result of earlier experiments we could not take the responsibility of complications of this kind. The same remark applies to the driving of one screw through two or more engines. In the latter case the necessarily large propeller diameter makes it, in addition, almost impossible to arrange the propellers in such a fashion that they are sufficiently protected against spray. In the plan in question, it showed in particular that especial difficulties would arise in satisfactorily arranging the screw surfaces for such enormous power as 6,000 hp.

'That the arrangement of the screws above the wing has considerably increased the lift is now generally acknowledged. We have particularly gone into the possibility of the use of pressure propellers running on the wing edge driven by engines in the wings, but have been forced to the conclusion that the long shafting, together with the heavy bearings necessary for this, would necessitate added weight, which would more than counteract any possible gain considered purely from an aerodynamic viewpoint.

"In the beginning I pointed out that there was no possible doubt that the first flying-ship must be a boat, and in particular, a boat with a central hull. At first we tried to obtain the necessary stability without the assistance of auxiliary displacements. It was found, however, that this was impossible with the measurements which came into question, without including many serious disadvantages. One was, therefore, forced to revert to the well-tried wing stump. The underwater formation, as far as this had any influence on starting, was very little altered from that used on former boats. The central step is retained. Behind this the bottom is horizontal to the line of flight, and continues forward in the form of a slight 'V.' The parts of the hull arranged on the side of the step are built slightly concave. The bows, especially in the portions which, when starting in still water are above the water line, are sharply wedge shaped. The wing stumps, at the point where they come through the side of the hull, are well-rounded towards the line of flight. This new

arrangement of the wing stumps was not allowed for in the original plan: it has static and hydrodynamic advantages. The depth of the stumps is considerably greater at the root, which allows for much stronger arrangement of the framework. When starting, with the arched shape, the water is thrown outward, whereas in the old design it was forced into an angle between the under part of the stump and the side walls of the hull.

'Of particular interest in the design of the flying ship Do-X is the division, used for the first time in aeroplanes, into three separate decks. The upper deck, the so-called 'command deck', contains pilot's cabin, captain's cabin, control cabin, and cabins for wireless and auxiliary engines. The second deck is intended entirely for passengers. The lower deck contains fuel, supplies, freight, and luggage.

'A great part of the researches which the design required was taken up by questions of a static nature. It was decided not to have cantilever wings, in order that the lightest possible wing surface could be obtained.

'The wing has been designed as a three-sparred triple-strutted structure. This system, used for the first time in the Do-X, gives, because of its peculiar compound action, exceptional rigidity and torsional strength. It offers the further advantage that damage to any single strut or support does not dangerously influence the structure taken as a whole.

'The manufacture of the templates for the building of the spars took up a great deal of time. The portion of the hull from the rear step to the stern was constructed entirely separately from the main hull. The tail-carrier which forms, as it were, the 'spine' for the whole ship, was built up on an iron former. The auxiliary wing complete with engines, engine cabins and bearers, as well as all necessary transmission for the running of the engines, was also made separately, and later mounted on the wings as a complete unit.

'The final erection, that is to say, the assembly, of the wings, hull, controls, and power plant, including the fitting of the supply pipes, took sixty days.

'The trials began on the early morning of July 12, 1929. First, somewhat lengthy rolling tests were carried out on the water. When it was tried to run the boat all out on the step she lifted, although this was not

below: Another important aeronautical achievement of the late 1920s was the gigantic Graf Zeppelin, shown here entering her hangar at Friedrichshafen, Germany. The era of the giant dirigible came to an end in 1937 when another German airship, the Hindenburg, was destroyed in a fire on landing at Lakehurst, New Jersey, having replaced the Graf Zeppelin on the North Atlantic run the previous year.

intended. After this unintentional start, very short jumps were carried out. On the next day the first real flight was undertaken. Up to the present a total of fifty-four flights have been undertaken.

'Even the very first flight proved that the oil temperature was much higher than was permissible. Also the temperature of several cylinders of the rear engines was too high. We succeeded in a comparatively short time in bringing down the oil temperature to required limits, but it took a large number of flights to achieve the same results in the case of the cylinder temperatures. A particular difficulty was the paucity of really reliable temperature-indicating instruments. It was very fortunate that, out of consideration for the rear engines, at first only comparatively short flights could be undertaken, during which the front engines had to be well throttled down.

'Naturally, we endeavoured to learn as much as possible during each flight. The stresses in the more important parts of the wings were measured by means of tensiometers: pressure conditions in the hull and in the wings were carefully examined. The streamlining of the cabins and the auxiliary wing was measured by means of Pitot tubes. The streamlining of the main wings was tested; bends in the spars were measured optically. The stabilizing properties of the ship were very carefully tested, and a succession of 'trimming' tests were also undertaken.

'Starting is surprisingly good. Water behaviour during this, excellent. The ship, even with heavy loads, begins to rise in a few seconds. Stability on the water fulfils all expectations; manoeuvring is simple. Even in the first test the ship was brought to the buoy under its own power. Visibility conditions are excellent. There are no difficulties during landing.

'The power plant is free from vibration. The time occupied in getting all twelve engines into operation is, on an average, four to five minutes (best time taken: three minutes).

'Flying properties are normal. The ship can be flown by average pilots. The rudders are easy running and effective. It was entirely unnecessary to mount servo controls to work the rudders. The elevator was at first over-compensated. Control is normally easy, but requires too much effort when large rudder alterations are necessary. The compensation and diameters

of the hand wheels were, therefore, increased. Centralization of engine controls and total separation from the pilot entirely justified itself. The measured stresses and strains of the various components on an average agreed with the calculated figures.

'According to contract arrangements made in 1927, a load of twenty tons was guaranteed. This means, a taking-off weight of forty-seven tons. For the fulfilment of these conditions on Lake Constance, with no wind, the ship needed sixty-five seconds. Converted to sea level, this start would take fifty-five seconds. The contracted highest speed of the flying ship, with a tolerance of five percent, was not to be less than 124 mph. With uncowled engines at a height of 1,370 feet, 131 mph was measured. There is no doubt that with still further improved cowling of the engines the speed can be further increased. All the flights carried out up to the present have been done with the same set of wooden propellers. Here again, with the use of different screws, and especially of metal propellers, a further increase in speed should be possible. When the engines are throttled down to 1,850 rpm, the cruising speed is 108 mph.

'The longest possible distance which can be made in unbroken flight is about 2,237 miles. For real long distance flights the ship would have to be fitted with even more economical engines. The flight limits of the ship in its present form, without intermediate landings for fuel replenishing, and under favourable meteorological conditions, can be set somewhere about 1,367 miles for all practical purposes.'

Specifications: Dornier Do-X

Engines: Twelve Curtiss-Conqueror water-cooled engines rated at 660 hp each
Maximum speed: 150 mph
Cruising speed: 122 mph
Service ceiling: 4,100 ft
Normal range: 1,367 miles
Weight empty: 72,036 lb, Gross: 123,459 lb
Wingspan: 157 ft 6 in
Length: 131 ft 4 in
Height: 33 ft 1 in
Wing area: 4,844 sq ft

The DO-X became a part of the great German Aviation Collection, Berlin, in 1936. In World War II a direct hit on the museum by an RAF bomb destroyed the once-proud flying-boat.

'I have nothing to declare except my genius.'
– Oscar Wilde

MARTIN

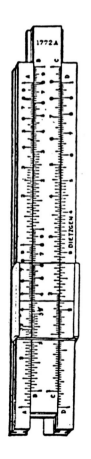

Before the Mars there was the XPBM2M-1, an experimental flying-boat whose development began in 1935 when the US Navy expressed interest in having a long-range, high-altitude patrol bomber. The Navy proposed that the Glenn L. Martin Company build the plane. Martin was eager to accept the challenge and started preliminary research on the project immediately. The company was awarded a Navy contract for a single prototype late in 1938, and the aeroplane was rolled out at the Martin Middle River, Maryland, plant in September 1941. They called her the 'Old Lady' and she was big, with a 200-foot wingspan, a length of 117 feet and an empty weight of 75,573 lb.

Glenn Martin himself drove in the first rivet when they laid the keel for the XPBM2M-1, which some referred to as the 'flying dreadnought', with its multiple gun turrets and ability to fly great distances carrying large bomb loads. Martin had constructed his first aeroplane in 1909 and by 1920 was prominent among the great aircraft manufacturers of America. The first bomber he built appeared too late to serve in the First World War, but Colonel Billy Mitchell later used it to demonstrate the capability of strategic air power. Martin designed and built a series of flying-boats, including the 'clippers' that made him famous and transoceanic commercial air travel a reality. He optimistically stated that the Mars, which would evolve from the XPBM2M-1, 'could capture an enemy island or totally destroy a rail centre or shipyard. A squadron of them could devastate Tokyo in one trip.'

When they launched the XPBM2M-1 at Dark Head Creek, Maryland, on 5 November 1941, she was launched stern first, and like a dreadnought, a bottle of champagne was broken over her bow. Four Wright 18-cylinder R-3350-18 Duplex Cyclone radial engines had been fitted, rated at 2,000 hp each and they drove 17-foot Schwarz wooden propellers. Actually, the flying-boat was unarmed but had been built with provision for nose and tail turrets as well as a retractable top turret and flexible machine-gun positions on both sides of the rear hull. All of the gun positions were intended to mount 0.30 calibre Brownings. The fuselage bombbay had doors in the wing roots and its racks could each hold five 1,000 lb bombs. Her interior layout preserved the military

class system by accommodating the officers and enlisted men with separate berthing, wash rooms and mess rooms. By the time of her first flight on 23 June 1942, she had been re-engined with uprated Duplex Cyclones of 2,200 hp each which drove three-blade 16 ft 6 in Hamilton Standard propellers, later replaced by four-blade 16 ft 8 in Curtiss Electric propellers with controllable pitch and full-feathering.

During a taxi test in Middle River on 5 December, two days before the Japanese attack on Pearl Harbor, one of the big laminated-wooden propellers threw a blade, causing an engine fire. The plane had to be towed close to the shore before the blaze could be contained. The engine burned off its mount and fell into the water. The damage to the nacelle and wing was substantial and led to a six-month repair period in which the aeroplane was re-engined. In that time, the Pearl Harbor attack and the sinkings of many supply ships in the Atlantic by German submarines, had led to a major reconsideration of the new plane's role. The Navy now felt that a greater need existed for a giant cargo flying-boat to overcome the U-boat menace.

It was then that the American industrialist Henry Kaiser suggested that he could rapidly produce hundreds of Mars aircraft in his various shipyards, to cope quickly with the long-distance cargo transport need. Glenn Martin agreed that producing the Mars in large numbers would certainly be cost effective, and more so than Kaiser's Liberty ships, but he had no interest in a partnership with Kaiser, or any other manufacturer, in the construction of his Mars. Kaiser then turned to Howard Hughes (see the chapter on the Hughes HK-1) to join him in the design and development of what would become the aeroplane popularly known as the Spruce Goose, the largest flying-boat ever built.

Martin had other plans. They included pushing for government support to build a much larger and more capable flying-boat based on his own 1937 design, a six-engined, 250,000-pounder. But the Navy redesignated the Old Lady a transport, the XPB2M-1R, and Martin workers stripped her turrets, armour plating and bombing gear and began to make a cargo plane of her.

A part of the conversion process to cargo carrier required reinforcing the decking to take far greater loads, as well as planning for cargo loading hatches and the related equipment. Following her conversion to the cargo role, the Old Lady was assigned to Air Transport Squadron Eight (VR-8) at Patuxent River, Maryland, in November 1943. Her career there began with a 28-hour non-stop flight from Patuxent to Natal, Brazil, hauling a 13,000 lb cargo a distance of 4,375 miles, and surpassing the existing record for a seaplane. She was transferred in January 1944 to VR-2 at the Alameda Naval Air Station near San Francisco, where she served until March 1945, making seventy-eight round trips to Honolulu and out to the western Pacific. During the Iwo Jima campaign, she delivered 120 tons of whole blood to the American forces there in a single month. In her service with the Navy, she delivered more than three million pounds of cargo before being retired and returned to the Martin

Company, which overhauled her and continued to use her for training purposes. The company organized a six-week training school in Baltimore to instruct pilots, mechanics and radiomen on the Mars.

So happy was the Navy with the Old Lady, they ordered twenty purpose-built flying boat transports based on her, and designated JRM-1 Mars. The *Hawaii* Mars was completed in June 1945, and had the same wing and float structure as the Old Lady, but the twin tail of the Old Lady had been replaced with a single vertical fin. The fuselage had been extended by three feet and large new cargo doors with electric hoists had been installed under the wings, with smaller cargo doors positioned further aft. There were fewer internal bulkheads. Once again, the engines had been uprated, this time to R-3350-8s of 2,400 hp each. The maximum take-off weight had increased to

below: This photo of the Caroline Mars is believed to have been made at Alameda, California. The Mars aircraft were the largest active-duty flying-boats ever built.

JRM-1 MARS

Glenn Martin had visualized his massive Mars flying boats becoming civilian airliners in the post-war years. It was not to be. The surviving planes, the Philippine, Marianas, Hawaii and Caroline Mars would ultimately become water-bombers, fighting fires for Forest Industries Flying Tankers Limited, Sproat Lake, Vancouver Island, British Columbia. Today only the Hawaii and Philippine Mars remain but they both continue to serve admirably.

148,500 lb. The carrying capacity of the plane was nearly sixteen tons and it could be configured to carry either 133 fully equipped troops or eighty-four litters in a medical evacuation mode, as well as twenty-five ambulatory passengers in reclining seats fore and aft. This first Mars aircraft was involved in a flight-test accident in Chesapeake Bay on 5 August 1945 and was damaged beyond repair. Within days, the war was over and the Navy's Mars order was cut back to just five aeroplanes, all of which were named after Pacific island groups. They were the *Marshall* Mars, the *Philippine* Mars, the *Marianas* Mars, a second *Hawaii* Mars, and a much-improved JRM-2 model, the *Caroline* Mars.

 The new JRM-1s were equipped with a hydraulic boost system for power-assisted controls, easing the workload of the pilots. Martin had designed the plane with a roomy, pressurized flight deck, adding to the comfort of the crews who flew it. The cockpit had complete sets of flight instruments for both pilots, along with tachometers and manifold pressure gauges, while other engine instruments and controls were at the flight engineer's station. On cargo flights the Mars required a crew of seven, which grew to eleven for passenger flights: an aeroplane commander, a first pilot, a second pilot, two navigators, two flight engineers, two radiomen and two flight attendants.

 On take-off, the procedure called for the pilot to control the throttles until fifty inches of manifold pressure was achieved. At that point the flight engineer took control of the throttles. When the aircraft lifted off the sea surface the pilot would call for cruise climb power and when the plane reached the assigned altitude for the mission, he would call for cruise power. The flight engineer was responsible for all power-setting changes in flight, cowl-flap settings, fuel transferring and monitoring of fuel consumption and engine readings. Once each hour he was required to climb into the wings and walk the catwalk to each of the four engines where he would tabulate readings from instruments located just behind the engines. During the landing, the pilot would again take control of the throttles.

 The Martin-trained crews and all of the Mars aircraft (except the *Caroline* Mars) had been transferred to VR-2 at Alameda by the end of June 1946. So effective

was the training of the aviation mechanics who had attended the Martin school, that from the beginning of the Mars missions across the Pacific, those aviation mechanics were able to replace flight engineers on the planes.

 Captain Albert Winchell, US Navy (Retd) had a unique experience with the JRM Mars aircraft, serving with VR-2 as both a navigator and pilot of the big flying-boats, as well as being what in modern terminology is a loadmaster, managing the loading of cargo, passengers and mail. He recalled his time in the JRM: 'It was a normal, stable aeroplane, but heavy on the controls, despite the seventy-five percent booster system. It was a lot different from the twin-engine, open cockpit flying-boat I had last flown during 1937/8. A plane commander designation from one squadron was never transferrable. A newly assigned pilot would start out as a co-pilot or second pilot, depending on his background and experience. After passing the required check rides and qualifying as a first navigator, the road was open to a Plane Commander designation. However, all pilots had to become qualified as first-navigators. Training was conducted in the squadron, both on the line and in a PBM Mariner that we used for local flights.' Of a normal mission between Alameda and Honolulu Winchell commented, 'We usually cruised at 9,000 or 10,000 feet with an average speed of 156 mph. Each engine used about fifty gallons of fuel per hour at cruise power.' And as a Mars navigator, 'I had to make sure that all charts and weather maps, two bubble octants, chronometer and HO manual were aboard before take-off. The Mars had a large navigation table located behind the plane commander's seat, and it would hold the chart for the entire trip. A radio and barometric altimeter was available, as well as a LORAN set, but I didn't place much faith in it. I'd take readings on the barometric and radio altimeters. After reading the difference between them I used a formula to determine the amount of left–right drift from our heading. Celestial was the primary type of navigation. We had to plot a fix and send a position report every hour. Our nav charts and math computations had to be turned in after every flight.'

 The Naval Air Transport Service (NATS) was formed in December 1941. In the Pacific theatre of the

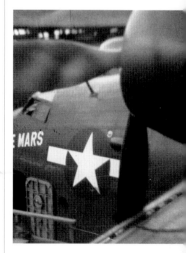

left: The Hawaii Mars passes near San Francisco's Golden Gate bridge; far left: A detail of the Marianas Mars at NAS Alameda, California; bottom left: The XPB2M-1R, known as the 'Old Lady', flying over San Francisco on 17 October 1944; bottom: The Philippine Mars at Alameda.

below: Another important wartime product of the Martin Company, the B-26 Marauder medium bomber.

Second World War, their supply lines extended right into the combat areas. Their prime objective was the quick delivery of critically needed supplies, materials and personnel. In some situations they air-dropped supplies to the combat groups. For their early operations they borrowed personnel and facilities from the commercial airlines and called up reserve officers with airline experience. Later in the war, the Navy developed a training programme to provide the crews that NATS required, but through the whole of the war, many of their routes were also flown by contract airlines. In 1943 NATS operated more than a hundred aircraft, flying more than 50,000 miles of routes. On their return flights to the USA they carried thousands of pounds of critical war materials such as mica and natural rubber, and they returned hundreds of sick and wounded servicemen. Using the large flying-boats, they were able to land alongside ships at sea to deliver vitally needed spare parts and pick up wounded men and fly them to the nearest medical facility. They were particularly useful in delivering supplies to the small atolls in the South Pacific where landing strips could not be built. In a reconnaissance role, they looked for submarines and for survivors of ship sinkings. The giant Mars boats were certainly fully utilized.

When a Mars logged 5,000 flying hours, it underwent a comprehensive overhaul, with ailerons, rudder, flaps, elevators, wingtips and beaching gear being dismantled, cleaned, resurfaced and reinstalled. The fuselage was vapour-blasted with grit and water to remove all the paint and corrosion. The engines and propellers were serviced and the aeroplane was then given a new coat of Navy blue paint. Usually within sixty days, the aircraft was back on operations.

Here is an excerpt from *The Martian*, the history of Air Transport Squadron Two, Naval Air Station, Alameda, California: 'Born in the early days of World War Two, and nurtured by the ever increasing demand for logistical support for our far-flung tactical operations, the Naval Air Transport Service grew in the course of three years from a single signature to a mighty machine that spanned oceans and continents, carrying the sinews of war to our embattled forces everywhere.

'Air Transport Squadron Two was the second of the transport squadrons to be commissioned. In April, 1942, less than a month after VR-1 had set up operations in Norfolk, Virginia, VR-2 was commissioned at Alameda, California, under the command of CDR Samuel LaHache. At that time the squadron consisted of six officers, sixty-six men, and one R4D. A humble beginning indeed for the vast operations that were to follow.

'VR-2 was soon ready to try its wings over the Pacific. A Sikorsky patrol plane had been delivered to the squadron, and departed on 15 May 1942, from Alameda for Honolulu. The two round trips within the month represented no mean achievement in those days.

'In July 1942, VR-2 began to receive the PB2Y flying-boats. For a time, with only four of these planes available, almost daily schedules to Honolulu were maintained. Squadron personnel were working day and night to maintain these aircraft which were transporting a pathetic trickle of desperately needed supplies. In addition to this terrific work load, there were the equally important jobs of preparing for the future, training pilots, navigators, flight crewmen and mechanics for the expanding operations to come.

'By November of that year, occasional flights were being made to Canton, Funafuti, Espiritu Santos, and Noumea in the South Pacific, in addition to the regular Hawaiian run. Scheduled trips went to Kodiak via Seattle and Yakutat. Detachments were established at Honolulu and at Noumea, in New Caledonia. PBMs, Martin-built flying-boats, were operating to Auckland, Sidney, Brisbane and Espiritu Santos from Noumea.

'On 4 March 1943, VR-2 split its land and seaplane operations which had covered the vast areas from Corpus Christi, Texas, to the Aleutians, and Alameda to Australia and New Zealand. The land plane section was commissioned as Air Transport Squadron Four.

'CDR. W.M. Nation was commanding officer of the squadron during most of its tremendous expansion. As the Central Pacific opened up, VR-2 planes began operations to Johnston Island and Kwajalein and later to Saipan and Manus in the Admiralty group.

'Early in 1944 the Martin Mars, the famed "Old Lady" and prototype of the current fleet of Mars air-

left: Two US Navy men on a trans-Pacific flight aboard one of the Mars flying-boats during the Second World War; below: The Sproat Lake, facility of Forest Industries Flying Tankers Limited.

below: The Marshall Mars, forced down at sea near Johnston Island in the mid-Pacific on 28 September 1946. On 5 April 1950, a fire broke out in one engine as the Marshall Mars passed near Diamond Head, Oahu, Hawaii. The crew had to put her down on the sea near the island. The fire could not be extinguished and the aircraft was completely destroyed.

craft was placed in operation with VR-2. Operating between Alameda and Honolulu, she completed seventy-eight round trips, and carried nearly three million pounds of cargo while serving with this squadron.

'When the Philippine Islands were recaptured in 1945, a route was opened to Manila, which, until the end of 1946, was the western terminal and turn-around point for the squadron. Flights from Alameda stopped at Honolulu, Johnston, Majuro, and Saipan.

'By August of 1945, with operations at their peak, VR-2 had 54 aircraft meeting a schedule of six departures daily out of Alameda. During this record month, a total of 1,813,892 plane-miles were flown, with a ton-mile load of 6,479,416. The squadron, which three and a half years before had consisted of seventy-two officers and men and one aircraft, had expanded until the roster showed 3,068 men and 800 officers aboard.

'Demobilization, of course, whittled down the squadron that was hanging up these records. Increasing numbers of men totalled up their "points" and headed for the personnel office with large, happy smiles. By June 1946, there were but 316 men and 63 officers permanently attached to the squadron.

'The Marshall Mars was delivered in February, 1946. By early summer, the Marianas, Philippine and Hawaii Mars had been delivered. The Mars aircraft were ready to start establishing new world's records. This has been done with almost monotonous regularity during their naval service. In April of that year, the huge Hawaii Mars even set a record for establishing records. Within eight hours after landing in Honolulu with a record payload of 35,000 pounds, she was unloaded, cleaned, and set up as a hospital ship with 100 evacuation patients from Aiea Hospital. With 120 persons aboard, including medical attendants and the crew, she returned to Alameda with the largest number of passengers ever carried on a flight of such duration, and with the largest number of patients ever evacuated in a single flight. In this manner, three world's records were smashed within 48 hours.

'Flight schedules for the giant Martin flying-boats were set up immediately, and the operation of PB2Ys was discontinued. The Mars aircraft were concentrated on main line runs to the Western Pacific areas until the end of the year, when the Philippine routes were closed, and a six-a-week schedule between Alameda and Hawaii was established. All VR-2 detachments west of Hawaii were demobilized at that time.

'In the spring of 1948, the engineering department undertook a task of herculean proportions. The Hawaii Mars was ready for its first major overhaul and the other aircraft were not far behind. The work was begun in April, and with considerable help from the Overhaul and Repair Department of the Naval Air Station in Alameda, the dismantling, rebuilding and modernization of all aircraft was completed in eleven months. When it is remembered that no aircraft of this size had ever been overhauled before, it is obvious that all hands had a thorough workout.

'Air Transport Squadron Two has a proud record. Although not engaged in actual combat operations, it contributed much to the success of our fighting forces by delivering strategic material and personnel when and where they were needed. The squadron has met each obstacle as a challenge, each task with a spirit of willingness and ingenuity which has been a credit to the Naval Service. Now, in the post-war era, VR-2 continues to carry out its assigned mission in that same spirit, and remains ready to face any new assignment—and deliver the goods.'

Retired US Navy man Edwin Gehricke remembers a flight he made on the Marshall Mars after the end of the Second World War: 'I was reassigned to the Cavite [Manila] JRM base of VR-2 in August of 1946. In Cavite we had a limited number of personnel and our duties consisted of maintaining the equipment and facilities. During a typhoon which swept the area all personnel slept in the NATS terminal building. The crash boat was used to sweep the area waters before the Mars could land or take off. The terminal building was operational twenty-four hours a day and fully equipped with telecommunications equipment. The manning of the terminal was shared by all of the personnel, with different time schedules. The telefax machine was our link to Alameda and all other military bases and the messages clicking during the night watches were always monitored for any action that might be required.

'On a night when I had the duty I sat at my post

monitoring the messages which notified us that a typhoon was on the way and the prediction was severe. This message was followed by an order that Edwin Gehricke return to Alameda as soon as possible for separation. The next incoming flight of the Mars was not scheduled at this time and my orders were to report at Alameda before October 1st 1946.

'I took a chance to catch a flight out of Clark Field on a military aircraft and was driven by jeep through the jungle via the village of Paranaque and Manila to Clark. Many planes were being lashed down because of the storm and the flight I was to take was grounded in Guam because of it. I returned to Cavite and learned that the *Marshall* Mars had departed Alameda for the Philippines via our Pacific bases. The typhoon would have passed by the time the Mars would arrive, around September 24th, so my hopes were up and I was looking forward to going home.

'The *Marshall* Mars arrived and all hands turned to for unloading and onloading, including the aluminum trunk I had made, loaded with all my belongings. JATO (jet-assisted take-off) bottles were attached to the Mars and we left in the evening for Saipan. As in Cavite, cargo from Saipan was loaded and, after two attempts, we lifted off the water. The harbor in Saipan was cluttered with sunken ships and debris, and the first take-off attempt had to be aborted because the take-off area was too close to the reefs. Another all-night flight took us to Majuro, an atoll in the Marshall Islands group, where we loaded more cargo. I met with my shipmates from Alameda who were very envious of my becoming a civilian.

'On September 27th we were flying from Majuro to Honolulu. It was a scheduled flight by NATS VR-2 Pacific Wing, the third leg of the trip from Cavite to Alameda. The JRM-1 Mars was the largest aircraft in the world. Only four of these giant aircraft were operational and were being used exclusively by NATS VR-2. Now that the war with Japan had ended, all four Mars aircraft were being used to transport equipment, supplies and personnel to and from Alameda and the Pacific islands.

'With heavy cargo on board, including Admiral Tower's furniture from Manila, we took off from the Majuro lagoon at 1800 hours. Lifting from the water

required the aid of twelve JATO bottles. All was normal. The all-night flight would bring us to Honolulu at about 0700 hours the next morning.

'At about 0330 hours, while the relief flight crew were resting on the flight deck, an engine problem developed on the starboard wing. Number three engine was experiencing a faulty prop motor and would have to be shut down. Inadvertently, the number four engine was put into full-feather, causing a tremendous vibration, and was immediately shut down along with number three. After correcting the propeller pitch on the number four, the engine was restarted. The Mars was now flying on only three engines. We had lost altitude from about 9,000 feet and it became apparent that we had an emergency as we could not maintain altitude.

'Our position was radioed to all area stations and the airplane commander ordered all of the crew to prepare for the possibility of having to dump cargo in the event of a dangerous open ocean landing in heavy seas. Our descent continued until we could visually confirm that the condition of the sea was rough, but suitable for a landing. Dawn was breaking as our commander brought the Mars down beautifully on the sea. Fortunately, we were in reasonable proximity to Johnston Island and the Marine Corps base there. With three engines, the airplane was able to taxi over water to the island where we anchored offshore.

'From Johnston Island a communication to Alameda resulted in a replacement prop motor being flown in by a NATS R5D from Honolulu. With on-board scaffolding removed from the aircraft and secured under the number three engine (over the water), the repair was made and the Mars was made ready to continue the flight.'

Other noteworthy flights of the Mars flying-boats included Operation Hayride, in which a merchant ship, the SS *Swarthmore Victory* had run out of food for its cargo of six elephants and a large assortment of tropical birds en route to the United States. The *Marshall* Mars was dispatched on a seventeen-hour, 1,500-mile mercy mission to deliver several tons of baled hay for the elephants, as well as containers of worms for the birds. Another type of mission frequently flown by the Mars planes were the Diaper Specials in which dependants of servicemen, wives,

'Don't talk to me about naval tradition. It's nothing but rum, sodomy, and the lash.'
– Winston Churchill

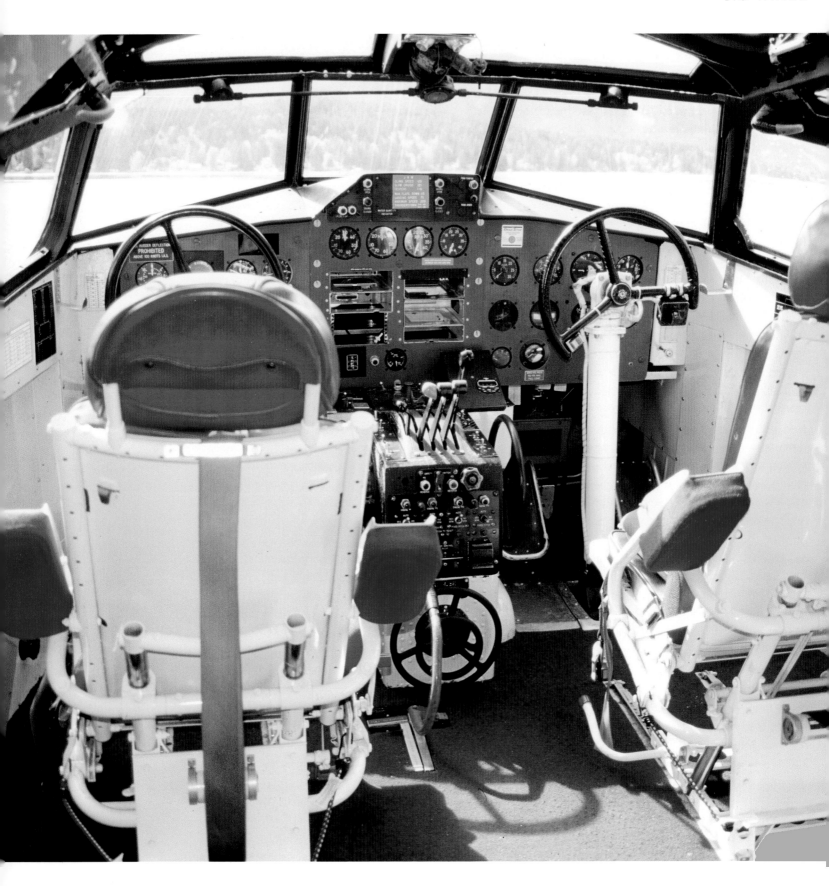

babies, infants and small children, were transported to and from the US mainland. The little ones were provided with kiddie life-jackets, bassinets and Playtex inflatable rubber mattresses. Each of these flights had a Navy nurse assigned to it to comfort anxious mothers and children.

On one occasion a cargo of live monkeys was being flown from the Philippines to Alameda in one of the JRMs. Chief Radioman Warren Mistler remembered, 'We were coming out of the Philippines and were hauling a cage with 160 monkeys, along with a Philippine lad who was responsible for their care and feeding. We had bags of peanuts and lots of bananas on board. Our crew took the monkeys from Sangley Point to Saipan, then another crew took over.

'The squadron had to rig the plane with humidifiers and heaters to maintain a constant temperature. I heard that twenty monkeys were stolen, but 140 arrived in Alameda. They were then put on a truck headed for Chicago and were used for polio research.'

On 15 December 1946 the *Philippine* Mars was approaching Oahu, Hawaii, and about to begin its descent to land when the pilot felt the plane yaw. He looked out of his side window and then yelled to the flight engineer, 'We've just lost number one engine.' The engineer responded calmly, 'Feather number one.' 'Feather, Hell!' said the pilot. 'We lost it. It fell off the wing!' The port outboard engine had indeed wrenched itself from its mount and fallen into the sea.

A far more serious incident involving the *Marshall* Mars occurred on 5 April 1950 during a short test flight following an engine change. The number three engine burst into flames and the crew was unable to extinguish the blaze when the bromide fire-bottle failed to function. The pilot, Lieutenant-Commander George Simmons, successfully landed the crippled plane south of Diamond Head, Oahu, and the crew quickly abandoned it. The *Marshall* Mars, which on one occasion had transported more people (308) than had ever been carried in an aircraft, lay in the water two miles off the famous Hawaiian landmark, burning furiously. The crew escaped from the area in rafts they had been able to launch and soon a fire-boat arrived and tried to save the aeroplane. The crew were rescued as the seamen aboard the fire-boat fought to douse

the flames of the Mars. Finally, they had to admit defeat and move away. The blaze advanced over the fuselage and wing and then the Mars exploded, 'flying to pieces like a clay pigeon' as Navy photographer Joe Martin, who witnessed the incident from a helicopter overhead, remembered it. The remains of the plane continued to burn on the water for fifty-five minutes before sinking to the bottom of Keehi Lagoon.

The JRM-2 *Caroline* Mars was the last of the Mars flying-boats built and was delivered to the Navy in July 1947. A considerable improvement on her elder sisters, the *Caroline* was powered by four Pratt & Whitney R-4360-4T 28-cylinder, similar to the powerplants of the giant B-36 bomber (featured in a chapter of this book), rated at 3,000 hp each. The aeroplane weighed 165,000 lb, cruised at 173 mph and had a range of 6,750 miles. Assigned to the Naval Air Test Center at Paxtuxent River, the JRM-2 finished her flight testing in May 1948 and was ferried to Alameda to join VR-2. On 27 August she flew non-stop from Honolulu to Chicago, a distance of 4,748 miles carrying forty-two passengers and 14,000 lb of cargo, in twenty-four hours and twelve minutes. She broke another record on 7 September when she carried a cargo payload of 39,500 lb on a flight from Cleveland, Ohio to Alameda, California.

VR-2 continued to operate its four JRM Mars flying-boats from 1946 through 1949, racking up a total of 32,997 hours in the air and carrying a total of 76,403 passengers in that period. Between 1950 and 1956 the big planes carried 108,198 passengers, 5,488 tons of cargo and 1,495 tons of mail in 1,940 trans-Pacific round trips. In all, the Mars planes had logged 87,000 accident-free hours in their trans-Pacific operations. All four surviving Mars aircraft, *Hawaii*, *Philippine*, *Marianas* and *Caroline*, were retired from service in 1956 and placed in outside storage at NAS Alameda until they were sold for scrap in 1959.

Dan McIvor was senior executive pilot for the Canadian timber company MacMillan Bloedel Limited in the late 1950s. McIvor was one of those who had pioneered the use of aircraft in fighting forest fires. His employer was frustrated by the frequent fires that destroyed large portions of its forests and was

left: The colourful flight deck of the Hawaii Mars on the Forest Industries ramp at Sproat Lake. Their pilots love the big Mars boats and wish they could fly them more often.

looking for ways to solve the problem when McIvor suggested that he should set out on a worldwide quest to find some flying-boats with sufficient speed, payload capacity, range and turnaround capability to attack the fires. The search was fruitless as the era of the large flying-boat was over. Most of the best such aircraft were military machines from the Second World War and most had already been scrapped. But then, in perfect serendipity, he happened on an old aviation friend who told him that the Navy was about to sell its four Mars flying-boats at Alameda. McIvor got on the phone to Alameda and found to his great disappointment that the bidding for the planes had been closed. The buyer turned out to be a scrap-metal dealer who had picked up the four aircraft for a shade more than $26,000. McIvor went to see the four Mars and knew he had to have them. He made a deal with the scrap-metal man, and bought the planes. For a grand total of about $120,000 he came away with the four Mars ready for ferrying, thirty-five spare engines, the Navy's entire ninety tons of Mars spare parts and its documentation archive including everything from hull templates to operational histories of the aircraft.

The new company was called Forest Industries Flying Tankers Limited, and had been formed in 1959 by a consortium of forest companies following several catastrophic fire seasons. Dan McIvor was appointed its chief pilot. In September 1959 he and two former Navy Mars pilots ferried the four planes to Patricia Bay near Vancouver Island, British Columbia.

A frightening incident happened during the ferry flight of the *Philippine* Mars to Canada. The plane was off the Oregon coast when a trainee flight engineer accidentally cut off fuel to all four engines. The Navy flight engineer on board happened to be visiting the head and was shocked by the sudden silence. Rushing back to the engineer station on the flight deck, he managed to quickly feather the propellers and get the engines restarted before an emergency ditching was required.

Fairey Aviation of Canada went to work modifying the Mars aircraft, converting them into water bombers, installing new 7,200-gallon water tanks and modifying some of the fuel tanks to hold water. They also added a secondary tank to hold a foam-concentrate thickening agent that is added to the water load to ensure deep soaking and helps the water to adhere to the trees in a viscous film. The company has estimated that this foam capability has increased the efficiency of the Mars by at least thirty percent. Fairey cut dumping hatches into the sides of some aircraft and the bottoms of the others; they also installed retractable aluminium scoops aft of the hull step. Meanwhile, some former Navy Mars specialists conducted courses about the type for the pilots and technicians of Forest Industries, followed by familiarization flying at the company's Sproat Lake, Vancouver Island base. It took the company crews six months to master the procedures and adjust to the idiosyncrasies of the big flying-boats, and a lot of trial and error in perfecting the after-hull water scoops that, when everyone does everything correctly, can replenish the water capacity of a Mars in just forty seconds of high-speed taxiing on the lake. The pilots had to adjust to the heavyness of the controls (even though partially power-assisted) and the matter of how to fly such a big, heavy bird with agility through the rugged passes and valleys of the western Canadian timberlands. They developed tactics for fighting fires, such as the use of a spotter plane to guide the great lumbering flying-boats into the fire areas. They learned that the best speed and altitude for water drops was 100 knots and between 150 and 200 feet. In their fire-fighting role, the Mars flying-boats are operated by a crew of four: a captain, a first officer, and two flight engineers, all working together efficiently and safely.

There were certainly some bad days . . . like the one in 1961 when a former military pilot was bringing the *Marianas* Mars around on a water-bombing run. The pilot disregarded the spotter plane and was too low in his approach. He did not drop his load, and instead began a steep turn away from the mountain. As he banked, the port wing clipped the trees and the Mars cartwheeled into the mountainside and tore itself to bits. The crew of four were all killed. Since that accident, it has been company policy that all pilots applying to fly for FIFT must have at least 7,000 hours in floatplanes or amphibians, with most

'Sometimes I think war is God's way of teaching us geography.'
Paul Rodriguez

of it in the British Columbia coastal region. Since the loss of the *Marianas* aeroplane, the Mars operation has been accident free, though nature struck in 1962 and the company suffered the loss of a second Mars, the *Caroline*, when a large and violent storm, Hurricane Frieda, hit the southern part of Vancouver Island, destroying the plane.

In addition to the two surviving Mars, *Hawaii* and *Philippine*, the company operates a much smaller 1944-vintage Grumman Goose as a lead-in aeroplane called 'The Birddog' and three Bell helicopters. The company's four pilots are proficient on both the Mars and the Goose. The helicopters are used to haul 145-gallon buckets of water to suppress small fires before they can get big. They are also used in routine daily fire-spotting patrols, for medical evacuation and for personal transportation.

When the company is called upon to fight a forest fire, it immediately launches the Goose, whose pilot contacts the Fire Boss on the ground. The Fire Boss provides an assessment of the size and nature of the blaze. While this is happening, the Mars flying-boat that will be employed against the fire is warmed up and out taxiing on the lake to scoop its first water load, usually within ten minutes of a callout. As soon as the Goose arrives over the fire scene, its pilot reports to the Mars pilot on the conditions for the water drop—the heights required for circling and for the drop, ingress and egress of the area. The Goose pilot will lead the Mars pilot into and out of the fire area for as many drops as are needed to quell the blaze. This highly capable team can begin the drops in little more than a half hour, and make as many as thirty drops in a six-hour mission.

Picking up water during a fire-fighting operation is possibly the most demanding part of the mission in terms of crew teamwork. The captain executes a normal landing, keeping the aeroplane 'on the step' and allowing the speed to decrease to seventy knots. The flight engineer then takes over the engine power and selects the water scoops to the "down" position. With ram pressure injecting the water into the tanks, the aircraft takes on water at the rate of a ton per second. To compensate for the rapidly increasing weight, the flight engineer advances the throttles to maintain a 'skimming speed' of sixty to seventy knots, to keep the plane on the step. The water pick-up time is, on average, twenty-five seconds. When the water tanks are full, the captain has the scoops raised and calls for take-off power for a full-load take-off. When the Mars is again airborne, the foam concentrate is injected into the water load, normally at a ratio of thirty gallons of concentrate to the 7,200-gallon water load. The concentrate disperses and remains inert until the load is dropped, when the tumbling action causes expansion which converts the water load into a foam. The process is repeated for each water drop.

Keeping these sixty-year-old workhorse aeroplanes in top shape is an extraordinary challenge and the people of Forest Industries Flying Tankers Limited are up to the task, servicing the Mars aircraft in an immaculate environment. Every detail is considered in the attentions lavished on the old planes which are kept on a rotating four-year maintenance schedule, with intensive annual inspections of the engines and the airframe components. The great enemies of aircraft, metal fatigue and corrosion, are meticulously addressed and defeated. The job of locating and acquiring spare parts for such elderly craft compounds the challenge of keeping them flying, but what the company can't find, they make. As the company says about its great old flying-boats 'No other aircraft can deliver a massive 60,000 lb payload as quickly as the Mars and continue to deliver it every few minutes for several hours or until the problem is solved.'

Specifications: Martin JRM-1 Mars

Engines: Four Wright Cyclone R3350-18 radials rated at 2,400 hp each
Maximum speed: 222 mph
Cruising speed: 158 mph
Service ceiling: 17,000 ft
Maximum range: 4,945 miles
Gross weight: 145,000 lb
Wingspan: 200 ft
Length: 120 ft 3 in
Height: 44 ft 7 in
Wing area: 3,683 sq ft
Maximum payload: 35,000 lb

far left: An interior view of one of the Mars flying boats during the Second World War.

HK-1

Howard Robard Hughes was a man of varied passions. Born in Houston, Texas, on 24 September 1905, Hughes was a renowned aviator, movie producer, recluse, multi-millionaire, aircraft manufacturer, playboy and eccentric. His inherited wealth came from Hughes Tool, the company that had made millions from the drill bit his father had invented for the oil industry. Rich, bright and extremely ambitious, the 18-year-old Hughes left Texas after the deaths of his parents to seek his greater fortune in southern California where he would indulge his two primary interests, movie making and aviation. There he gained experience in motion picture production with a brief series of films, some moderately successful, before producing the movie that he most wanted to make, the First World War aerial epic *Hell's Angels*, the film that made a star of Jean Harlow, one of the many Hollywood women in his life. At a cost of four million dollars, *Hell's Angels* was the most expensive film of the time and it would never show a profit, but Hughes' involvement added to his prestige in the movie industry. Two of his films, *The Racket* in 1928 and *The Front Page* in 1931 received Academy Award nominations. His best known and most successful film was *The Outlaw* in 1943, starring Jane Russell, for whom he is supposed to have designed the first cantilevered push-up bra. The ladies in his life then included Harlow, Katherine Hepburn and Bette Davis, but aviation was his one true love.

He founded the Hughes Aircraft Company in 1933, and in September 1935 set a world speed record of 351 mph in the H-1, a racing plane his engineers had built. Through the 1930s he became as well known in the aviation world as he already was in Hollywood, and in 1939 he purchased the majority ownership in Trans World Airline (TWA). American federal law would not allow Hughes to build planes for his own airline, so he contacted Lockheed in Burbank, California, who had built the plane that he had used in a round-the-world record flight a few years earlier. Working in relative secrecy at Hughes' insistance, Lockheed created the Constellation, a revolutionary new airliner with a fully pressurized cabin, providing greater flying comfort to passengers by operating at higher, less turbulent altitudes. The aeroplane was also quite fast

and commercially successful.

In the 1950s Hughes sought to make TWA a jet airline by ordering a $400 million fleet of the new Boeing 707s, but his creditors were pressuring him to give up his total control of the airline, which marked the beginning of his decline and that of his company. By 1960 Howard Hughes had been forced from power at TWA and in 1966 a federal court ruled that he must sell his shares in the airline.

In his book, *The Sky's the Limit*, Charles J. Kelly said of Hughes, 'Over the years, almost everyone has tried to explain Hughes' behavior in complex psychiatric terms. My opinion is quite simple. I think Howard Hughes has grown old without changing his little boy's fascination for aeroplanes, movies and girls. To the tired, middle-aged ethos of our business world, Hughes' intrigues and eccentricities are an enigma— but any small boy would instantly understand and appreciate the secret night negotiations and delight in his complicated dealings. Unpressed, unshaven, tieless and in dirty sneakers, Howard Hughes is the Huck Finn of American Industry.'

As he aged, Hughes's behaviour became ever more quirky, bizarre and paranoic. Terrified of germs and infection, he adopted a lifestyle in which he frequently moved from one hotel to another; an insominiac living in darkened rooms and addicted to pain killers. After years of declining health and many moves between residences in Los Angeles, Las Vegas, the Bahamas, Vancouver, London and Mexico, Hughes died in April 1976 while en route from Mexico to a Houston hospital. Of all the achievements of this strange man whose stated goals in life were to become the world's best golfer, the world's best movie producer and the world's best pilot, one of his most impressive accomplishments was the largest aeroplane ever to fly, the legendary 320-foot-wingspan HK-1 flying-boat, commonly called the "Spruce Goose."

The HK-1 was in many ways years ahead of its time, particularly in heavy-lift capability and giant aircraft technologies. Like other grand-scale aircraft projects, the Hughes-Kaiser flying-boat generated a range of new and extraordinarily challenging design and engineering problems. Hughes engineers had to design a

left: The "Spruce Goose", as it is popularly known, being trailored from the Hughes Aircraft plant in Culver City, California, to Long Beach, where its maiden and only flight took place. It is the largest aeroplane ever to fly and was designed, built and flown, briefly, by the reclusive billionaire, Howard Hughes. It was originally conceived by steel maker and builder of the famed Second World War Liberty ships, Henry J. Kaiser. The ribs and airframe were made mainly of birch stock and the skin of the plane was made using a process called Duramold, which involved laminating and moulding thin sheets of veneer together. The end product material was amazingly light and strong.

2 November 1947. In a surprise move following a brief taxi-test at Long Beach, California, Howard Hughes thrilled thousands of people watching as he advanced the eight throttles of the magnificent HK-1 flying boat, and at 75 mph, lifted the giant craft from the water to cruise for a distance of one mile at a speed of 80 mph and a height of 70 feet. The big plane flew in the faces of Hughes' Congressional detractors in Washington and went on to become an aviation icon.

below: A Second World War three-view identification drawing of the British Short Sunderland flying-boat. The Sunderland figured prominently in the Allied campaign against Germany's U-boats during the Battle of the Atlantic.

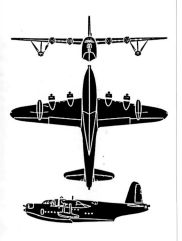

system to provide power-assisted control for the pilot. They had to experiment with complex flying boat hull designs to find efficiency in giant scale and they had to devise a new fuel storage and supply system for the long-range requirement of the wooden monster slowly taking shape in the Hughes Aircraft plant on a small airfield near Ballona Creek in Culver City, California.

Henry Kaiser had visualized a fleet of giant wooden flying-boats crossing the Atlantic and delivering hefty cargoes to share the burden of the Liberty ships which had become prime targets for German submarines. President Franklin Roosevelt liked the idea and initially proposed that Donald Douglas and his aircraft company build the big planes, but Douglas declined on the basis that it was technologically too difficult and impractical. Kaiser then took the concept to Howard Hughes who received it with considerable interest. With his experience of building ships rapidly, Kaiser believed that such a giant flying-boat could be constructed in as little as ten months. The two men arranged to build a prototype flying-boat and the Hughes design staff went to work on it.

When the Second World War began, Hughes Aircraft had only four full-time employees. When the war ended in 1945, it employed 80,000. While involved in the development of several experimental prototype aircraft for the military during the war, the bulk of the company's activity was the manufacture of aircraft components, the designs of other military contractors.

During the Battle of the Atlantic in 1942, German U-boats were sinking Allied cargo ships faster than they could be replaced. These losses were slowing the vital flow of supplies, fuel, food, war equipment and troops to Britain and the combat zones, as well as reducing the amount of essential raw materials reaching American factories for war production. Additionally, the construction of ships to replace those lost put further heavy demands on America's scarce raw materials and resources. This was the background against which the US War Production Board met in May to look for a solution. Board member F.H. Hoge Jr proposed a radical way around the U-boat problem—moving enormous loads of cargo by

air, in massive flying-boats, the largest ever built. Hoge reasoned that, not only would such aircraft not be subject to the submarine threat, they could make many Atlantic crossings in the time it took a cargo ship to make one. He wrote of the greater fuel efficiency of a giant cargo aircraft over that of smaller planes. He emphasized the value of a flying-boat in that it required neither a runway nor heavy landing gear, and the availability of appropriate sheltered harbours around the world, including the combat zones.

The idea for the massive flying-boat came from Hoge, but the visionary behind its implementation was the American steel maker and ship builder Henry J. Kaiser, who had earlier been involved in the construction of America's largest dams including Hoover, Bonneville and Grand Coulee. Kaiser had directed the programme to build hundreds of "Liberty" ships, essentially pre-fabricated cargo vessels. Patterned on a British tramp steamer, the Liberty ship was 441 feet long, 57 feet wide, displaced 14,100 tons and could transport 10,000 tons of cargo. These ships were designed to be constructed quickly and inexpensively. Utililzing welded hulls, which could be produced faster than their riveted counterparts, they were powered by reciprocating engines, allowing most of American naval turbine engine production to be used in US Navy warships. A total of 2,770 Liberty ships were built, some of them in less than two weeks from their keel laying. The life expectancy of the Liberty ships was just five years, all that Kaiser thought would be required of them.

Initially, Kaiser was interested in the possibility of converting some of his shipyards to the production of the giant flying-boats proposed by Hoge. He was also keen on the idea of building small, anti-submarine escort aircraft-carriers using hulls destined for his Liberty ships, a notion not viewed with enthusiasm by the US Navy. Ironically, the Vancouver shipyard run by his son Edgar was launching one such vessel a week by 1944, and in company with destroyers and land-based naval aircraft, his escort carriers were proving so effective against the U-boats that the giant cargo flying-boat programme would become irrelevant.

Kaiser wanted to begin with a programme to build a quantity of Martin Mars seventy-ton flying-boats in shipyards on the Atlantic, Gulf and Pacific coasts. With a fourteen-ton payload, he reckoned, 'That ship could carry a hundred men fully equipped. Five thousand of them could land 500,000 equipped men in England in a single day. And the next day they could fly over again with 70,000 tons of fresh milk, beefsteaks, sugar, and bombs. No submarine could shoot them down.' His plan called for building the flying-boat hulls in the shipyard slipways, launching them like ships and then towing them to outfitting docks where the wings, engines and other components would be added. Word of his plans reached the Roosevelt administration, Congress, the aviation industry and the American public, and the wrangling began. Kaiser was ultimately denied the opportunity he sought, but then he received a telephone call from Glenn Odekirk, a friend and associate of Howard Hughes.

Odekirk had heard of Kaiser's plans and his congressional meetings about them. He had talked with Hughes about seizing this apparent chance to involve Hughes Aircraft in the construction of the giant flying-boats and his boss was intrigued by the prospect. On 16 August 1942, Odekirk called Kaiser and the partnership began.

Kaiser joined forces with Howard Hughes to create the HK-1 (Hughes Kaiser-1) flying-boat. After several days of discussing the project, conversations involving Hughes, Kaiser, his son Edgar, and Odekirk, it was agreed that Hughes would design the great flying-boat and Kaiser would build it. Kaiser told the press that he and Hughes had agreed to proceed with 'the most ambitious aviation programme the world has ever known'.

It seemed, however, that virtually everyone in the American power structure then, except President Roosevelt, was vehemently opposed to the Kaiser plan. But not quite everyone. Donald Nelson, head of the War Production Board, and his principal aviation adviser, Grover Loening, who in 1910 had received the first master's degree in aeronautics in the United States, from Columbia University, seemed keen. Loening was an old seaplane man who became a proponent of the Hughes-Kaiser flying-boat. And Henry Kaiser had his share of friends in high places, whose influence was felt throughout Washington. But

before signing the letter of intent to go ahead with the project, Nelson had both the Army and Navy agree in writing that the Hughes-Kaiser project would not interfere with current programmes and that the Army agreed to make available standard engines and instruments for three of the proposed flying-boats. Both services stressed in their letters that the Hughes and Kaiser organization was to be specifically prevented from pirating key personnel from existing government aircraft contractors. In September the Defense Plant Corporation subsidiary of the Reconstruction Finance Corporation authorized Kaiser and Hughes to go ahead with the engineering design and construction of three flying-boat-type cargo planes, one for static testing and two for flight test. The work was to be under the direction of Howard Hughes in his Culver City plant. The authorization required that the construction of the aircraft should use a minumum of any critical or strategic materials; that no fee or profit to Howard Hughes, Kaiser, or companies with which either was affiliated could be included in the cost; that no engineers, technicians, or other skilled personnel who were then working for manufacturers engaged in the war effort could be employed without the prior written consent of their respective employers; that the Kaiser-Hughes organization could spend no more than $18 million; and that the authorization was limited to a period not to exceed twenty-four months from its inception. Howard Hughes had grave misgivings about these conditions and said as much to the deputy director of the War Production Board's aircraft division. Still, a contract was signed on 16 November and Hughes and Kaiser went to work.

It was intended to carry 750 fully equipped troops or two Sherman tanks. Typically of Hughes' endeavours, the great flying-boat was seen by many then as the most prodigious project in the history of aviation.

An important characteristic of the new plane was that it would be built, not of conventional aircraft aluminum, which was then a high-priority product for the war effort, but primarily of wood (birch). Actually, it was built of something called 'Duramold', which was birch impregnated with plastic and moulded

In late 2004, *The Aviator* was released to critical acclaim. The movie, which depicted events in the life of aircraft builder and film maker Howard Hughes between the 1930s and the 1950s, was directed by the widely-respected Martin Scorcese and starred Leonardo DiCaprio as Hughes. *The Aviator* looked at the filming of Hughes' World War I flying spectacular, *Hell's Angels,* his near-fatal test flight of the elegant XF-11 photo-reconnaissance plane

he had built for the US Army Air Force in the mid-1940s, the 1947 Congressional hearings in Washington where Hughes was interrogated about the giant HK-1 flying boat under construction at his Culver City, California factory, and finally, the dramatic first (and only) flight of that aeroplane, which has come to be popularly known as the Spruce Goose.

below: A detailed view of one enormous wing under construction for the Hughes flying-boat; bottom right: The fuselage of the HK-1 under way from Culver City to the Long Beach facility where final assembly would take place in 1947.

WORLD'S LARGEST AIRPLANE

uses Plaskon Resin Glue!

PLASKON
RESIN GLUE

INSTRUCTIONS
FOR
AMERICAN
SERVICEMEN
IN
BRITAIN
1942

into components of the sizes and shapes required. The Duramold process was the creation of Colonel Virginius Clark, one of the great early aerodynamicists, in collaboration with aircraft manufacturer Sherman Fairchild. Clark, like Hughes, was unconventional and somewhat eccentric. His clever process for plasticizing wood and moulding it enabled the creation of large structural elements whose strength could be tailored to their specific requirements within the airframe. The ribs and frame were constructed from birch and the skin of the aircraft was made of thin sheets of Duramold veneer laminated together. Hughes had previously obtained the licence for the Duramold process when he had come to the financial aid of Fairchild during the hard times of the Depression era. Hughes also purchased the rights for the Duramold process for aircraft weighing more than 20,000 lb, a deal which included the services of Colonel Clark.

Birch was used as the primary structural material for the flying-boat because it made the best moulded ply, had an excellent strength-to-weight ratio and was much more readily available than spruce. But spruce, maple, poplar and balsa were used as well. An incredible amount of research, experimentation and trial-and-error went into making the process work in the massive flying-boat and progress came very slowly.

Nearly the entire airframe was composed of the Duramold laminate, which used 1/32-inch veneer in layers arranged perpendicular to each other. The layers were bonded with special glue and the components shaped with steam. The resulting product was very light and extremely strong. Others, including Fairchild Aviation and Northrop had also built (much smaller) aircraft using Duramold or other molded wood laminate techniques in the 1930s.

The trouble started in the spring of 1943. At a meeting held on 4 May to review the progress of the HK-1 project, Grover Loening signalled a warning of what was to come: 'The use of wood, because of strategic shortages, is not now needed.' A US Navy representative took it from there: 'The Bureau of Aeronautics is definitely on record against wood construction for a

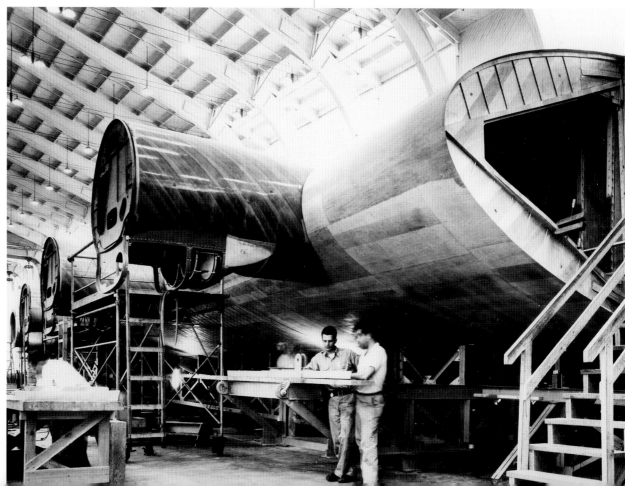

project of this character. The Navy feels the design is very good, but we're skeptical of wood and the time of construction.' Loening, after a visit to the Hughes plant in early August: 'The general progress of the Kaiser-Hughes project can be reported on as satisfactory. It is, of course, difficult to appraise work of this character, but the progress on the engineering seems particularly noteworthy. The design of the HK-1 aircraft, aerodynamically and hydrodynamically, appears excellent. It is in no sense a freak, but is, on the other hand, a very fine and graceful layout in a fairly conservative but thoroughly modern type of aircraft in which giant size alone is the principal new contribution.' He then turned to the matter of the wooden construction: 'Several times in the past your consultant has called attention to the serious question involved in building the huge 320-foot span wing of this design out of wood. Originally this was mandatory upon Hughes, because it was and still is distinctly understood that this project must not "raid" strategic materials from military aircraft production. However, since that time the situation has reversed itself in

that wood, particularly birch veneer, is becoming very scarce, and metal is becoming a great deal easier. For this reason, the question of developing a metal wing for this design was again taken up in detail with Mr Hughes. In the discussions on this subject, Mr Hughes finally expressed agreement and said that he would be entirely willing to proceed at once with the metal wing.' At the same time significant management changes were taking place at Hughes Aircraft. Loening's view on his visit to the Culver City plant, that Hughes's management and organization were in running order, changed considerably over the next three weeks and he reported further to his boss at the War Production Board that he was concerned about the finishing of the stabilizer, 'which indicated a very great overweight—far beyond what would be permissible and of a nature requiring immediate review of the project'.

Loening was again sent to the Hughes plant to check on the project in September. In his report of this visit he stated, 'As a matter of fact conditions in the fabricating end of the plant were generally

During the Second World War, an odd little character called Kilroy, possibly the creation of an actual American serviceman by that name, turned up all over the world. In what was probably the broadest application of graffiti in history, Kilroy appeared virtually everywhere that GIs found themselves, usually scrawled on fences, building exteriors, bathroom walls, and sidewalks.

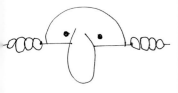

**KILROY
WAS HERE**

reported as greatly improved since the recent resignations . . . There is not, therefore any particular necessity for appraising the progress of this contract and the future plans for it in the light of management difficulties, but only in the light of technical considerations of the design itself. The most serious thing that is taking extra time . . . is that the method of construction has not yet been wholly devised and *actually, the government is financing an experimental development of a new wooden construction method*—at a time when it thought it was financing the development of a giant aircraft built on known structural fabricating methods.'

The method of construction—on such a gigantic aircraft—certainly was experimental. Tolerances were critical and considerations such as the chemistry and nature of the glue involved was a major headache. With glue that was too heavy or thick, the strength of the bonds would be questionable and the weight would be increased. If the glue was too thin, the quality of the bonds would suffer. Many components were rejected as a result of insufficient bonding. Loening: 'Unlike the ability we have in metal with Magnaflux and X-ray devices to determine the character of metal joints, these wooden joints must be taken on faith and on their external inspection only. Yet structural loads including vibrations, flutters, etc., and finally, weathering effects, will definitely strain these joints with forces other than shears (in which they are manifestly strong) and thus give to the entire structure an element of unreliability that is definitely "scary" for aircraft. It is the details of construction material used and [the] likelihood of serious overweight, the miscalculating of time needed and cost, the choice of engines, and consequently the practical availability of the aircraft for this war that warrants a very serious review of the desirability of this project from here on.'

That review followed in October. The Aircraft Production Board of the WPB held a detailed consideration of the flying-boat project and Loening's reports about it and the board then ruled that the contract for the HK-1 would be cancelled, 'inasmuch as the project offers no useful contribution to the War effort, and the facility is required for production

of important military types.' There followed a Washington meeting in which Howard Hughes and Henry Kaiser had been invited to address the various points of contention about the aeroplane. Hughes put up a thoughtful and spirited defence of the wood construction method and the use of wood rather than metal for the plane. He gave cogent reasons why, in his view, there were objections to the use of wood in the aircraft and was asked by Loening at one point if he considered wood satisfactory in the construction of seaplanes as well as land-planes. Hughes answered, 'With phenolic glues wood might even be considered superior to metal for seaplanes.' The committee chairman, Charles E. Wilson, raised his doubts about the plane being completed before the end of 1944, and Hughes replied that he could deliver the first HK-1 within one year, and to guarantee that, his company would forfeit half a million dollars if that schedule were not met. The exchanges grew darker and Kaiser suggested that one plane be built of wood and one of metal in order to test and compare them, to which Loening said that he favoured proceeding in metal only, but that he was unsure about the qualification of Hughes's design staff to work in metal, to which Hughes responded emphatically that they were perfectly capable of making the switch to metal. By the end of the meeting there seemed to be a consensus that it would be desirable to save the HK-1 project. Following that meeting, Kaiser and Hughes managed to wring a significant concession from Wilson, in which they were given a further thirty days to perform static testing of several HK-1 subassemblies, the results of which would then be examined by a board of engineering experts who would report their findings to the WPB Aircraft Production Board which would then decide the final disposition of the project.

The testing turned up a number of serious glue joint failures in the stabilizer, and despite repairs and more testing, the results continued to be unacceptable. By the end of the thirty-day test period, Loening had written to Wilson that further engineering investigations would simply mean additional delay in ending this expenditure of public funds. He urged that the project be terminated immediately. He mentioned too, that the static testing performed on the stabilizer was not as important as testing for flutter would have been 'because the possibility of flutter is very serious in wooden aircraft. Due to the peculiar action of wood in various humidity conditions, one day it will be perfectly okay, and the next day its rigidity will be quite different, and that has always been one of the reasons why aircraft engineers would like to leave wood and go to metal, because they can count on it more surely. The stress can be figured more accurately.'

The Aircraft Production Board considered Loening's opinion, but opted to allow the investigation to go ahead as planned. At that point it seemed that nearly all of the principal figures involved, except Hughes and Kaiser, believed that, if there was to be any future for the big flying-boat, it would be as a *metal* aeroplane, and that there was little value to the wooden aeroplane under construction and little value in completing it. All the work of all the committees, study groups, and individual experts appeared to conclude that the project should be cancelled.

Then, for whatever reason, the tide turned. It is clear that President Roosevelt, an original supporter of the flying-boat project, and a confidant of his, Jesse Jones, who headed the Defense Plant Corporation that had contracted with Hughes and Kaiser to build the plane, still favoured continuing the project. In this climate, after a series of lengthy and at times heated phone conversations between Hughes and Donald Nelson of the WPB, followed by a 17 March 1944 letter from Hughes to Nelson to 'advise strongly against stopping construction of the HK-1 flying-boat now being built by Hughes Tool Company for Kaiser-Hughes . . .', on 27 March the contract was reinstated, with Hughes. Kaiser had been excluded.

Friday 1 August 1947. Howard Hughes was subpoenaed to appear before a United States Senate committee to investigate the National Defense Program. The assistant chief counsel for the committee, Francis Flanagan: 'Based on my investigation to date, it is my opinion that this entire flying-boat project, which never had the wholehearted approval, and in some cases actually had the disapproval of responsible government agencies, must have received strong backing from

some persons with considerable influence in high government places.' The committee would be co-chaired by Senator Homer Ferguson of Michigan and included Senator Owen Brewster of Maine (chairman), who had agreed to pass the gavel to Ferguson in order to be free to tangle with Hughes in the hearings as a 'private citizen'. Brewster had sponsored legislation called the Chosen Instrument Bill which, had it become law, would have resulted in Pan American Airways being named the US flag carrier in international air transportation. The bill was blocked through the lobbying efforts of TWA and other US airlines and that led to Brewster stumping for a similar bill introduced by Nevada Senator Pat McCarran with the same intent as that of Brewster's bill.

On the first day of the committee hearings, it emerged that these would be the first congressional hearings to be televised, though only a relative handful of people would be viewing them in those early days of the medium. Procedural haggling dominated the first session followed by a series of sometimes angry exchanges between Ferguson and Hughes, Brewster and Hughes, and Ferguson and Florida Senator Claude Pepper, one of the committee Democrats who supported Hughes and tried to moderate the escalating exchanges. As the hearings continued, Hughes and Brewster concentrated on savaging each other. Hughes appeared to be winning most of the points, both argumentatively and with the gallery and the American public. On the third day the hearings were finally focused on the flying-boat that the public and many in the aviation world now referred to as the Spruce Goose, and Senator Brewster called the Flying Lumberyard. Ferguson immediately squared off with Howard Hughes. In that session Hughes responded to the grilling with clarity and confidence in the defence of his company's work on the plane and his own involvement with it.

The fourth day of the hearings elicited a dramatic comment from Hughes: 'Yesterday I said that I spent between eighteen and twenty hours a day for a period of between six months and a year. Now that was the concentrated, heavy design work on this plane; but from that point on I spent hours and hours every day for, oh, a period of years, on this project, and I am still

'Join the army, meet interesting people, and kill them.'
– anon

below right: On the water in the Port of Long Beach. For nine years the HK-1 was displayed at Long Beach by the Disney corporation. When Disney decided to part company with the big plane, the owner, the Aero Club of Southern California, needed to find a new home for it, one where it would be properly preserved and displayed. The winning bid came from Captain Michael King Smith and his father, Evergreen International Aviation founder and chairman, Del Smith. The Smiths wanted the HK-1 to be the centre-piece of their planned air museum at McMinnville, Oregon, near Portland, and persuaded the Aero Club that their museum would be the best home for the plane. The task of disassembling the big flying-boat began on 12 August 1992 and was completed in six weeks, reducing the plane to 38 separate elements to be shipped to Oregon by land and sea. The propellers, engines and smaller parts were crated and moved overland. the giant fuselage, wings, rudder, ailerons, elevators, flaps and horizontal stabilizers made the sea journey from Long Beach by barge, all of it arriving in Oregon by 18 October.

spending a great deal of time on it. I put the sweat of my life into this thing. I have my reputation rolled up in it, and I have stated that if it was a failure I probably will leave this country and never come back, and I mean it.' Then, at Senator Pepper's behest, he described the aeroplane to the committee and responded to charges by Ferguson of inefficiency and lengthy delays by Hughes Aircraft in relation to the flying-boat contract: 'I would like to say at this point that I have researched all of the airplanes that were designed and built during the last seven years [which included the war years], and I have discovered that this flying-boat, which is now being criticized so violently, will cost the government less per pound and has taken less time per pound to complete than any other airplane, the first of a design . . . The criticism that has been levelled at our supposedly inefficient operation does not really

seem to be justified when you consider the result, because you can always find somebody around a factory who will bellyache and say that things are not going right, but just the same, if the result, the proof of the pudding is in the eating–if that measures up in relation to the other projects, I don't think the criticism is well founded.' Pepper asked Hughes if the aeroplane was relatively completed and relatively ready to fly. Hughes responded that it was structurally complete, except for the control system, which was delaying testing of the plane. He deftly explained the unique difficulties the company had faced in virtually inventing much of the aircraft and solving many extraordinarily complex problems, and the knowledge gained in the massive effort which 'will be of considerable value to everyone in the building of bigger planes hereafter.'

Hughes'ss performance before the committee had

been sensational, leaving Ferguson eager to conclude the hearings, but with the announced intention of resuming them on 17 November. Hughes left Washington in a jubilant mood.

Three years after the eleventh-hour WPB decision to continue work on the flying-boat, it was finally ready for testing. The taxiing tests were set to begin on 1 November 1947 at Long Beach, down the coast from the Culver City plant. Howard Hughes had been coming down to the aeroplane every night for three months to check on the operation of the electrical and hydraulics systems, to watch the eight great engines running, and to insinuate himself into every aspect of his creation as the maiden flight drew near. His planning extended to orchestrating the media show that would surround the debut of his new plane. He saw that reporters and photographers, celebrities, dignitaries and VIPs were invited to the occasion, entertaining them in Hollywood style. A large press tent had been set up on Terminal Island and had been filled with long tables, phones, typewriters, and plenty of good food and refreshments catered by Hughes's friend, the Hollywood restaurateur Dave Chasen.

The question was not really whether it would fly, but whether Howard Hughes would fly it? Some in the government believed that to protect the huge investment of the taxpayers in the new plane, someone better qualified to pilot large flying-boats should be at the controls on the all-important first flight. Others, in a position to know, were sure that there was no one better qualified to fly it than Hughes, who knew the aircraft and its systems thoroughly. And Hughes had made thousands of water take-offs and landings in the Sikorsky S-43 amphibian that he had bought in 1937.

The great plane lay in its custom-built drydock at Terminal Island, Long Beach, on that grey Saturday morning, 1 November. All obstructions had been cleared from the area and the dry dock was being filled with water. Hughes' people prepared to tow the flying-boat out into the harbour. There was a chop on the sea in the outer harbour and the forecast for the day was not promising. It appeared that no testing would be conducted, but the launching

process was continued. Hughes wanted the aeroplane to be ready when the weather improved. Hours later it lay at anchor in Long Beach harbour.

The scheduled testing on Sunday was to be taxiing to evaluate the water-handling characteristics of the big plane and some of the systems. Hughes' chief engineer, Rae Hopper, stopped him briefly at the aeroplane to mention what he considered a minor problem in the aileron operating mechanism, saying that it was easily fixed but that it would be better not to fly the plane until the work had been done. He said that if Hughes wanted to go ahead and fly it, he should not exceed 140 mph.

Some members of the press were invited to go aboard the flying-boat at around noon as passengers on the first taxi tests, three miles across the harbour and back. He told them that, owing to the amount of chop on the water, it was doubtful that they would reach more than 40 mph. Hughes deliberately chose a non-pilot to occupy the co-pilot seat beside him so that no one could ever claim that Howard Hughes had not actually been flying it. He had asked Dave Grant, the designer of the flight control hydraulic system for the plane, to share the cockpit with him that day.

Hughes relied on walkie-talkies to communicate with company and press boats. One of his main concerns as the big plane was towed out to the test area, was the possibility of striking floating debris and he had employed some small craft to check the test area for such flotsam. They reached the test area and the tow lines were cast off. Then Hughes and his flight engineers started the eight R-4360 engines. The initial test would be a slow run and would give the first indication of the plane's handling on the water. It handled well. The second run would be at speed and Hughes found it exhilarating as the flying-boat quickly accelerated through sixty and seventy knots to seventy-five knots, where the sleek hull lifted onto the step. As the run ended, the pilot was satisfied with the performance.

Hughes now paused to answer the questions of some of the reporters on board. One of them asked if Hughes planned to fly the giant plane that day, and got this response 'Of course not. As I have explained,

In 1939, Howard Hughes quietly began buying a majority interest in Trans World Airline in order to take over the company. US federal law prohibited him from building planes to be used by his own airline, so Hughes went to his friends at the Lockheed Aircraft Corporation, asking them to build a new and revolutionary airliner for him. He stipulated though, that the plane must be built in total secrecy. It was the famous and highly successful Lockheed Constellation. Its pressurized cabin allowed it to fly above most turbulence, providing its passengers with an entirely new standard of comfort in the air.

During the 1950s Hughes and TWA profited greatly from the success of the Constellation and its successor, the Super Constellation. He wanted to take TWA into the jet age and in 1956 placed a $400 million order with Boeing for a fleet of 707s. His creditors, however, insisted that Hughes give up control of the airline. Unable to cover the cost of the huge purchase, but unwilling to relinquish control of TWA, Hughes's empire then began to crumble. As his fortunes slowly waned, his eccentricity grew and he began to alienate some of his closest advisors and executives. The TWA board eventually forced him from power at the airline, and after a lengthy legal battle, he was compelled by a federal court in 1966 to sell his shares in the airline. His mental and physical health continued to decline and he died in 1976.

I estimate it will be March or April before we're really ready to fly this airplane.' The reporter then wanted to know if it would be possible for him to go ashore and file his story at that point. Hughes said it would, and called for a boat to come alongside to pick up any news people who wanted to depart. Several of the journalists, worried about their deadlines, accepted the opportunity, leaving about ten media people on board for the remainder of the day's testing. One of these was James McNamara, news editor of Los Angeles radio station KLAC and 'pool reporter' for all of the radio news people. With the departure of the press boat, Hughes restarted the engines and prepared for the third taxi test of the day.

'This is James McNamara speaking to you from aboard the Howard Hughes two-hundred-ton flying-boat, the world's largest aircraft. At this moment as we speak to you from the spacious flight deck, this mighty monster of the skies is slowly cruising along a northwest course in the outer Los Angeles Harbor.

'Howard, do you have time at this moment to explain for our radio listeners exactly what you're doing—the operation?'

'Yeah. We're taxiing downwind very slowly to get into position for a run between the entrance to Long Beach Harbor and Myrtle Beach and San Pedro. It's about a three-mile stretch there and we're gonna make a high-speed run in that direction. The wind is changeable—it's been changing all day—but it's not too serious. The water is fairly rough for the outer harbor here. You see, there was quite a heavy wind last night, up to forty-five miles an hour, I believe, which created quite a sea here and that shortens the length of runway we have available because down toward the southeast end here there's effectively an open sea coming around the end of the breakwater and it's very, very rough. But I believe we have an area there that's sufficient and pretty soon we'll be ready to make a run.' Hughes then told his engineer to lower the flaps fifteen degrees.

McNamara stood behind Hughes and called out the speeds as the flying-boat accelerated on this third taxi run. He called 'seventy' and before he could say 'seventy-five', the great hull left the surface and the plane was airborne. The noise and

vibration levels dropped in the aircraft as the resistant water fell away. Then Hughes felt the pull of a crosswind and immediately over-corrected, uncertain of the amount of correction he needed in the untried aircraft. The wing was level again. The altitude: seventy feet. Gradually, he eased the throttles back and began the landing process. According to 'co-pilot' Grant, Hughes made a perfect landing. 'You couldn't even feel it hit the water.' Another crew member, stationed in the forward part of the cargo deck, later commented, 'You could hear the wood creaking, but once we were off the water, everything just smoothed out. I could tell the minute it left the water. When it settled in the water again it started creaking again.' After the landing, McNamara asked Hughes 'Howard, did you expect that?' Hughes replied, 'I like to make surprises.' He added, 'She sure jumped off easy. I think the airplane is going to be fairly successful. I sort of hoped it would fly but didn't want to predict it would and make people disappointed. The controls operated well. We will follow the original testing schedule. That schedule called for a first flight in March 1948.'

The report of the Senate committee investigating Howard Hughes was not released until April 1948. The committee had split in its opinions entirely along party lines, with only the Republican members approving the report which said of the flying-boat project '[It] produced no planes during the war, was an unwise and unjustifiable expense as a wartime project. The manpower, facilities, and public funds devoted to it during the war were wasted at a time when military planes were urgently needed . . . The conclusion was inescapable that the decision of the War Production Board was influenced because of the wide and favorable public acceptance of the proposal of Henry J. Kaiser for the mass production of huge cargo planes which Kaiser claimed would overcome the existing submarine menace to ocean transportation. The technical side of the war cannot be waged from day to day in a manner to accord with public opinion.' The report continued, referring to the failure of the procuring agency to follow normal channels as 'a costly mistake. The Defense Plant

Corporation did not have personnel qualified to supervise an aircraft construction programme. Because of this inadequacy in personnel, the Civil Aeronautics Administration and the National Advisory Committee for Aeronautics, each were given some supervisory authority . . . This divided authority . . . together with the inefficient management of the Hughes organization resulted in allowing Hughes Aircraft Company to carry on the project in an inefficient and wasteful manner.' There followed a dissenting report from the Democrats on the committee in which they stated, 'Howard Hughes and his companies were entitled to a positive finding by the committee, especially so far as fraud, corruption, and willful wrongdoing are concerned. There is absolutely nothing in the evidence which discloses any fraud, corruption, or wrongdoing on the part of Howard Hughes or his associates.'

Hughes built a special hangar on Terminal Island, with controlled humidity for the flying-boat which, since the departure of Henry Kaiser from the project, had been redesignated H-4 and nicknamed *Hercules*. The plane was kept under 24-hour guard. Year after year, Hughes had the aeroplane cared for there, with all of its systems in functioning order, on a fixed maintenance schedule. Noah Dietrich, his executive vice-president, urged him to scrap the plane and save the heavy annual expense. He would not scrap it, nor would he ever fly it again. Hughes was proud of the aeroplane and his company's achievement in creating it. When the General Services Administration, which held the actual legal title to the plane, considered selling it in 1949, Hughes threatened to sue if it were sold to any of the promoters who were the only interested parties. Eventually an arrangement was made in which the Smithsonian Air and Space Museum agreed to accept title to the H-4 and then give it to Summa Corporation (which was all of Hughes's companies), in exchange for the famous Hughes H-1 racing plane, which the museum wanted. Some Summa cash was included to further compensate the museum for the difference in the estimated values of the two aeroplanes, as determined by experts represent

ing the American Institute of Astronautics and Aeronautics.

In 1975 the flying-boat had still not found a home, and there was talk of cutting it up into several sections, each to be donated to a different museum. Such talk infuriated Hughes and when the general public heard about it there were protests against Summa. With the death of Howard Hughes in 1976, Summa explored other possible futures for the H-4, including a proposal for a major evaluation programme by the US Navy, but that idea collapsed in March 1977 because the funding could not be made available.

An agreement was reached in July 1980, in which Summa donated the aeroplane to the Aero Club of Southern California, a non-profit organization, and agreed to finance the move of the plane and the construction of a special dome building in which to display the H-4, in Long Beach adjacent to the liner *Queen Mary* which had been an attraction in the port city for several years.

The Hughes flying-boat was visited by many thousands of people in the near-decade that it resided in Long Beach. Then in 1990, the Aero Club of Southern California was informed that the old flying-boat was to be evicted. The Club solicited proposals from organizations interested in providing a good home for the aeroplane and displaying her proudly, and they chose the Evergreen Aviation Museum of McMinnville, Oregon, (thirty-six miles south-west of Portland), where she is still beautifully preserved.

Specifications: Hughes HK-1 (H-4)
Engines: Eight Pratt & Whitney R-4360 Wasp Major 28-cylinder air-cooled radials rated at 3,000 hp each
Maximum speed: (approx) 218 mph
Cruising speed: (approx) 175 mph
Service ceiling: 20,900 ft
Maximum range: (approx) 3,000 miles
Weight gross: 400,000 lb
Wingspan: 320 ft
Length: 218 ft
Height: 80 ft
Wing area: 11,430 sq ft
Maximum payload: 130,000 lb

The Hughes HK-1 Hercules, reassembled and restored for display, is now on view at the Evergreen Aviation Museum, McMinnville, Oregon.

'During the Second World War, a German prisoner of war was sent each week to tend my garden. He always seemed a nice friendly chap, but when the crocuses came up in the lawn in February, 1946, they spelt out 'Heil Hitler'.'
– Irene Graham

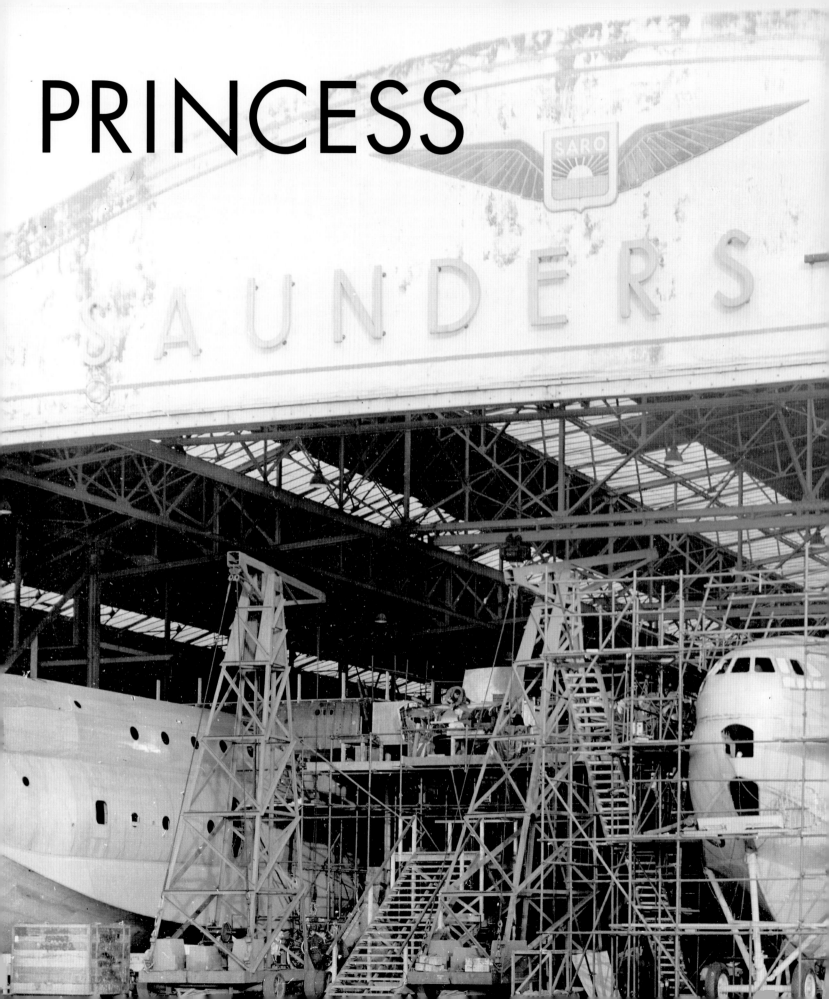

In the 1920s and 1930s the flying-boat seemed to be the way of the future for long-distance commercial aviation. It was thought, by many aircraft designers and airline industry figures, to be the most appropriate type of aircraft for crossing the oceans, for unlike land-planes, if trouble occurred in flight the flying-boat could readily land on the sea and remain there until repairs were made and then it could take off again. The capablility of taking off from, and landing on, the sea, a lake or river, obviated the conventional land-plane requirement for an airfield and its facilities, and the flying-boat could be safely moored in a minimally sheltered harbour or lagoon, with no need for the protection of a large hangar. Physically, the flying-boat offered the great structural, aerodynamic and hydrodynamic advantage of not requiring a large, bulky and complex undercarriage, which also meant a considerable weight saving, always an important consideration with aircraft.

In 1913, the London Daily Mail was offering a £10,000 prize for the first aircraft to successfully cross the Atlantic. The Curtiss H America flying-boat was being prepared for the attempt when the First World War ended that effort. The coming of the war energized the British Royal Navy into mounting long-range flying patrols against German submarines, and to do so they employed the America, together with some smaller Curtiss flying-boats. They were soon ordering several larger Curtiss H-16 flying-boats for the patrols.

Britain's Imperial Airways was formed in 1924 with the merger of four small short-range airlines, in order to connect the British Empire with world-wide air service using flying-boat aircraft. Airfields could only be constructed with great difficulty in the far-flung outposts of the Empire, whereas such destinations had an abundance of rivers, lakes and harbours. The new airline began its service using a small fleet of Calcutta flying-boats built by Short Brothers of Rochester, England, and derived from the Royal Air Force's Singapore I aircraft. These three-engine long-range planes were initially employed on a route to India. They were used on a cross-Mediterranean route and, in 1931, were partnered with another Short flying-

left: Two fuselage hulls of SARO Princess flying-boats under construction probably in 1950 at the Saunders-Roe East Cowes facility on the Isle of Wight; top: Lerwick flying-boats by Saunders-Roe.

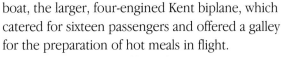

right: The flight deck of a Princess, G-ALUN, at East Cowes. Aimed at the trans-atlantic market, the flying-boat was planned for a cruising speed of 380 mph at an altitude of 37,000 feet. The range was intended to be 5,720 miles. Power was supplied by ten Bristol Proteus two-propeller turbines arranged as four coupled and two single units, all fitted with four-blade sixteen-foot airscrews with coupled units driving the contra-rotating airscrews. The crew consisted of two pilots, two flight engineers, a navigator and a radio operator. There was to be provision for 105 passengers in tourist- and first-class cabins.

boat, the larger, four-engined Kent biplane, which catered for sixteen passengers and offered a galley for the preparation of hot meals in flight.

To capitalize on the effect of the British government's Empire Airmail Scheme, under which air mail letters could be sent between any British Empire countries for only 1d for two ounces, Imperial Airways ordered a fleet of twenty-eight new Short S-23, or 'C Class' flying boats in 1935. The first of these new streamlined all-metal seaplanes made its maiden flight in July 1936. The four 910 hp Bristol Pegasus engines of the C Class aircraft gave it a respectable cruising speed of 160 mph over a range of 1,500 miles. It offered passengers a comfortable, spacious interior that seated twenty-four, or nineteen sleeper passengers, and was operated by a crew of five. Its unique wing-flap system allowed it to operate from shorter stretches of water than were used by the smaller flying-boats it replaced.

The level of luxury experienced by travellers aboard the Empire C Class flying-boats was unprecedented in air travel. The airline had the planes fitted out for first-class accommodation, with individual passenger cabins, separate bathrooms for men and women, a promenade cabin and a substantial galley. The passengers were efficiently attended by two stewards and luncheon menus included such entrées as poached salmon and roast lamb. Those flying from Britain first travelled by train to Southampton where they spent the night in a first-class hotel. After breakfast the next morning they would arrive at the aircraft and their journey would begin. It was a time of unpressurized passenger aircraft and the otherwise luxurious experience was frequently made less comfortable by the inability of the aircraft to operate at altitudes high enough to avoid much of the weather and turbulence. The fatigue factor must have been extremely high on the journey out to Australia, which required an incredible twenty-nine landings and take-offs.

The C Class flying-boats were only flown for two years on the Empire routes before the Second World War disrupted the service. In that brief time they were operated with relatively few significant problems, but some were noteworthy. In June 1938, the

Empire *Ceres* was forced to make an emergency landing on a lake near Karachi. It had run short of fuel after bucking exceptionally strong headwinds. The aircraft had to be lightened substantially in order to be able to take off again from the small lake and the passengers and their luggage had to be taken off and carried to their next port of call by cart and train. In a famous incident of March 1939, the Empire *Corsair* was damaged when it struck rocks while taking off from a river in the Congo. It had been serving Juba from Lake Victoria when the incident occurred, and again, the passengers and their luggage were required to continue on their way by train. Airline personnel arrived from England to repair the flying-boat, a job that took nine months to complete.

In April 1940, a merger of Imperial Airways and a short-haul airline called British Airways, resulted in the creation of British Overseas Airways Corporation. The new company was equipped with the remaining twenty-one Empire C Class aircraft, three Short S.26 and two Short S.33 flying-boats. With war raging in Europe, the Royal Air Force utilized the S.26s and two Short S.30s, on North Atlantic submarine-patrol flights. Both of the S.30s were destroyed by the enemy during the Battle of Norway in May 1940 and two of the S.26s were lost in wartime accidents. BOAC operated a wartime service on routes from Britain to South Africa, Australia and India from its base at Poole, Dorset, from 1940. With the entry of Italy into the war on the side of Germany, several important refuelling stops were lost to BOAC, restricting its service. As the summer of 1940 wore on, and Nazi expansionism in Europe and the Mediterranean gained momentum, C Class flying-boats of BOAC were pressed into making several unscheduled rescue flights, evacuating hundreds of Allied troops, until May 1941.

The BOAC route to Australia was cut late in 1941 when the Japanese invaded Singapore and Malaya. Some of the airline's flying-boats then in Australia were taken over by the Royal Australian Air Force and by Qantas, the Australian airline. As the Japanese gained territory in the Pacific, BOAC suffered casualties when three of the C Class planes were shot down or destroyed on the water by enemy fighters and bombers, with the loss of thirty-seven passengers. Three more of the planes were lost in accidents in Africa and a fourth was destroyed in a German air raid on Poole harbour.

Pan American Airways founder Juan Trippe had long championed the flying boat and in 1927 he launched the first regularly scheduled international airline service on a 90 mile run between Key West, Florida and Havana, Cuba (using Fokker Trimotor landplanes.) But he aimed to expand the service to Central and South America, and to serve coastal cities along these new routes he invested millions of dollars commissioning large and luxurious "clipper" flying boats. In 1936 he followed these with still larger flying boats, the China Clippers, with far greater range to serve a pioneering route from San Francisco to Manila, an 8,000-mile, five-day journey. He called them China Clippers in advance of a service he intended with regular flights to China, a service predicated on the use of refuelling and resupply bases that he had built on Midway, Guam and Wake Island. The coming Pacific war would defer those plans.

With the war came new work for the flying boats of the world. American twin-engine PBY Catalinas built by Consolidated, and British Short Sunderlands, played an important part in long-range reconnaissance and anti-submarine patrol. RAF Coastal Command Sunderlands and Catalinas prowled the Bay of Biscay, attacking German U-boats there and in the Atlantic approaches to the British Isles. PBYs and Martin Mariner flying boats patrolled great areas of the Pacific in US operations against the Japanese Navy. One of the largest flying boats of the war was the Japanese Kawanishi H8K with an impressive range of 4,475 miles. Larger by far, however, was the US Navy Martin JRM Mars (featured in a chapter of this book), at a gross weight of 145,000 pounds. The five Mars flying boats had a range of 4,700 miles and served as effective cargo carriers in the Pacific. 59 years after that war, two surviving Mars aircraft are still in service, as water bombers against forest fires in the western United States and Canada.

In the years immediately after the Second World

overleaf: A taxiing trial of the Princess on the Solent off Stokes Bay at Gosport in August 1952.

The Saunders-Roe Princess was the last of the very large commercial flying-boats. The age of the flying-boat airliner had already finished by 1946, a year before construction of the first Princess had even begun. The Second World War had left a plethora of big airports with long runways which had been designed and built for the great bombers of that war. The Princess was meant to ply the BOAC trans-atlantic route between Southampton and New York, carrying more than one hundred passengers in considerable comfort. But the time of the Princess had come and gone even before it appeared. The two examples were fated to remain moored and largely forgotten for years until they were finally scrapped in 1967.

'I don't hold with abroad and think that foreigners speak English when our backs are turned.'
– Quentin Crisp

War, two really big flying-boats were built. One was the Howard Hughes HK-1 Hercules, commonly known as the Spruce Goose, (discussed in another chapter), which had been in design and construction through much of the war and made its one and only flight in November 1947. The other was the Saunders-Roe SR.45 Princess, which was built for British Overseas Airways Corporation to provide a two-class passenger service between England and New York. Unfortunately for Saunders-Roe, the first flight of the Princess wasn't until August 1952, nearly two years after the British government and BOAC had decided against further large flying-boat development.

In 1910 the brothers Humphrey and Alliot Verdon Roe founded a firm in England called A.V. Roe and Co. Ltd, to build the world's first all-enclosed aeroplane. They produced it in 1912, and by the start of the First World War, were building aeroplanes that the Royal Flying Corps was using to bomb targets like the great Zeppelin sheds at Friedrichshafen. A.V. Roe and Co. (Avro) prospered, and in 1928 became part of the Armstrong Siddley Group. Thereafter, the brothers associated themselves with the S.E.Saunders Co., a firm engaged in building flying-boats, forming a new company called Saunders-Roe Ltd, which in 1952, produced the SARO Princess.

Long before the Princess project, the British Air Ministry was keen on building large flying-boats and by the end of the war had ordered Saunders-Roe and Short Brothers to collaborate on the design and construction of a new aircraft to be called the Short-Saro Shetland. At fifty tons it was physically impressive, but it was not a success. The two examples were scrapped in 1951. For Saunders-Roe the Shetland had been a learning experience, but was nothing like the flying-boat they wanted to create. Before engaging in that project they would be involved in something else quite revolutionary. In 1944 the British Admiralty asked the company to design and build three prototypes of a single-seat jet fighter flying-boat, the SR.A1. The first flight of this aircraft took place at Cowes, Isle of Wight, on 15 July 1947 and it soon established a

speed record for flying-boats of 0.8 Mach, which was later eclipsed by the Convair Sea Dart, which exceeded the sound barrier in a shallow descent. By the time the SR.A1 arrived, the war had ended, defence budgets had been slashed and the Admiralty could not afford to order the aircraft in quantity.

Germany had been the world leader in the design and construction of the long-distance flying-boat in 1929 with its magnificent twelve-engined Dornier DO-X (described in another chapter). Britain had created flying-boat routes throughout her empire with Short Brothers planes and the Americans had entered the

left: The lovely hull of a SARO Princess under construction; below: The East Cowes, Isle of Wight facility of Saunders-Roe, with an incomplete Princess on the ramp.

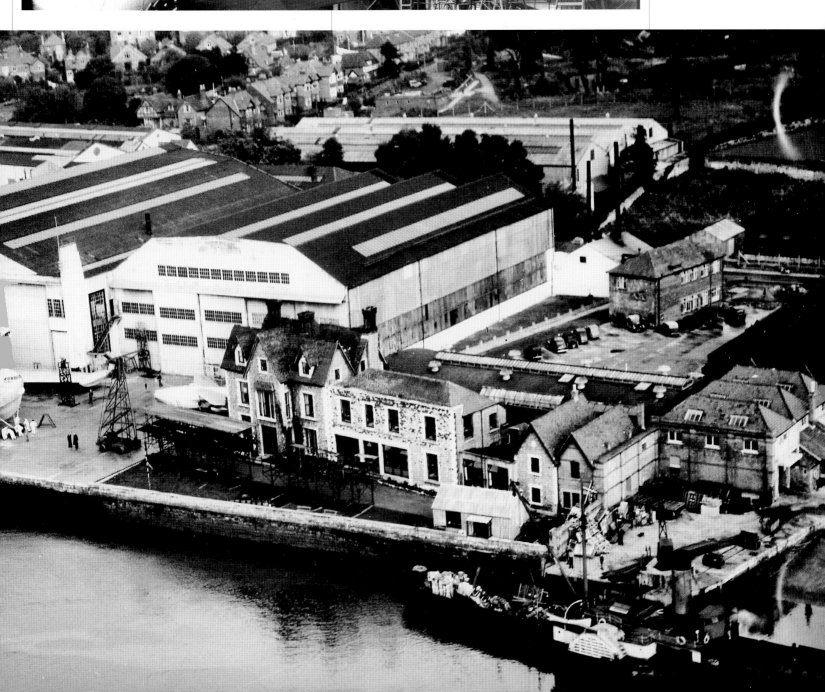

'There is no destination in
life. The journey is everything.'
– anon

market with flying-boat routes from Florida to
Central and South America, as well as from the US
west coast across the Pacific, using Martin, Sikorsky,
and Boeing aircraft. The future development and
uses of the large flying-boat appeared promising.
However, when war came great changes came with
it. Hundreds of long, hard-surface runways were
constructed around the world, and many of these
would be developed later with efficient airport and
communications facilities for peacetime use, eliminating one of the fundamental advantages that had
been touted for the flying-boat. Still, Saunders-Roe
continued to focus on what they believed would be
a viable postwar commercial air transport market
for very large long-range flying-boats. They saw the
golden age of travel by flying-boat extending from
the 1930s, past the Second World War, into the
1950s and beyond to a new age of elegance and
luxury. While they laboured away on the Princess,
many key figures in the airline industry were looking at the way large land-based aircraft had developed as a result of the war. They were interested in
aircraft that would evolve from those wartime successes and in their potential for hauling large numbers of passengers over long distances in reasonable comfort and safety with good economy at an
affordable fare.

Arthur Gouge went to work for Short Brothers at
Rochester, in 1915. He was employed as an appren-
tice mechanic, but by 1930 had become the company's
General Manager and Chief Designer. He was also
acknowledged in the industry as one of the foremost
authorities on flying-boat design, based on his considerable experience with the Empire Class and
Sunderland flying-boats. An outspoken advocate of
the large flying-boat, he collaborated with Henry
Fowler, chief designer of Saunders-Roe in 1943, and
the pair developed the design proposals that led the
British Ministry of Supply to contract with Saunders-
Roe in 1946 for the design and construction of three
long-range SR.45 flying-boats.

Work began on the plane that was to be known as
the SARO Princess, and almost immediately the project was dogged with schedule slippage and higher

costs than had been projected. These triggered questions in the House of Commons about what was
seen by many as a high-risk project, the costing of
which was at best difficult. The matters under discussion were the greater-than-anticipated expenditures
on airframe design and testing and the significant
under-estimation of the cost of developing the Bristol
Proteus engine, something over which Saunders-Roe
had no control.

Preliminary conceptual design for the Princess had
actually begun during the war, when Messrs Gouge
and Fowler agreed on the specifications for such an
aircraft, should they ever be fortunate enough to be
able to build it. Their design called for a flying-boat
that would weigh 140 tons, with a pressurized
'double bubble' hull. It was to be the largest all-metal
flying-boat ever built, with a 219-foot wingspan, the
wing being a high-mounted cantilever monoplane,
built in five sections around two spars. The aircraft
would have a length of 148 feet, a height of 55 feet 9
inches and accommodation for 105 passengers. It
was intended to serve the transatlantic market with a
cruising speed of 380 mph at an altitude of 37,000
feet. Depending on the payload carried, the anticipated range of the plane would be between 3,640
and 5,190 miles.

The Princess was to have power-assisted flight controls to help the pilots cope with the great surface
loads she would present. Some thought was given to
the possibility of fitting her with an early 'fly-by-wire'
control system, but the designers settled on a system
of mechanical linkages connected to electrical power-
assist units. Such an enormous craft would clearly
require enormous power to lift and propel her and,
after evaluating the possibilities, the design engineers
opted for an arrangement of ten Bristol Proteus turboprop powerplants, positioned as four coupled pairs
and two additional engines outboard of the pairs,
with all engines having four-bladed 16 foot 6 inch propellers; the coupled pair units driving contra-rotating
pairs of propellers. The rate of climb was to be 1,900
feet per minute and the maximum take-off weight
would be 330,000 lb. The flight deck of the Princess
accommodated two pilots, two flight engineers, a navigator and a radio operator.

The planned launch of the first SARO Princess was delayed one day by bad weather, to 21 August 1952. The next morning she was taken out for taxi testing on the Solent by Saunders-Roe's chief test pilot Geoffrey Tyson, in command of a company flight-test crew. The taxi testing continued for half an hour and then Tyson proceeded along the Solent to Stokes Bay near Gosport and turned the graceful seaplane into the wind, facing a clear seventeen-mile expanse of water, in excellent conditions. Supposedly, the test plan for the day only called for taxiing, but the conditions must have been just what Tyson wanted as he advanced the ten throttles to full power. The Princess gathered speed and a cloud of spray spread from her hull. Of the moment, Tyson later said, 'Well, she simply wanted to fly, so I let her!' She became airborne at 12.28 p.m. on a thirty-five-minute flight in which Tyson circumnavigated the Isle of Wight with no significant problems.

In advance of an appearance by the Princess at the Farnborough International Air Display on 2 September, the aircraft was put through a number of further test flights, during which the first indications of engine reliability trouble appeared. An engine failure in this period led to the cancellation of a display by the plane at the Farnborough Public Preview Day, 5 September, with flight testing resumed after replacement of the engine. As the testing went on, reliability problems with the engines and the gearboxes increased, but the flying and the evaluation continued through 1953, with emphasis on isolating and correcting the troubles. The aeroplane was displayed again at Farnborough in 1953, and flight testing went on until 27 May 1954, her 46th and final flight. By then it had been established that the perfected and fully rated Proteus engines would indeed power the Princess to her projected performance numbers. By the end of the flight-test period, she had logged about ninety-seven flying hours and had earned a very good report.

The British government now had to decide what to do with the elegant new flying-boat. That first flight test aeroplane and the two additional unflown airframes were placed in storage pending the decision. A lengthy period of indecision followed. BOAC, for whom the planes had been built, finally stated that it no longer wanted them, having permanently terminated its flying-boat services in 1950. Faced with the prospect of no future for its big flying-boat, Saunders-Roe looked for other potential users, including the US Navy, which in 1958 expressed an interest in the construction of a nuclear-powered version of the Princess, but dropped the idea the following year.

Two further flying-boat projects were explored by Saunders-Roe. The Duchess was planned to be a smaller, jet-powered six-engine aircraft capable of carrying seventy-six passengers at 500 mph. The second idea, Project P192, involved a much larger version of the Princess, a flying cruise ship with a wingspan of 313 feet, a length of 318 feet and a gross weight of 670 tons. Neither of the projects went beyond the preliminary stage.

Across the River Medina from where it was built at Cowes, Isle of Wight, the first Princess sat on jacks, cocooned in storage, awaiting her fate. Her two sister ships, uncompleted airframes, were also cocooned and were in long-term storage at Calshot until 1965 when they were scrapped. In July 1967, unable to find a buyer for its lovely Princess, Saunders-Roe finally had the original flight-test aeroplane towed from Cowes over to Southampton, where it was broken up, closing the era of the large, passenger-carrying flying-boat, perhaps forever.

Specifications: Saunders-Roe SR.45 Princess
Engines: Ten Bristol Proteus 600 Series turboprops arranged as four coupled and two single units, rated at 3,780 hp each, all fitted with four-blade propellers; the single outboard units driving single propellers; the coupled units driving contra-rotating propellers.
Maximum cruising speed: 380 mph at 37,000 ft
Service ceiling: 39,000 ft
Maximum range: 5,720 miles
Weight, empty: 190,000 lb. Weight, gross: 330,000 lb
Wingspan: 219 ft 6 in
Length: 148 ft
Height: 55 ft 9 in
Wing area: 5,019 sq ft
Capacity: 105 passengers

'I have found that there ain't no surer way to find out whether you like people or hate them than to travel with them.'
– Mark Twain

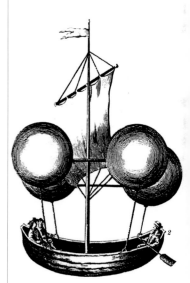

ME321
ME323

German aviation pioneer Willy Messerschmitt, the son of a wine merchant, was born in Frankfurt am Main in 1898. He began his aeronautical design career in 1923 when he formed his own company at Augsburg. Before that he had assisted the gliding pioneer Friedrich Harth at a military flying school during the First World War. Together they designed a glider, the S8, which set a world record for time aloft (twenty-one minutes) in 1921. This led to their work on an undistinguished series of powered gliders, one of which crashed in 1925 with Messerschmitt on board. His injuries required hospitalization.

In 1927, Messerschmitt merged his company with *Bayerische Flugzeugwerke* (Bavarian Aircraft Works). There his M20 light transport plane was a disastrous failure when Lufthansa airline M20s were involved in a number of crashes. The airline subsequently cancelled the balance of their order for the aircraft. But with the rise of the Nazis and the establishment of their government in 1933, Messerschmitt's reputation was restored. He and fellow designer Robert Lusser collaborated on the model M37, known by its *Reichsluftfahrtministerium* (Reich Aviation Ministry) designation as the Bf108 *Taifun*, an excellent four-seat sport plane. Following that success the pair designed a derivative of the *Taifun*, the Bf 109 fighter, which became the mainstay of the German Fighter Command for much of the war. It won Messerschmitt worldwide acclaim and more 109s were built than any other single-seat aircraft in aviation history.

Unfortunately for Messerschmitt, he had acquired a powerful enemy in Erhard Milch, the head of Lufthansa, who had lost a dear friend in one of the M20 crashes. When the Nazis took power, Milch was made head of the Reich Aviation Ministry and he vowed that Messerschmitt would get no government contracts in that time of resurgence for the German aircraft industry. To keep his company in business, Messerschmitt accepted orders from Romania for the M37 and for his M36 transport plane. On learning of these contracts, Milch called Messerschmitt a traitor, which resulted in the designer being interrogated by the Gestapo. His fortunes improved markedly, however, when the German First World War hero, Ernst Udet, was appointed leader of the Luftwaffe's devel-

left: An Me 323 on final approach with flaps lowered. The giant Me 321 was originally planned as a transport glider, to deliver tanks, guns and soldiers in the German invasion of Britain during the Second World War. Even though that invasion was cancelled, the Nazis still needed such a craft when they turned east to invade the Soviet Union. Messerschmitt and Junkers each received contracts for 100 of the gliders, but the Junkers entry, the Ju 322, proved unacceptable and the work went to Willy Messerschmitt's company.

right: The Me 321 V1 at Leipheim just before its first flight on 25 February 1941; below: The cross insignia used on all Luftwaffe aircraft during the Second World War; far right: The Me 321 was capable of carrying up to 175 fully equipped troops, with some of them seated in the wing.

opment section.

The Bf 109 was a remarkably advanced aircraft. A compact monoplane airframe of all-metal construction, it incorporated leading-edge slats to reduce the landing speed, a retractable undercarriage, an enclosed cockpit and high-lift devices—all revolutionary features in the 1930s. Udet was sceptical when he first saw the Bf 109, but when he flew it he declared it the best flying machine in the world at that time. He was greatly impressed by the aeroplane and it was soon adopted as the principal fighter of the German Air Force. Willy Messerschmitt was then in full favour with the Hitler regime. He had given Germany a superb fighter that would serve it with distinction throughout the war.

The little Bf 109 was not the only contribution that Messerschmitt made to his country's war effort. In a particularly clever but ill-fated attempt to develop a high-performance twin-engine two-seat aircraft with remotely controlled guns and all the best qualities of the superb British Mosquito (more than a year before the Mosquito became operational), the Messerschmitt chief designer Waldemar Voigt created the Me 210. But Messerschmitt applied excessive weight-saving demands on the plane and it became unstable. He tried to save the project through development of the Me 410, which arrived far too late to be effective as the 'German Mosquito'. Later, Luftwaffe chief Hermann Goering commented that his own epitaph should be, 'He would have lived longer but for the Me 210.'

Other interesting aircraft to emerge from the company works were the Me 110 twin-engined fighter, a menace to the Allied bombers attacking Germany; the huge Me 321 and 323 programmes, enormous aircraft that could carry tanks and troops to the battle zone; and the Me 262 twin-engined jet fighter which, had it appeared in greater numbers, could have seriously challenged the Allied bombing campaign.

The Me 321 glider led to a powered version, the Me 323 *Gigant* (Giant) that was capable of ferrying 130 fully equipped troops. In their construction, the Me 321 and 323 were both based on steel tubing airframes and main spars, while their wings, ailerons and flaps were largely of pine and plywood, with fabric covering most of the structure. With the early 1941 termination of the planned invasion of England by German forces, a new role was given to the Me 321 glider, that of ferrying over-sized or extremely heavy war materiel or equipment by air to wherever it was needed in the war zone. The big glider was perceived as a single-use

aircraft, to be disposed of on the completion of its assigned sortie. A delayed-action explosive charge was provided in the cockpit of each aircraft. Fitted under the pilot's seat, the device could be set to explode ten minutes after it was activated. The 321 had a forty-two-foot cargo hold with a hardwood floor that could accommodate a twenty-two ton tank, a variety of vehicle types, or an 88 mm anti-aircraft gun with its tractor and crew. Other loads that it could carry included twenty-two tons of general cargo or up to 175 fully equipped troops. The cargo hold was fitted with several plexiglass windows to provide light. Frontal access to the large cargo bay was through a pair of fabric-covered outward-opening clamshell doors. A loading ramp was provided as was a non-steerable two-wheel undercarriage which could be jettisoned after take-off, along with two smaller wheels in the nose section. For landing, the Me 321 alighted on four sprung skids. It was also equipped with a braking parachute which could be released to shorten the landing distance if needed.

To assist the take-off when the Me 321 was overloaded, or in short-field situations, four Walther rockets could be fitted under the wing. These devices had a thirty-second burn duration, and when their fuel was expended, the rockets could be jettisoned at low altitude to land by parachute. They could then be recov-

ered, repaired if necessary, cleaned and made ready to be re-used. The wood and plexiglass roof of the cockpit could be jettisoned if necessary, and the entire cockpit was fitted with protective armour, including armour-glass panels on the front and sides. The two pilots had dual controls and sat side by side. The release mechanism for the tow coupling, and the braking parachute lever, were located between the two pilots.

Their utilization of relatively small troop and cargo-carrying gliders against the Belgian Eben Emael fort in May 1940 had convinced the German Army that large gliders could be employed successfully in the coming Operation Sea Lion, the invasion of Great Britain. In early October, Willy Messerschmitt wrote to Ernst Udet, then Chief of German Air Armaments, proposing the design and construction of a very large, tank-carrying glider which would be towed by four Ju 52 transport aircraft. Apparently, Udet was impressed by the concept and within a few days preliminary work on the bold project was begun under the supervision of the former Arado aircraft engineer, Josef Frölich. But *Reichsmarschall* Hermann Goering's Luftwaffe was unsuccessful in its efforts to defeat the pilots of the Royal Air Force Fighter Command and gain air supremacy over the British Isles and the English

below: An exercise in which the efficient exiting of troops from the Me 323 is tested.

Channel in the Battle of Britain that summer and fall. The planned invasion was postponed and then, in January 1941, formally cancelled. Work on the new Messerschmitt high-capacity glider, now designated Me 261, had continued however, and in November 1940, Willy Messerschmitt personally convinced Adolf Hitler of the big glider's importance and promise. In a design competition between Messerschmitt and Junkers, the Messerschmitt entry, now called *Gigant*, was selected. It would be built of steel tubing, wood and fabric and was to be capable of carrying a twenty-two ton Panzer IV tank. By late November, Messerschmitt had discussed

the concept of a powered version of the new glider with Udet. It was to be designated Me 323. It would be powered by four Daimler Benz DB 601 engines and, by February 1941, its technical specifications had been resolved. Meanwhile, initial work on the Me 321 glider was under way at Leipheim, an airfield near Ulm.

With completion of the first Me 321s came a lengthy and incident-filled programme of towed flights during which a wide range of aircraft combinations was tried in order to determine the safest and most efficient method of getting the 321 airborne and to its release point. In addition to the use of Ju 52s, Messerschmitt

Bf 110s, Junkers Ju-90s, and Heinkel He 111 bombers were tried, along with various mechanical adjustments, but as the programme continued into late 1941, and increased use was made of the Bf 110s in the tug role known as *Troika-Schlepp*, the accident rate increased alarmingly. The worst of these incidents occurred when an Me 321 carrying a load of 15,000 litres of water was taken aloft by a group of the *Troika-Schlepp* aircraft on a flight test. As the *Gigant* approached to land at the Obertraubling airfield, it was caught in a sudden updraft, which caused a catastrophic structural failure and the loss of the tail section. The glider plunged 400

feet and crashed near the village of Barbing, killing the crew of five. The famous woman test pilot, *Flugkapitän* Hanna Reitsch, took part in the flight testing of the Me 321 at Obertraubling, but fortunately for her, was not involved in that particular test. To stem the increasing number of accidents, Udet decided to experiment with another entirely new concept, the Heinkel He 111Z; two standard He 111s grafted together with a central wing addition and powered by a total of five engines.

The troubled tow-testing programme, and the less than satisfactory performance in the rocket-assisted take-off trials, gave added impetus to the already rapidly developing Me 323. The 323 would be propelled initially by four, and later by six engines. In his excellent book *Messerschmitt Me 321/323*, Hans-Peter Dabrowski describes the construction of the 323: 'The cargo compartment and cockpit (referred to by the crews as the 'lower house' and the 'upper house') were joined by a ladder inside the fuselage on the port side.

'The three-piece wing was trapezoidal in outline with a straight leading edge. It consisted of a one-piece centre-section with two-part landing flaps on each side and two upswept outer sections with two-part ailerons. The wing ribs, stiffeners and leading edge skinning were made of wood, while the rest of the wing plus the flaps and ailerons were fabric-covered. The 30-meter [97 ft 6 in] centre-section spar, which was welded to the fuselage framework, was a box-shaped structure made of steel tube. Steel tubing of varying diameters and thicknesses was welded together to form the tapered box spar. This spar absorbed the bending and torsional forces exerted on the wing. Welded to it were fishplates, to which the ribs were attached. The wing was stiffened by glued-on longitudinal and transverse strips. The plywood leading edge skinning was also glued to the ribbing. Three outriggers were attached to each side of the wing to support the trailing edge flaps and these were also supported by bracing wires. At the outer extremities of the box spar were flanges for attachment of the outer wings. The wing framework was attached to the fuselage framework by four bolts. The wing-fuselage joint was covered by a fabric-covered filet. The wing spar was braced on each side by a single strut extending to the fuselage. This in turn was braced

'Generals detest generals on their own side far more than they dislike the enemy.'
– Peter Ustinov

How are the mighty fallen,
and the weapons of war
perished!
– Old Testament, 2 Samuel

above: Fitting the nose
doors of Me 321 A gliders;
right: An Me 323 which
escaped damage during an
Allied air raid on Lecce.

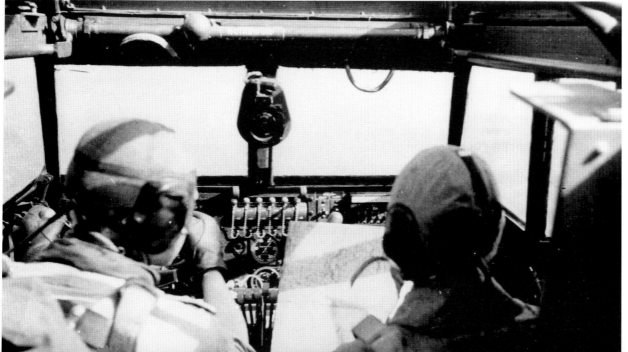

above: An Me 323 D-1 which has been retrofitted with guns in its nose doors; left: Pilots Obfw. Kandzia and Fw. Binder in an Me 323.

against bending and twisting by two V-struts. All struts were covered by streamlined fairings. The pitot tube for the airspeed indicator was mounted on the port bracing strut.

'An outer wing was attached to each end of the wing centre-section. Here, too, the spar was a tapered box structure, 12.5 meters [40 ft 6 in]in length. The rib structure and attachment of the leading edge were similar to that of the wing centre-section. The wingtips consisted of slightly-rounded rib boxes covered with fabric. The upper and lower girders of the centre-section spar were attached to the corresponding girders of the outer wings with the aid of flanges. The joint was covered with fabric.

'A cutout in the centre of the leading edge of the wing centre-section was designed to accept the cockpit, which was a separate component. It was attached to the front wall of the box spar at four points. On the port side of the cockpit was the pilot's seat, with the co-pilot's seat mounted on the starboard side. Both were bolted to the floor. The seat tub and back were padded as were the arm rests on each side. In front of the pilot seats was the instrument panel in shock-absorbing mounts and a common throttle lever box. Cockpit ventilation was provided by adjustable ventilation inlets on each side. To provide crew protection against enemy fire, the cockpit was designed as an armoured box: the floor and the front and rear walls, including the cabin door, consisted of 8mm armour plates which were bolted together. A two-part superstructure covered the cockpit. It consisted of a load-bearing welded steel tube framework, partly covered with *Sekuritglas* (safety glass) and part with plexiglass.

'The pilots were provided with the following instrumentation: airspeed indicator with heated pitot, coarse (0 to 6,000 m) and fine (0 to 1,000 m) altimeters, vertical speed indicator, electric turn-and-bank indicator, chronometer, remote reading compass, emergency pilot compass, mechanical stabilizer incidence indicator, position indicators for all three Flettners. There were no engine monitoring instruments, however, just an ignition switch which allowed the pilot to cut each magneto independently or all simultaneously. Mounted on the port side of the

cockpit was a pressure gauge (0 to 50 atm) for monitoring the compressed air pressure for the brake system.

'Flight engineer positions were placed in the leading edge of the wing between the inboard engines (2 and 3, 4 and 5). These could be reached by means of crawlways inside the wing. The crawlways from the cockpit to the flight engineer positions had a clear height of about 1.3 meters [4 ft 4 in. In each cabin a cushioned seat was attached to the front wall of the box spar. Several windows were incorporated into the leading edge. Above the flight engineer seats were jettisonable glazed escape hatches. The flight engineer thus had a limited view up, down and forward. In front of the seats were instrument panels with engine instruments and to the sides were control boxes with the control levers. The flight engineer's chest parachute lay on the floor, half under his seat, and in an emergency he had to clip it onto his parachute harness.

'The ten-wheel (initially eight-wheel) undercarriage, which consisted of three 1200 x 420 wheels aft and two 875 x 320 wheels forward on each side, was designed in such a way that it could cross uneven ground in a manner similar to a caterpillar track. Furthermore, the wheels were so arranged that the aircraft always remained in a horizontal position regardless of load. A retractable strut in the extreme rear of the fuselage prevented the aircraft from tipping backward during loading. In order to spread the shock of landing between several wheels, the two aft wheels acted upon the same shock absorber.

'All production Me 323 aircraft were powered by 14-cylinder air-cooled Gnôme-Rhône 14 N radial engines.

'In order to prevent engine vibration from being transmitted to the wing structure, the engines were installed on two-piece welded steel tube mounts each, consisting of a forward shock-absorbing section and an intermediate section.

'The two flight engineers in their wing cabins, each had to operate and monitor the three engines on their side of the aircraft. The only engine controls available to the pilots were the throttle levers and ignition switches for all six engines. Using the pitch switches of the propeller pitch control system, the flight engineers could regulate engine output in

flight independent of rpm and boost pressure. The
engines were prone to failure in flight, however, and
the Me 323 was capable of flying on just three engines
provided all of the non-functioning engines were not
on the same side.

'Various pilots have also stated that the engines
tended to catch fire when started after sitting idle for
some time.

'[The Me 323 had] one MG 15 [machine-gun]
mounted on the roof of the armoured cockpit canopy
and operated by the radio operator or another
crewmember, with a field of fire above and to both
sides. Located behind the cockpit, between the steel
wall and the wing bearer, was the radio operator's
compartment. Above it was a rearwards-sliding hatch
which could be used as an escape hatch or makeshift
gun position.

'Forward defense was provided by two MG 15
(later MG 131) machine-guns in the clamshell doors.
One or two rearward-firing MG 15s were mounted in
the fuselage underside. Additional crew members
had to be carried to man these weapons. A simple
modification made it possible to mount MG 34s in
the fuselage side walls, for example when the aircraft was used as a troop transport. The MG 34 was
designed for use by the infantry and was not an aircraft machine-gun, however, it could be installed in
the above-named locations instead of the MG 15.
Beginning with the E-2, defensive armament was
bolstered by the addition of two EDL 151 power turrets on the upper surface of the wing centre-section,
each mounting one MG 151/20 cannon. These were
manned by gunners or, in an emergency, the flight
engineers. The *Gigant*'s armament varied from aircraft to aircraft. In some cases gun positions were
not used, while in others improvised positions were
added. As development of the Me 323 progressed,
operational experience resulted in field modifications which were subsequently adopted as standard
equipment.'

With the final cancellation of the invasion of England,
Me 321 production and operational training were
reduced in priority and redirected towards operations
on the Eastern Front, beginning late in 1941. As the
production of the powered Me 323 version got under

way, engines were installed on many Me 321 gliders to convert them into Me 323s.

The first major operational deployment of the Me 323 occurred in November 1942 when Nos. 1 and 2 *Staffeln* of 1/KGr.z.b.V. 323 departed Leipheim for Eleusis, Greece. After flying several sorties to Crete, the *Gruppe* was transferred to Lecce, Italy just as the Allies launched Operation Torch near Oran in West Africa. For three weeks the *Giganten Gruppe* operated from Lecce before being transferred again, this time to the Alfa Romeo airfield at Pomigliano d'Arco, near Naples. Between 1 November and 10 December, the *Gruppe* flew eighty-two sorties in which it carried 865 tons of cargo, with forty to sixty per cent of its aircraft available for use, the latter figure towards the end of the period. The two relocation moves hindered the maintenance capability of the *Gruppe*. The primary servicing problem was engine maintenance, with propeller pitch motors failing at a high rate.

Operationally, the Me 323 was proving to be relatively easy and efficient to load and unload and the unique undercarriage provided superb ground manoeuvrability in all load configurations. All was not positive about the handling characteristics of the aircraft, however. Crews complained about inadequate aileron effectiveness in certain conditions and about how uncomfortable the aircraft was in low-level flight. Controllability problems were evident during low-light and evening landings in the reduced visibility. The Ratier variable-pitch propellers presented continuing problems, as did refuelling, which took too long. There were complaints about the armament system and improvised field installation of dorsal turrets from Heinkel He 111s were made to help resolve the problems. Other crew complaints—unnecessarily difficult emergency exit accessibility for the pilots and the radio operator, the lack of provision for the pilots to communicate with the gunners, the lack of direction-finding equipment, and inadequate visibility for the pilots during formation flying and landing approaches.

With the start of 1943, several Me 323s, and many Ju 52s, fell victim to Allied fighter attacks as the German transports struggled to deliver supplies to Afrika-Korps units. These operations were especially harrowing for the crews of the Me 323s. Owing to the aircraft's great size, they were easily spotted from long distances and readily attacked by enemy fighter aircraft.

In December 1942, the four *Staffeln* of II./KG.z.b.V. returned to Leipheim from the Eastern Front, to be re-equipped and retrained on the Me 323. During this time *Generalfeldmarschall* Erhard Milch was gathering as many transport aircraft and crews as he could in preparation for a massive airlift to resupply the German Sixth Army, which was surrounded by Soviet forces at Stalingrad. This included elements of II./KG.z.b.V.323, inexperienced in their Me 323s, as well as He 111Z / Me 321 tow-plane and glider combinations, in spite of these aircraft being required just as urgently in

right: The first Me 323s to be sent to the Mediterranean theatre in late October 1942.

the Mediterranean theatre to resupply the Afrika-Korps. But the *Gigant*s of that *gruppe* were not employed at Stalingrad, as *Generalfeldmarschall* Paulus was compelled to surrender his Sixth Army there to the Soviets on 2 February 1943.

II. *Gruppe* was transferred to the Mediterranean where it suffered its share of bad days, the worst being Thursday, 22 April 1943. Early that morning fourteen Me 323s and ten Ju 52s took off from Pomigliano on a mission to resupply Army Group Tunis, the remains of Rommel's vaunted Afrika-Korps. The *Gigant*s were hauling fuel and ammunition and the whole formation was to be escorted by 104 Bf 109

fighters. On the day before this mission, the crews had been specifically briefed to avoid the area around Cape Bon, which was considered quite dangerous. Their route was to be over Cape Farina and the aircraft were flying through a heavy haze. The formation was roughly half way between Sicily and Tunisia, and flying at just 150 feet above the sea when, for whatever reason, the *Gigant*s turned away from the Ju 52s onto a new heading *towards* Cape Bon. There must have been much confusion at that point, with the majority of the fighter escort remaining with the Ju 52s on the prescribed course, while thirty- six of the Bf 109s continued with the *Gigant*s.

above: An exercise in the loading of horses aboard an Me 323; centre: Training a new pilot on the Me 323; far right: The wreckage of a six-engined Me 323 in Tunisia near the city of Tunis. It is believed to have been destroyed by the retreating German forces.

The Ju 52s reached Cape Farina safely at 9.35 a.m., but at 9.25 the Me 323s and their fighter escort were attacked by two groups of enemy fighters between the island of Zembra and Cape Bon, while flying at an altitude of approximately 7,800 feet. As the first group of enemy attackers engaged the Bf 109s, the second group, identified by the Me 323 crews as Curtiss P-40 Kittyhawks of the South African Air Force, bore in on the *Gigant*s. As they were attacked, the *Gigant*s attempted to scatter and take evasive action. But the great, bulky transports stood no chance of evading the Kittyhawks, which quickly scored a number of hits on them. Carrying the highly

volatile cargoes, many of the *Gigant*'s were soon burning, with some exploding on being hit by the enemy machine-gun fire. The *Gigant* crews fought tenaciously, their gunners bringing down between five and seven of the Kittyhawks, but the situation was hopeless for the big transports. By the end of the attack, all of the Me 323s had been shot down and destroyed. In the action, 119 of the 138 men aboard the *Gigant*'s were killed. By the end of October, Axis fortunes had changed considerably. Mussolini, the Italian leader, was deposed in late July, leaving the Germans without their Mediterannean ally. Continuing Allied air attacks on their few remaining Italian airfields took a further toll of their *Giganten*.

The final evolutions of the *Gigant* were the Me 323D and E models, and by 1944, 201 of these aircraft had been constructed. The six engines of the D model produced a total of 4,320 horsepower and the plane now had self-sealing fuel tanks. Later, more powerful engines were fitted, producing a total of just under 6,000 hp. For armament, five MG 15 machine-guns were standard (eventually replaced by five MG 131 13 mm machine-guns) and ten of the plexiglass windows were fitted with rubber seals which could accommodate MG 34 machine-guns. These weapons were intended to be manned when necessary by infantry troops being transported in the aircraft. With the introduction of the E model, the Me 323 received uprated engines generating a total of 6,600 hp. A final variant, the Zeppelin/Messerschmitt ZMe 323F, was produced. Its six Jumo 211R engines had a total power rating of 8,040 hp. A further version of the E-2, the *Waffenträger* (Weapons Carrier), also known as the *Flakkreuzer*, (Flak cruiser) was heavily armed with eleven 20 mm cannon and was manned by a crew of twenty. It is believed that the *Waffenträger* concept resulted from the disastrous *Gigant* losses incurred in the resupply flights to North Africa. It carried no payload and was strictly a weapons-carrying escort for other Me 323s. Major modifications by the firm of Luftschiffbau Zeppelin, of Friedrichshafen, in September 1943 had added the cannon armament

and bullet-proof glass to protect the crews. The gun-containing clamshell front-loading doors were permanently sealed shut. When the Leipheim base was bombed on 24 April 1944, a number of Me 323s that were being converted to *Waffenträgers,* were destroyed.

Mechanically, the 323s were continually troubled by overheating problems with their French Gnôme-Rhône engines, which had originally been selected to power the big planes because they could be built in occupied France without interfering with German aero-engine production.

The end of Me 323 production came in April 1944, when Willy Messerschmitt received the following letter from Major Mauß, *Gruppenkommandeur*, I.TG 5:
Dear Professor,
The *Gruppe* is sending you a commemorative print on the occasion of its 2,000th sortie on the Me 323.
While the first 1,000 sorties were flown in the south, the second 1,000 were completed in the difficult conditions of the Russian winter. We approached this new mission with the same enthusiasm as when we began operations and with the same belief in the practicality and necessity of large-capacity transport aircraft and mastered it. The success of this mission, which was ordered by the *Führer*, was greatly influenced bringing the *Gruppe* up to strength with E-series Me 323s. With the exception of the uncorrectable shortcomings which are known to both you and us, we are very satisfied with the E-series. Unfortunately the engines are becoming even worse and the situation has caused us serious concerns such as never existed before with the Messerschmitt. We therefore hope to see a German engine in this airframe. Coincident with the 2,000th sortie, the first Me 323 airframe reached 500 flying hours.
The decision not to continue building the *Gigant* has hit us hard, because we have become so used to the aircraft. Nevertheless, we continue to hope that, following a decisive turn in the war which is expected soon, the *Gigant* will be developed and built on a much larger scale than was previously the case. For us there is no fonder wish than to be a part of this.

As creator of the *Giganten*, you, Herr Professor, will surely be allowed to realize your ideas in the area of large-capacity transports, for this type of aircraft will also be part of the future after the war.

With best wishes for you personally and for your work, which is decisive to Germany's life and death struggle, I respectfully salute you with *Heil Hitler*, —Mauß

The big Me 323 did not achieve the kind of success its planners had anticipated, but it had been produced utilizing relatively inexpensive and low-priority materials in a minimal number of man-hours. It was the first transport aircraft of the war capable of carrying outsized and very heavy cargoes to combat areas without the need for paved runways. It was the largest land-based aircraft of World War Two.

Specifications: Messerschmitt Me 323E-2

Engines: Six Gnôme-Rhône 14N radials rated at 1,140 hp each

Maximum speed: 149 mph

Service ceiling: 14,760 ft

Normal range: 808 miles

Weight, empty: 64,066 lb Weight, maximum take-off: 99,210 lb

Wingspan: 180 ft 5 in

Length: 93 ft 6 in

Height: 31 ft 6 in

Wing area: 3,229 sq ft

Armament: one 20 mm MG 151 cannon in each of two turrets (one on each wing), two 13 mm MG 131 machine-guns in the nose doors and five additional MG 131s firing from beam positions and the rear of the flight deck

'Always forgive your enemies. Nothing annoys them so much.'
– Oscar Wilde

CONVAIR

right: The Convair XC-99 was the world's largest land plane. Its maiden flight took place on 24 November 1947 at San Diego. It is shown here landing after that initial flight. Capable of carrying up to 400 fully equipped troops or 100,000 lb of cargo, the six- engined heavy lifter resulted from Convair's effort to develop a cargo version of its B-36 bomber. A proposed production model, the C-99, would have had fore and aft loading ramps and could have transported large armoured vehicles and other bulky military equipment. Operated by a five-man crew, the XC-99 had a range of 8,000 miles with a reduced cargo load.

Japan's attack on Pearl Harbor in December 1941, and her subsequent naval and air superiority in the Pacific theatre of the Second World War, caused a number of concerns in the United States. American officials worried about their ability to maintain US forces in that theatre with supplies, weapons, ammunition, food, spare parts, medical and other equipment, with the hazards posed by the enemy on the sea lanes. This concern provided the impetus in 1942 for the priority development of an entirely new range of heavy lift and transport aircraft, including the mammoth Consolidated-Vultee XC-99.

This giant cargo carrier would emerge from design work already under way on Consolidated's new intercontinental superbomber, the B-36. The big bomber, which was still four years away from her first flight, had come about early in 1941 with the notion that, should Britain be taken over by Germany, and the United States enter the war, the Americans would be left with no air bases from which to conduct bombing raids in Europe against the Nazis. The US Army Air Corps believed that it required a truly intercontinental heavy bomber capable of striking targets anywhere in Europe from bases in the United States. The new plane would require a 12,000-mile maximum range, a cruising speed of 275 mph and a top speed of 450 mph. She would have to bring a bomb-load of 10,000 lb over a radius of action of 5,000 miles and would need a service ceiling of 45,000 feet. The B-36 would ultimately achieve much of what was expected of her, though not during the remaining years of the war. But, as the backbone of the American strategic bombing force until the coming of her replacement, the Boeing B-52, the B-36 helped hold the line for America and the Western nations during the early years of the Cold War with the Soviet Union.

In May 1942, Consolidated designers began a consideration of a new ultra-long-range heavy-lift double-deck cargo aircraft based on the specifications of the developing XB-36 design. The project was called the Model 36 Transport, and though slightly smaller, resulted in a design that was quite similar to that of the final XC-99. The XC-99, however, would not be built with the 'trade mark' Consolidated B-24-style twin vertical stabilizers. It would have a single vertical fin much like that of its B-36 antecedent. It would be the largest piston-engined cargo plane ever built.

Consolidated planned the new aircraft to incorporate the wing, piston engines and engine arrangement of the B-36, but with a much larger, fully pressurized fuselage which would accommodate 144 passengers and up to 12,000 lb of cargo in a combined version. The plane was to be operated by a crew of five with additional provision for a five-man relief crew for extremely long-haul trips. Clearly, the company was thinking about the post-war airlines market from the initial brainstorming sessions of the XC-99. An aircraft of such specifications would, in their view, certainly fill an important niche in that market, providing far greater passenger and/or freight capacity, and more comfort than any airliner likely to emerge from the decade.

A magazine article that appeared in the 1940s hyped the potential and speculated about the power source of Consolidated's proposed Model 37, as the company's intended commercial version of the XC-99 was known: 'No one knows when or where the legend of Pegasus first became popular. Nor does the date really matter. For as long as history records, men of the world have seen the flying beast of burden as the epitome of mortal ambition. Now Consolidated-Vultee has come forward with a single vehicle which moves through the air on the power of 30,000 winged horses—to prove conclusively that the sky alone is the limit where practical airplane size is concerned.

'That the recently announced Model 37 is far and away the largest flying machine on the immediate post-war docket is obvious. Although size alone does not spell greatness in aviation, it is interesting to note that the single slender wing of the Model 37 would outreach a 21-story building if upended on a metropolitan street corner. Similarly, the single fin and rudder stands approximately five stories above the runway. Twice as large as the Consolidated-Vultee Liberator, the Model 37 has a wing span of 230 feet and measures 182 feet in length. Nearly ten Piper Cubs could be parked in the tarmac space occupied by a single Model 37.

'Actually this new transport is something more than a very large airplane, with external lines and internal

XC-99

design unlike anything previously offered to the commercial airline operators of the world. It has, first of all, six engines buried in the wing to match the largest pre-war German, French and Russian commercial types in number of engines. Unlike the latter types, however, the Model 37 carries the engines in the trailing edge of the wing and becomes the first pusher type likely to see commercial service. Because the Model 37 is derived from a new Consolidated design, all information on power plants is necessarily restricted at the present time. However, the manufacturer has announced total power output equal to that of 353 automobiles–approximately 30,000 hp if we accept 85 hp as the average for American motor cars. It would be possible to obtain this output in one of two ways. The Model 37 may have a pair of inline engines in each nacelle, with a lone uni-twin head and shaft driving the three-blade propellers. Or it may be fitted with individual engines each developing 5,000 hp for take-off. The former would seem impractical in the light of Consolidated's thin wing with maximum camber inadequate for accommodation of the Allison 3420, the only announced inline, which develops more than 2,500 hp. It is possible that wartime ingenuity has brought radial engines which develop considerably more than the 3,000 hp announced some time ago. However, air-cooled engines, never too successful in pusher mountings, could hardly obtain sufficient cooling on the ground while buried in the Model 37 wing. So this sky gargantua is probably powered by either a gas turbine or a diesel engine of 5,000 hp efficiency–a remarkable power plant if it exists.

'In operation, the Model 37 follows a performance pattern which is more or less general in projected multi-engine transports, although its load is obviously greater than that of the Boeing Stratocruiser, the Douglas DC-7, the Lockheed Constellation, and the Martin Mars. Cruising at speeds between 310–342 mph, the big ship will carry a payload of 50,000 lb composed of 204 passengers and seven and one-half tons of mail or express. Operating above the weather at 30,000 feet, the Model 37 is designed for a range of 4,200 miles with the previously mentioned load. A double-deck interior will embrace two-passenger staterooms, oversize berths, two lounges, and a number of rest rooms, with Henry Dreyfuss interiors assuring colour and comfort for passengers on the long over-water routes.'

Development of the XC-99 was seen by Consolidated as an avenue on which important aspects of the XB-36 could be evaluated before the bomber entered its flight-test phase. Company officials were pleased at the prospect of constructing an XC-99 prototype aircraft that could serve that purpose, and doing so in far less time than it was taking to get the bomber up and running, since the cargo plane would not be carrying the complex military systems earmarked for the B-36. They especially liked the fact that the developmental costs of the XC-99 prototype would go on the government tab, making the company's financial position particularly rosy relative to the likely sales of an airliner version in the post-war years. Enthusiasm for the Model 36 project was running high when an Army Air Force contract was received by Consolidated in late December 1942 for the prototype aeroplane. After that the aeroplane was designated XC-99 and the work on the programme relocated to the Consolidated plant at Fort Worth, Texas, from San Diego where priority construction of the B-24 Liberator bomber, flying-boats and the development of the new B-32 bomber, demanded most of the California facility's space. The move was seen as a further efficiency in that the main mock-up for the XC-99 would now be assembled next to that of the XB-36.

In wartime, production priorities frequently shift up and down with the projected consequences of world events. Both the B-36 and XC-99 programmes were subject to such priority adjustments, and both progressed more slowly than their proponents and participants liked. Later, as manufacturing activity at the Consolidated Fort Worth division increased, company officials decided to return the XC-99 programme to the San Diego facility, a move that took place in the spring of 1944. However, there was no building at the San Diego plant high enough or wide enough to completely house the big plane whose 57 foot tail fin towered over the Consolidated experimental project building there. While much of the craft could be

left: Convair chief test pilot Beryl Erickson in the left seat of the XC-99, with his co-pilot, Russell Rogers in November 1947; below: The XB-36, first of the B-36 line from which the gargantuan XC-99 evolved.

'If God had intended us to fly, he would have sent us tickets.'
– Mel Brooks

sheltered in that structure, the last thirty feet of the
fuselage and tail structure was left protruding from
the building.

In San Diego, work on the fuselage of the giant
cargo plane continued and the design evolved somewhat. What had originally been planned as a fully
pressurized fuselage would now become unpressurized,
and the original twin-tail configuration would now be
a B-36-style single fin. Development continued inexorably until the last years of the war, with final
assembly taking place in San Diego's Pacific Highway
plant during 1947. Those elements common to both
the B-36 and XC-99, the wing and other parts, were
manufactured at the Fort Worth facility and rail-
shipped to the California plant for final assembly.

As specified, the XC-99 was designed to transport a
100,000 lb cargo load or 400 fully equipped troops or
up to 300 litter patients. The fuselage contained two
decks with a total cargo area volume of 16,000 cubic
feet. She was to be operated by a crew of eight: a
pilot, co-pilot, two flight engineers, a navigator, a
radio operator and two observers called scanners.
The latter were on board to visually monitor the
engines and the landing gear from windows in the
rear of the fuselage. The 265,000 lb (gross weight)
aeroplane was meant to cruise at 292 mph with a top
speed of 335 mph at 30,000 feet and had a 21,116-
gallon fuel capacity. This enormous, heavy aircraft
with its immense wing area, was not equipped with
modern power-assisted flight controls. Her doped,
fabric-covered control surfaces were operated directly
through the control column by the same 'spring-tab'
system employed in the B-36.

The maiden flight of the XC-99 took place at San
Diego's Lindbergh Field in the afternoon of 24
November 1947. The pilots were Beryl Erickson and
Russell Rogers, accompanied by a seven-man
Consolidated flight-test crew. The flight lasted
approximately one hour and was considered to be
uneventful. Contractor flight testing continued on
the giant plane for a year and a half and no significant
problems were encountered other than the ongoing
engine-cooling concern with the R-4360s that aggra-
vated engineers with the B-36 programme. During

the initial flight-test phase, the great 110-inch wheels of the main landing-gear, and the entire main gear arrangement, were replaced by the more efficient four-wheel bogie arrangement of the B-36 production aircraft. In this first flight-test phase, the XC-99 clearly established herself as the new heavyweight lifting champion when she hauled 100,000 lb of cargo, the unofficial heaviest payload ever lifted by an aeroplane, on 15 April 1949.

Phase Two of the flight test was the province of the US Air Force, which completed it in May 1949. The Air Force was satisfied that the XC-99 had met all of the performance criteria set for her in the original contract with Consolidated. The giant aeroplane was officially handed over to the Air Force on 26 May 1949. A month later, she was flown to Kelly AFB, Texas, where she received new, uprated R-4360-41 engines, a new fire extinguishing system and an engine-oil warning system.

While undergoing operational evaluation by the Air Force, an incident occurred in October 1950 when the XC-99 was being used to bring forty-two aircraft engines for C-54 transport planes, from Kelly to McClellan AFB, California, with a first stop scheduled for McChord AFB, Washington. Engine overheating problems developed in flight and excessive fuel consumption plagued the early hours of the trip. Later, one of the observers reported an apparent 'wobble' in the number two engine propeller. The condition worsened, requiring the engine to be shut down. The excessive fuel consumption then compelled the crew to make an unscheduled landing at Kirtland AFB, New Mexico, where the offending engine and propeller were inspected and a long crack was discovered in the propeller shaft. After an engine and propeller change, the XC-99 continued on to McChord.

The series of Air Force evaluation flights ended late in 1950, and technicians at Kelly then began a six-month period of modification work on the giant cargo plane. This included reworking the cockpit with new sound-proofing, the addition of several crew bunks and an improved galley and dining facility. The fuel tanks were resealed, an elevator/lift was installed to improve the cargo loading and unloading capability, B-36-style square-tipped propellers

replaced the original props and the landing-gear/undercarriage was strengthened, enabling the aircraft to operate with a slightly increased gross weight.

By mid-1951 the XC-99 was being flown on a fixed schedule, making two trips a week from the San Antonio, Texas, Air Materiel Depot to the McClellan AFB depot in northern California, with frequent stops at other California air force bases. By 1952, loading and unloading efficiency was increased with the advent of preloaded cargo bins, similar to those currently in use in the cargo holds of wide-body airliners. The loading/unloading operation of the aeroplane was facilitated through two electric sliding doors in the bottom of the fuselage. These were supplemented by two separate sets of clamshell doors aft of the rear sliding doors. Electric hoists were installed on tracks in the ceilings, two each in the upper and lower cargo compartments and angled ramps in the lower compartment allowed vehicles to be driven aboard the aircraft.

The next major modification of the XC-99 came in June 1953, when a weather radar unit was installed within a large black radome at the centre of the nose and directly below and ahead of the cockpit.

The plane continued carrying large cargo loads, serving the Air Force efficiently and well for several years with relatively few problems. Her first intercontinental flight came in August 1953, when she hauled 61,000 lb of cargo and a crew of twenty-three from Kelly to Rhein Main Air Base, Germany, with stops in Bermuda and the Azores. Then, in June 1957, inspection established that the airframe was showing signs of significant structural fatigue, including a broken main spar. So extensive, and expensive, was the projected cost of repairing the big plane, that the Air Force elected to permanently ground her. By August of that year she had hauled more than 60,000,000 lb of cargo in more than 7,400 flight hours.

Consolidated's planned Model 37 commercial version of the XC-99, was to have been powered by six gas turbine engines of 5,000 hp each, but these engines failed to materialize. And as the fuel and oil consumption of the 3,500 hp R-4360 radial engines used to power the XC-99 were deemed too high for airline

left: The cavernous cargo hold of the XC-99. The mammoth plane established the first in a long series of records by lifting a 100,000 lb payload from the Carswell AFB, Texas, runway on 15 April 1949.

In January 1945 Convair executives talked with Pan American World Airways representatives about Pan Am's need for an aircraft like the Convair Model 37, the planned commercial version of the XC-99 for use on the airline's San Francisco-Hawaii route and its New York-Europe routes. Pan Am ordered fifteen of the planes and production was to start as soon as the war ended. But when that happened, the postwar economy of the US was not as vigorous as the airline had predicted and it cancelled the planes. The Model 37 was never built and the era of wide-body airliners was deferred for twenty years.

profitability, and early post-war projections for airline passenger traffic were interpreted as insufficient to justify the sort of capacity that would be offered by the Model 37, the commercial project was cancelled.

Having no further use for her, the Air Force passed title for the XC-99 to the Disabled American Veterans organization in November 1957. For the next thirty years the DAV displayed her to the public in a field adjacent to Kelly AFB. Over that time the aeroplane fell victim to the forces of nature, gradually deteriorating, and in 1993 she was sold to a group called the Kelly Field Heritage Foundation. She was then towed back to the Kelly AFB ramp and was eventually donated to the United States Air Force Museum, which announced in January 2004, that the XC-99 was being dismantled to be shipped to the museum for a detailed restoration and reassembly. It will then be on public display at the museum.

Specifications: Consolidated XC-99
Engines: Six Pratt & Whitney R-4360-41 Wasp Major twenty-eight cylinder air-cooled radials rated at 3,500 hp each, in pusher configuration, driving 19-foot reversible-pitch propellers
Maximum speed: 335 mph at 30,000 ft
Cruising speed: 180 mph
Service ceiling: 30,000 ft
Normal range: 8,100 miles with a 10,000 lb load
Range with a 100,000 lb load: 1,720 miles
Weight empty: 130,000 lb, Maximum gross weight with 100,000 lb load: 265,000 lb
Wingspan: 230 ft
Length: 182 ft 6 in
Height: 57 ft 10 in
Wing area: 4,772 sq ft

In 1957 the XC-99 was retired from active service with the Air Force and was put on public display in a field at Kelly AFB near San Antonio, Texas. There it sat, rotting under the south-western sun, until it was finally rescued in 2004 by the United States Air Force Museum, Dayton, Ohio. It is being restored there and will ultimately be displayed as part of the museum's extensive aircraft collection.

'The Army is a place where you get up early in the morning to be yelled at by people with short haircuts and tiny brains.'
– Dave Barry

LOCKHEED

right: The first C-5 Galaxy heavy lifter at the rollout ceremony for the press and dignitaries, 2 March 1968, at the Lockheed Marietta, Georgia, plant. US President Lyndon B. Johnson was the keynote speaker.

It was during the administration of US President John F. Kennedy that the American military doctrine of 'flexible response' to Communist aggression in limited-war situations was born. To make such a policy work, the nation had to have the capability to rapidly transport a large force and an enormous quantity of supplies anywhere in the world at very short notice with great efficiency. US officials saw the threat of invasion posed in western Europe by ever-expanding Warsaw Pact countries as intolerable for NATO forces and concluded that a new air transport system was urgently needed. The mainstays of the US Air Force Military Air Transport Services in that time were the Douglas C-124 *Globemaster* with reciprocating engines and the C-133 *Cargomaster*, with turboprop engines. The new Lockheed C-141 *Starlifter* jet turbofan cargo transport was just entering service with the Air Force and was able to haul a 70,000 lb load at high speed over intercontinental distances. But what was required to support the *flexible response* was an aircraft able to move twice the payload of the *Starlifter* in up to five times the volume in order to accommodate virtually any type of equipment, armoured vehicles, trucks, palletized loads, etc. that the US military possessed. Time was of the essence—and not just time en route to a destination, but turn-around time on the ground. Loading and unloading operations would require an aircraft able to be accessed at both the front and rear to eliminate slow backing manoeuvres by large or heavy vehicle cargo.

When the armies of Syria and Egypt began their surprise two-front advance on Israel from the Golan Heights and across the Suez Canal on 6 October 1973, the United States acted quickly with Operation Nickel Glass. The Israelis urgently needed a quantity of M48 and M60 tanks for their defence, together with ammunition, other military equipment and supplies. Such supply by sea would have taken weeks and the need was immediate, but European allies of the US denied landing (for refuelling) and overflight rights to the Americans because of Arab oil producers' refusal to sell to nations that supported Israel. With aerial refuelling, US Military Airlift Command Lockheed C-5A *Galaxy* aircraft were able to fly non-

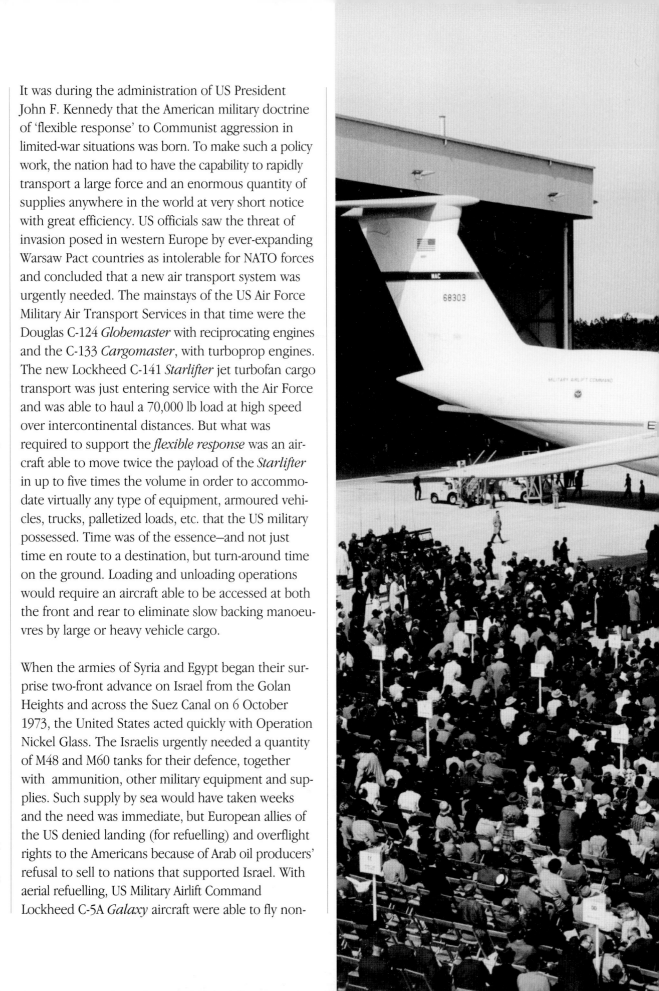

C-5

U.S. AIR FORC

stop from their base at Dover, Delaware, to Tel Aviv, 6,450 nautical miles. However, most C-5 crews at that time were inexperienced in the technique of air refuelling from the KC-135 tanker planes. Therefore, most of the C-5 resupply sorties were flown with the cooperation of Portugal, which allowed the USAF to use its airfield at Lajes in the Azores for refuelling.

Nine hours after President Nixon ordered the resupply flights to Israel, the first C-5A took off with a 193,000 lb load of cargo. A total of 144 similar flights would follow before the Arab–Israeli ceasefire of 24 October. The performance of the C-5s was especially impressive alongside that of the Russians, who were supporting their Arab allies in the war through Soviet Transport Aviation. In their 935 flights during a forty-day period, they were able to deliver an average of just sixteen tons per flight, less than a quarter of the load delivered by the C-5s to the Israelis. This poor record spurred the Soviets to develop their Antonov An-124 transport, which is a bit larger and heavier than the C-5, and first flew in late 1982.

With the Iraqi invasion of Kuwait in 1990, came another opportunity for the big Lockheed lifter to prove its worth and capability. During the Desert Shield and Desert Storm operations, 577,000 tons of cargo and a half-million passengers had to be airlifted to the Persian Gulf region. Together with the smaller C-141, the C-5s delivered approximately seventy-five per cent of the cargo and a third of the passengers in the biggest airlift since the Second World War. Employed in the operation were 110 C-5s, or ninety percent of the entire Galaxy fleet, including C-5 Air Force Reserve and Air National Guard Unit aircraft and crews, bringing into the theatre fifteen complete field hospitals and the medical personnel to operate them, among many other priority cargoes.

In the build-up to Operation Iraqi Freedom, the second Gulf War, USAF C-5s flew 5,150 sorties, averaging nearly fifty-four tons per sortie, though the reported mission capability rates of the C-5s were the lowest of the Air Force planes participating in the conflict. Still, it was a nearly accident-free deployment for both the C-5s and the C-17 partner aircraft in the operation. There were no crashes and the C-5s experienced just four incidents in which relatively minor damage was sustained. The C-17s suffered seven such incidents.

Sub smasher

To smash a sub, you first find the sub. That takes a fairly large bomber with a fairly long range, for subs are big and subs are small.

After you find your sub you go into a power-dive, quick, and drop your bombs. U-boats now somedive to just 30 seconds. Obviously you can't do much of a power-dive with a medium bomber weaving and stay in one place.

But you can in a Lockheed Hudson bomber! Lockheed Hudsons hold the official RAF Coastal Command record for having strafled more subs than any other submarine. The Lockheed Hudson, like the Lockheed Lightning and the Vega Ventura, was designed, engineered and built to provide extra strength and extra dependability. It has been used by the RAF longer than any other American bomber.

For protection today, and progress tomorrow, look to

Lockheed

FOR LEADERSHIP

right: The impressive bulk of the Galaxy on take-off. The aeroplane, one of the largest in the world, was conceived as part of the US military conventional forces rapid response doctrine of the 1960s. Design work began on the plane as American involvement in the Vietnam War began to escalate. In the period of its development, controversy surrounded it and it was roundly criticized by Congressional and media personalities as a prime example of government excess and wasted tax dollars.

The C-5 Galaxy heavy lift transport was designed for the strategic deployment and supply of fully equipped American combat and support forces to wherever they may be required. It can move exceptionally heavy loads enormous distances at jet speed. It is capable of taking off and landing from relatively short runways. Having both front and rear cargo doors, the mammoth plane can be loaded and off-loaded simultaneously. Both the nose and rear cargo doors open the full width and height of the cargo compartment, enabling drive-through loading and unloading of both wheeled and tracked vehicles and easy loading of bulky or unusually-shaped equipment. The landing-gear system allows the aircraft to kneel, lowering its cargo floor to truck-bed height. A roller system covering the entire length and width of the cargo floor facilitates the rapid handling of palletized cargo. The twenty- eight-wheel landing-gear efficiently distributes the great weight of the C-5. The plane is also equipped with an ingenious Malfunction Detection Analysis and Recording System. Its digital computer identifies malfunctions in replaceable units, recording trend and failure information on magnetic tape for analysis. The system monitors more than 800 test points of the various subsystems in the aeroplane.

In 1964, the US Air Force Systems Command awarded small design study contracts to Douglas, Boeing and Lockheed for the airframe of a new, heavy-lift jet cargo transport which would carry extremely heavy and bulky military equipment on ultra-long-range deployments, jobs that the existing C-141 *Starlifter* transports could not handle. At the same time, similar design study contracts were awarded to General Electric and Pratt & Whitney for high-bypass turbofan engines that would provide the new plane with high speed and good fuel economy. The C-5 programme began when the Defense Department asked the three airframe manufacturers and the two engine builders to submit their proposals for the design, construction and testing of five prototype aeroplanes, a firm production run of fifty-three aircraft and a conditional production run of a further fifty-seven aircraft, for a total force of 115 C-5s, which would equip six Military Airlift Command squadrons. These aeroplanes would be required to perform a maximum-weight take-off from an 8,000-foot runway, land on a semi-prepared 4,000-foot strip, carry a 125,000 lb payload, unrefuelled, on sectors of up to 8,000 miles, carry a maximum payload of 250,000 lb, and have a design life of 30,000 flying hours.

All of this was in the context of Defense Secretary Robert McNamara's new policy called Total Package Procurement, which was intended to define and control the actual or true cost of the military weapons and systems purchased for the armed services. The policy called for all aspects of such orders, including research, development, testing, evaluation, and production, to be purchased under a single, fixed-price contract, but with negotiated performance incentives.

The final production contracts were awarded in 1965 to the Lockheed-Georgia Company and General Electric. The key factors in the decisions in favour of the two companies were price and technology. All three original proposals had incorporated the same basic design features, including front and rear ramp-equipped doors to facilitate flow-through loading, high-wing configuration, and power from four under-wing-mounted turbofan engines. In addition to submitting the lowest bid of the three competing contractors, Lockheed's proposal featured an upward-lifting visor-type nose that enabled maximum clear access to the cargo hold for loading and unloading of extremely large and bulky cargoes. The Boeing and Douglas proposals provided side-hinged doors and the Air Force preferred the Lockheed feature. Another consideration in the C-5 awards may have related to spreading large-project work among the nation's primary defence contractors. In 1965, for example, huge contracts were being let for the Manned Orbital Laboratory project, the C-5, and the American supersonic transport plane. With the C-5 going to Lockheed-Georgia, the Manned Orbital Lab would go to Douglas (in California) and the SST to Boeing (in Washington). Of these three major programmes, only the C-5 would reach fruition.

The first flight of the first C-5 aeroplane in the initial order of five took place on 30 June 1968 from the Dobbins AFB runway shared with the Lockheed-Georgia Company in Marietta, Georgia. It was an uneventful ninety-four-minute outing and early flight testing continued with no significant problems. In June 1969, the second C-5 was flown to Edwards AFB, California, to participate in a six-month joint Air Force/contractor test series which included a gross weight take-off at 762,000 lb, for a new world record, followed a few months later by one at 798,200 lb. In August, the aeroplane successfully flew a 20-hour 29-minute unrefuelled test flight.

Throughout the entire four-year test period, possibly the longest for any modern aircraft, many aspects of the C-5 design and performance justified the choices of airframe and engine manufacturers. Among them were the speed and efficiency with which the loading and unloading of such massive cargo as Army and Marine Corps main battle tanks, the 74-ton mobile scissors bridge, a double row of vehicles, twenty-four AH-64 attack helicopters, etc. The Air Force liked the fully pressurized main cargo compartment, 121-foot length, 19-foot width and 13-foot height. Another extremely useful function was the aeroplane's ability to 'kneel' on its landing-gear system, to lower the cargo floor to truck-bed height at either end of the aircraft. Other features included accommodation for a long-mission relief crew in a compartment behind the cockpit, a galley and a lavatory, and similar compartments in the rear of the plane for drivers of the vehicles being transported. While not intended for use as a troop transport, the C-5 can accommodate up to 290 troops in seats on the main deck. The aeroplane is operated by a crew of five—a pilot, co-pilot, flight engineer, navigator, and load master, and on some flights a second load master.

Systems that were validated in the flight-test programme included the high-flotation landing-gear and its four-wheel nose gear and four six-wheel main trucks. This system also provided two further aft-mounted trucks to improve crosswind steering. A computerized malfunction-detection, analysis and recording system (MADAR) monitored 800 separate test functions both on the ground and in the air. The C-5 was the first transport plane to have an aerial refuelling capability via a receptacle inset in the top of the fuselage immediately behind the cockpit. It was the first aircraft to use the General Electric TF-39 high-bypass turbofan engines. The aeroplane seemed to be an important concept, well executed.

The full-scale ground fatigue-testing programme produced very different results, however. In July 1969, a C-5 wing failed in a structural ground static test at only eighty-four per cent of the scheduled maximum test load, the first indication of major trouble for the aeroplane. The enormous wing was discovered to have a fatigue life expectancy of only one-quarter of the specified 30,000 flying hours, restricting the payload capacity to 50,000 lb, less than one-third of the specification. Lockheed came up with the appropriate solutions, but the Air Force could not then afford to fund them, and their implementation had to be deferred.

Compounding the troubles of the company and its customer were a rather high-profile series of cost overruns due, at least in part, to Lockheed having submitted an unrealistically low bid on the plane, and made worse by that Defense procurement policy that seemed not to take into account the many unknowns and inevitable bugs that are a normal part of development in a complex new military system. New technology employed in the aeroplane probably stretched the capabilities and resources of both Lockheed and General Electric well beyond what they had anticipated for the programme. The war in Vietnam, production changes to both airframe and engine, increased

redesign costs, labour and materials increases, overtime, delays, shortages, inflation, and work stoppages, all were factors leading to costs that could not be recovered under the framework of the overall fixed-price contract. Added to the problem was $295 million in essential spare parts and ground equipment that the Air Force had failed to include in the agreement.

In 1968 it became public knowledge that cost overruns on the C-5 project were nearing $2 billion, a price tag that many American taxpayers were loudly decrying as scandalous. Meanwhile, Lockheed, at that point, was six months behind in the delivery schedule for the aeroplane, triggering performance penalties that exacerbated the company's financial position, it having borrowed hundreds of millions of dollars to cope with the massive costs relating to its various commercial and defence programmes.

Fed by the media and Congressional criticism, the American public was angered at what it perceived as the most extreme example yet of the excesses and rotten management in the 'military industrial complex'. The public perception encompassed a cast composed entirely of villains—the company, the Air Force, the Pentagon, the Congress, and probably the national leadership which, to many, must have seemed to want the 'wasteful and unnecessary' C-5 as a means with which to drag the country into prolonged and hugely unpopular wars like Vietnam. Congress went on the warpath, initiating several investigations of the C-5 project.

To help itself and Lockheed in the dire situation, the Air Force gave the go-ahead in January 1969 for the second production run of the C-5, but reduced the order from fifty-seven to just twenty-three aircraft and 176 engines, pending a further Congressional appropriation to fund the remainder of the order. It also reduced the delivery schedule from four aircraft a month to three, which was intended to help Lockheed with its annual financial burden. The press and media blasted the C-5 programme relentlessly and that, coupled with public outrage over the costs of the war in Vietnam, required a more mollifying move on the part of the Air Force. In November, it announced that the eighty-one C-5 aeroplanes contracted for would be the total purchased. Lockheed

The Galaxy has two galleys for food preparation and are located in the forward and rear upper-deck compartments. Lavatories are also located in the forward and rear upper-deck areas. The troop compartment is in the upper-deck and has a galley, two lavatories and seating for seventy-three passengers. In the full troop-carrying mode, up to 267 additional passenger seats can be installed on the cargo floor.

'If anything can go wrong, it will.'
– Murphy's Law

above: The flight deck of a C-5 while on display at the Royal International Air Tattoo at RAF Fairford, England, in July 2004. The square display on the panel is the weather radar, a retrofit item that replaced the earlier multi-mode unit originally supplied.

reacted swiftly, bringing in its lawyers to insist that the government was already committed to the purchase of 115 C-5s. The spectre of bankruptcy now hung over the company, and with the possibility of having to default on the remainder of the C-5 programme, it had to have help. The US government clearly could not afford to let Lockheed collapse, with the loss of many vitally needed military and weapon systems, not least being the Galaxy programme itself, which to date had produced just four aeroplanes.

below: A Galaxy wearing the distinctive European One camouflage scheme that caused some Air Force personnel to refer to it as 'The Flying Pickle.'

The impressive capability of the C-5 was dramatically demonstrated during the Gulf War of 1990-91, when the heavy lifters transported nearly a half-million passengers and more than 677,000 tons of cargo to the Gulf region. The effort included fifteen air-mobile hospitals and 5,000 medical personnel to run them as well as 211 tons of mail to and from the men and women in the area each day. Ninety per cent of the Air Force's C-5s were utilized in Operations Desert Shield and Desert Storm along with eighty per cent of its C-141 fleet.

More recently, during Operation Iraqi Freedom, the combination of C-5s and C-17 Globemaster IIIs flew 11,400 sorties. In it the C-5s delivered an average of 53.8 tons per sortie. By the end of the Operation, the mission-capable rate of the C-5s rose to nearly seventy-two per cent. In the effort the C-5 fleet incurred only four minor incidents, compared with seven for the C-17s.

Heavy-lift air cargo requirements of the US military in 1969, with the increased level of combat activity in South-East Asia, had burgeoned to a point where the Air Force simply could not wait any longer to replace its ageing, obsolete C-124 and C-133 aircraft, and despite the limitations placed on the C-5A because of the wing static-test failure, the new plane was rushed into operational service. Accelerated transition training of crews for the C-5A began in December 1969 at Altus AFB, Oklahoma, and the first missions to Vietnam were flown from Travis AFB, Fairfield, California, in April 1971.

In operations related to the Vietnam War, three tragic accidents occurred involving C-5As. The first, in September 1971, resulted from corrosion and structural fatigue when an engine and pylon separated from an Altus AFB aircraft on take-off, causing the destruction of the aircraft. On 27 September 1974, a large fire broke out in a wheel well of an aeroplane of the Altus Wing, shortly after take-off from that base. The pilot headed the giant jet for the nearest landing ground, the Clinton-Stewart Municipal Airport, but the fire had destroyed the braking capability of the aeroplane and it rolled off the end of the runway and across an irrigation ditch where it broke up. Far worse was the fate of a C-5A that was evacuating South Vietnamese civilians, many of them orphaned children, in the first flight of Operation Babylift, from Tan Son Nhut Air Base on 4 April 1975, shortly before the end of the war. Again, in an incident just after take-off, the aft pressure door blew out, ruining a number of control cables and hydraulic lines. Three of the four hydraulic systems of the aircraft were lost as was control of the rudder and elevators. The pilot and co-pilot tried desperately to get the plane back to the field for a landing, but with very little control or power, the C-5 crashed into a rice paddy short of the runway, with the loss of 175 of the 328 people on board, most of the dead being children. In an accident related to the first Gulf War, a C-5A of the 60th Military Airlift Wing crashed shortly after take-off from Ramstein Air Base, Germany, on 28 August 1990, with the loss of thirteen of the seventeen service personnel on board. Notwithstanding these tragic losses, the C-5 had proved its worth beyond any doubt when, in the final

phases of the Vietnam War, it hauled 1,650,000 lb of tanks and helicopters in just ten flights during the siege of Da Nang. In thirty-two years of operation by 2003, and two million flight hours, only four C-5s were lost in flying accidents, an excellent safety record for any aircraft type, especially a military one.

In one of history's greatest rescues, the US government acted in May 1971, guaranteeing $250 million in loans to Lockheed, and Congress voted for a contingency fund of $200 million to fix the aeroplane. With most of the money going to Lockheed, it was provided on the basis that the company, and General Electric, would finish the C-5 programme, delivering all the aircraft at a rate of just two a month, which still proved unsustainable for Lockheed.

By January 1973, when the final C-5A was completed, the aircraft were in normal operations, their primary problems having been corrected. With the cost overruns and the modifications, the unit cost of the aeroplane had ballooned to more than $55 million, almost twice the original price, and the customer had thirty-one fewer aircraft than had been ordered. But the C-5 was operating effectively, and the Air Force wanted and needed more of them. Lockheed was most anxious to restart the C-5 assembly line and, hopefully, recoup some of its losses in the programme. But with the end of the war in Vietnam there was little political sympathy for buying more of the aeroplanes.

In the early design stages of the C-5A, the company was constantly aware of the need to minimize the weight of the aeroplane in order to meet the Air Force performance specifications. It is believed that some of the measures employed in this weight-reduction programme contributed to the inability of the C-5A wing to pass the structural ground static test in 1969. The severity of the problem surfaced when a number of the planes had been in service long enough to have accumulated 5,000 flying hours. One such aircraft was subjected to a wing tear-down procedure, and the ensuing inspection revealed significant cracks in the wing structure. This critical revelation meant that, on an average basis, only 2,500 to 3,000 additional flying hours could be expected for the C-5s once they reached the 5,000-hour mark. Performance restrictions were imposed by the Air Force and Lockheed faced the problem of how to rebuild the wing to achieve the originally specified 30,000 flying hours.

The solution to the wing fatigue problem came in three parts. The company proposed development of a system to alleviate gust loading on the wing through the use of active ailerons. Secondly, it suggested the incorporation of local modifications to lessen fatigue, and finally it proposed the redistribution of fuel within the wing, to minimize the bending that the wing was subjected to. Between 1975 and 1977, seventy-seven C-5As were equipped with the active ailerons and the company received an Air Force contract for the design engineering of a major wing modification. This work was completed in June 1978 and the solution was the Pacer Wing project. Two new sets of wings, incorporating a new centre wing, two inner-wing boxes and two outer-wing box sections, were manufactured by the Aerostructures Division of Avco Corporation, from alloys that were not available to Lockheed when the original wings were produced. Flight testing of the new wing began in August 1980. The flight and full-scale ground fatigue and damage tolerance test results were so good that all performance and service-life restrictions on the aeroplane were lifted with the modification of all C-5As. All re-winged C-5As were re-delivered to the Air Force between February 1983 and July 1987.

In the aftermath of the Vietnam War, there was no support in Washington for restarting the C-5 production line, which the Air Force wanted to do in order to meet its growing strategic airlift needs. With no chance of securing the required funding, the Air Force instructed Lockheed to store the C-5 tooling, jigs and fixtures pending the availability of such funding at a later date. The decision paid off in 1981 when a Congressional mobility study resulted in authorization of additional heavy-lift aircraft. Without being asked, Lockheed proposed production of an additional fifty C-5 Galaxy aircraft on a fixed-price basis and the proposal was welcomed by both Congress and the Department of Defense, which authorized the company to go ahead with production in October 1982. While retaining the basic C-5 airframe, these new aeroplanes, designated C-5B, would incorporate the strengthened

wing boxes, be powered by uprated General Electric TF-39-GE-1C turbofan engines, be built of stronger, more durable aluminum alloys, and be equipped with an improved MADAR system and new state-of-the-art avionics. In another change from the C-5A, the B-model eliminated the complex crosswind landing-gear system. The aeroplane had a triple inertial navigation system allowing it to operate without ground-based navigational aids. The first C-5B began flight testing at Marietta on 30 September 1985 and initial aircraft deliveries to the Air Force began late in 1986, with the final plane being delivered to the 436th Military Airlift Wing at Dover AFB, Delaware, in April 1989.

To give NASA the capability of transporting complete satellite and space station components, two C-5As were modified in the late 1980s. Their aft upper-deck troop compartments were removed and the aft cargo doors were modified to accept larger cargo items. Designated C-5Cs, the two aircraft were assigned to the 60th Airlift Wing at Travis AFB, California.

The first (early) C-5As were reassigned to equip some of the Air Force Reserve and Air National Guard units in December 1984. In addition to their participation in a variety of US military actions during the 1980s and 1990s, C-5As and Bs were used effectively in relief work following disasters such as earthquakes in Mexico and Armenia in 1985 and 1988, and Hurricanes Hugo and Andrew in 1989 and 1992 respectively, and after the man-made tragedy at Chernobyl in 1986. This great heavy-lift workhorse has proved itself many times over the years to be tough and capable when needed.

Specifications: Lockheed C-5

Engines: Four General Electric TF-39-GE-1C turbofans rated at 41,000 lb thrust each.
Maximum speed: 541 mph. Cruising speed: 518 mph
Service ceiling: 34,000 feet
Normal range: 5,940 miles empty, Range with maximum payload: 3,749 miles
Weight, basic operating: 337,937 lb Weight, maximum takeoff: 769,000 lb
Wingspan: 222 ft 9 in
Length: 247 ft 10 in
Height: 65 ft 1 in
Wing area: 6,200 sq ft

How do you get six Apache helicopters to fly in formation with their engines off? According to the Lockheed Martin Aeronautics Company, you put them inside a C-5 Galaxy. Two M1A1 Abrams main battle tanks weighing 135,400 lb each; six M2/M3 Bradley Infantry Vehicles; or a quarter-million pounds of relief supplies—all can be carried by the C-5. According to Lockheed, there is no piece of army combat equipment that the C-5 cannot carry, including a 74-ton mobile bridge. Yet, say the makers, the C-5 is amazingly versatile. Even with a payload of 263,200 lb, the latest version of the big lifter can fly non-stop for 2,500 miles at jet speed. With aerial refuelling, it has nearly unlimited range. It can load outsized cargo from both ends at once (at either truck-bed height or ground level) and its high-flotation landing-gear system enables operation even from unpaved airfields without ground-support equipment.

In 1973, C-5s essentially saved Israel, flying desperately needed supplies to Tel Aviv and Jerusalem during the Yom Kippur War. The big planes delivered more than 885,000 lb of earthquake relief supplies to Armenia in 1988, and in 1989 C-5s took two million pounds of clean-up gear to the Alaska oil spill area. The Galaxy has proven itself big enough and tough enough to handle virtually any heavy airlift mission.

BOEING

The key to the selection of a design based on the McDonnell Douglas DC-10-30CF by the United States Air Force as its advanced tanker/cargo aircraft in the 1970s was that it could lift heavier payloads and operate from shorter runways than Boeing's entry in the competition, a militarized 747 refuelling aircraft. Choosing the -30CF over the Boeing plane obviously demanded consideration of other factors, including price, overall capability, special features and life-cycle costs, but of primary importance were payload and short-field operating capability. For McDonnell Douglas, the programme began with an initial $28 million contract for preliminary engineering and tooling.

The KC-10A derives from the McDonnell Douglas DC-10 jetliner, which entered commercial airline service in 1971. In that year the company began preliminary engineering work on what would ultimately become the military KC-10A Extender tanker/cargo plane. The -30CF is the long-range version of the DC-10, which went into production at the Long Beach, California, Douglas Aircraft Company plant in January 1968. That plant is now the Long Beach Division of Boeing Commercial Airplanes. Production of the DC-10 continued until 1989, with 386 commercial aircraft being built, as well as sixty KC-10s for the Air Force. The DC-10 series of aircraft raised industry standards as it brought out major improvements in aerodynamics, structures, avionics, propulsion, flight-control systems and envi-

'The first step in having any successful war is getting people to fight it.'
– Fran Lebowitz

ronmental compatibility. In all, six series models were designed to meet a broad range of customer requirements. Beginning with Series Ten, an aircraft intended to serve routes of up to 4,000 statute miles, Douglas created a vehicle with power from three General Electric CF6-6 engines which were rated at 40,000 lb thrust each for take-off. The maiden flight of the first Series Ten aircraft took place on 29 August 1970, with Federal Aviation Administration certification being given on 29 July 1971. Deliveries to United and American Airlines began that year with scheduled service starting on 5 August 1971.

The Series Forty followed in 1972, a DC-10 with an intercontinental range of 5,800 miles. Power was

KC-10

supplied by Pratt & Whitney JT9D turbofans. A slightly longer-ranging variant, the Series Thirty, also entered service in 1972, powered by General Electric CF6-50 fanjets. The first convertible freighter DC-10 was delivered in 1973. The model was made available in all of the basic series and in all its versions offered cargo space equal to that of four forty-foot railroad freight cars. In 1979, Series Fifteen was introduced, with uprated engines on the smaller airframe of the Series Ten, for improved performance from high-altitude airports with full loads in warm climates. And in 1984, in response to an order from Federal Express, an all-freighter model was developed from the Series Thirty, the 30F, which is able to carry up to 175,000 lb of palletized cargo over a range of more than 3,800 miles. Following the development of the 30F came the KC-10 tanker/cargo plane.

The DC-10 was the first commercial transport plane to be FAA-certified under the strict Stage Three FAA regulations governing sound levels for commercial aircraft. Douglas was determined to make its plane 'a good neighbour', complying with international noise standards, and its engines were considerably quieter, while far more powerful, than those of the first-generation jetliners. The large flight deck is quite roomy, accommodating a three-person crew with two additional seats for observers. The thinking behind the design of the cockpit gave priority to minimizing crew workload through simplicity, efficiency and organization. Unusually large windscreens were provided to allow for exceptional visibility. And for low-visibility conditions, the aeroplane is certified for Category IIIA automatic landing in near-zero visibility.

The technology of the Pratt & Whitney and General Electric engines used to power the various DC-10-series aircraft is considerably advanced over that of the engines that powered the first-generation jetliners. Delivering far more power and far more environmentally friendly, the big high-bypass turbofans operate at much lower noise levels with virtually smokeless exhaust. Their fuel efficiency is far greater and they are highly reliable, requiring somewhat less maintenance which is easier to perform. The engines of the DC-10 family are positioned with two mounted

below left: The KC-10 at RAF Fairford, England. Derived from the DC-10 jetliner, the KC-10 Extender is a US Air Force Air Mobility Command advanced tanker and cargo aircraft intended to provide increased global mobility for the US armed forces. While its primary role is aerial refuelling, the KC-10 can combine the tasks of a tanker and cargo aircraft by refuelling fighters and simultaneously carrying the fighter support personnel and equipment on overseas deployments. The KC-10 can transport up to seventy-five people and nearly 170,000 lb of cargo a distance of nearly 4,400 miles unrefuelled.

below: A US Air Force KC-10 in flight, the aerial refuelling boom clearly visible under the rear of the fuselage.

beneath the wings and the third above the aft fuselage at the base of the vertical stabilizer.

The DC-10 has a wide-body cabin interior offering the same sort of spacious environment found on the Boeing 747. For its time, the DC-10 two-aisle cabin provided a new standard of comfort with wider aisles and wider seats than those of earlier commercial jets. Of course, seat width and pitch are determined by the individual customer airline and can and do vary greatly, even in the economy sections. Many well-travelled people have experienced some of their most and least comfortable flights on DC-10s, depending on the carrier and its particular level of interest in passenger comfort. Many travellers, including myself, have been so heavily influenced by a particularly miserable flight as to vow never again to fly with that particular airline. The reverse can also happen. An unusually pleasant flight, made so in part by the consideration of the airline in providing an extra few inches of seat pitch, can certainly buy the loyalty of a passenger who, in many cases, has a choice of airlines for his trip. Unfortunately for the

DC-10, a number of the air carriers who have operated it elected to stuff it with the absolute maximum number of seats that their economy sections would hold, guaranteeing a high misery quotient for the long-haul flyer. Indeed, the final fading memory that many folks share of the DC-10 is one of unparalleled discomfort. But to fairly apportion blame look not at the aircraft which, after all, did not devise its own seating plan, but to the greed and mismanagement of certain airlines which, to this day, continue to operate with the same philosophy about their passengers that they had during their DC-10 days.

In the early years of DC-10 operation, the reputation of the plane was seriously marred by a number of catastrophic accidents. One of these events occurred on 25 May 1979, when American Airlines Flight 191, bound from Chicago's O'Hare International Airport to Los Angeles International departed its gate at 2.59 p.m. Central Standard Time, and taxied out to Runway 32R where it was cleared for take-off at 3.02 pm. The aeroplane was a McDonnell Douglas DC-10-

10, registration N110AA, which had been built in 1972 and had accummulated 19,871 flight hours on its airframe. There were 258 passengers and thirteen crew members on board.

The aircraft started its take-off roll and all was normal. But, as it approached the point of rotation, the pylon structure of the number one engine began to come apart. As the nose came up, the entire number one engine and pylon separated and flipped over the top of the wing before falling to the runway in the wake of the heavy jet. The DC-10 was airborne and climbing in a relatively stable attitude. It had lifted from the run-way at about the 6,000-foot mark and was approaching 300 feet of altitude. Its wings were still level. Then, it began to turn and roll to the left. The nose pitched down and the big plane ceased its climb and began to descend. It continued rolling to the left even after the wings had passed the vertical. At 3.04 pm the DC-10 crashed into a field, exploded and slewed into a trailer park just under a mile beyond the departure end of Runway 32R. In the massive ground fire that ensued, two people in the trailer park were killed. All 271 persons aboard Flight 191 perished.

The accident report of the crash indicated the prob-able cause: 'The asymmetrical stall and the ensuing roll of the aircraft because of the uncommanded retraction of the left wing outboard leading edge slats and the loss of stall warning and slat disagree-ment indication systems resulting from maintenance-induced damage leading to the separation of the no. 1 engine and pylon assembly procedures which led to the failure of the pylon structure. Contributing to the cause of the accident were the vulnerability of the design of the pylon attach points to maintenance damage; the vulnerability of the design of the leading edge slat system to the damage which produced asymmetry; deficiencies in FAA surveillance and reporting systems which failed to detect and prevent the use of improper maintenance procedures; defi-ciencies in the practices and communications among the operators, the manufacturer, and the FAA which failed to determine and disseminate the particulars regarding previous maintenance damage incidents; and the intolerance of prescribed operational proce-dures to this unique emergency.'

The design and procedural problems associated with the DC-10, as a result of this and other operational accidents, were analysed and corrected, and the aero-plane went on to re-establish itself as safe and reliable.

The DC-10 has evolved further since the end of production in 1989. Following the acquisition of McDonnell Douglas by Boeing in the 1990s, the MD-10 model conversion was created for Federal Express, in which both current DC-10 air freighters and ex-airliner freighter conversions were converted to a two-crew flight-deck. With an instrument-panel layout identical to that of the MD-11, pilots can be readily qualified to fly both aircraft. The initial MD-10 delivery to FedEx was made on 4 April 1999, the first of an 89-aircraft order from the air shipper.

Nearly two billion dollars was invested by McDonnell Douglas and its subcontractors in the development of the DC-10 series of aircraft, and the US Air Force has been able to benefit greatly from this investment, and that of the worldwide support network set up by the airlines that have operated the plane. These investments have made it possible for the Air Force to purchase and maintain its fleet of KC-10A Extender aircraft at substantially less cost than in a new military aircraft development programme. The KC-10A Extender advanced tanker/cargo aircraft is designed to increase the mobility of American forces in contin-gency operations by refuelling fighters while concur-rently hauling support equipment and personnel for these same fighters, in overseas deployments. In addition, the Extender can enhance the US airlift capability by refuelling the C-5 and C-141 strategic air-lifter aircraft during their overseas deployment and resupply missions. Effectively, aerial refuelling of a fully loaded C-5 by a KC-10A can nearly double the nonstop range of the giant airlifter. The duality of the KC-10A makes it possible for the Air Force to do a job like supporting the deployment of a fighter squadron (through aerial refuelling) and its support personnel and equipment (through delivery) with the use of a single aircraft type, rather than having to employ both tanker and cargo planes. It has earned the nickname Extender for its ability to do both aerial refuelling and the cargo mission without requiring forward basing

In addition to the three main DC-10 wing fuel tanks, the KC-10 has three large fuel tanks under the cargo floor, one under the forward lower cargo compartment, one in the centre-wing area, and one under the rear compartment. Combined, the capacity of the six tanks is 356,000 lb, almost twice that of the KC-135 Stratotanker. Using either an advanced aerial refuelling boom, or a hose-and-drogue centreline refuelling system, the KC-10 can refuel a wide variety of US and allied mili-tary aircraft within the same mission. The aircraft is also equipped with lighting for nighttime operations.

The KC-10's boom operator controls refuelling operations through a digital, fly-by-wire system. Sitting in the rear of the plane, the operator can watch the receiving aircraft through a wide window. During boom refuelling opera-tions, fuel is transferred to the receiver at a maximum rate of 1,100 gallons per minute; the hose-and-drogue refuelling maximum rate is 470 gallons per minute. The Automatic Load Alleviation System and Independent Disconnect System greatly enhance safety and facilitate air refuelling. The KC-10 itself can be air-refuelled by a KC-135 or another KC-10, to increase its delivery range.

facilities. The aeroplane is able to carry up to seventy-five people and 170,000 lb of cargo over a distance of 4,400 miles; 11,500 miles unrefuelled, without the cargo.

The KC-10A first flew on 12 July 1980, and on 30 October of that year it completed its first air refuelling test, delivering jet fuel to a thirsty C-5 Galaxy heavy lifter. The US Air Force has maintained a fleet of sixty KC-10s, basing them initially at March AFB, California, and Barksdale AFB, Louisiana. A spate of base realignments, closings and downsizing, however, has seen the relocation of the KC-10s to McGuire AFB, New Jersey, and Travis AFB, California.

When the Air Force chose the DC-10-30CF as the

basis for its KC-10A Extender, it called for a number of changes to tailor the plane to its special needs. In its tanker role, the aeroplane had to provide both the boom-type refuelling system utilized by Air Force aircraft, and the hose-and-drogue refuelling nozzle system used by the US Navy and some foreign air forces. This dual refuelling system capability provided the Extender with unique versatility among tanker planes. The cargo compartment floor had to be strengthened to cope with up to 170,000 lb of payload. A tanker boom operator position and a refuelling boom had to be provided at a ventral location on the centreline of the rear fuselage. The refuelling capability required that a hose-and-drogue refuelling nozzle system be

right: The KC-10 cockpit, console and instrument panel. Power is supplied to the aeroplane by three huge General Electric CF6-50C2 turbofan engines of 52,000 pounds thrust each. They can bring the plane to a top speed of Mach 0.825 or 619 mph. The service ceiling is 42,000 feet and the range is 4,400 miles with cargo and 11,500 miles without cargo.

installed in the starboard lower rear fuselage. An aerial refuelling receptacle had to be installed above and behind the flight-deck in a dorsal position. When refuelling other aircraft, the boom operator can off-load up to 1,500 gallons a minute. The total fuel capacity of the KC-10A is 54,455 gallons and 30,000 gallons of this is available to aircraft arriving to 'tank'. The maximum fuel capacity of the Extender allows it to cruise up to 2,200 miles from base, orbit while serving the 30,000-gallon maximum, and return to its base with a reasonable fuel margin for safety. More than half the USAF Extender fleet aircraft are capable of refuelling three aircraft simultaneously through the use of under-wing pods.

In the years since the closure of the DC-10 and KC-10 production lines, and the acquisition of McDonnell Douglas by Boeing, there has been some interest on the part of other countries in having an aerial refuelling capability of their own. In shopping for it they have started to acquire commercial DC-10s, many of which have been resting in the desert, part of a massive fleet of airliners retired from service (at least temporarily) as one side effect of the terrorist events of 11 September 2001. The DC-10s converted to cargo/tankers have been designated KDC-10, and are able to carry up to twenty-six cargo pallets or 300 passengers, or a combination of the two, along with the refuelling capability. The Boeing Company has offered the advanced aerial tanker technology for the conversion of DC-10s to military tankers which, unlike the technology utilized in the current KC-10A fleet, provides a new Remote Aerial Refuelling Operation system (RARO), a system that is only available for installation on Boeing DC-10 aircraft. It is based on three-dimensional operator displays and controls that are located on the forward main deck. The sensors of the viewing system enable wingtip-to-wingtip viewing of the area aft of the tanker, unlike current tanker systems in which the operator is at a station at the rear of the tanker, either seated at a window position as in the KC-10A, or prone as in the KC-135R. With the RARO system, the operator uses a closed-circuit video camera and monitoring facility in the forward area of the cabin to view the in-flight refuelling operation. This technology delivers greatly improved provision for operation in poor weather and at night as well as enhanced depth perception, taking advantage of the infra-red and stereoscopic capabilities of the RARO camera. The operator's console is mounted on a pallet that can be removed to allow for additional cargo or passengers. These Boeing-modified DC-10s (KDC-10) can also be furnished with hose/drogue pods that are attached to pylons under each wing, enabling the aircraft to serve fuel to a wider range of aircraft types, including most US and NATO planes. A bonus for KDC-10 customers is the commonality with DC-10 commercial airliners that are still operating worldwide and providing a huge network for FAA-approved maintenance and spare parts.

below: The tail structure of a KC-10 showing the third engine position; bottom: The Douglas DC-3, a worthy troop and cargo carrier in the Second World War and a family forerunner of the versatile KC-10.

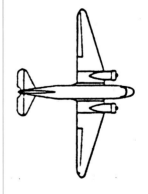

In Operations Desert Shield and Desert Storm in 1990 and 1991, the USAF KC-10 fleet provided in-flight refuelling to aircraft from the US armed forces as well as those of other coalition air forces. In the early stages of Operation Desert Shield, in-flight refuelling was key to the rapid airlift of materiel and forces. In addition to refuelling airlift aircraft, the KC-10, along with the smaller KC-135, moved thousands of tons of cargo and thousands of troops in support of the massive Persian Gulf build-up. The KC-10 and KC-135 conducted about 51,700 separate refuelling operations and delivered 125 million gallons of fuel without missing a single scheduled rendezvous.

The Extender is a big aeroplane, meant to play a big role. It can bring up to 200,000 lb of fuel to a point in the sky 2,200 statute miles from its home field, orbit, dispense, and return, or carry a full cargo load of up to 170,000 lb 4,370 statute miles. The engine power for this hefty tanker comes from three General Electric CF6-50C2 high-bypass-ratio turbofans, each putting out 52,500 lb of take-off thrust. The CF6 engine has achieved an impressive record of reliable operation, helping to power the USAF KC-10 fleet to 650,000 flight hours by the year 2000. To that year, the fleet had established a superb safety record, with only one aircraft written off, the result of a ramp accident at Barksdale AFB in September 1987.

The Extender retains an enormous commonality of 88 per cent with the commercial DC-10, with additional modifications such as provision for extra crew members, the elimination of most upper-deck windows and lower-deck cargo doors, accommodation for additional support personnel, an in-flight refuelling receptacle, military avionics, extra fuselage fuel tanks, an improved aerial refuelling operator's station, an advanced aerial refuelling boom, an improved cargo-handling system, and a hose reel/drogue system. The fuel tankage system of the KC-10A comprises seven unpressurized integral-body fuel cells with three forward and four aft of the wing. All the cells are located in vented cavities of the under-deck area. A major effort has been made to build in substantial crash-resistance, with keel beams and energy-absorbing material placed to give maximum protection for the tanks. Easy access to the fuel cells is provided via under-fuselage panels making installation, system inspection, maintenance and removal efficient.

McDonnell Douglas designed the aerial refuelling boom system for maximum safety, fuel-flow rate and efficiency, operated by a a digital fly-by-wire control system with automatic load alleviation, position rate sensing for assured disconnect control, precision hand controls and operator-selectable disconnect limits. The operator is also able to switch from boom to hose refuelling and vice versa in flight. The operator is stationed just aft of the rear lower fuselage tanks. There he is situated in a relatively comfortable little area where he is able to sit upright in an aft-facing crew seat, with excellent visibility through a wide viewing window. Along with his refuelling controls, he has a periscopic viewing capability. The fully pressurized operator station can be reached from the upper deck and there is a facility for him to control the heating for his area. Two extra seats are provided near his station for the use of an instructor and an observer on training flights. The operator watches the approach of the receiver aircraft and 'flies' the boom via the digital fly-by-wire control arrangement. The transfer rate of fuel in the boom system is 1,100 gallons a minute, while in the hose and drogue mode it is 470 gallons a minute.

In the cargo-handling mode the KC-10A is considerably improved over the commercial DC-10 air freighter. The Extender is equipped to cope with a wide range of load types, having a power winch to help move various kinds of cargo fore and aft in the hold, along with a powered roller system, cargo-pallet couplers to create pallets for larger items, and an extended ball-mat area for the loading of oversize cargo. A 102-inch by 140-inch cargo door on the left side of the forward fuselage swings upward for loading and unloading. The usable cargo area of the plane is more than 12,000 cubic feet and the cabin is nineteen feet wide with a ceiling height of 8 feet 6 inches and a floor area of 2,200 square feet. It can accommodate up to twenty-seven standard cargo pallets in a single-aisle configuration. Accommodation for the crew and for additional personnel can be configured to a variety of arrangements. Commonly, provision is made for a crew of five with six additional seats for extra crew members and four bunks in a crew rest area. It can also be configured for a total of eighty crew and support personnel.

In 1986, the United States responded to several Libyan-sponsored acts of terrorism against American citizens when, on 15 April US Air Force and Navy aircraft hit alleged terrorist targets in Libya. It was called Operation El Dorado Canyon and nineteen KC-10As of the 2nd Bombardment Wing at Barksdale AFB, Louisiana, the 68th Air Refuelling Group at Seymour Johnson AFB, North Carolina, and the 22nd Air Refuelling Wing at March AFB, California, flew to RAF Fairford and RAF Mildenhall in England on 11 April to assemble for the attack. Shortly thereafter, thirty-four USAF KC-135s also deployed to Mildenhall and Fairford in preparation for it. The attack would be carried out by USAF F-111F bombers from RAF Lakenheath and EF-111A defence suppression aircraft from RAF Upper Heyford. These planes would have to circumvent France and Spain on their way to Libya as those nations had refused to allow the F-111s to overfly their territory *en route* to the targets, necessitating a 5,500-mile round trip mission. Thus, a number of in-flight refuellings would be required. In planning the raid, it was decided to try to maintain an element of surprise, which meant that all aerial rendezvous and refuellings would have to be carried out under complete radio silence. In servicing the F-111s, the KC-10s provided four in-flight refuellings on the outbound leg and two on the return. In the attack itself, the F-111s struck and destroyed four MiG 23 fighters, six Il-76 transports, one Boeing 727, two Fokker F.27s, two Mi-8 helicopters and the Al Jamahiriyah barracks. One of the F-111s failed to return.

In other actions, when the USA sent forces to Panama in 1986 to restore democratic rule in that Central American nation, USAF KC-10s and KC-135s were employed to dispense more than twelve million pounds of aviation fuel to more than a hundred participating aircraft. The KC-10 fleet was called on in 1990 and 1991 during Operations Desert Shield and Desert Storm for the in-flight refuelling of both US military aircraft and those of other Coalition air forces. The Extenders, and many of the KC-135 fleet, were also used to haul thousands of tons of cargo and thousands of troops in the build-up to the Persian Gulf operations. Forty-six KC-10s were sent to the Gulf in support of the war ops there in a powerful demonstration of their ability to refuel a variety of military aircraft, utilizing both the flying boom and the hose-and-drogue methods. In the Gulf, the Extenders and the KC-135s carried out 51,700 separate refuellings, dispensing 125 million gallons of fuel and not missing a single refuelling rendezvous. In a 1998 attempt to persuade the Iraqi leader Saddam Hussein, to allow United Nations weapons inpectors to go on with their monitoring of his capability to produce weapons of mass destruction, Extenders again participated in a build-up of supplies and personnel in the Gulf region. There followed the NATO air campaign against Yugoslavia in March 1999,

in the aftermath of the failed negotiations between NATO members and the Yugoslavian government over Yugoslav oppression of ethnic Albanians in the Serbian portion of Kosovo. By May 150 KC-10s and KC-135s had deployed to Europe where they were involved in refuelling the fighters, bombers and support aircraft participating in the campaign. The KC-10s flew 409 missions in the Kosovo operations.

With a projected service life of 30,000 hours, its relatively low purchase and maintenance cost, state-of-the-art technology and updates, and its commonality with commercial DC-10s for the availability of spare parts, the KC-10A fleet has a theoretical projected service life to the year 2043. But there are other considerations. The KC-10s amount to only a small portion of the DC-10 aircraft still operating around the world in 2004. Most of what are referred to as 'first-tier operators' of commercial DC-10s are expected to take their planes out of service by the year 2010 as these high-time aeroplanes reach retirement age. Some of these aircraft will continue to be operated by small carriers, but the majority of the old planes will be retired and their departure is very likely to change the economics of the USAF KC-10 fleet operation. The good news for the Air Force is that its rate of utilization of the planes is much lower than that of the commercial airlines, making for a longer service life for the Extenders. But as the world pool of commercial DC-10s goes to grass, the sources for spares and other requirements to keep the KC-10s airborne will inevitably dry up and the costs associated with running the big planes will rise.

Specifications: KC-10A

Engines: Three General Electric CF6-50C2 turbofans rated at 52,500 lb thrust
Maximum speed: 619 mph
Service ceiling: 42,000 ft
Normal range: 4,400 miles with cargo; 11,500 miles without cargo
Weight: maximum take-off 590,000 lb
Wingspan: 165 ft 4 in
Length: 181 ft 7 in
Height: 58 ft 1 ins
Wing area: 3,958 sq ft

The NATO air campaign against Yugoslavia began on 24 March 1999, following the breakdown of negotiations between NATO members and the Yugoslavian government over the its oppression of the ethnic Albanian majority in the Serbian region of Kosovo. The campaign, dubbed Allied Force, followed months of preparation. The mobility part of the operation began in February and was heavily tanker-dependent. By early May 1999, some 150 KC-10s and KC-135s were deployed to Europe where they were used to refuel bombers, fighters and support aircraft engaged in the conflict. The KC-10 flew 409 missions throughout the Allied Force campaign and the continued support operations in Kosovo.

ANTONOV

AN-124
AN-225

overleaf: A majestic An-124
on short final approach for
a landing at Hannover,
Germany, in September 2003.

In the fairy tale of the Russian poet Aleksander Pushkin, the lovely Ludmila, daughter of Prince Vladimir of Kiev, marries the mighty knight Ruslan. On their wedding night the young bride mysteriously disappears and the rest of the tale follows the trials of Ruslan as he searches for his love. In the end, after many struggles, they are reunited and live happily ever after back in Kiev, which also happens to be the home of the Antonov Design Bureau and the Antonov Aeronautical Scientific Technical Complex, creators of the An-124 *Ruslan* cargo transport, currently the second-largest commercial heavy-lift aircraft in the world, exceeded only by its younger sister, the larger derivative An-225 Mriya.

The first flight of the An-124, called Condor by NATO, took place on 26 December 1982, fourteen years after the first flight of the Lockheed C-5 Galaxy heavy lifter, an aeroplane to which the An-124 bears more than a passing resemblance. Like the C-5, the big An-124-100 is fitted with an upward-swinging nose door, the largest nose door of any cargo aircraft except the An-225. This great gap can swallow a cargo load up to four metres high by six metres by twenty metres long and weighing up to 120 tons. Like the Galaxy, the An-124 was designed with a front and rear drive-on loading and unloading capability thanks to its rear fuselage ramp/door configuration. Unlike the C-5, however, the Antonov utilizes a system of two electric traveling cranes to position its loads.

The An-124 has a pressurized upper deck with a rear compartment aft of the wing that can accommodate up to eighty-eight passengers or troops. The lower deck is also pressurized and is dedicated for freight only. The big plane is designed to fly air-drop and airlift missions day and night in both visual and instrument flight conditions. Its twenty-four-wheel undercarriage comprises two steerable nosewheels and ten main-wheel bogies, five per side, each with two wheels, which allow it to operate from and onto many unprepared and unimproved fields, frozen land and hard-packed snow.

Four of the same Lotarev D-18T turbofan engines that power the An-225 drive the An-124, providing a total thrust of 206,360 lb and its ten huge wing fuel tanks, with a capacity of 507,000 lb of aviation gas, give the fully loaded plane a range of 2,800 miles.

Twenty-one of the forty-eight An-124s that have been built to date are being flown by civilian cargo air carriers

Antonov Airlines, Volga-Dnepr, Poliot, and others, to destinations throughout the world. In addition to more standard commercial missions, a large and eclectic mix of outsize cargoes are carried regularly, including large assembly sections of other aircraft such as the Airbus A330 and A340 airliners between manufacturing plants in Canada, Britain, France and Germany.

With Perestroika in the mid-1980s, the organizational restructuring of the Soviet economy and bureacracy in the Gorbachev era, most Soviet government military programmes were in slow decline, as was the financial condition of the Antonov Design Bureau. With the prototype An-124 and two additional An-124 test aircraft in hand, the company had exhibited the aeroplane internationally and had received many inquiries about carrying commercial cargo, but it was not permitted to offer such a service. The An-124 was, after all, still a military strategic transporter aircraft whose movements were controlled by the Soviet General Staff or Ministry of Defence. But the people at the Antonov Design Bureau were intrigued by the idea of operating the plane commercially and eventually, in March 1989, they received government permission to operate the An-124 on a commercial basis, worldwide. To fly commercially, the Antonov Design Bureau created its transport division, Antonov Airlines.

The lineage of the Ruslan and Mriya heavy lifters goes back to the 1950s when the Antonov Design Bureau first flew its eighty-four passenger turboprop-powered An-10, which was soon developed into the An-12, an aircraft equipped with a rear cargo-loading ramp. The evolution continued with the famous An-22 Antheus, which made its first flight in 1965. The An-22 is a large, four-engine turboprop of 60,000 hp whose Kuznetsov NK-12MA engines drive eight-blade contra-rotating propellers, giving it the ability to haul a 99,000 lb payload more than 6,800 miles at a cruising speed of 370 mph. The aeroplane can carry a maximum 176,400 lb payload in its cargo hold. The forward cabin compartment is fully pressurized and seats a crew of five and twenty-nine passengers. Observers in the West first saw the An-22 at the June 1965 Paris Air Show, only a few months after its first flight. The plane appeared to be a larger version of the An-12 Cub, both aircraft being powered by four turboprop engines and having a high, straight wing, main landing gear arranged in fairings on the fuselage sides, and a pressurized crew compartment and unpressurized cargo compartment. But unlike the Cub, the An-22 has twin vertical tailfins for improved handling and stability, and with its wing design and long double-slotted flaps, it can take off fully loaded in a bit more than 4,200 feet.

When operating from rough, unimproved strips, the crew can adjust the tyre pressures. The cargo capacity of the An-22 is 88 tons. In the production run of the plane, which ended in 1974, approximately one hundred were built, with roughly half delivered to the airline Aeroflot and the rest to the Soviet military airlift service. In the course of its operational career, the An-22 has been heavily employed flying cargoes to the Soviet Far East. It is believed that as many as a dozen An-22s continue in service.

It was an early 1980s Soviet requirement for a technologically advanced strategic military transport aircraft that could haul extremely large cargoes over great distances with an economic performance far greater than its predecessors, that led to the development of the An-124 Ruslan and its serial production at the Aviant State Aviation Plant, Kiev, Ukraine, and Aviastar of Ulyanovsk, Russia. By January 1987, the new plane was operating with the Soviet military. It had been designed primarily to transport heavy military combat and support equipment, other large and outsize heavy cargoes, including missile launchers, transport vehicles, guidance stations, all existing battle tanks, infantry combat vehicles, armoured personnel carriers, self-propelled guns, construction and excavation equipment, graders, bulldozers, trucks and fully equipped paratroops.

The An-124 is a high-wing monoplane with a swept wing, a single vertical tail fin and a fuselage-mounted fixed horizontal tailplane. The An-124-100 commercial variant was issued its type certificate in 1992. Its D-18T turbofan engines are relatively light in weight and offer both a low noise level and low fuel consumption. The engine nacelles are fitted with hush kits to guarantee compliance with international noise standards. The upper-deck front cabin accommodates the flight crew and a relief crew. The flight deck includes positions for a pilot, co-pilot, two flight engineers, a navigator and a communications officer. There is a station for a loadmaster on the lower deck. The aircraft is fitted with two aux-

iliary power units equipped with electric generators and turbopumps for independent operation of the aircraft.

As a cargo transport, its capability is enhanced by the simultaneous loading and unloading of outsize cargo from both directions utilizing the front and rear access ramps. Provision has been made for two overhead traveling cranes able to lift 20 tons, and two mobile floor-mounted electric winches. The plane also has roller equipment enabling the loading and unloading of single-item cargoes of up to 50 tons. It can carry a normal 120-ton payload and can para-drop cargoes of up to 100 tons. Among the many modern features of the An-124 are its automated radio communications system and navigational radar, an automatic control system, the TCAS-2000 collision-avoidance system, a ground-proximity warning system and a four-channel hydraulic system. It carries new avionics designed by Honeywell (USA) and by Aviapribor and Leninets (Russia). All of the systems are quadruple redundant. The aeroplane also offers a 'kneeling' system wherein the fuselage can be lowered at either front or rear, decreasing the slope of the loading ramps to assist the loading and unloading of certain cargoes. To kneel at the front, the nose landing gear can be partially retracted and the nose settled on extendible 'feet.'

Among the many impressive accomplishments of the Ruslan are the delivery of 3,500 tons of humanitarian aid to the people of Armenia following the devastating earthquake there and the 1985 transport of 152-ton Euclid rock-hauling dump trucks from Vladivostok to Polyarny, the delivery of 110-ton mine-clearance equipment to southern Angola, Lynx anti-submarine helicopters, 90-ton hydraulic turbines, a 109-ton locomotive, and a 135-ton Seimens electric generator. Its record-breaking achievements are numerous, including lifting a 171-ton cargo to an altitude of 35,000 feet and a 25-hour non-stop flight in 1987 that covered 15,000 miles. Since 1994, the An-124s of Volga-Dnepr have been flying cargo missions for the United Nations and its World Food Programme.

The aeroplane and its crew are heavily computer reliant, with thirty-four separate computers on board allowing the flight and ground crews to monitor all aspects of the aircraft operation with warnings and recommendations about malfunctions, real and potential. The computers are combined into four primary systems—automatic

The An-124-100 heavy transport was designed and manufactured by the Antonov Aeronautical Scientific Technical Complex, based in Kiev, Ukraine. It was planned for the long-range delivery and air-dropping of heavy and over-size cargo, including machines, equipment and troops. An-124s serve in the Russian Army where they are called the Ruslan. They have the NATO reporting name Condor.

Based on the An-124 military transport, the An-124-100 has been developed and certified for cargo operation. The unique transport capabilities and the high performance of the aircraft have been proven in lengthy operation around the world. The aeroplane has served several nations, moving cargoes such as 90-ton hydraulic turbines, Euclid dump trucks, an ocean-going yacht and a 109-ton railway locomotive.

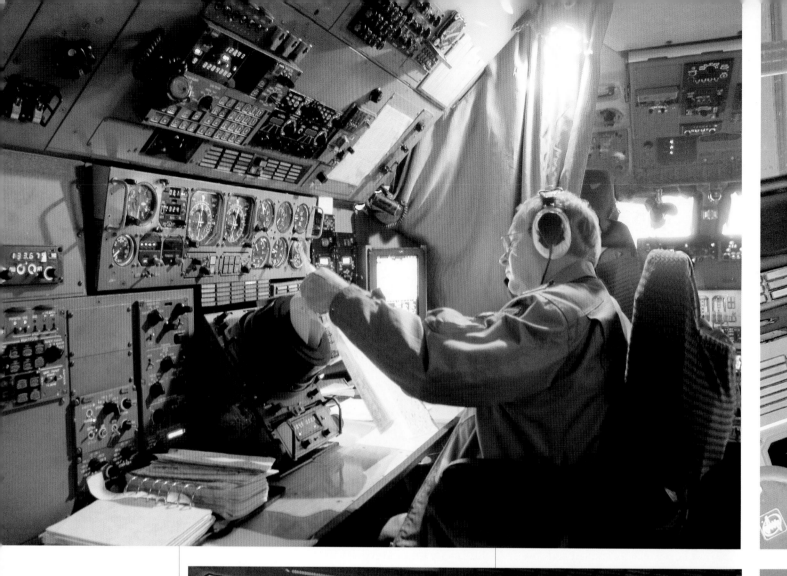

above, right, and centre:
Views of the massive An-124
in flight; far right: The enormous cargo compartment
of the An-225; far right top:
The
flight deck and instrument
panel of the gargantuan
An-225 Mriya heavy lifter.

Designed to carry twice as much cargo as a Boeing 747 freighter, the An-225 Mriya is staggering in its scale. Both nose-to-tail and wingtip-to-wingtip, the Mriya measures nearly the length of a football field. At its maximum take-off weight, it is half again the weight of a fully loaded Lockheed C-5. From the beginning of its development, the An-225 took just 3 1/2 years to complete, making its maiden flight on 21 December 1988. With the collapse of the Soviet Union a year later, the Ukraine, home to the Antonov Design Bureau creators of the aeroplane, became an independent republic.

The An-225 made its first public appearance at the 1989 Paris Air Show where it arrived spectacularly, carrying a Buran space shuttle on its

piloting, navigation, remote control, and monitoring.

Antonov Airlines, Aviastar and Air Foyle have planned for the development of two new versions of the An-124: the An-124-210, which would be powered by Rolls-Royce RB211-52H-T engines, and the An-124-100M to be powered by Series 3 D-18 engines made by Progress Design Bureau. The service range of the new planes would be ten per cent greater than current An-124s and they would require a shorter take-off roll. Honeywell (USA) and Aviaprobor (Russia) would provide the digital flight-deck instrumentation, which would enable the operators to fly the aircraft with a crew of four rather than the current six needed on the An-124-100.

Specifications: An-124

Engines: Four ZMKB Progress Lotarev D-18T turbofans rated at 51,590 lb thrust each
Maximum speed: 535 mph
Cruising speed: 500 mph
Service ceiling: 39,335 ft
Range: 8,905 miles with maximum fuel; 2,430 miles with maximum payload
Weight: 385,810 lb empty; 892,870 lb maximum take-off
Wingspan: 240 ft 6 in
Length: 226 ft 6 in
Height: 69 ft
Wing area: 6,760 sq ft.

And now we come to the biggest of the big, the flying superlative, an aeroplane large enough to dwarf a Boeing 747, with a maximum take-off weight 553,750 lb *greater* than that of a Lockheed C-5 Galaxy. She is called Mriya, Ukranian for 'dream', and she must have seemed rather far-fetched, even to the dreamers of the Antonov Design Bureau when they first thought about creating an aircraft with a 250-ton internal carrying capacity, twice that of a 747 air freighter, or 200 tons on top of the fuselage. The super-heavy lifter An-225 became airborne for the first time, for seventy-five minutes, in December 1988, three and a half years after they began her design work.

By any measure, Mriya is the world's largest, heaviest and most powerful aircraft. Even her wingspan, when measured from root to wing-tip, is greater than that of the Hughes HK-1 flying-boat. Mriya is a man-made vehicle capable of lifting from the ground at a maximum

weight of 1.32 million pounds and cruising at 500 mph (497 officially) for more than 2,800 miles. She achieves this with six huge ZMKB Progress Lotarev D-18T turbofan engines, each rated at 51,590 lb thrust and fitted with thrust reversers. With its integral fuel tanks in the wings and additional tankage in the added wing centre section, the Mriya has an estimated maximum fuel capacity of more than 660,000 lb.

Known to NATO as Cossack, the An-225 was a Cold War design requested by the Soviet Ministry of Defence and meant to haul the now-defunct Soviet Buran space shuttle or the Energia launcher external tank, on its back, and other shuttle components internally, from a service area to a launch site. In addition to this role, it was hoped that the superplane would serve the Soviet cause by transporting huge power plant and oil exploration cargoes to the far reaches of Siberia. The An-225 is actually a cleverly enhanced derivative of the Antonov An-124 Ruslan military transport, with a high degree of commonality and standardization with the An-124. Piotr Balabujew and the Antonov Design Bureau staff created a stretched, pressurized fuselage forty feet longer than that of the An-124, and powered the new plane with six engines instead of four. The fuselage cross-section dimensions are the same as those of the An-124 and the aircraft retains the nose visor of its predecessor, but sacrifices the rear loading-ramp/door assembly of the 124 design to save weight. The basic wings of the An-124 were used with the addition of a new centre section, increasing the overall wingspan to 290 feet. The addition of two more engines than were used on the 124 resulted in an enormous thrust rating of the 309,540 lb. While not designed as a military aircraft, the An-225 would certainly be of great military value with its ability to deliver cargoes of a size and weight no other existing aircraft can manage.

The main design concerns in planning the giant cargo lifter were weight distribution and maneouvrability on the ground and in the air. The problem of weight distribution was solved by fitting the aircraft with a unique thirty-two-wheel landing-gear arrangement that included twenty steerable wheels (including the four nose-gear wheels). The manoeuvrability issue was resolved through the use of a modified twin tail design which greatly reduced buffeting and improved the lateral stability and the handling of the plane when carrying a large external load in the piggyback configuration. The An-225 flying control system is fly-by-wire and all control surfaces are hydraulically actuated. Each wing is equipped with two-section ailerons, three-section single-slotted Fowler flaps on the outer panels and single-section on the centre section, as well as six-section leading-edge flaps on the outer panels only, with eight air brakes (inboard) and eight spoilers (outboard) on each wing upper surface and centre section forward of the flaps. The nose landing gear is two independently steerable, forward-retracting twin-wheel units. Like the An-124, the An-225 can kneel by partially retracting her nose wheels and settling on two extensible feet, to assist the loading and unloading process. Utilizing many of the An-124 components allowed the ADB designers to keep the development cost of the An-225 down.

In one of the most spectacular events in aviation history, the An-225 arrived at the June 1989 Paris Air Show carrying the Buran space shuttle on its back, for a most impressive world debut. But the lustre of that day soon faded with the grounding of the Soviet shuttle programme and its discontinuance in 1993. Lacking its *raison d'etre*, Mriya was the world's biggest white elephant, sitting unwanted on an airfield near Kiev, where she was cannibalized for engine spares and other parts for use on An-124s. After the collapse of the Soviet Union, however, she was re-acquired by the Antonov Group. They determined to find a new role for their massive creation, to take advantage of her ability to carry almost anything on her back that would not fit inside her immense cargo bay. An important alliance was soon formed between Antonov and the Ukranian aero-engine maker Motor-Sich. The joint-business collaboration invested approximately twenty million dollars in modernizing the aircraft and installing updated avionics, a collision avoidance system and engine noise reduction.

In October 2001, a joint venture was announced between the British outsized and heavyweight cargo specialist firms Air Foyle and HeavyLift Cargo Airlines. The new company was called Air Foyle Heavylift Ltd and was formed to market and promote commercial charter operations by the Ukranian carrier, Antonov Airlines. With their An-124 fleet, the reintroduction of the An-22, and the commercial launch of the An-225

(having been issued its commercial transport type certificate in May 2001), Antonov Airlines and co-venturer Air Foyle HeavyLift Ltd enjoyed a 2002 turnover in excess of $140 million. Antonov Airlines Vice President/ Commercial, Vince Seeger, 'For us, the market [in 2003] is exceptionally strong. In general terms there are ongoing flights into Kabul on behalf of the German and Italian militaries and operations into the Gulf for the British and American forces. We are extremely pleased to see the An-225/ An-22 taking an active role within the commercial market.' Some of the cargoes carried by Antonov Airlines to the Gulf region have included sanitation equipment, medical supplies, food, pre-fabricated housing, and vehicles. Christopher Foyle, chairman and joint chief executive officer of Air Foyle HeavyLift Ltd, stated in March 2003, 'The last twelve months have been the busiest ever for us, not just in revenue but in flying hours as well. Special situations in central Asia, the work resulting from the American West Coast port strike, and military flights to Kabul and Kuwait have added huge amounts of flying hours. With our fleet of seven An-124s, an An-225 and a newly refurbished An-22, all commercially available, the market share achieved by Antonov Airlines has now increased to approximately fifty per cent.'

Antonov Airlines anticipates a growth cycle for world air cargo traffic in which it will triple by 2015. The company operates world-wide cargo operations in competition with many major airlines, including Poliot, Volga-Dnepr, and Aeroflot, all of which also operate the An-124.

With its specialized aircraft, Antonov Airlines has been able to haul many outsized and extremely heavy payloads that the cargo arms of some other airlines could not accommodate. In addition to these commercial activities, it has provided a number of humanitarian relief flights. Among its assignments have been the delivery of a 135-ton Siemens power generator from Dusseldorf to Delhi; United Nations peacekeeping supplies and materials from Brindisi and Lisbon to East Timor, and the transport of nuclear fuel from Iraq to Russia in the implementation of a UN Security Council resolution. And, in an example of the colossal carrying capability of the An-225, the aeroplane transported a 285,000 lb transformer from Linz, Austria, to

back. The Soviet space programme, however, was discontinued and the giant plane was left without a mission. It sat, parked by its hangar near Kiev, unused and unneeded, except as a source for scavenged engine parts. With the Soviet Union break-up, title to the plane passed to the Antonov group, which began searching for a way to make the Mriya profitable. The group partnered with the Ukranian aero-engine maker, Motor-Sich, investing $20 million to repair and modernize the plane and its avionics.

Now the firm Air Foyle HeavyLift Ltd, through its association with Antonov Airlines, is hopeful of putting the massive Mriya into regular heavy lift service.

The world's largest operating aircraft, the An-225 Mriya, resulted from the Soviet requirement for an aircraft able to transport very large items for the Soviet space programme. In 1985 the Antonov Design Bureau was assigned the task with the added demand that the new aeroplane be capable of transporting the Buran space shuttle orbiter. Antonov's experience with the An-124 led to their design for the larger An-225, retaining the same cross-sectional dimensions, but with greater length. Standard An-124 wings were used on the new plane, but were grafted onto a new centre section. An additional pair of D-18T turbofan engines was fitted to the new wing centre section, raising the total thrust to 309,540 lb, sufficient to easily lift the mammoth aeroplane at its maximum take-off weight of 1,322,750 lb.

right: An in-flight view of the wondrous An-225; top right: The Mriya landing at Luxembourg in late 2003, far right: Another view of the aircraft landing.

Williams Gateway Airport, Arizona, for the SRP Kyrene/Santan Generating Plant at Tempe, Arizona. According to Air Foyle Heavylift, 'The An-225 has an unmatched payload and is a realistic proposition in today's outsized cargo market.'

Mriya is operated by a crew of six on the flight deck and a loadmaster in the lobby area below. There are two pilots, two flight engineers at starboard-side stations, a navigator and a communciations specialist at stations behind the pilot on the port side. A rest area for a relief crew is provided behind the flight deck and there is provision for up to seventy passengers aft of the wing carry-through. The completely unobstructed cargo hold is 141 feet long and has a titanium floor. The hydraulically operated hinged nose-visor door opens in a seven-minute cycle in syncronization with the folding-nose loading ramp.

The avionics of Mriya are like that of its An-124 elder sister. There is an automatic flight-control system, a moving-map display, forward-looking weather radar and downward-looking ground-mapping/navigation radar, along with quadruple INS, Loran and Omega.

Antonov has built a second An-225 airframe, but at the time of writing there are no firm plans to complete the aircraft. According to Igor Babenko of Antonov Airlines, if a second An-225 is completed, it will be built with a rear cargo door and the tail will be redesigned as a single tail. It would then be more effective for cargo transportation.

Specifications: An-225
Engines: Six ZMKB Progress Lotarev D-18T turbofans rated at 51,590 pounds thrust each
Maximum speed: 530 mph
Cruising speed: 497 mph.
Service ceiling: 39,000 feet (estimated)
Range: 2,795 miles with 440,900 lb internal payload; 5,965 miles with 220,450 lb internal payload; 9,570 miles with 220,450 lb internal payload and maximum fuel
Weight: 385,800 lb empty; 1,322,275 lb maximum take-off weight.
Wingspan: 290 ft
Length: 275 ft 7 in
Height: 59 ft 9 in
Wing area: 9,741 sq ft

'– What do you think of modern civilisation?
– I think it would be a good idea.'
– Mahatma Gandhi

BOEING

'They all laughed at Joan of Arc, but she went right ahead and built it.'
– Gracie Allen

Among the most interesting features of the Boeing C-17 Globemaster III is its 'propulsive lift system'. This ingenius idea utilizes the engine exhaust to enhance lift generation and significantly reduce the take-off run and landing roll of the aircraft. Large flaps in the plane's 'supercritical' wing design can be extended into the jet exhaust stream, enabling the C-17 to fly very steep landing approaches at amazingly slow speeds, giving the plane the ability to bring huge payloads of more than 170,000 pounds onto runways as short as 3,000 feet. This 'externally blown-flap' or powered-lift system lets the pilot make extremely precise landings on a variety of runway surfaces. The wing design itself, through its higher efficiency and reduced drag, improves the range, fuel economy and cruising speed of the aeroplane, helping it achieve truly impressive performance.

During the Vietnam War in the 1970s, American military planners identified an increasing requirement for the rapid deployment of armed forces and equipment that went beyond the capacity and capability of the existing fleet of C-141 Starlifter and C-5 Galaxy transport aircraft. These planes had been hauling their vitally needed cargoes from the United States to major base facilities well behind the battle zones. Once delivered, the cargoes then had to be reconfigured in order to be reloaded aboard the smaller C-130 transports that would fly them on to airstrips nearer the front lines. This slow, inefficient procedure delayed delivery of often urgently required supplies and equipment. Thus was born the Department of Defense Cargo-Experimental (C-X) Program in December 1979, established to define a highly capable new aircraft that could bring a wide spectrum of combat equipment across great distances, air-drop troops and equipment, land on a 3,000-foot runway, and operate on unprepared runways, with excellent ground manoeuvrability, low maintenance, high reliability and durability. This aeroplane had to be able to deliver combat-ready troops and their equipment to the sharp end of the combat zone without the need to stop at an intermediate staging area. It had to be able to bring their tanks, helicopters, and other outsize cargo, only previously airlifted by the Lockheed C-5, into that same location, in a substantially improved

global threat response.

The DoD invited proposals by Lockheed, McDonnell Douglas, and Boeing for the new plane in 1980, with the design of the Douglas Aircraft Company arm of McDonnell Douglas being chosen in August 1981. The winning design incorporated many aspects of the YC-15, a McDonnell Douglas aircraft designed and built during the 1970s for a project called the Advanced Medium Short Take-off and Landing Transport (AMST) Program. Then began a lengthy series of tests and programme evaluations and assessments, as well as many substantial delays, technical problems, cost overruns, and a reduction in the original purchase number from 210 to 120 aircraft. Finally, on 15 September 1991, the first C-17 was flown, nearly eighteen months after the scheduled first flight date stipulated in the contract. At one point, the US Congress and the Air Force tangled over accusations that the wing of the C-17 was structurally weak and unsafe, and that the Air Force was believed to have been making improper 'progress payments' to McDonnell Douglas in an effort to help bail them out of a financial struggle in that period. When the aeroplane began flight testing, some fuel leaks were discovered, as was cracking in the aluminium/lithium-alloy flooring. The resulting production delays caused the Department of Defense to announce that the C-17 production line would be closed after completion of the fortieth aircraft unless the company could fix the problems and deliver the rest of the planes on schedule at the agreed cost.

Congressional pressures, and the eventual cutbacks in the number of aircraft purchased, left the company in an even more difficult position, both internally, for having to lay off many workers from the C-17 programme, and externally, with regard to its subcontractors, placing the programme in great jeopardy. A staggering effect of this sad, chaotic situation surrounding the C-17 project, and the reduction in the order, was an outrageously high unit cost for the planes. By 1995, however, the company was able to correct the major problems with the aeroplane, improve production efficiency and effect significant cost savings, opening the way for additional orders from the Air Force and bringing the per-plane cost down to an acceptable level.

C-17

In 1995, the C-17 proved itself one of the finest aircraft ever built, passing an extraordinarily demanding government Reliability, Maintainability and Availability evaluation, in which it was put through realistic operational scenarios including a week of simulated wartime activity. This involved several C-17s, loaded with 125,000 lb M1A1 Abrams main battle tanks, flying from North Carolina to the Mojave Desert of southern California, where they were required to land and stop in a distance of less than 2,800 feet. In more than 2,200 flying hours, the C-17s in the test demonstrated a mission-capable rate of ninety per cent and an on-time departure rate of better than ninety-nine per cent. In flight testing at Edwards AFB, California, during 2001, C-17s set thirty-three world records—more than any other airlifter in history—including payload to altitude, time-to-climb, and short-takeoff-and-landing marks in which the aeroplane took off in less than 1,400 feet, carrying a 44,000 lb payload to altitude, and landing in less than 1,400 feet.

So impressive was the new plane that, in May 1995, McDonnell Douglas, its subcontractors, and the US Air Force, became joint recipients of the Collier Trophy for aeronautical achievement during the year 1994. The award, made by the National Aeronautical Association, was given 'for designing, developing, testing, producing, and placing into service the Globemaster III, whose performance and efficiency make it the most versatile airlift aircraft in aviation history.'

By the summer of 1996, the Secretary of the Air Force had ordered eighty C-17s from McDonnell Douglas, and the engines for them from Pratt & Whitney, to be delivered over a seven-year period. This order raised the total C-17 buy to 120 aircraft, with the final aeroplane delivery scheduled for November 2004. By the end of December 2001, the DoD had authorized a plan to purchase an additional sixty C-17s under a new contract running until 2007.

In the run-up to a decision as to which manufacturer would win the competition to build the AMST, Boeing and McDonnell Douglas each designed and built demonstrator aircraft, the YC-14 and YC-15, respectively, and these aircraft efficiently demonstrated the concept that powered lift devices could actually reduce the critical take-off run and landing roll-out of such heavily loaded cargo transports. This proof was essential in the developmental progress of the aircraft that would become the C-17, as it had to be able to operate easily from thousands of marginal, unimproved landing fields.

The C-17 Globemaster III programme got under way in late August 1981, when the US Department of Defense chose McDonnell Douglas to produce the new plane. Large-scale production was authorized in February 1985 and that was followed late in the year by a fixed-price incentive-based contract worth more than three billion dollars to McDonnell Douglas, with a further $725 million for tooling.

Although the McDonnell Douglas Company, and its C-17 programme, were taken over by the Boeing Company later in the 1990s, the C-17 actually went aloft on its maiden flight on 15 September 1991 from the Long Beach, California, plant of McDonnell Douglas. The flight-test programme was conducted from September 1991 through December 1994, establishing the performance of the big plane: 540 mph with a service ceiling of 45,000 feet and a maximum gross weight of 585,000 lb.

The first production aeroplane was delivered to Charleston Air Force Base, South Carolina, in June 1993 and the first USAF squadron to become operational with the aeroplane was the 17th Airlift Squadron, achieving that status in January 1995. In addition to the C-17s based at Charleston AFB, others are with squadrons of the USAF Air Mobility Command at McChord AFB, Washington, Altus AFB, Oklahoma, and with the Air National Guard at Jackson, Mississippi. The Air Force has announced that McGuire AFB, New Jersey, has been selected as a preferred site for basing further C-17s coming into the inventory, along with alternative sites at Dover AFB, Delaware, and additional aircraft for Charleston AFB, South Carolina. These Air Mobility Command locations are preferred for their relative proximity to the military forces the aircraft would likely deploy, most of which are located in the eastern United States.

In Britain, the C-17 is operated by No.99 Squadron of the Royal Air Force. The use of the C-17 by the RAF resulted from a $1 billion+ contract with the British government in September 2000 for the leasing of four

The C-17 is the newest heavy airlift aircraft in the US Air Force inventory. It is capable of rapid strategic delivery of troops and all types of cargo to main operating bases, or directly to forward bases in the deployment area. The aircraft can also perform theatre airlift missions when required. Utilizing advanced aerodynamics and an innovative NASA powered-lift concept, the C-17 combines the load-carrying capacity of the Lockheed C-5 Galaxy with the short take-off and landing performance of the C-130 Hercules. McDonnell Douglas, the originator of the C-17 (now merged with Boeing) was awarded the Collier Trophy, the highest award in aviation, in 1994 for the greatest achievement in US aviation that year in recognition of its work on the C-17 Globemaster III.

below: The Douglas C-124 Globemaster II, piston-engined forerunner of the amazing C-17 heavy lifter; right: A Globemaster III rotates from a runway at Frankfurt Rhine-Main in September 2003.

of the aircraft with delivery set for the following September. The agreement enables the UK Joint Rapid Reaction Force to shift both personnel and out-sized cargoes to crisis zones at very short notice. Previously, the British have had to hire appropriate aircraft on the open market. Now, the capability is under the immediate direction of the UK Permanent Joint Headquarters at Northwood, north of London. Of the agreement, the British Defence Procurement Minister, Baroness Symons, stated, 'This is a significant step towards providing, in the short term, the rapid deployment capability promised in the Strategic Defence Review conclusions. With C-17 we are joining the successful partnership of the United States Air Force and the Boeing Company, and the UK is benefitting from the success of this established management team.' The Strategic Defence Review referred to by Baroness Symons had clearly identified the shortfall in Britain's strategic airlift capability along with its long-term need to replace its ageing air-transport aircraft. To meet that long-term requirement, the UK has planned to purchase twenty-five A-400M Airbus aircraft. For the interim period, until the delivery of the A-400Ms, the four RAF C-17s will be covered for aircrew and maintenance training, as well as maintenance and spare parts management, by foreign military sales contracts with the USAF. The British Defence Procurement Agency and the RAF have established C-17 project teams at Wright-Patterson AFB, Ohio, as part of the USAF C-17 programme office, at the primary USAF C-17 base, Charleston AFB, South Carolina, and at the Boeing C-17 production centre at Long Beach, California.

Airbus Industrie, Paris, has called its A-400M military transport programme 'the most ambitious military procurement programme in European history'. The 20 billion Euro (US $23.7 billion) programme was scheduled to proceed by the end of 2003, with Airbus having orders for 180 planes from Belgium (7), France (50), Germany (60), Luxembourg (1), Spain (27), Turkey (10), and the United Kingdom (25). The first aircraft deliveries are expected in 2009. The A-400M is intended to replace the European nations' ageing fleets of C-130 Hercules and C-160 Transall transport aircraft. In the A-400M, customers are expecting an aircraft that

has significantly increased load-carrying capacity, with essential tactical short-field and soft-field take-off and landing capability. The new plane is expected to have about twice the cargo capacity of the C-130, in both weight and volume. While there are similarities between the A-400M and the C-17, there are significant differences too. Both aircraft are high-wing designed, four-engined heavy lifters. Both have rear cargo doors and cargo holds designed to maximize the payload-to-weight ratio. The C-17 cruises at 450 knots (Mach 0.74), carries a maximum payload of 170,900 lb and can take off and land on runways as short as 3,000 feet. The A-400M is planned to cruise at a similar speed, but is powered by turboprop engines for greater economy. It's carrying capacity, however, at just 81,570 lb, is only half that of the C-17 and it will need at least 3,500 feet of runway to take off and land. While eight per cent of the C-17's structural weight comprises composite materials, between thirty-five and forty per cent of the A-400M will be made of such materials.

Britain's C-17s are operated from RAF Brize Norton in Oxfordshire. The typical loads to be carried by the RAF version of the big transport include: a Challenger tank, or thirteen Land Rover light trucks, or three Apache helicopters. The commander of the British Army's 16 Air Assault Brigade, Brigadier Peter Wall, commented on the role of the British Globemaster IIIs: 'If we're allocated the C-17, it will transform our ability to take heavy elements to within C-130 Hercules range of an area of interest. The potential is to use a strategic airlifter to operate in a tactical way.'

Among the newest and most advanced aircraft in the inventory of the US Air Force, the C-17 Globemaster III represents the third generation of transport aircraft to carry that name, its predecessors being the C-74, which saw service in the Berlin Airlift and the C-124, which was a mainstay in the Vietnam War era of the 1960s and 1970s. The latest Globemaster is utterly unlike its ancestors and not much like anything else in the air today. What makes it special and separates it from the pack are features like its supercritical wing design and the "winglets" (the small wing-like vertical surfaces positioned at each wing-tip), which work

together to significantly reduce drag, providing considerably increased fuel efficiency, enhanced cruising speed, and extending the aircraft's range. They achieve this by producing weaker shock waves that create less drag, permitting higher efficiency. Taking full advantage of the knowledge accumulated by NASA through its 1970s wind-tunnel research on winglets, the C-17 uses winglets that curve airflow at the wing-tips to pro-

duce a forward force on the aeroplane, not unlike that produced by the sail on a sail boat. The supercritical wing also features full-span leading-edge slats.

The T-tail empennage configuration of the C-17 design gives the aerosplane important aerodynamic advantages over more conventional design approaches. Positioning the horizontal tail so high puts it in relatively undisturbed airflow in normal cruise conditions, maximizing stability and control, but the decision to do so was hardly a cavalier one and came only after extensive wind-tunnel testing to ensure that acceptable handling characteristics would follow even at extreme pitch attitudes. There were concerns about the flow phenomena where, at high angles of attack, the low-energy wake of a stalled wing could impinge on the horizontal tail and cause a loss of longitudinal stability, making the plane pitch up and reducing longitudinal control. In the 1960s, another T-tail transport plane, a British BAC 111, suffered a fatal accident when the aircraft entered a deep stall and fell in an uncontrollable condition at a high rate of descent with the fuselage in a nearly horizontal attitude until the impact. Worldwide interest in this accident led to a major research programme by the Langley Research Center in the USA on the behaviour of T-tail design configurations at high angles of attack. A Langley team conducted wind-tunnel and piloted-simulator studies into the aerodynamic characteristics associated with deep-stall trim conditions and the development of design methods and piloting techniques to recover from such conditions. Many design configurations were evaluated in the Langley high-speed wind tunnel and the data resulting from these studies have since been utilized in the designs of many civil and military transport aircraft. The quadruple redundant digital fly-by-wire flight-control system of the C-17 provides automatic limiting of the angle of attack in high-angle-of-attack circumstances, to prevent the aircraft entering an uncontrollable deep-stall condition.

In addition to its receiver in-flight refuelling capability, the plane has an externally blown flap configuration and direct-lift control spoilers. Its high-impact landing-gear system enables it to be operated into and out of some of the most austere unimproved airfields in the world. The C-17's wide-spectrum capabilities allow it not only to haul enormous cargo loads or great numbers of passengers or troops over extreme distances, but to provide theatre and strategic airlift performance in both air-land and air-drop modes, as well as effectively performing special-operations missions and aero-medical evacuation. But its principal virtue is its long-range direct-delivery capability, the ability to accomplish the rapid delivery of combat-ready troops and/or all types of cargo either to main operational bases or directly to bases in the forward combat area.

Besides all of the above, this exceptionally capable transport aircraft is equipped with forward and upward thrust reversers, allowing the C-17 to back up when necessary, reducing its ramp-space requirement as well as the amount of noise, dust and debris in the ramp area. One loadmaster is all that is needed to handle the cargo door and cargo restraint systems, and the rapid off-loading of cargo and equipment. On the flight deck the plane is manned by a pilot and a co-pilot who operate it at a state-of-the-art four cathode ray tube (CRT) panel (with analogue back-ups), of greater reliability and less complexity than previous large aircraft cockpit displays. It also makes maximum use of built-in test features that reduce the amount of maintenance needed and perform much of the trouble-shooting function; this is in addition to an easy-access walk-in avionics bay located beneath the flight deck.

When the Air Force made up its requirements for the C-17, it included an extremely demanding reliability and maintainability requirement. For a mature fleet of the aircraft with 100,000 flying hours, the customer insisted on what it referred to as "an aircraft mission completion success probability" of 93 per cent, "aircraft maintenance man-hours per flying hour" not to exceed 18.6, and "full and partial mission-capable rates" of 74.7 and 82.6 per cent respectively.

In the structure of the C-17, more than 16,000 lb of modern composite materials are employed for greater strength, durability and reduced weight over conventional aluminium construction techniques. Major control surfaces and secondary structural components are formed with the composites, as are the rudders, whose graphite-epoxy structure has been proved in over 500,000 flight hours on the DC-10 jetliner. Both the Boeing Company and Vought Aircraft Industries Inc. of Dallas, Texas, worked on a redesign of the C-17's horizontal tail during 1999, to replace the aluminium horizontal stabilizer with a carbon fibre composite structure. All of the Globemaster IIIs built since then have the composite tails, requiring 2,000 fewer parts and 42,000 fewer fasteners than the earlier aluminium version. The newer tail also weighs 470 lb less than the old one. Like the upper-aft rudders of the time-proved Douglas DC-10 airliner, the control

'Sometime they'll give a war and nobody will come.'
– Carl Sandburg

surfaces of the C-17 utilize a multi-rib configuration of carbon fibre/epoxy. The ailerons, elevators and rudders, built mainly by Vought, are also primarily of composite construction and the nacelles for the Pratt & Whitney jet engines are largely carbon fibre-reinforced epoxy and polyimide composites.

Among the many practices instituted in the construction of the C-17 to significantly cut the cost of the plane, is the use of pre-coated rivets. Fastener technology, as it is known in the aircraft industry, went through a revolutionary change in 1997 when McDonnell Douglas, the Hi-Shear Corporation, and Aerospace Rivet Manufacturing Corporation, combined to introduce a new pre-coated rivet with the C-17 programme. The company and its suppliers developed a pre-coated dry sealant for aluminium rivets and titanium pins that enables faster, cleaner, better and more efficient work. Previously, the 1.4 million such fasteners required to hold an aeroplane like the C-17 together had to be installed 'wet', using a sealant that cost more to dispose of than to buy, because of its hazardous waste condition. Line workers claim that the use of the new product enables a 'better squeeze' on the fastener and eliminates the situation where a rivet doesn't fill the hole tightly. The new pre-coated dry sealant reduces variability in installation quality of the 733,000 rivets and 590,000 titanium pins employed in the assembly of a C-17, as well as ensuring better corrosion protection in each hole.

Just three men operate the C-17—a pilot, a co-pilot and a loadmaster. Nearly all out-size air-transportable combat equipment can be carried in the large cargo hold, including military vehicles and palletized cargo. All cargo is loaded and unloaded through a large, inward-opening aft door specially designed to enable out-size cargoes to be loaded and for low-altitude parachute extraction. The plane is designed to air-drop both paratroops and cargo. Spearheading army force projection in tactical, operational and strategic missions are the airborne forces, which have to be ready to deploy at very short notice and fight immediately on arriving in the drop zone. Included in the tactical operations are military freefall and personnel static-line air-drops, container air-drops, low velocity air-drops of heavy equipment, container delivery sys-

tems and the previously mentioned low-altitude parachute-extraction system. Use of the large C-17 means fewer aircraft are needed to deliver required personnel, supplies and equipment into a combat area and thus less exposure of aircraft and personnel to enemy ground fire. The C-17 enables use of the Dual Row Airdrop System (DRAS) in which equipment is delivered more efficiently and safely than was possible with the old single-row system. Using a two-row side-by-side rail system, cargo loads leave the aircraft sequentially, by row. Such airdrops are made between altitudes of 750 and 1,200 feet at airspeeds of 130–150 knots. The DRAS of a single C-17 can deliver eight platforms of Humvee vehicles and 105mm howitzers. It can also be used to deliver food, medicine, ammunition, trailers, water purifiers, power generators and other supplies and equipment. Damage to items on impact is minimized through the use of special energy-absorbing material packed under the items. With load-master stations located both forward and aft, the C-17 cargo bay is even reconfigurable in flight, making it possible to change the interior from passenger seating to all-cargo, or a combination of both. The compartment contains fifty-four permanent seats, with provision for the installation of 100 seats in a palletized form. A total of thirty-six aero-medical stretcher patients can be accommodated in litters.

Able to carry 102 fully equipped parachutists at a time, these personnel can exit the aircraft through a dual-door arrangement in just fifty-five seconds, but problems can and do happen in such deployments. One such occurred during routine flight developmental testing at Edwards AFB, California, in August 1994. During a mass drop of paratroops, two jumpers were involved in a high-altitude entanglement. They were able to successfully extricate themselves and both landed without injury, but the Army and Air Force studied the problem to find a solution. While not unique to the operation of the C-17, the vacuum effect of the draft from the design and 'wake' of this aircraft does tend to 'form' paratroops into a single file after they exit the dual-door arrangement, creating the possibility of their bumping into each other. Subsequent testing in mass jumps was carried out without incident. The dual side doors are now pro-

Probably the most interesting feature of the Globemaster III is its propulsive-lift system. It utilizes engine exhaust to augment lift generation by directing engine exhaust onto the large flaps extended into the exhaust stream, enabling the C-17 to fly steep approaches at amazingly low landing speeds. This allows the aeroplane to make very slow and steep landing approaches with heavy cargo loads. Such approaches help pilots make precision landings, touching down as required on runways of very limited length and surface quality. By diverting the engine exhaust downward, the wing achieves more lift. The C-17 uses a supercritical wing design like some other military transport aircraft, to increase the range and improve the fuel efficiency and cruising speed of the aeroplane by producing weaker shock waves and less drag for higher performance.

right: An RAF C-17 airborne over Oxfordshire; bottom left: The cargo hold of a USAF C-17 bringing a load of paratroopers to jump as part of the sixtieth anniversary of the June 1944 D-Day landings commemoration on the Normandy coast of France; below: A USAF C-17 manoeuvring on a busy taxiway in Germany.

vided with paratrooper platforms and wind deflectors. Its overall size and shape, and the vortices created by the C-17 (with a much wider cargo compartment than that of its predecessor, the Lockheed C-141 Starlifter), cause much greater wake turbulence than that created by the Starlifter. This requires far greater separation between element lead aircraft during jumps, for the safety of the jumpers.

It takes a lot of power to move the big, heavy C-17, and all that thrust has to be matched by unquestionable reliability. Both are provided by four Pratt & Whitney F117-PW-100 turbofan engines on underwing mounts. So powerful are the F117s that, with their reversers operating, the aeroplane can be backed up a two per cent slope. The engine thrust reversers are operable in flight, giving the aircraft the ability to carry out rapid decelerations and descents. They are the same engines that power the Boeing 757 jetliner and their reliability has been established over many years of demanding service. The Pratt & Whitney Division of United Technologies also builds and supplies spare engines, as well as providing logistical support to Air Mobility Command. Use of the F117 engine came under a pilot scheme of the office of the Under-Secretary of Defense (Acquisition and Technology) in which a commercial engine is used to meet a military requirement. In such a scheme, the development cost of the engine does not have to be borne by the government. Cumulatively, the four F117s produce just under 162,000 lb of thrust, and some of that masssive power is put to unusual use when the huge fixed-vane, double-slotted flaps are angled down behind the exhaust nozzles of the jets to deflect some of that thrust downward. The effect is increased lift for take-off. Engine exhaust is also directed over the top of the flaps to create additional lift, and it is largely this effect that lets the C-17 take off in a shorter distance and approach a landing at a slower, more controllable air speed, often in steeper descents onto short runways in which it requires a shorter than conventional roll-out. It is the combination of these features that allow the big transport to bring a cargo load of more than 170,000 lb onto a runway of less than 3,000 feet.

In a most unusual feature for a large transport air-

left: In the cockpit of the C-17 Globemaster III, nearly all devices are duplicated and located for left-right flight crew split. Still, each pilot can operate control panels and configure his or her displays, as required, independently of the other pilot.

The Royal Air Force leases four C-17s from Boeing to meet the interim strategic airlift need of the UK until the twenty- five Airbus A400Ms ordered by the RAF are delivered. The C-17s began operating from RAF Brize Norton, Oxfordshire in September 2001. The RAF C-17s are similar to those of the USAF, each capable of carrying a variety of heavy equipment, from a Challenger tank or three Warrior armoured vehicles, to three British Army Apache attack helicopters or thirteen Land-Rover light trucks.

craft, a full-time, full-function head-up display (HUD) is provided for each pilot on the C-17 flight deck. The HUD allows the pilots to check all of the principal flight parameters while looking ahead through the cockpit front windows. The plane is operated through a fly-by-wire control system which is quadruple redundant, and even with all of that, there is a mechanical back-up system.

The design of the C-17 has allowed for the greatest possible use of standardized US Air Force avionics and readily available off-the-shelf equipment. Redundancy is a primary characteristic of the plane, to give it a high degree of survivability and mission success. Computers play a large part in the operation of the C-17, with engine condition data, built-in test data and structural integrity data collected as maintenance data and loaded into a ground support system. The data are then transferred to a central database management system for analysis and the use of maintenance personnel. An advanced computer flight-planning programme is used by the pilots of Air Mobility Command, in which generated flight plans are downloaded to the Base Flight Planning Computer. Additional data can be added as available and the final flight plan is then uploaded to the mission computer of the C-17 in preparation for flight. Mission functions implemented through the software include the flight-control computers, flight-plan manipulation, and the display-control of computer-operated flight instruments. The mission computer software acts as management for the communication and navigation databases, with the capability to load and manipulate data from the mission-planning system. An Aircrew Laptop Computer System provides the loadmaster's Form F weight and balance calculations, uploaded mission data and downloaded avionics and non-avionics fault data.

For its self-defence, the C-17 is equipped with BAE Systems Integrated Defence Solutions countermeasure flare dispensers and a missile-warning system. The latter includes an array of surface-mounted thermal sensors around the aircraft to detect the heat signature of a missile exhaust plume. Frequent, quick selection and processing minimizes the number of false alarms and the system warns the crew through a cockpit indicator unit of the presence and direction of any

missile threat to the aircraft. The system can carry a formidable mix of expendable countermeasures, which includes jamming devices and it interfaces with the sensors of the aircraft. From manual to semi-automatic, through to fully automatic operation, the C-17 crew can select the system mode preferred for each situation. Input of mission data and the types and numbers of expendable countermeasures can be made through the cockpit control unit which updates and displays the status of the dispenser and the quantities and types of expendable countermeasures remaining. This system is capable of dispensing the new-generation active expendable decoys GEN-X and POET, as well as standard chaff and flare decoys that are compatible with earlier-generation dispensers.

In its operational career to date, the C-17 has proved itself the versatile, adaptable and thoroughly efficient airlift system it was designed to be. In the run-up to the 2003 Operation Iraqi Freedom, C-17 Globemaster IIIs combined with C-5 Galaxys to fly 11,400 sorties, with the C-5s flying fewer sorties than the C-17s, but hauling 11,500 tons more than the smaller aircraft, and 5,300 more passengers. The average cargo load for the C-5 was 53.8 tons while that of the C-17 was 33.1 tons. But the C-17 was easily the more reliable airlifter. For the four-month period ending in April, the average availability rate of the C-17 was 88 per cent, while that of the C-5 was 67.5 per cent. It was the first opportunity for the C-17 fleet to bring heavy army cargoes directly into a combat area. It marked the first occasion in which an M1A1 main battle tank was delivered by a C-17 into a battle zone for immediate combat deployment. That April, C-17s of the Air Mobility Command flew five main battle tanks, five M-2 Bradley fighting vehicles and fifteen M-113 armoured personnel carriers from Ramstein Air Base, Germany, to Bashur, Iraq. C-17s also carried out their first low-altitude combat air-drop in that conflict as well as the first large army unit drop when the 173rd Airborne Brigade parachuted into northern Iraq. Losses to Coalition forces during the war amounted to twenty aircraft including one A-10 and six helicopters. The C-17s were involved in seven minor incidents and the C-5s in four. For the high sortie rate, performance of both types of airlifters was virtually accident free.

In September 1997, eight Globemaster IIIs flew non-stop 7,780 miles in just under twenty hours, from Pope AFB, North Carolina, to a drop zone at Kazakhstan in central Asia where 500 troops of the US Army's 82nd Airborne Division parachuted in the exercise CENTRAZBAT '97, the first field training exercise using C-17s to drop American troops over central Asia and the longest airborne operation (in distance) ever achieved. With the support of aerial tankers from Travis AFB, California, McConnell AFB, Kansas, McGuire AFB, New Jersey and MacDill AFB, Florida, the C-17s operating from their bases in Oklahoma and South Carolina flew the mission with three aerial refuellings.

In Afghanistan, C-17s have flown more than 230 humanitarian missions in Operation Enduring Freedom, air-dropping more than 2.4 million ration packages to refugees as well as landing bulk food and blankets. The aircraft continue to fly daily missions carrying troops, supplies and heavy equipment into austere fields in Afghanistan and airfields in neighbouring countries.

Two of the USAF C-17 Globemaster IIIs have become dedicated commemorative aircraft. In April 1997, Dr Shiela Widnall, the US Secretary of the Air Force, spoke at the dedication of 'The Spirit of Bob Hope': 'We're here today to extend a symbol of thanks to a man who has brought cheer and moral support to men and women of the service for well over fifty years. Bob Hope began his humanitarian tours even before the Air Force, now celebrating its fiftieth anniversary, came into being.' To the 93-year-old comedian, Secretary Widnall added, 'We thought we'd give you, in a sense, an aeroplane—an aeroplane which, like you, will go visit troops in some of the least enviable locations on the planet. After all, the folks crawling through mud and jungles don't really expect to see this plane any more than they expected to see you—but the plane, like you, will show up. And this airplane will, like you, carry the spirit of American patriotism and freedom to the furthest reaches of the world.' In May 1998, the German Chancellor Helmut Kohl joined US President Bill Clinton and 7,000 invited guests at Templehof airfield

in Berlin for the dedication of 'The Spirit of Berlin'. The event marked the fiftieth anniversary of the Berlin Airlift, when American and British airmen defeated the Soviet blockade of the German city. 'The constant drone of an airplane every ninety seconds became a symphony of freedom', Clinton told the audience that morning at Templehof, which he referred to as 'the first battlefield of the Cold War'.

The Berlin Airlift was the first large-scale, peacetime use of an airlift in the execution of national policy. The first missions were flown to Berlin on 26 June 1948, airlifting eighty tons of milk, flour, medicine and other cargo—the payload equivalent of a single C-17—on thirty-two C-47 flights. 'The experience of the airlift caused us to join together as allies, and we still are today', said Chancellor Kohl, who paid tribute to the veterans of the airlift who were in attendance at the ceremony. He continued, 'Millions of Americans have been stationed here since then to defend our freedom. The Americans got rid of the barbed wire and created the climate for reunification.' The Berlin Airlift proved enormously successful. The aircrews delivered more than 4.4 billion pounds of food, fuel and supplies to Berlin in fifteen months. They brought 227,655 people into or out of the city. At the height of the airlift, the planes were flying three to four minutes apart, twenty-four hours a day, seven days a week. Some 75,000 Americans, Britons, French and Germans took part in the effort. The airlift demonstrated the peacetime utility of transport aircraft and led to the present era of big cargo aircraft like the C-17 Globemaster III.

Specifications: Boeing C-17
Engines: Four Pratt & Whitney F117-PW-100 turbofans rated at 40,440 lb thrust each
Maximum speed: 570 mph
Cruising speed: 540 mph
Service ceiling: 45,000 feet
Normal range: 3,200 miles, unrefuelled with 130,000 lb payload
Weight: empty 227,000 lb, maximum 585,000 lb
Wingspan: 170 ft
Length: 174 ft
Height: 55 ft 1 in
Wing area: 3,800 sq ft

In the original McDonnell Douglas specification for the C-17, a service life of 30,000 hours was indicated. Planned modification programmes are expected to keep the aircraft updated in current and future requirements for communincations, navigation, threat avoidance and other enhanced capabilites. Commercially available avionics and mission computer upgrades may also be employed to improve performance and lower aircraft life-cycle costs.

'How long was I in the army? Five foot eleven.'
– Spike Milligan